Lou –

May this book
bring back some
memories and
the incentive to
write your story.

Dick

Events in the Life of an Ordinary Man

RICHARD R. PARISEAU

Copyright © 2014 Richard "Dick" Pariseau.

All rights reserved. No part of this book may be used or reproduced by any means, graphic, electronic, or mechanical, including photocopying, recording, taping or by any information storage retrieval system without the written permission of the publisher except in the case of brief quotations embodied in critical articles and reviews.

LifeRich Publishing is a registered trademark of The Reader's Digest Association, Inc.

LifeRich Publishing books may be ordered through booksellers or by contacting:

LifeRich Publishing
1663 Liberty Drive
Bloomington, IN 47403
www.liferichpublishing.com
1 (888) 238-8637

Because of the dynamic nature of the Internet, any web addresses or links contained in this book may have changed since publication and may no longer be valid. The views expressed in this work are solely those of the author and do not necessarily reflect the views of the publisher, and the publisher hereby disclaims any responsibility for them.

Any people depicted in stock imagery provided by Thinkstock are models, and such images are being used for illustrative purposes only. Certain stock imagery © Thinkstock.

ISBN: 978-1-4897-0361-3 (sc)
ISBN: 978-1-4897-0362-0 (e)

Printed in the United States of America.

LifeRich Publishing rev. date: 12/05/2014

Contents

Introduction

My intent is to share some personal stories from my life that I think might be of interest to my friends, my family, and readers who are curious about everyday life in America between 1938 and 2014.

In the title, "ordinary" implies middle class American without the special privileges of wealth or title, and without the hardships of poverty. America, my family, and occasional hard work provided me with many opportunities and I tried to take advantage of most of them. Memorable events in one's life include successes and failures, some humorous, others sad, motivational, or educational - that cumulatively are called life's experiences. That is the subject of this book and since each person's life is different, my story is unique.

Writing this book was an educational experience for me. Since I am no longer so young that I know everything, some research was involved. While searching for facts, I discovered that people recall what they believe to be the truth, but individuals remember the details of an event differently. In reality, "a fact" is what actually happened and "the truth" is what it meant to the individual telling the story. I have provided documentation for some of the stories, however I acknowledge that stories from many years ago have been clouded by life experiences and that what I, or a witness, believe to be the truth may not be precisely a fact. Therefore, if you were witness to an event described in this book and remember it differently, please accept that I have portrayed the event as factually as I, or the individuals who provided input, could remember it and there has been no intent to deceive. It also became clear to me that several events, disturbing to me when they occurred, turned out to be opportunities.

Although the words, errors, and omissions, are my responsibility, the fact that they have been written and bound together belongs to my wife Becky. She not only encouraged me to write this book, but as an anniversary gift, gave me a card that said, "Please accept this, Writer's Package for Inspirational Stories, from Life Publishing Company as a present from your most devoted fan." As a fiscal conservative who stops to pick up a stray penny, the thought of wasting the money she had pre-paid for publication of a book left me no recourse. I had to put my story on paper. So here it is. I hope you find it interesting, occasionally humorous, perhaps informative, and useful as a catalyst to the recollection of adventures in your life.

CHAPTER 1

Background and Early Memories

Family Album

"All happy families are alike, but each
unhappy family is unhappy in its own way."
L. N. Tolstoy, 1828-1910

I was born at the Sturdy Memorial Hospital in Attleboro, MA. Until sometime before age four and a half, when I began school, we lived in an apartment on Fisher Street in North Attleboro, MA. My only recollection of living there is that the backyard was deep and ended at a small brook surrounded by large, mature trees. I heard stories about having a white duck as a pet and that it would follow me around the yard. I also heard that the duck enjoyed eating in the neighbor's garden. After numerous complaints from the neighbor, I was told that my pet had run away. It seems that one Sunday noon meal the traditional roasted chicken was a bit smaller and had more dark meat than usual – but I only heard about that much later.

The setting for my earliest memories is the LeBlanc's house in North Attleboro, MA. Grandfather LeBlanc was a kind hearted, crusty, no nonsense, Canadian who worked as a butcher. At home he favored a very large, dark brown, smoke stained chair where he read the paper and relaxed. A tall pipe stand with a center ashtray surrounded by several

1

occupied pipe-holding clamps was the chair's constant companion. He loved the vegetable and flower garden that populated his entire backyard and he would let me tag along while he weeded, harvested, or simply admired his garden. Fresh vegetables, picked just before being cooked were washed and sliced by grandmother. I was just tall enough to see the countertop when on tip toes and would be allowed to pilfer a vegetable slice or two to eat while raw. That apparently ended when I successfully grabbed and began eating a long green vegetable that I thought was a green bean, but was a jalapeno pepper. My most vivid, early, memory is of grandfather Leblanc in the large, dirt floored, cellar below the house. It had an oversized door that opened to the backyard garden and stairs at the far end leading into the kitchen. The cellar housed garden tools, fresh vegetables packed in brine, an icebox, a wringer washing machine, and other assorted items. I watched grandfather tie a string around the doorknob of the large, opened, cellar door, sit in a four-legged, wooden chair and tie the other end to one of his teeth. He leaned back slightly in the chair, put both feet against the door, and violently, kicked it shut. He applied his handkerchief to his bleeding mouth and went to the icebox to get a piece of ice to help stop the bleeding. When I saw the blood and asked what happened, he said that he'd had a toothache for a couple of days and that the tooth had to come out. I still dread visiting a dentist for fear that he will tell me that I need a tooth pulled!

Attleboro, MA is where I began school and where I lived until age seventeen. It is located in southeastern Massachusetts along the US Route 95 corridor, 10 miles north of Providence, RI, 39 miles south of Boston, MA and about 50 miles from the Cape Cod Canal. English settlers arrived in 1634, the Community was incorporated in 1694, and on June 16, 1914 the city charter was signed and the town of Attleborough became the City of Attleboro. The main railroad line along the east coast passes through the city center and city land was cleared for the north-south Interstate Highway, Route 95. Between 1900 and 1914 the population increased from 11,000 to 18,000, the number of factories expanded dramatically, and manufacturing (jewelry, tool, and textile) output more than doubled.

During my youth, Attleboro was a city of approximately 25,000, where many residents had lived for generations, recognized one another, drove slowly, and supported the high school basketball and football teams. The only high school was Attleboro High.

Attleboro was known as, "The Jewelry City," because of its many jewelry companies, e.g., Swank, Balfour, and Evans Case, and because a large billboard at the southern edge of the city on Route 95 read, "Welcome to Attleboro. The Jewelry City." Today, a few of the tool & die companies that supported the jewelry making industry remain, but most of the jewelry companies are gone or have reverted to making school rings, trophies, and touristy items. The city still supports the Capron Park Zoo, the LaSalette Shrine, an Art Museum and the Attleboro Industrial Museum.

There were three grammar schools: Willett, a protestant school, west of the city; Bliss, a protestant school, east of the city; and St. Joseph's, a French Canadian, Catholic school, south of the city. Further south was South Attleboro, a rural community without a town center. It may have had a grammar school, but students eventually came by bus, to Attleboro High School. North of us was North Attleboro, about our size, whose one and only high school was our dreaded rival during the annual, Thanksgiving morning, high school, football clash. In 1870 North Attleboro split from Attleboro and became a separate municipality and school system.

I attended St. Joseph's school from grades one through eight. It was a French, Catholic, parish school. St. Joseph's church was across the street from the school and the entire liturgy at mass that was not in Latin, including the gospel and sermon, was in French. Not surprisingly, we were known as the "French School." It was actually a very appropriate moniker, because we were taught our lessons half a day in English and half a day in French. During one semester Arithmetic would be taught in French, and History and Geography in English. The next semester they reversed. I have copies of my Palmer Method writing workbooks, filled with continuous circles and slashed lines at the proper, right-facing, angle. There was no kindergarten, but if your family's attendance at church was good and you turned in an envelope during collection each Sunday, you children could begin first grade before age five. And that was my case. I began school in September, but my fifth birthday was still five months away in February. (It does sound like my parents were trying to get me off their hands doesn't it?)

When I was about ten years old we moved within Attleboro's east side about two miles, from 108 James Street to 6 Orange Street, affectionately and easily remembered for a child, whose grandfather owned a bakery, as half-a-dozen Orange Street. The move was from a second floor rental to ownership of a duplex house. The school was two blocks away from our house on Half A Dozen Orange Street, and I was in a class of 8 boys and 11 girls. The teachers were French Canadian Sisters of the Sacred Heart who wore long black habits and head coverings. Like nuns everywhere they believed that boys were inherently bad and girls were good. Consequently they kept the genders separated to keep the boys from corrupting the girls. In church, the girls sat on the left side of the main aisle and the boys sat on the right side. In class a similar separation occurred and at recess there was an imaginary line, never to be crossed, separating the yard into boys' half and girls' half. None of the boys in my class graduated without stretched ear lobes from being lifted from a desk chair and dragged to the front of the room to sit in the dunce chair after being caught doing "something." The offense may or may not have also warranted a smack on the knuckles with a ruler, before having their earlobes brutally, pinched between a thumb and forefinger.

I met my best buddy, Ronnie Boivin, at French School. We ran the school yard together, at least the boy's section, delivered the pint bottles of milk to each classroom mid-morning, were altar-boys, and were selected to get out of class one day per year, to ride with the parish priest and deliver the little boxes of church donation envelopes to parishioners. Ronnie told me early in our friendship that he "intentionally stayed back a year" in the second grade so we would be classmates. Now that's a real friend.

Only because I have not experienced all other choices, would I hesitate to say that my childhood, growing up in Attleboro, was idyllic. It was a small city where I could walk or take my Schwinn bicycle (with a bell on the handle bar and a couple of playing cards kissing and clicking the rotating wheel spokes) to the sand lot for a pick-up football or baseball game, to the marshes to chase frogs and turtles, to the market for a missing meal item, or to the city center to visit the library, YMCA, movie theater, museum, or the family bakery. "Be home in time for supper," was the mantra in my home. Of course Mom always wanted to know where I was going, but any of the above choices - except perhaps the library - would result in, "Have fun." No cell telephones, no organized sports to be driven to, no worry about being kidnapped or molested, and no bicycle helmets. Helmets were not new to football, but that's about the only time they were worn. We felt free and it was fun. I played "cowboys and Indians," loved western movies, thought Tarzan was a real hero, and earned a few dollars setting pins at the local bowling alley. Except for comic books (The Lone Ranger, Red Ryder, Gene Autry, Roy Rogers, Archie, and Dick Tracy) I was not much of a reader. The exception was the "Hardy Boys" books. When I left home I had collected and read the entire Hardy Boys series, all 32 books. They were proudly displayed on a shelf above my bed.

I have a brother and two sisters. Brother Bob is four and a half years younger than I and that was just enough to keep us from playing together on the same high school teams. He is a great athlete and we would have done very well as teammates. My sister, Lynne is eleven years my junior and Joan is thirteen years my junior. When I left for the Academy and life in the navy, Bob was starting high school and the girls were five and seven years old. I missed the excitement of being present as a big brother and watching my siblings grow up. We get along well, enjoy one another's company, have never had family issues, and still try to get together for Halloween, Thanksgiving, Christmas, Easter, Bastille Day, and for no reason at all.

Mom was the homemaker and the one who raised us. She was born, Viola Elizabeth LeBlanc, in Cocagne, New Brunswick, Canada. She came to the USA with her family when she was ten years old and lived in North Attleboro, MA. Dad met her through her brother, Al, who played ice hockey with Dad and his friends at the local ponds. My Dad and his brothers were very good hockey players and I remember when I asked him, "How good was Al?" I was told, "How good do you have to be when you have five pretty sisters?" Mom was a splendid cook and loving woman who took great pride in her home, but was a very nervous mother - at least while her first born was growing up. How nervous was she? Well she was too nervous to attend any of my high school football or basketball games. In her defense, I think she had a heart arrhythmia that caused a very rapid heartbeat when triggered by excessive excitement, (Your son is shooting two foul shots to win or lose the game.) or worry, (Your son did not get up after that last tackle.) She did come to Philadelphia for the Army vs. Navy football game, the last year I played. Of course, the game may not have been as memorable to her as sitting four rows behind Cary Grant and a Navy Admiral. (The football players were given prime seat tickets for their family and guests!) While the women discussed the movie star's attire, looks, and career, Dad commented that it was not that big a deal because he had met Cary Grant before. In fact he said, "I probably should go and say hello to him." Without further ado, Dad walked four rows down the aisle, extended his hand in front of the Admiral who was sitting on the end seat, and shook hands with the actor. Upon returning to his seat and asked what he had said to the famous actor, he replied, "Hello Mr. Grant. My name is Rollie Pariseau. My son will be playing for Navy in the game today. I'm glad to see that you're sitting on the winning side. Enjoy the game."

As a cook, Mom was renown among friends and relatives for her chocolate chip cookies and hermit cookies. She strung cranberries and popcorn for our Christmas tree and I will never forget the many times she made us molasses popcorn balls and cooled them on a large pan, out on the front porch, on top of a pile of winter snow. Having claimed that my favorite meal was roasted turkey with mashed potatoes and cranberry sauce, whenever I came home on vacation or military leave she would make a turkey dinner. As a young child, I have fond and vivid memories of the two of us making frequent trips to the woods to pick blueberries, to a community art studio where she painted ceramic figurines - she was a meticulous and very creative artist - and tagging along while she went grocery shopping. Her grocery shopping methods never wavered and selecting a melon or a couple of tomatoes was an event that could take tens of minutes. Each one available had to be sniffed, squeezed, and carefully examined visually, before a selection could be made. As an adult shopping for myself, I tried it because, if Mom did it that way, it must be the thing to do, but after making so many careful choices that resulted in the melon not being ripe or the tomatoes having "no taste," I gave it up. I have had good luck if I notice a housewife examining a display of vegetables or fruit like Mom did, by simply waiting until she made her selection and was about to leave and asking, "Which one was your second choice?" and taking that one. In reality it was only possible for me to make jest of Mom's fruit and vegetable shopping until I was old enough to help Dad buy a piece of lumber. Every piece was eyeballed to insure that it wasn't curved and placed on the floor to insure it touched at every point. If you were after several pieces or something larger than a 2" x 4", you had better bring gloves and have lots of time.

Dad had two brothers and two sisters. The three Pariseau brothers were good athletes. A Pariseau was captain of the Attleboro High School football team three years in a row. When my father was finally able to take a sabbatical from working full time in the family bakery he finished high school at La Salle Military Academy on Long Island, New York. His school yearbook mentions him as a football star at halfback, the best hockey player on the team, a basketball player, and member of the track team.

Dad became a high school algebra teacher, sports coach, baker, and played saxophone & clarinet in a dance band. These were not sequential occupations, but rather trades frequently performed, by a hardworking man, all in the same day. As the oldest child in his family, he would report to the family's "Ideal Bakery" in the city center, at 2 AM to begin baking. He would leave in time to get to school by 7:30 AM, teach until 2:30 PM, coach (at various times football, tennis, swimming, boys ice hockey and girls ice hockey) until 5 PM and come home to dinner unless he played with the dance band at a party or wedding reception. Dad hated the bakery (celebrating when it closed) and was extremely passionate about education. His high school education was delayed several years because he had to work full time in the bakery and later, when he was having success and enjoyment as a high school football coach with his brother, he was told he could no longer coach because he did not have a college degree. He went to Providence College and received a Bachelor of Philosophy Degree, ten years after he had graduated from high school, so he could coach and teach. I recall a visit home when I was a young naval officer on military leave and my three siblings were still going to school. Mom and Dad sat me down to explain the intent of their Last Will, since I would be the Executor. My instructions were, "If any of you want to go to school, any school that offers a diploma, certificate, or letter of completion, we want to pay for that first. After that, split everything four ways." He also aggressively sought scholarships and wrote numerous letters of recommendation to help students and his players get into college or to convince them that it was possible for them to attend a college. To him education was a key to success. For as long as I can remember, he was receiving letters from former students and players thanking him for his support and crediting him with their success in life.

I didn't get much time with Dad until I was old enough to go places with him. He taught and coached at high schools in Rhode Island. In southeastern Massachusetts, high school football games were Saturday afternoon affairs, but in Rhode Island they played on Friday nights. Eventually, when I was in the 5th or 6th grade, I was allowed to go along with him to the Friday night games. On the bus to the stadium with the players, watching the game from the sideline, carrying a water bucket onto the field during time outs, getting a worldly education listening to the high school football players whose on field performance kept me in awe and whose stories I was hearing, was as good as it gets for a ten or eleven year old boy? After the game, when we returned to the school, I was allowed to carry the large metal baking trays of pies, cakes, cookies, and anything Dad didn't think the bakery would sell or could spare, into the team locker room. No silverware needed, requested, or required, just jostling bodies and hungry hands breaking a pie in half and eating half a pie in two bites. Wow! This was exciting. Once the food was gone and I had piled the pans near the door I was given a basketball and told to go upstairs to the gym and shoot baskets while the team showered and got dressed. Shooting on a real court where I had seen the high school team play real games was another thrill. Then, on the way home we would stop at a diner in Pawtucket, RI that sold wieners. It was tiny and smelled of fried onions, grease, celery salt, and oregano. It was also invitingly warm after a night on the football field. Its specialty, at least what we ate every time we stopped, was their wieners. These were not hot dogs like you bought in the grocery store, these came in one huge link wrapped around a metal bar hanging alongside the grill. The cook would unroll a section and cut bun length wieners with a large, butcher knife. They would be served on a squashed, white bread bun that had neither been toasted nor heated, and topped with a thin meat sauce, chopped onions, and a generous amount of celery salt. We got two each. I still remember how great they tasted and would drive there right now, for "a couple of wieners."

Dad was an expert at, "showing not telling." He never said I should not smoke, but frequently would nod towards a swimmer who had lost a close race or a football player who had been caught from behind and mention to me in a low, conspiratorial voice, "I think he's been smoking. He doesn't have the wind he used to have." I never wanted that to happen to me, so smoking was never a consideration.

My father and his brother, Anthony, "Gig," coached high school football together during their thirty-five year career. It began in 1942 with seven years at St. Raphael Academy and ended in 1977 after twenty-eight years at Pawtucket East (re-named Tolman in 1955) Senior High School. The schools are located in the same city, about ten miles apart, and their football season climaxed on Thanksgiving morning when the two lined in against each other. When this private Catholic vs. public school game occurred, the teams were usually battling for more than city bragging rights; they were more often that not, playing for the championship in their football division. The field where they play their games has been renamed, "Pariseau Field."

"PARISEAU FIELD"
(Personal Photo)

Dad was always interested in sports medicine and watched the football team doctor whenever he was administering to an injury. He learned to tape injured joints, restore a dislocated digit, and find unique ways to protect an injury that allowed a player to play in a game. The one our family remembers most was for a Tolman football player who broke his nose in the next to last game of the season. This was in the early 1950s when there were no facemasks. The player was a senior and the big game on Thanksgiving morning would be his last. He had pleaded unsuccessfully with the team doctor to let him play and asked Dad to help him. Dad consulted with the doctor and was told that if he could find a way protect the player's nose that the doctor approved of, he would let the player play. I watched Dad build a "nose cup" in our basement – his workshop. He painted the white tape on the outside of the device with red and white stripes (Tolman school colors) and padded the inside with thin pieces of sponge. Two elastic straps would hold the device in place over the player's nose. The doctor approved the device and the player played his final game. Only our family and the doctor knew that the nose protector started out as a plastic, jockstrap cup used by an ice hockey goalie.

Noting our interest in basketball, Dad retrieved an old, discarded telephone pole, planted it in our back yard, and added a homemade backboard and basket. Mom eventually gave up replanting a couple of her flowerbeds. One took a beating whenever a shot missed the backboard and another was just a little too close to the spot where we wanted to stand when we were trying to make corner shots. My brother and I, and two cousins grew up shooting basket in our yard and we all played on the high school team.

After a snowstorm, Dad would flood the back yard upon request so we could ice skate during the week in addition to going with him to the ponds on the weekend. Snow ice is relatively soft, bumpy, and not great for hockey, so it was my two young sisters and their friends who enjoyed backyard skating the most.

For many years, Dad played on an ice hockey team called Rhodie's Oldies, (with Rhodie identifying them as coming from Rhode Island.) It was a team for old hockey players. Initially the minimum age was 55, but the waiting list got so long they changed it to 63. There was no maximum age and most players were in their 70s and 80s, because no one left until they couldn't get up in the morning. One player mentioned to me that he gets a kiss from his wife when he leaves in the morning to go play and two kisses when he gets back home. During the groups' first eleven years, 1983 - 1994, two players died on the ice. After one death, a newspaper reporter tried to get the deceased player's wife to condemn the games, but her only response was, "When it's your time to go, what better way than doing what you love with the friends you love." The players, including the brother of the deceased, concurred.

No body-checking was allowed, but the passing, shooting skills, and overall intensity was remarkable. They did relax the age requirement to get goalies, but it was not a very successful ploy. Their favorites were the women goalies from Dad's girl's high school hockey team. The girls received good practice and experience playing against men and the men enjoyed having the young ladies present. It was easy to be fooled by only considering the ages of these men. They were very good hockey players with high school, college, and semi-professional experience. They raised money putting on exhibitions, e.g., during a period break at a Boston Bruins hockey game. On more than one occasion I witnessed a couple of them at a weekend frozen pond, where they were not known, participating in a pick-up game. Two popular local boys would alternately select members for their team and the old guys would be selected with reluctance when no other choice was available. It would take about ten minutes before it became apparent that the skill of the old guys was significantly better than any of the younger, weekend only, hockey players and someone would propose that team selection be redone. In the ice skating arena and during exhibition games, the Rhodie's Oldies wore jerseys that had the last two digits of their birth year on the back. In a photograph dated 1992 the jersey numbers included 08, 10, 11, 13, 20, and no one cared if there were duplicates or triplicates. Dad wore number 11. Weekly ice time was free since they were willing to use the ice in the early morning, before any paying team wanted to use it, and because they had the Zamboni driver (who had a key to the rink) as a teammate. Dad stopped playing at age 87 when he started taking blood thinner and was advised by his doctor to avoid falling or getting hit. It was a very, very, great disappointment for him.

With one or more of us running off to play at a sporting event, it became routine when leaving the house to hear, "Bye. Hope you win." The wish for the departing individual went from commonplace, to traditional, to automatic. I remember occasions as a 50-something year old, departing my folk's home in Attleboro after a visit, to drive back to Virginia, when the final words were, "Bye. Hope you win."

I took music lessons for a few months one spring. I chose the drums. Likely because of input from Mom, Dad cut me a 6-inch by 6-inch block of wood on an angle that faced me like a drum and covered the top with a ¼ inch piece of rubber that rebounded like a drum when hit with a drumstick. My music teacher thought Dad's creation was wonderful and I learned a few beats. Simply repeating the same beat for an entire song or piece of music is not what I recalled of Gene Krupa banging away on the drums during a solo performance. I got bored, wasn't any good anyway, and went back to playing sports. Dad's musical genes went to Lynne who sings and plays the ukulele, and Bob and Joan who play with guitars.

We became a Cape Cod beach family in the summer when school ended for teachers and students. We tried a few different locations, but ended up with a small cottage, Dad called it a "shack," in Dennis Port, on the southern shore of the Cape. The cottage was in an area called Chase's Ocean Grove and was one of about 180, small, summer only, cottages that were built as replacements for the summer tents that originally populated the area. There was barely space to walk between cottages, but there was also no paved road between the cottages and the beach. As children we were free to roam "the Grove" in safety and without supervision. Dad would work to avoid getting bored and despite all the high school and college students looking for summer work at the beach, he always found a job. Most summers he would try a different type of work, "to learn something new" and for one or more summers worked as a plumber, carpenter, electrician's helper, roofer, delivering bottled gas, and repairing septic systems. If he learned something new or interesting he would call brother, Bob and me, to come and witness or hear about what he had learned today. We also learned that he got his summer jobs by telling the boss that he would work the first week for free to learn the trade and show his value. He always ended up getting paid for the first week. We did a lot of swimming and fishing, dug soft shell clams (steamers), raked quahogs, picked mussels, and played on the beaches. After dinner there was always a card game going on. Kitty Whist, the favorite of the LeBlanc's, was the most popular, but I also learned to play Gin rummy, cribbage, and High-Low-Jack (played the Canadian way with a joker worth two points.) Summers were a treat for all of us. Today each of my sisters owns a cottage in Chase's Ocean Grove to go along with the "family cottage." The after dinner games continue but have become a bit more sophisticated since we have matured. The traditional card games are now occasionally interspersed with domino games such as "Mexican Train," a card game called "Wizard," and a game played with numbered tiles called "Rummikub."

The other lesson that Bob and I learned from Dad was to always have a trick ready to entertain a youngster. Card tricks do nicely but others are often as exciting. Bob became especially proficient at magic tricks during his years living and sailing the oceans on his sailboat. Our younger cousins, friends who came to our house, and even some of Dad's students can tell you about a trick of Dad's they witnessed.

I was born on February 3, 1938 and have proof. I have a one-penny postcard addressed to me and stamped by the post office at 11:00 AM on that date. The card, my first piece of mail, reads:

Dear Son,

A Happy Birthday to you. I'm so lucky to have your mother as my wife. I want God to know that I'm thankful for the happiness he has given me, in having her as my wife and giving you to us both.

/s/ Your Loving Father

Born in February, I am a hard-core Aquarian. The daily newspaper's horoscope is often pertinent and I can identify with the commonly advertised, positive and negative, traits of the Aquarius-born: They are always up for excitement. They love to make people laugh because it makes an Aquarian feel good. They are bored by routine and will often come up with new ways to do things. They are constantly looking for intellectual stimulation and are interested in a variety of subjects. They have a strong preference for financial and emotional independence, and any attempt to tie them down will make them run away. They are loyal and will keep their word. They are often called eccentric because what they will do next is not easy to predict. They believe in a, live and let live policy, because for them, getting attached to something or someone is like losing their valuable independence.

Add to those traits the strong desire of a first born to please others - parents, teachers, coaches, and peers - and you will be less surprised at what follows!

Childhood Holidays
"Children have more need of models than of critics."
Joseph Joubert, 1754-1824

While growing up, my two favorite holidays were Christmas and Easter. This is why.

Grandmother Pariseau lived at one-dozen Orange Street. I have a photo of three generations of Pariseaus. Dad is standing behind his seated mother and father and holding me, a baby, but I have no recollection of my grandfather. He died when I was young and left his family (a wife, three sons and two daughters) with the Ideal Bakery in the city center of Attleboro.

Twelve Orange Street housed a family on each of its three floors. Dad's sister, "Sis," and her husband, Clarence "Gus" Gurn, lived on the second floor above Grandma. Their son, Paul, is two years younger than me. Paul's younger brother, Dennis, is about the age of my oldest sister, but I don't remember him or my sisters participating in "Christmas Eve at grandma's." My sisters may correct me on this and I'd be delighted if they did remember celebrating Christmas Eve at Grandma's.

After dinner, the night before Christmas, we would walk the half-block to Grandma's. Bob and I would be wearing pajamas under our winter coats. Upon arrival we had to check out the Christmas tree one last time - no presents for us yet 'cause Santa had not yet come - but to insure that the lowest branches still left plenty of room for presents, then insured that the fireplace was clean, the chimney clear, and chocolate chip cookies and milk were left for Santa. One year we concluded that we might get an extra present if we left something better for Santa than cookies. Grandma owned a bakery after all so why not leave Santa something special. That year Santa was left a glass of milk, a slice of chocolate cake, and a piece of blueberry pie.

At bedtime, we (Paul, Bob, and I) were sent to sleep in a single bedroom while the adults walked to midnight Mass at St. Joseph's Church, two blocks away, and then return for a big breakfast. Ham, bacon, eggs, French toast, French Canadian meat pies, baked beans, rolls and pastries (remember the bakery!) By the time they finished eating, cleaning up, (and putting presents under the tree?) it was usually around 3:00 AM. If there was snow, Dad would walk across the yard dragging a 2" x 4" under each arm - tracks of Santa's sleigh. He would then go upstairs to the room directly above where we were sleeping. Wearing heavy boots and carrying strings of bells, he would stomp on the floor and wildly rattle the bells to wake us up. Racing from our bedroom to the dinning room, wide eyed, yet still half-asleep, we would find the adults braving freezing air while looking out wide open windows and shouting: "Santa's leaving the roof." "Look at the tracks from his sleigh and the reindeer." "There he is." "I can see his sleigh." "He's got Rudolf with him tonight. I can see his red nose." "Look, Santa's waving at us. Wave goodbye to Santa." "There he goes."

We were always asked, "Did you see him?" I'm certain we replied in the affirmative, but most of the time we got to the windows a little late, missed him, and silently vowed to get up faster the next year. However, no one had to convince me there was a Santa. I had heard his sleigh bells and seen the tracks from his sleigh more than a couple of times, and I believed that I had seen him, at least in my mind. I knew he was real.

Then it was a race to the Christmas tree in the living room. It was always surrounded by presents; real presents. At Grandma's, Santa left toy trains, baseball gloves, Lincoln logs, a model boat or airplane to put together and paint, Chinese checkers, monopoly, new ice skates, a hockey stick, or a football game with players that would move when we turned on the game's vibrating field. I don't ever remember Santa leaving any of us a shirt, pants, or socks at Grandma's house.

The morning after we left Santa the chocolate cake and blueberry pie, he left us a note. We noticed that only one bite had been taken from the piece of cake as we read, "Thanks for your kind thoughts, but I have a full sleigh of gifts to deliver and only have time for a cookie. Love Santa."

We were allowed to open all our presents, before going back to bed. We finished about 4:30 or 5:00 AM and were sent back to bed and told to sleep until at least 8:00 AM, at which time we could get up and quietly play with our presents. Making a pack to remain quiet and for the first one awake to get the others up, I think 8:00 AM occurred between 6:00 and 7:00 AM for us on most Christmas mornings. Later that morning, after the adults had eaten again, we gathered our gifts from Santa and returned home to open presents and exchange gifts left under our Christmas tree. For me these Christmas events were exciting and eagerly anticipated. They ended when Grandma's cancer kept her in bed and eventually killed her.

My other favorite holiday was Easter because of our Easter tradition. It went on years longer because it was only our family and I remember Lynne and Joan being involved. Our house at half-a-dozen Orange Street had three bedrooms on the second floor. The girls had the front bedroom, Mom and Dad had the middle bedroom, and Bob and I had the back bedroom. We would each get our own Easter basket with chocolate bunnies, marshmallow chicks, Easter eggs, and jellybeans, but we had to find it. We would each have one end of a ball of kite string tied to the foot of our bed and at the other end was our basket. Following our string was however, neither direct nor unencumbered. Our strings would criss-cross, could lead us into closets (sometimes two or three of us at one time), under and behind furniture, down to the basement, through several rooms, into cabinets, up stairs and downstairs or even up into the attic. We would be bumping into one another and attempting to keep our string (they were all identical in type and color) sorted out, while trying to be the first to find our basket. Once our baskets were found some trading of candies went on - the girls liked the marshmallow chicks that Bob and I eagerly traded for jellybeans - but overall we each had several days worth of goodies.

It was another childhood holiday filled with good fun and great memories provided by parents who spent time showing us love and making us laugh.

Learning To Ice Skate
"The object of teaching a child is to
enable him to get along without a teacher."
Elbert Hubbard, 1856-1915

In southeastern Massachusetts there are no hills for skiing; the outdoor winter sport was ice skating on frozen ponds and rivers. Favorites included the pond at LaSalette Seminary, the Mud Hole in North Attleboro, and the Ten Mile River next to the Highland Country Club where it was wide and accessible. LaSalette was home to a large stone monastery where the brothers (preparing to become catholic priests) lived, studied, prayed, ate, and slept. From the highway, a divided, two lane, road crossed a quarter-mile of grassy field that elevated towards the end where the monastery was prominently located above its surroundings. Midway up the road, on the right hand side, there was a spring fed lake about half the size of a football field. This was Dad's favorite skating location because there always seemed to be a sufficient number of the French Canadian, resident brothers available to insure enough players for a hockey game. That's where I learned to ice skate.

By age six or seven I had apparently pestered Dad to go along on his weekend games at LaSalette sufficiently that he tired of hearing my pleas and was able to convince mother that I was old enough to go along. He had found a pair of double-runner blades somewhere and had riveted them to the soles of an old pair of ankle high shoes that youngsters my age wore in those days. They were my first ice skates. My dress code requirement was that I wore a toke - a knitted, woolen cap, made by

Mom - at all times. Helmets, in the 1940s, were made of thin leather, were worn by football players, but never ice hockey players.

My first day at the pond, after putting on my ice skates, Dad held me up between his legs and skated quickly across the pond. "Feel the wind, you can go as fast as you want. Isn't it great?" It was and I wanted to learn. In a far corner of the pond, a safe distance from where the hockey game would be played, he showed me how to push with alternating feet and glide in between. He said to pick two spots on the ice, a few yards apart, and skate back and forth so I would learn to turn or stop and change direction, like a hockey player. My final instruction, alas the hockey game was beginning, was, "Count the number of times you fall. When you reach 100 you will know how to ice skate." That was cool, a goal was in sight, and I could do that.

During breaks in the hockey game, Dad would come over, ask me to show him how I was doing, provide encouragement, and do a bit of coaching. I remember being eager to tell him, and Mom when we got home, how many times I had fallen as a measure of my improvement. One weekend I was given a hockey stick that Dad had cut down to my size. The stick may have been a prop to help me remain upright, but I saw it as a clear sign of my improvement and first step to playing ice hockey. I don't recall how many falls I counted, but I did learn to skate that winter. I know because the next year I was given a real pair of ice skates with single blades.

I now recall that little episode as a terrific lesson in leadership. Identify a goal, demonstrate the thrill of success, provide the means of accomplishment, offer periodic advice and encouragement, and let the person earn it. It means more if you earn it.

CHAPTER 2

High School Years

Attleboro High School

"There isn't much to be seen in a little
town, but what you hear makes up for it."
Frank McKinney Hubbard, 1868-1930

When my buddy, Ronnie Boivin, and I graduated from St. Joseph's
grammar school we let the nuns talk us into attending Coyle High
School. It's located in Taunton, a forty-five minute bus ride from the
Attleboro city center and was the only Massachusetts, Catholic, high
school in the area. Academically it was probably a good year, but for
everything else it was a disaster. We had to catch the school bus in the
city center, about a mile from home, at 7:00 AM to get to school and
the bus left on the return trip as soon as school ended for the day. If we
wanted to remain at school to play a sport, join a club, or participate
in an after-school activity we had to thumb a ride home. It was a
regrettable choice and we both switched to Attleboro High School
(AHS) after the first year.

Beginning with my sophomore year, I attended the old Attleboro
High School on County Street, about one mile from the town center,
before the new high school was built. I walked the mile or two from
Orange Street, over the railroad tracks via Olive Street Bridge, to the
school. It was the first place where I had the opportunity to play on an
organized sports team.

Although I believe it was originally built to be the high school, it was only a little larger than some of the houses that surrounded it and was small relative to newer high schools in nearby towns. It was an imposing stone structure, but it had no adjacent fields, no parking lot, and a gym suitable only for physical training (PT) classes, not for athletic events. The building was located on a small hill that accommodated a split-level, design style. From most of the doors, one went down a few steps to the 1st floor or up a few steps to the 2nd floor. There was also a third floor.

The gym was an eight-foot deep rectangular hole in the middle of the 1st floor. It had basketball baskets at each end, with the floor lined as a basketball court that left twenty-four inches of space between the edge of the basketball court boundary lines and the eight-foot high wooden wall that defined the gym. Just enough room to step out of bounds or land after a layup before crashing into the wall. The 1st floor encircled the sunken gym and one could look down over a metal railing into the gym. On the 1st floor, opposite the sunken gym, were located the cafeteria, boys & girls locker rooms and restrooms, and offices for the coaches behind which was a locker room used by sports teams. The gym was not used for basketball games because with only a sixteen-foot overhead clearance (8' to the 1st floor whose ceiling was 8' high) any shot taken beyond the foul line would hit the ceiling before reaching the basket. The gym was used for PT Classes, school dances, and our senior class banquet with the walls decorated with posters used at class activities during the year.

Staff offices, the auditorium, and classrooms filled the 2nd floor. The school library, a laboratory, and additional classrooms were on the 3rd floor.

The teachers, like in many small towns, were long term, generally supportive, and had reputations that had been passed down and embellished for many years. For example, our biology teacher, Mr. Cooper, was famous (infamous?) for his lectures and final exam on birds. In his lectures he described the life and feeding style of his avian friends, their discriminating visual and audible characteristics, and would display examples from his private collection of stuffed birds. For his final exam he would hide behind his desk, raise one of his stuffed aviary boarders and swing it rapidly right-left-right, simulating a bird in flight, before lowering it behind the desk. Students were to identify each bird. The story on Mr. Cooper was that one year during his final exam, as one of his stuffed animals flew right-left-right its head left its body after only two of the three direction changes. After that there was always excitement throughout the school on Mr. Cooper's bird exam day as student waited for stories about the exam hoping to hear of another failed flight or spectacular casualty.

The High School was part of the community. Townspeople attended the football and basketball games, and the local radio station, WARA, carried the games live. The bleachers were always full for our home basketball games, (basketball was more popular than football in Attleboro) and I recall frequently hearing radio station reports such as, "All the seats for tonight's 7 PM basketball game were sold by 5 PM." And the High School gave back to the community. I remember speaking at Bliss Elementary School as part of the town's "Sportsmanship Program." In pairs, varsity members of the basketball team would visit the local elementary schools. Coach Howard Tozier, our basketball coach, would introduce his two players and we would talk to the students about sportsmanship and our game experiences at a special assembly.

The local Rotarians were major supporters and their events always embraced country, honor, hard work, ethics, and god. They hosted members of the High School that had made the National Honor Society and the year I made it, presented each of us with a pen and pencil set with perpetual calendars and a Rotarian insignia. The speaker that year was Canon Roebuck, the rector of St. Paul's Episcopal church in Pawtucket, RI and his message was, "Know yourself, know your world, and know your god because success is not based on material and physical things alone." Annually the Rotary Club hosted Attleboro High School athletes who had earned a varsity letter and presented a small gift to each of the seniors. My senior year, the Speaker was Coach Sheary, the head basketball coach at Holy Cross College. He gave a pep talk with advice and counsel that included: "You can be all you want to be if you're willing to sweat. Good athletes can sit quietly knowing they don't have to make noise. The biggest sign of character is respect for the rules, your coaches, your parents, and yourself. Don't be poor advertisements. And for you girls in the group, know that you can get as much respect as you ask for." His closing remark was, "Having said all that, natural endowments are nice too. If a basketball candidate holds a ball over his head and brings it down covered with snow, I'll be very, very, interested."

One day each Spring the school celebrated Student Teacher Day. On that day seniors filled every position at the school including the principal and his staff, classroom teachers, and even the custodians. Those interested ran for election to their position of choice. My good friend, known mischief-maker, and member of the National Honor Society, Bernie Barrett, wanted to be guidance counselor. Graduation was approaching, college applications were being answered, letters of recommendation written, and the school's announcing system was frequently calling individuals from class to report to the guidance counselor's office. There were some football teammates Bernie promised to call out of a class and a girl he thought he could impress if he could spend a period with her in "his office." He convinced me to run for principal, because it would be fun (and since the two offices were adjacent, occupancy by a buddy would allow him leeway to do his thing!) He also suggested - in jest - that we might have access to everyone's attendance record and grades. We both won election. Two football players from the trade school became custodians for the day. The individuals we were replacing for the day spent the early morning describing their daily routine and responsibilities then turned the jobs and office over to us. I looked over the invitations and speaking requests that Principal Gibbs had received and left him notes on which ones I thought he should attend, then I visited classrooms to insure that "my teachers" were performing admirably, and periodically I joined

Bernie in his office when teammates had been called from class. Neither Bernie nor I did any harm, or broke any rules that day. We both had a marvelous time with lots of laughs between us and with favorite classmates, and he got a date.

During my high school years, I probably exuded confidence, but felt insecure in social settings especially when interacting with girls. I was uncomfortable making small talk and exchanging gossip with classmates that went to Bobby's Diner for a soda in the afternoons after school. It took me years to get comfortable talking with girls. I blame the nuns.

Our graduating class in 1955 was the largest, at the time, from Attleboro High School, 169 plus 15 from the trade school for a total of 184. The graduation ceremony was held on a warm, sunny morning, on the grass at Haywood Field. I was one of the thirty-seven that graduated with honors.

AHS Football Season

"Advertisements contain the only
truths to be relied on in a newspaper."
Thomas Jefferson, 1743-1826

Football practices and games were held at Haywood Field, a ten-minute bus ride north of the school. It was a city athletic park. There was a baseball diamond with a football field across the outfield that had permanent bleachers along the fence-line, and several unmarked fields for general community use.

Rollie Kerkhoff, our fullback, was our best player. He weighed close to 190 pounds and was a sprint record holder in track. Bernie Barrett, one halfback was a tough, 5' 7" fighting Irishman whose father was know to occasionally celebrate excessively and take it out on Bernie and his brother. Our other halfback was 5' 11", Ronnie Boivin, my buddy from French school, who played at about 165 pounds. I was 6' 1", 180 pounds, and played quarterback.

For our first game of the season we traveled to Fall River and beat Durfee High School by a score of 20 - 7.

The next week we lost to Taunton High School at their field by a score of 13 - 19. Rollie Kerkhoff missed most of that game and the next game, after getting an eye severely gouged and scratched in a pileup after carrying the ball. Taunton did not have a reputation for good sportsmanship when we were playing.

Without Rollie Kerkhoff, we then lost to Fairhaven by a touchdown, 7 - 14.

We won the next four games, beating Coyle 20 - 4, New Bedford Vocational 14 - 0, and Braintree, in a driving rainstorm, 7 - 6. We scored against Braintree on a two-yard pass to Rigby who immediately lateraled the ball to Kerkhoff, who then sprinted 67 yards down the sideline for the touchdown. Our fourth consecutive win, was over Milton by a score of 24 - 13.

North Attleboro High was favored to win the annual, Thanksgiving morning game. We were playing at home, at Haywood Field, but they had beaten Milton by a score of 40 - 0. Post game statistics for our contest favored North Attleboro High, but the game ended in a scoreless draw, 0 - 0. We must not have seriously threatened to score because the local newspaper, *the Attleboro Sun*, under the headline, "Pariseau's Punting Cool Stuff," reported; "It's rare to point to a player's defensive doings as the outstanding feature of a football game, but senior Dick Pariseau rates as Attleboro's outstanding performer yesterday based on his great punting. Called on several times to punt . . . late in the game after North had been stopped at the Attleboro 5 yard line . . . Pariseau dropped back into his end zone and boomed a 53 yard punt to get Attleboro out of trouble."

Rollie Kerkhoff made All-Bristol County first team. Bruce Rigby an end, Joe McKenna our center, and I made the second team, with me as team captain.

On a historical note, the first national color television broadcast occurred in 1954; it was the Rose Bowl Parade on New Year's Day.

And late in 1954, just in time for the Christmas holiday sales, Texas Instrument put the transistor radio on the market.

"AHS 1954 Football Team"
Front row from left, Sinclair, Salley, Maloof, Tozier, Jensen, Frova.
Middle row, Boyd, DeLutis, LaCroix, McKenna, Jost. Zarek, Rigby.
Rear row, Barrett, Kerkhoff, Pariseau, Boivin.
(The Pawtucket Times, November 24, 1954)

AHS Basketball Season
"A good story teller is a person who has a good
memory and hopes other people don't."
Irwin S. Cobb 1876 - 1944

The AHS basketball team practiced and played its home games at the Pine Street, East Side Armory. It was a large, stone, building that housed the National Guard's vehicles and accommodated their musters and drills. There was a small, popular, neighborhood bar next door. A basketball court had been built in the center of the armory and temporary bleachers that could seat 900 spectators were erected on both sides of the court for home games. The armory was a ten-minute ride east of the High School. The heating system could not heat the cavernous space so the temperature was between chilly and cold when we practiced. During home games, spectator body heat helped warm the court. We used the locker room on the second floor to change for both games and practice, the only difference being there might be warm (never hot, but warm) water in the showers after a game. The basketball area of the armory was frequently swept - we were told - and that kept us from tripping over debris that might have come in with the National Guard vehicles, but left sufficient dirt to cause instantaneous infection when one fell and skinned a knee, elbow, or hand. It was unique, not quite as unique as the gym in the high school, and we learned to like it. The warm water for showers on game night was likely a concession to our opponents to keep them coming back. The only gym that gave the home team more of an advantage than our armory was at the Fall River Boy's Club where Durfee High played their home games. They had one basket solidly bolted to a large running track that circled above the court and the other basket hung from the middle of the roof by a pair of 30' pipes. Hit the backboard with a shot at one end and the ball would rebound like it hit concrete while the same shot at the other basket would cause the backboard to vibrate and the ball to drop straight down rather than rebound. For visiting teams, the routine changing of baskets required several shot to adjust. I'm certain they loved their gym as we did ours.

Five seniors formed the first team and so often played the entire game that we were dubbed the "Iron Men" by the local press. Bowen "Dutch" Dieterle played center, Bruce Rigby and Dick Gawlik were the forwards, and Lee Baker and I were the guards. Gawlik may have been able to stretch to 6' 2", but the rest of us were between 5' 11" - 6' 1". Our sixth man, another senior, was Don Sinclair.

We had a 14 win and 4 loss record, losing to Durfee twice, and splitting with New Bedford Vocational and New Bedford High. Durfee and New Bedford High ended the season with identical records and were Bristol County league co-champions. Durfee's, Al Attar led the league in individual scoring. He scored 31 points against us when we played in the Fall River Boy's Club. New Bedford Vocational was always challenging, because they used a full court press defense the entire game. The games against Brockton were fun because I had met their high scoring center, Ed Burke, on an outdoor basketball court on Cape Cod the previous summer and we had played some basketball together. We beat Brockton twice, but Ed scored 21 points in their 61 - 54 loss to us. Attleboro led the Bristol County league in team scoring. North Attleboro favored football over basketball and our basketball games were no contest.

By virtue of winning over 65% of our games we were eligible to compete in an elimination round for the Eastern Massachusetts Tournament at the Boston Garden.

Despite a student body enrollment that would have placed us in Class D, we played in Class A that included the large schools around Boston. The play-in games were held at Brandeis University in Boston and we were matched against heavily favored Lawrence Central Catholic. The Iron Men played the entire game and won 61 - 60.

New Bedford won the coin toss with League co-champions Durfee, and entered the tournament as Bristol County League champions. Durfee won their play-in game against Boston Latin, 47 - 41.

With three teams in the quarterfinals from "far away" Bristol County and the tournament directors counting on Greater Boston team supporters to fill a good portion of the 13,800 Boston Garden seats, we expected to play either Durfee or New Bedford in the quarterfinals, our first game in the Boston Garden. It was New Bedford.

In the quarterfinal games in our bracket, we, Attleboro, won our rematch with New Bedford, 60 - 51, and Somerville trounced Cambridge Latin, 75 - 52. In the other bracket, Durfee squeezed by Rindge Tech 52 - 51, and Quincy beat Dorchester.

In the first semifinal game, a full-house crowd watched the five Iron Men play the entire game finally losing to highly favored Somerville 55 – 53. We were down by as many as eleven points mid-way through the last quarter before making a run. With time running out Gawlik scored from the corner, I made two foul shots to make the score 53 – 51, and Baker scored on a driving layup to tie the score. With only seconds left Somerville missed a shot, but their 6'5" center, Paul Howard got the offensive rebound and threw up an off balance shot while falling to the court on his back. The ball bounced around the rim a few times and dropped through the basket. We inbounded the ball and threw a long pass to Gawlik in the corner whose shot hit the far rim and was rebounded by Somerville. Game over. Howard was the game's top scorer with 21 points, mostly from rebounds and shots from under the basket. McGovern had been Somerville's top scorer all season and Coach told me if I could hold him to ten points or less we would win. I held him to nine points and we could have won. Lee Baker and I had 15 points each, and Gawlik had 13.

Dick Pariseau, of Attleboro, Mass., leaps high to score again.

"Dick Pariseau drives for a layup against Summerville"
(The Pawtucket Times, March 12, 1955)

In the other semifinals Durfee lost to Quincy (63 – 47.) In the tournament final Somerville and Quincy were tied at the end of the game and again after a three-minute overtime. They went to a "sudden death" format where the first team with a two-point advantage would win. Somerville won the championship 60 - 57.

Post Season Honors

Truth is stranger than fiction; fiction is
obliged to stick to possibilities, truth isn't."
Mark Twain 1835 - 1910

The Boston Herald's All-Eastern Massachusetts Quintet in Class A was: Forwards, Attar (Durfee) and McGovern (Somerville); at Center, Howard (Somerville); and for Guards, MacDonald (Quincy) and Pariseau (Attleboro.)

Both Lee Baker and I received nominations and applications for participation in the North-South All Star game to be played in Murray, KY. Neither of us was selected, but it was an honor to be nominated.

A group of Attleboro businessmen hosted a "Citizens Testimonial Dinner" for the team, the Iron Men and our sixth man, senior, Don Sinclair. About 300 parents and supporters were present to hear tributes piled upon the team. The Master of Ceremony was Hal Peterson, the sports radio broadcaster for Attleboro's WARA. One guest-speakers was Coach Sullivan of the Somerville team that beat us, "I was glad when the final whistle blew. This team gave us our toughest game of the season. They were in wonderful condition." The second was Mr. McCarthy, the tournament director who came down from his home in Winthrop, MA to praise the team and acknowledge the character building lessons we were getting from Coach Tozier. During the fourth quarter of our play-in game against Lawrence Central Catholic, that we won 61 - 60, there was a flurry under the Lawrence basket that sent one of their players to the floor with an apparent leg injury. He got up hobbling, but since they had no time out left, Coach Tozier called our final time out to let the injured player get off the court and a substitute enter the game. It was another example of a small town character lesson and local support for the High School and their athletic programs.

Pawtucket Boys' Club Tournament

"Anybody can win, unless there happens to be a second entry."
George Ade, 1866-1944

After the high school basketball season is over, the city of Pawtucket, RI holds an open basketball tournament that usually results in some good competition. My Dad invited the Iron Men to enter the tournament with the proposition that he would pay the entrance fee and he would keep the trophy if we won. We could keep the jackets given to the winners. We invited our sixth man, senior classmate, Don Sinclair, to join us and we all agreed to play. The games were played in the Rhode Island Auditorium, in Providence, RI.

The tournament team names didn't provide much of a clue about team capability, but some information surfaced. The number one seed and early Rhode Island press favorite was the Pawtucket Rockets, a team that included the year's five Rhode Island All State high school players. The Somerset Raiders, a team from Massachusetts made up of players from Somerset and Durfee High Schools, including Durfee's star, Al Attar, was being touted by the Massachusetts newspapers as the team to watch. Other teams included the Barrington High School Eagles, Orabona Oil from Providence, the French Aces from Cumberland, the Woonsocket Grid Iron Club, the Pawtucket East High School Grads, the St. Raphael Academy Saints, the Valentines, the Pawtucket East JVs, the Attleboro Jewelers, St. Paul's CYO (Catholic Youth Organization) team from Blackstone Valley, and a team called Santo Christo. The four teams that made the semi-finals were:

First. St Paul's CYO, an early underdog that became the tournament darling after beating the Pawtucket East High School Grads, then upsetting the top seeded Pawtucket Rockets by two points (64 - 62), followed by an overtime win over the Woonsocket Grid Iron Club 69 - 67.

Second. Somerset, led by Al Attar of Durfee. They embarrassed the Pawtucket East JVs 72 - 40, beat Orabona Oil by a score of 74 - 61, and became the projected tournament winner after the Pawtucket Rockets were beaten.

Third. The Iron Men, who beat the Barrington Eagles 87 - 57 and the second-seeded, Valentines 87 - 75. Because each of the five Iron Men were scoring in double figures in every game and making over 80% of their free-throws they were touted as being, "Very difficult to defend."

Fourth. The St. Raphael Saints who beat Santo Christo and the Attleboro Jewelers to become the only team from Rhode Island to make the semi-finals.

The semi-final match ups were Iron Men vs. St. Paul's and Somerset vs. St. Raphael. We received a telegram the night of the semifinals, April 2, 1955 addressed to The Attleboro Iron Men c/o Providence Auditorium. It read, "Wishing every one of you luck tonight and tomorrow night. Your old coach, Howard Tozier."

The press anticipated a final matchup between Somerset and the Iron Men, but hoped St. Paul's would continue its storybook run to the finals.

And that was the extent of the newspaper clippings about the tournament that I found among the bureau drawers and attic boxes of "stuff" when we cleaned out the family house after my mother died. Based on volume, I thought they had saved every event program, newspaper and magazine article, letters, cards, etc. that mentioned or had anything to do with one of their children, but there was no final tournament results. Dad had taken home a tournament trophy, one of the largest and most ornate trophies prominently displayed among the other family awards and recognitions in the family's TV/den/trophy room. The trophy was two tiered, classic marble and brass, about 20" tall, with a figure shooting a basket adorning the top. Seeing the trophy year after year on my return visits home, I knew that we had won the tournament. Hoping that the trophy itself might reveal the score and teams in the final game

I retrieved the trophy from its resting place deep in the bottom of a box, stored for years in the back of my basement closet.

The plaque on the trophy said,

Pawtucket Boys Club Basketball Tournament 1955
The Iron Men
2nd Place

What!!! In disbelief I looked again, but it had not changed. I immediately decided that a massive, all-inclusive search for the truth, sparing no expense, was required.

During a telephone call to the Pawtucket Times newspaper, I discovered that newspaper archives are maintained by local libraries not the newspapers themselves. An e-mailed archival request to the Pawtucket Library yielded a reply from "Matt B." which included a photocopy of the sports page of the Pawtucket Times dated April 14, 1955. I learned that the semifinal results were the Iron Men 88 - St. Paul's 63, and in the second game it was Somerset 74 - St. Raphael 61. But, the main headline read, *"Somerset Five Tops Attleboro In Final With a Thrilling 75 – 74 Victory"* and that, *"Davenport pushed in a rebound with 39 seconds left for the winning points"*

With a four point lead and minutes left in the game we tried to freeze the ball (never a good idea) and Somerset went on a five point run with a basket by Attar giving them a one point lead. A traveling violation (obviously a bad call) gave the ball back to Somerset without us getting a final shot.

Dad received the second place trophy. We did not get the jackets.

This was the first but not the last time I discovered while writing of the events in this book, how one's memory is selective in retaining the details of events. I seem to remember happy outcomes over sad, good over bad, and in this case, even fabricating desired results in my mind!

Al Attar led Durfee High to the State Basketball Championship the next year, his senior year. He became the Principal of Durfee High

School and was inducted into the New England Basketball Hall of Fame in 2009.

AHS Track Season
"All I know is what I read in the newspaper."
Will Rogers, 1879-1935

In 1955, Attleboro High went undefeated in seven dual meets, won the Bristol County Dual Meet League Championship, captured the State Relay Team Championship, won the State Meet Championship, and won the All Bristol County Meet.

Rollie Kerkhoff at 100 & 220 yards and Lee Baker at 440 yards were our stars. Baker completed three years of competition in the 440 with 21 straight wins and without a dual meet loss. His best was 52.0 seconds. Kerkhoff ran the fastest 220 in the history of Massachusetts high school track in the state championship meet winning with a time of 21.8 seconds. He was clocked at 10.1 seconds in the 100-yard dash.

Except for being part of the 440 & 880 yards relay team, I was mostly "cannon fodder." That is, I was entered in multiple sprint events (100 and 220 yards), the 110 yards high hurdles, and/or the high jump, shot put, or whenever and wherever the coach was hoping to pick up an additional second, third, or fourth place. My best high jump was 5' 7", this was before the Fosbury flop was introduced, and it actually took first place in one dual meet, but 5' 10' or higher usually won. I held the Attleboro high school record in the 110 yards high hurdles (17.8 seconds) and placed 5th at the State meet in that event. In dual meets, I occasionally contributed points in the 100 and 220-yard dashes.

The Attleboro High School 440 and 880 yards relay team was unbeatable. Kerkhoff to Pariseau to Gerry Gravel to Baker won the school's 1st ever State Relay Championship and set school records in the 440 yards relay (46.4 second) and the 880 yards relay (1:33.3) that may still remain today. Towards the end of the season, Coach Falk would take the four of us in his automobile, which we dubbed, "the relay-team bus" to meets such as the Belmont Relays where the four of us, as the AHS Track Team, competed against 35 other schools. At 440 and 880 yards, our relay team remained undefeated and continued to set records.

Backfield Reunion
"Why get good luggage when you only use it when you travel?"
Yogi Berra 1925 - 2014

The Attleboro High School class of 1955 holds a reunion every five or ten years, but once settled in our careers the four of us who comprised the football backfield began a tradition of annual reunions.

After graduation our fullback, Rollie Kerkhoff, accepted a football scholarship and graduated from Michigan State. I was the quarterback and went on to graduate from the US Naval Academy. Our left halfback was Bernie Barrett who played football, lacrosse, and graduated from University of Massachusetts. Ronnie Boivin, our right halfback, decided to remain in Attleboro, forgo college, to attend trade school to become a plumber.

Ronnie Boivin hosted all our reunions because only his home had a tennis court and swimming pool, and he was the only one with a summerhouse and sailboat. Obviously we tried to share the costs, but Ronnie, who owned his own plumbing business, was our financial hero. Our backfield reunions stopped too soon. We met once after Rollie Kerkhoff died and before Bernie Barrett died. Now there are only two of us living, (the two from the French School) and we see each other occasionally and informally.

Although commonly accepted that everyone needs a college education it is not true. Unfortunately, what that old saw has done is to spread a general attitude of disrespect for non-college graduates rather than embrace the necessity and usefulness of trade schools. Today some individuals take five or six years to complete college (they likely lack motivation and/or capability and should be in a trade school), others graduate with large student loans and cannot find a job while it takes four or five days of lead time to get an electrician, plumber, or heating expert.

Enough from my soapbox on the value and need of trade school educational opportunities in America!

"Backfield Reunion 1999, Dick, Bernie, Kirk, Ronnie."
(Personal Photo)

CHAPTER 3

My Year at Tabor Academy

Life Among the Elite
"The Good, the Bad, and the Ugly."
The Title of a 1966 movie starring Clint Eastwood.

In the spring, before graduating from Attleboro High School, I went with my Dad to visit Tabor Academy, meet Mr. Markham, the football coach, and speak with the headmaster, Mr. James Wickenden. I had been notified in March of my admission to Brown University and Bates College, along with letters of congratulations from their football coaches, but I was not aware of how much financial aid/scholarship they were offering. There was a chance that I could go to the Naval Academy to play football, at no financial expense to my parents if I spent a year maturing at a prep school. Tabor's annual charge of $1900, covered tuition, room and board, lab fees, infirmary service, and athletic equipment except for gloves and shoes. Deposits for laundry, textbooks, and weekly allowances ($1.50 to $2.00) were kept at the school bank. Money seemed to be an automatic qualifier for admission. A limited number of scholarships, based on need and a boy's potential were granted. All I remember about the visit was sitting in the headmaster's office while Dad discussed his work, salary, and family size while requesting financial aid for my year of schooling. He was successful and I was admitted as a fifth year senior with financial aid, but I never wanted to put Dad in the position of begging on my behalf again.

What we didn't know when we accepted admission was that the headmaster had major changes in store for the school. Between the time I was admitted in early spring and my arrival in the fall, Mr. Wickenden fired Mr. Markham, the aggressive football coach, and had stopped accepting fifth year seniors, especially those requesting financial aid. The football coach had been recruiting fifth year seniors for his football team for several years and was beating comparable size private schools so badly; few would play against Tabor any longer. The football schedule reduced to four games and trying to schedule a fifth, was now filled with games against college freshmen teams and large high schools. We learned about these changes in July while spending the summer at our cottage on Cape Cod.

One early summer evening, we received a telephone call from Jules Luchini, announcing that he had recently been appointed Tabor's varsity football coach. He was working on Cape Cod as a wholesaler, delivering coke-cola, and invited us to have coffee with him in downtown Dennis Port the following morning. We gladly accepted and met an Italian gentleman of medium height and build, with graying hair, and a trace of Italian accent. My impression was of an honest, sincere, hardworking, blue-collar individual. Someone you could trust. We had a brief and friendly meeting during which time he told us about the changes going on at Tabor Academy. He also revealed that as the Tabor JV football coach he had always used single wing style football, but that he had recently received a telephone call from the football coach at Brown University who was hoping that I would play T-formation quarterback for him at Brown, so Tabor would use the T-formation this fall. I thanked him and told him that I hoped to attend the Naval Academy in Annapolis the next year and had been told by a football coach that if I passed the entrance exams they would get me an appointment. My grades were fine, so they did not offer me a year at the Naval Academy Prep School, but since I had just celebrated my 17th birthday four months before graduating from high school, they wanted me to spend a year maturing somewhere. He said that he would use the T-formation anyway, because he'd told the coach at Brown that he would.

Tabor Academy is a college preparatory boarding school located in Marion, Plymouth County, MA on Sippican Harbor off Buzzards Bay, a few miles south of the Cape Cod Canal. Marion is a small residential town (population 2,000 in 1956) that once was a whaling port. Tabor Academy was an all boys, private, boarding school that catered to wealthy families from MA, CT, and upstate NY. James W. Wickenden had been the headmaster since 1942. Students and faculty wore jackets and neckties to class, in the dinning hall at all meals, and to vesper services.

The campus centered around Lillard Hall, whose ground floor housed the school's kitchen facilities, dinning room, and a large living-reception room where vesper services were held on Sunday evenings. The upper floors contained the infirmary, faculty apartments, and living quarters for underclassmen. One resident of Lillard Hall during my year at Tabor was Jose Bacardi, from Cuba and the eventual heir to the Bacardi (rum) Company, whose dormitory room closet had more suits than Macy's men's department. Adjacent to Lillard Hall was a large well-manicured field/ parade ground that fronted the Hoyt Gym and sailing center.

Seniors were housed in Dexter House, Bushnell House, Hiller House, and Knowlton House. Across the street from Lillard Hall was Dexter House where fifteen, socially elite, seniors had rooms. The headmaster's house was next door to Dexter House. Moving west, away from the campus center, there was the Academic Building, where all classes were held, three large athletic fields, and the three additional senior residences in decreasing order of status. The furthest from the campus center, just inside the school's boundary, was Knowlton house. It was across the street from the football field, was known for housing the football playing 5th year seniors and the varsity football coach had traditionally been the housemaster. This three storied, old house, housed twenty-six students, and was known as the "Animal House" - and that was over twenty years before the movie called Animal House, that spoofed college life in the 1960s, came out in 1978. When I arrived, Mr. Dibble, the varsity basketball coach, had become the new housemaster as part of the football program de-emphasis. Coach Dibble and his family lived on the first floor and I was assigned a second floor room with Milton "Buddy" Robinson, another 5th year senior. Buddy Robinson was a short, muscular, fireplug of a guard from Reading, MA, a good size town outside of Boston. He was a very good football player, less of a student, and is still a good friend. After Tabor he attended the University of New Hampshire and became a very successful, and envied, women's lingerie salesman. The other 5th year student who had been admitted before the policy change and who had played football in high school, Tom Curran, was either not recruited or was paying full fare because he was not assigned a room in Knowlton House.

During my year in Knowlton house when Buddy and I were the only football recruits, the other residents were either non-WASP (mostly of Jewish lineage), socially individualistic, or geeks in the broadest sense of the word. Some had been to several other schools and were not much interested in academics. Knowlton House's academic average after the first semester was 74.73 and ranked 7th out of 8 despite the fact that four of us were Cum Laude. Others residents had strange all consuming passions, e.g., a photographer never without a camera hanging from his neck, always taking photographs, and pretending to be working for National Geographic's Magazine. Another unique character was Tom Teele. Tom, neither a good student nor undersized, spent all his time alone in his room practicing his six shooter quick draw from a holster worn low on his hip. And he was good. I witnessed him, in his room of course, fully extend his right hand with his palm facing down and a wooden match on the back of his hand, draw his gun, cock the hammer, and pull the trigger before the match hit the floor. By graduation time his goal was to complete the maneuver standing beside his bed and fire his weapon before the match landed on the bed. Yes, he really was good; unfortunately it was the 20th century! Another exception was Joe Miller from Rye, NY. Joe had apparently been to several high schools before ending up at Tabor and trying - not very hard - to get admitted to a college. He was 6'1" tall, about 190 pounds, and our hard running fullback. The type who enjoyed contact and whenever he broken through the line while carrying the football, he would look for a defensive back to run over rather than "run to daylight." Last I heard, Joe was in jail for killing a man in a bar fight; a broken beer bottle was somehow involved. It could be argued that lacking football players, the least socially acceptable/elite from each house was sent to Knowlton House. I have personally heard from housemates that only white, Anglo-Saxon, protestants (WASPs) could gain elite status at the school and that's why several Jewish classmates were sent to Knowlton House. Most residents were comfortable being called a geek by a housemate and Buddy and I answered to "dumb jock" with a smile. To us being called a Knowlton House jock or geek was a badge of honor.

In support of my contention that there was a social hierarchy within the school consider that in the Yearbook, the page for Dexter House, identified it as, "THE House On Campus," their photo caption was, "WHERE THE ELITE MEET," a footnote stated, "Inter-House Track Champs," and the 15 residents were identified as: Bruce Evans, Jim Wickenden, Ralph Hines, John Gada, Russell Wootton, Jules Worthington, etc. The Yearbook's photo of Knowlton House identified it as, "The House of Champions," it had no photo caption, and identified the twenty-six residents as: Ed, Max, Gaucho, Mouse, Bal, Jay, Kos, Dick, Bat, Neil, Un, Stew, Milt, Seaweed, Ira, etc.

The only Tabor Academy graduates I've been in contact with have either been football teammates or from Knowlton House. The Knowlton House geeks are successful and happy.

Tabor Football Season

"If this is coffee, please bring me some tea; but
if this is tea, please bring me some coffee."
Abraham Lincoln, 1809-1865

With only three 5th year seniors and a schedule predicated on many more, we were in trouble. Add to that the fact that Coach Luchini was changing, for my benefit, from the single wing formation that he and the team were familiar with, to the T- formation and we could be in trouble. The first day of practice the team met in a section of the large field across the street from Knowlton house. There was no football field lined off with yard markers, but the grass was nicely cut and manicured, and we could see goal posts in another part of the field. John Gada, who played center and was our team captain, led us in calisthenics. That, and running laps, was how football teams warmed up before stretching and weight lifting became fashionable. As we were finishing our calisthenics routine, Coach Luchini came over to me and said, " Dick. I'm going to send those who want to play in the backfield over here with you so you can show them how to take a handoff." I still believed that handoffs were basic football 101, so how inexperienced were these backs? I quickly found out how much Tabor had been relying on 5th year seniors to carry their football team. I had the backs form two lines, five yards behind me, in halfback position. I lined up behind our center, alternately call "Right-half . . . hike." or "Left-half . . . hike." got the ball from center and turn to put the ball in the stomach of the right or left halfback running straight ahead. When I found most of them watching me and the ball instead of where they were running, and grabbing for the ball instead of letting me put it in their stomach, I began to realize two things: My teammates had little or no playing experience because the recruited 5th year seniors got all the playing time and our schedule, all "away games" against Tufts Frosh, MIT JV, Boston's very large Hingham High School, and Thayer Academy, was likely to be a disaster. And those were the "easy" games that Tabor did not cancel.

The Tabor football season was summarized in the December 15, 1956 issue of the school's quarterly newspaper, the "Tabor Log." It is the primary source of the game details provided below and has been used with permission.

TABOR 6 - TUFTS 33

Tabor was overmatched by a strong Tufts Freshman team. Tabor's best first half drive ended with a fumble at the Tufts' 30-yard line. Tufts controlled the ball for most of the first half and repeatedly got close to the Tabor end zone, but could only score once. Dick Duffy recovered a Tufts fumble at the Tabor 5-yard line to end one drive and Dick Pariseau intercepted a Tufts pass in the end zone to end another. The score at the half was Tufts 7 Tabor 0.

In the second half Tufts' depth and size began to have an impact. Pariseau was frequently tackled before handing off the ball and when dropping back to pass, before he could turn to look downfield for a receiver. On defense, Tabor's secondary was making most of the tackles. Tabor lost four starters to injury during the game. Team Captain and center, John Gada (knee), guard Buddy Robinson, the team's best lineman (bruised/cracked ribs), halfback John Storkenson (leg), and Pariseau with a right shoulder strain near the end of the game when he got sacked while half way through his passing motion. Tabor's "total yards gained" statistic may have had a minus sign in front of it. The final score was a valid reflection of team performance.

Coach Luchini, in an interview with the New Bedford Standard Times, said that he remained optimistic about the season because he considered Tufts the strongest team on Tabor's schedule. He was more concerned with team injuries and would continue with the Wing-T formation as long as quarterback, Dick Pariseau, could recover and play. The article in the New Bedford Standard Times on September 22, 1955 titled, <u>LUCHINI REMAINS CONFIDENT AT TABOR</u> concluded with, "Pariseau, a solid 180-pound, triple threat, eased his coach's concerns somewhat today when he tested his arm with a few soft passes without shoulder pain. At practice he was also booming punts that averaged about 50 yards"

TABOR 6 - MASSACHUSETTS INSTITUTE OF TECHNOLOGY JV 13

Miller scored on an 8-yard run and Buddy Robinson recovered two MIT fumbles. Tabor missed its extra point kick attempt again this week. At the half it was Tabor 6 – MIT 0. MIT scored in the third period to lead 7 – 6 and scored again in the final period, on a four yard run by their fullback.

TABOR 0 - HINGHAM HIGH 39

The scenario was much like Tabor's first game against Tufts. Buddy Robinson left the game early after reinjuring his ribs and suffering a concussion. Bruce Kosman broke his hand. Fumbles ended several Tabor offensive series.

TABOR 12 - THAYER ACADEMY 6

And then Tabor won a game. Both teams entered the game without a win and three losses. Thayer received the opening kickoff and fumbled on their first play from scrimmage. Tabor moved the ball to the Thayer 1-yard line, was backed up by penalties and could not score. Thayer scored in the first half on a 5-yard run set up by a 50-yard punt return. Tabor responded with a 43-yard drive to tie the score at 6 – 6 just before the end of the first half.

Tabor scored its second TD early in the second half following an interception at midfield and then missed its fourth consecutive kick for the extra point. Score: Tabor 12 Thayer 6. Thayer was held to only four first downs, most occurring on their final drive near the end of the game. Cheered on by the home field crowd and knowing that a touchdown and extra point would win the game, they marched downfield on a fourteen-play drive. With a first down on the Tabor 3-yard line they were kept from the end zone during three attempts to run the fullback up the middle. On fourth down, Al Blake, stopped an end run for a four-yard loss. Tabor could not move the ball from the shadow of its goal posts and on third down Pariseau lined up in punt formation. Instead of punting, he threw a pass to Miller for a first-down that gave Tabor time to run out the clock.

Back at Tabor Academy it was announced that in two weeks Tabor would host a final game, a home game, against Nantucket High School. It was orchestrated to coincide with the announcement of next years schedule (all prep schools and "small" high schools) and to encourage underclassmen to come out for the team.

TABOR 39 - NANTUCKET 0

The Tabor football team gave the student body and visitors more than they expected from a team that had won only a single game. Nantucket received the opening kickoff, made one first-down then had to punt. On Tabor's first play Miller gained 20 yards and on the next play Tabor scored on a long pass from Pariseau to Sickles. That sequence set the tone for the afternoon. Nantucket's next offensive series ended with an interception on their 34-yard line. Again it took Tabor only two plays, scoring on a 21-yard pass from Pariseau to Duffy.

In the second period, another intercepted pass by Pariseau, set up Tabor's third TD. Crawford broke through the line on a dive play and another Pariseau to Sickles pass made the score 18 - 0. Nantucket drove to the Tabor 7 yard line before the first half ended, but could not score.

Tabor received the second half kickoff and wasted no time driving 78 yards for another TD. Crawford ground out 67 of those yards and scored on a one yards plunge. Miller ran for the extra point and a 25 - 0 lead. Tabor scored again on the first play of the 4th quarter as Ladner ran it in from 5 yards out. Pariseau passes to Duffy for the two-point conversion and a 32 - 0 score. Nantucket put on one last drive, but was held at the Tabor one-yard line. On Tabor's first play from its 1 yard line, Pariseau, who had already thrown for three touchdowns, took the ball on a quarterback sneak and sped 99 yards for another score. Ed Kiernan kicked the extra point. During the final minutes of the game, Ira Gavin intercepted a pass to insure the 39 - 0 shutout. Coach Luchini revealed that he was far from dissatisfied with the team despite its 2 - 3 record and was convinced that it simply took the team three games to get use to the new system and Wing-T formation. If the team had begun the season as they ended it, the record books would reveal a different story. He was proud of how the team performed before the student body and fans in their final, and only, home game.

In my opinion the team did toughen up and become a cohesive unit. With the experience gained during this season and a more compatible schedule in the future, they will do more than hold their own. I wish them luck and good fortune.

COACHES AWARD TROPHIES

At the Annual Fall Sports' Rally, on December 15th, superior athletic performance during the fall sports season was recognized. Coach Luchini presented individual awards for excellence in football to team captain and center, John Gada of Fishers Island, NY and quarterback, Dick Pariseau of Attleboro, MA.

Dick Pariseau also received the Rip Perry Award, a trophy, as the team's "Most Valuable Player." (Possibly in sympathy for the beating I was taking each week?)

My Singing Career
"Sleep is an excellent way to listen to opera."
James Stephens, 1882 - 1950

Returning from Christmas vacation at Tabor Academy the latest rumor was that they were looking for new singers to join the choir and that the choir would have two joint concerts with the choirs from two girls' prep schools. So of course I signed up. Unfortunately, not much later, I discover that new applicants had to audition with Mrs. Wickenden in her living room, with her playing the piano. Oh my god! What have I gotten myself into?

In anticipation of my audition, I was summoned to the headmaster's residence during evening study hall. When the audition of the student preceding me ended, Mrs. Wickenden greeted me, and we exchanged brief pleasantries. She then took a seat at her piano and indicated that I should stand alongside.

"What key do you sing?" she inquired.

"I have never been in a choir before. I don't know."

"OK." she responded, "What would you like to sing?"

"Well, I really don't have a favorite song. What do you suggest?"

"How about God Bless America?" she suggested with a smile.

I agreed and we began.

Then we began again.

And then we began at least one more time. I was getting concerned.

Apparently the restarts were in different keys, because she finally said, "You have a very wide range, but I think you're a baritone. Welcome to the choir."

Walking back to Knowlton House I thought, "What the hell was I thinking?" It was about girls rather than singing, obvious. I had no business going to the audition and except for the grace and goodness of a very elegant lady I could have been very badly embarrassed.

I sang with the choir during all their events and am listed as a "second tenor" in the Spring Day Concert program. The two joint concerts with the girls were fun, although less exciting than anticipated. Such is life and the frequent chasm that exists between expectations and reality.

I did continue singing with the Catholic Choir during my years at the Naval Academy. That was a pleasant experience, but alas it was also the end of my brief singing career.

The Inter-House Track Meet

"A highbrow is a person educated beyond his intelligence."
Brander Matthews, 1852-1929

This event was held outdoors in the parade ground area during the days when the emerging spring sun melts the winter snow sufficiently to create mud that freezes overnight. The small, (16 laps per mile) wooden, banked track used for meets was there along with a cinder straight-away for sprints that was 120 yards long and wide enough for four running lanes. The shot put occurred over in a corner of the field and the high jump took place in the gym. The event was well advertised and held on a Wednesday afternoon with classes cancelled. Several of the geeks in Knowlton house were getting annoyed at all the fuss and trash talk about how Dexter house (home to the track team and track coach) had established a tradition of beating the football jocks and geeks from Knowlton house in the annual Inter-House Track Meet. They were taking it personally and wanted to win this year. These organizers called a Knowlton House residents meeting and explained that their plan was to enter several people in every event in the hope of getting enough second and third place finishes to win. (Not a bad idea, I thought.) They also mentioned that several of the geeks were surprisingly fast over short distances (a skill learned running from bullies, I wondered?) and convinced all of us to follow their plan.

The day of the track meet it was cold, the field was wet from recent rain and melted snow, and the ground was still frozen. Buddy Robinson, Joe Miller, and I, won all three places in the shot put. The geeks and I won places in the 50 and 100 yards dashes. I won the 110 yards high hurdles and placed 3rd in the high jump. The distance runs, on the banked wooden track belonged mostly to the Dexter house residents who were on the track team. Students from the other houses earned a few points, but did not have many people participating. With only the mile run remaining, the rumor was that Knowlton house and Dexter house were close in total points. The Knowlton House group gathered to plot a strategy for the mile run. While I was trying to convince one of the geeks to run the mile they were trying to get me to run the race. I had run the 50 and 100-yard dashes at least three times each, because with only lanes for four runners at a time, and no one denied entry, there were several qualifying runs. Four runners would compete at a time and the two slowest would be eliminated. This would continue until there were four or fewer remaining for the final race. I had also competed in the high jump, shot put, and 110 yards high hurdles (only two heats.) I was tired and the longest race I'd ever run, while on the track team at Attleboro High School, was 220 yards.

Mr. Howe, the assistant basketball coach and a history professor in the lower half of the administration's social hierarchy, had ambled over to our little group and was listening to our discussion. In a soft, but authoritative voice he said, "I think you should run it Dick."

Individuals in our group were quick to express agreement, "Yeah. Dick should run." "Great idea." "We agree. Thanks coach."

I responded, "Coach, I would not know how to pace myself. I only know how to run at full speed in sprints. I would run out of gas by the third lap."

He advised, "Just get behind Wootton let him set the pace and try to pass him when they ring the bell for the last lap."

From the group, in a chorus, some with excitement and others with relief that they would not have to run, I heard, "Yeah Dick, that's what you should do. It's been decided. Dick's going to run." Drifting, not so slowly, away before any change occurred, they continued, "We will all be cheering for you Dick." "We will go and add your name to the list of runners." "Yeah, and we will make sure you hear the bell for the final lap." "Good luck Dick. We know you can do it."

Alone with Mr. Howe, I asked, "Why did you volunteer me, coach. I'm bushed already and we have basketball practice in about 90 minutes."

"Because Coach Luchini told Mr. Gowing that you were going to win it." He said without emotion.

"What? What's going on? What's he talking about?" I replied as I looked around without seeing Coach Luchini anywhere on the field.

"Gowing was bragging to Coach Luchini about how good his track team was, how smart athletes could beat dumb jocks anytime, and how his Dexter house was going to beat Knowlton house again because Russell Wootton, his track team co-captain was his miler and there was not a boy in the school who could beat him."

"Well, yeah. They've won most of the distance events." I agreed.

Mr. Howe looked me in the eye and said, "Before ending their conversation and walking away, Coach Luchini told Gowing, 'There may be a man in the mile race.' I think you should run the race for Coach Luchini."

Argument over. How could I refuse? So, I ran the race.

I had to sprint briefly at the start to get out of the pack and get behind Wootton who immediately took the lead. I stayed behind him and, since he was about my height, tried to match his stride. The pace was not fast, we were not going to set any records, and by the 4th (of 16) lap I was comfortable enough to "zone out." The way you can get while performing a boring, monotonous task that takes little or no concentration and you daydream. I remained on his heels; my daydreams occasionally interrupted by shouts of encouragement from my Knowlton housemates. The geek who had promised to insure that I heard the bell signifying the final lap actually got a group together to loudly count down the final five laps for me. Their encouragement worked. Wootton and I were running side by side when the bell for the final lap sounded and I was able to pick up the pace, pass him, and win the race. Pausing only briefly for the back pats, hoots, and holler from the geeks, I walked to the gym, crawled under the stage at the end of the basketball court where the wrestling mats were stored, laid down and slept until basketball practice.

I don't recall which dorm house won the event, but since there was no announcement at dinner that evening we might have won. I may try to find out. I'm sure some of the geeks know and remember.

Dinner routine was for a rotating table member to carry out the food, served family style, from the kitchen to their table. The evening of the inter-dorm track meet it was my turn to serve our table. I was in the queue with serving tray in hand waiting for my turn to get our food from the kitchen. As I passed the headmaster's table, occupied by the Wickendens and the Gowings, Mrs. Wickenden turned and said to me, "I heard you had yourself quite a day. Congratulations." No one else at the table looked my way or said anything.

I said, "Thank you." and moved on.

She was a lady with a lot of class and unique among the Tabor academic elitist.

Tabor Basketball Season
"There is no time like the pleasant."
Oliver Herford, 1863-1935

Basketball season was better than football season. There were two returning letter winners, Bob Hoagland, a not very tall, junior who played guard and had a nice outside shot, and James Wickenden Jr., the headmaster's son, a senior, about my size, who played forward and could score. I played guard with Hoagland. We ended up with a 12 - 2 record. Before the first game the team voted and elected me team captain. An honor, that I later discovered, could have ended my Naval Academy career because the heir apparent before my arrival was James Wickenden Jr. I was also awarded the Coach's Trophy at the end of the season. Here's how the season unfolded, again primarily using details and quotations from the school's newspaper, the "Tabor Log," with permission.

TABOR BEATS THAYER TO WIN FIRST GAME

The visiting Tabor team started out cold against an accurate Thayer team, playing before a home crowd and fell behind by 17 points, 23 - 6. In the first quarter, Tabor made only two field goals to Thayer's eight, and two out of seven free throws to Thayer's seven out of eight. In the second period Thayer was held to six points while Tabor scored seventeen. Half time score was Thayer 29 -Tabor 23.

Coach Dibble must have delivered a motivational speech during halftime because in the second half Tabor took control. The third period ended with Tabor leading 44 - 38. During the fourth period Tabor opened its lead to 20 points before winning 68 – 54. Individual scoring honors went to Bob Hoagland with 24, and Dick Pariseau & Bruce Evans each with 16.

TABOR BEATS MASS. MARITIME 61 - 46

Tabor held the high scoring Mariners to 20 points below their average. Playing without Bob Hoagland, Dick Pariseau led the scoring with 20 points, almost all of which were scored on rocketing drives to the basket. Jim Wickenden had 18 points, Bruce Evans 11 and Dick Duffy 10 points. Jim Shaw grabbed 13 rebounds.

BASKETBALL TEAM DOWNS MILTON

Tabor held an outclassed Milton team to only 25 points while scoring 64. The Tabor second team played the entire second half of the game. Dick Pariseau and Jim Shaw were high scorers, each scoring 14 points before turning the game over to the second team.

TABOR TOPS SWAIN SCHOOL in 85 - 50 Romp

Tabor's added New Bedford's Swain School of Design to their list of victims. Swain started the game in a zone defense and Bob Hoagland put on a one man show scoring 12 straight points from outside the zone, to give Tabor a comfortable 19 - 7 lead after just four minutes of play. Tabor led at the half 42 – 26. In the second half, when Swain switched to a man-to-man defense, Dick Pariseau (15 points) began scoring on driving layups. When Wickenden scored his 16th point, Coach Dibble inserted his reserves.

ANDOVER ACADEMY BOWS TO TABOR

Tabor made adjustments to beat Phillips Andover 71 - 58. Captain Dick Pariseau was moved inside on defense and helped controlled both boards against a much taller and bigger Andover team. Evans and Shaw teamed up to get the rebounds that Pariseau couldn't reach. Tabor maintained a lead, which varied between 15 and 20 points, throughout the game. Individual scoring: Hoagland 29, Wickenden 21, Evans 7, Shaw 5, Pariseau 5.

TABOR SWEEPS ST. GEORGE'S

Tabor was faster and bigger than the St. George's quintet and coasted to a 62 - 31 victory. Led on offense by Wickenden's 15 points and Shaw's 13 points and the rebounding of Pariseau, Evans, and Duffy, Tabor had a decisive win.

TABOR BEATS MASS. MARITIME FOR 2nd TIME

Tabor defeated Mass. Maritime for its seventh straight victory. Tabor led the entire game and won 56 – 33.

Meet the Captains: RICHARD R. PARISEAU
The Tabor Log - March 15, 1956

Each fall of a new year there rings forth around the Tabor campus a name that boys regard with respect. Usually the boy whose name is used so freely excels in some type of athletic or curricular activity. Such a name of an outstanding boy is that of Richard R. Pariseau.

Word spread around the campus the first week that Dick Pariseau was the man to watch. Tagged as a finished football and basketball player, much speculation arose as to the type of football team that would be made up around this T-quarterback. The team's record did not back up the speculations. Dick did his utmost ability to help the course, such as a ninety-nine yard quarterback sneak against Nantucket High. At the annual football banquet, Dick was rewarded for his efforts by being awarded the "Donald 'Rip' Perry" trophy for outstanding performance and ability, and the quality of representing team sportsmanship and leadership.

This winter term Dick was elected to lead the basketball team. Thus far the team has compiled an excellent record. The leading scorer and rebounder is Dick.

At Attleboro High, Dick participated in spring track. Here, Dick will go out to play lacrosse during the spring term.

Dick's marks excel, as does his athletic ability. He compiles an 86.3 average and he "hopes to make Cum Laude." Along with his work he is a member of the glee club.

Dick hopes to attend the U.S. Naval Academy and plans to make the Navy his career.

TABOR LOSES TO HARVARD FRESHMAN

With a 6' 8" center and three teammates at 6' 5" Harvard dominated the rebounding and frequently got two or three shots from offensive rebounds. Tabor played without the injured Bob Hoagland. Pariseau led the individual scoring with 18 points. Duffy had 10 and Wickenden had 7 points. Final score was Tabor 40 Harvard 59.

ANNUAL SENIOR SPORTING EVENT

Tabor annually hosts a weekend of sporting events and an evening dance for its senior class. This year the sporting events were a track meet vs. New Bedford High School and a basketball game vs. Thayer Academy. Tabor was crowded with guests and students escorting young ladies. Tabor won the track meet and the crowd filled the gym for the basketball game.

Both teams began with a zone defense and Thayer took the first quarter lead 14 – 11. Tabor outside shooter, Bob Hoagland, spent the quarter on the bench nursing a leg injury and Tabor had problems beating the zone. During the second quarter with Thayer leading by nine points, Coach Dibble put Hoagland into the game. Left alone outside the zone, he scored four baskets and with half time approaching threw one in from half court just before the buzzer sounded. The score was tied at the half 26 – 26.

Tabor opened the second half with a full court press that caught Thayer by surprise, quickly took the lead, and led by ten points at the end of the third period. Tabor continued to dominate during the fourth quarter and won the game 56 – 43.

A reporter from the New Bedford Times covered the events and on February 12, 1956 the New Bedford Sunday Standard Times, under the heading, Tabor Wins in Basketball and Track, reported, " . . . (In track) *Tabor swept the Shot Put event won by Pariseau with a toss of 43 and 1/2 feet, with Miller 2d and Robinson 3d. . . . Dick Pariseau dressed in basketball togs after the event to lead his basketball team to victory. . . . Pariseau matched his fine shooting with that of Dick Sullivan, Thayer's top scorer.*

TABOR 55 - BROWN UNIVERSITY FRESHMAN 43

Tabor playmaking and shooting beat a taller Brown team in what Tabor considered one of the season's "big" games. Brown led at the end of the first period 13 - 8 and at the half 27 - 26. In the third period

Tabor went on a run scoring nineteen points to five for Brown and when the quarter ended it was Tabor 45 Brown 32. Tabor played a very cautious fourth period, held off a final surge by Brown and left the floor with a credible 55 - 43 win. Pariseau led the Tabor scorers with 16, Wickenden had 13, and Hoagland had 10.

TABOR BEATS PROVIDENCE COUNTRY DAY

Tabor dominated the game played at the Providence Country Day School. Tabor led by ten points at the half and won 60 - 46.

TABOR DEFEATS ARLINGTON HIGH 62 – 47

Arlington High, the second place team in the Class A Suburban League entered the game with a 9 win 3 loss record. Arlington led by three-points at the end of the first quarter and 25 – 21 at the half. Tabor outscored Arlington in the third period 20 - 6 and by five points in the fourth quarter, for a 15 point win. Dick Pariseau led the Tabor attack with 22 points; Bob Hoagland had 15.

WORCESTER ACADEMY TOO MUCH FOR TABOR

There seemed to be a cover on the Tabor basket and the team could never threaten a stronger Worcester team. Individual scoring: Hoagland 18, Pariseau 13, Duffy 10, Shaw 5, Wickenden 4, Evans 3, Gray 1. The final score was Worcester 57 Tabor 44.

TABOR WINS AT GOVERNOR DUMMER ACADEMY

Tabor was too powerful for the Governors, jumped out to an early lead and held a comfortable lead the entire game. Captain Dick Pariseau once again ran the show and was high scorer with 21 points. Bob Hoagland was next with 10. Shaw 9, Evans 8, Duffy 7, and Wickenden 6. Final score was Tabor 61 Governor Dummer 51.

SEASON ENDING GAMES

Tabor ended the season with wins over the Sippican High School Indians (61 – 48) and Hebron Academy (68 – 42) before losing to the

Swain School in the last game by two points (55 – 57.) Tabor had a 12 win and 3-loss record. A season highlight was the victory over Andover Academy. The team will be remembered as one of the finest ever to play at Tabor.

TROPHY AWARD BANQUET

At Tabor Academy's Winter Sports Banquet, team captain and high scorer, Dick Pariseau was awarded the "Coaches Trophy" and fourteen players were presented with varsity letters.

Introduction to Lacrosse

"And what is a weed? A plant whose
virtues have not been discovered."
Ralph Waldo Emerson, 1803-1882

In the spring, George Trautman, the lacrosse coach, invited me to join the lacrosse team. This was the first time I ever held a lacrosse stick or would see a lacrosse game. I ended up playing crease defense as the enforcer who would knock down any midfielder who dodged their defender or anyone crossing in front of the goal for a pass and quick shot. I struggled with my stick work when I had the ball, but got good reviews for knocking down players who had some finesse with the lax stick, but who were not accustomed to being hit. Our season record was three wins (the Alumni, Harvard Freshman, and Nichols Jr. College) and four losses (Brown University, Exeter, Andover, and Governor Dummer.)

Coach Trautman had just graduate from the University of Pennsylvania where he played football and lacrosse. It was his first year at Tabor and his first job. He spent several years at Tabor, and then became headmaster at the Groton School, which he built into a well respected, and financially sound school. On one occasion, after I had retired from the Navy, I was honored to be their graduation week Commencement speaker.

The Ugly

"Believe everything you hear about the
world; nothing is too impossibly bad."
Honore de Balzac, 1799-1850

I never had a conversation, received a word of encouragement, nor even a, "Well done," from the school leadership, i.e., the headmaster or his favored faculty member and First Lieutenant, James Gowing. Mr. Gowing, who came to the school in 1942, the same year as the headmaster, was Head of the English Department, track coach, and housemaster of Dexter House. The only exception among the school's elite was Mrs. Wickenden, the headmaster's wife, who was a gem among the briquettes. She was always pleasant and ready to exchange a "Hello" when our paths crossed and overtly displayed her elegance and graciousness on several occasions.

As I was leaving the dinning hall one pleasant evening in late May, only a few weeks before graduation, to walk back to Knowlton house, Coach Luchini approached and offered to give me a ride.

"Not necessary Coach, but thanks for the offer." I naively replied.

"Actually Dick, I'd like to talk to you."

"Oh! Sure Coach. My pleasure. Thanks."

We drove to Knowlton house in silence and he parked at the far end of the long circular gravel driveway that fronted the house. Turning to me he said, "I want to apologize to you Dick. I let them fool me again."

I sat quietly, not knowing what was going on, until he continued, "The coaches and senior faculty voted for the school's best athlete this evening before dinner. The vote resulted in a tie between you and Billy McKenzie. He starred in soccer as you did in football. He ran track while you starred in basketball. He starred in lacrosse while you were learning the game. In the midst of a very lively discussion to determine the winner, I was told that I had a telephone call and that I should take the call in the lobby. While I was gone Billy McKenzie won. I'm sorry."

"It doesn't matter coach. Thanks for supporting me, but it really doesn't matter."

"I should not have let them pull such a cheap trick on me. I'm truly sorry."

I was getting embarrassed, because it looked like coach was getting teary eyed, but he continued, "You should know that there are people at this school who really dislike you. You had better watch your back."

"I haven't gotten into any trouble at the school. I don't know what you mean coach?"

"Well Dick, you know you won the football MVP trophy when John Gada's parents, big donors from Larchmont, NY, were led to believe their son, the team captain, would win it. Then you were elected basketball team captain when Jimmy Wickenden likely had already included 'basketball team captain' in his college applications. Gowing didn't like it when you embarrassed his track team captain in the inter dorm track meet and he won't forget that. You're a 5th year senior, which is no longer acceptable. And as the product of a public education system your athletic and academic record is not good advertisement for a private school that is trying to convince people that only they can provide such success."

"Wow coach. I had no idea about any of this."

"If things go badly for you, I would be pleased to get you a scholarship to Colgate, my alma mater."

I thanked him, but told him that I was still counting on going to the Naval Academy, and our conversation ended.

Both chronologically (a year older, bigger and stronger) and academically, the year at Tabor did me a lot of good. The professors I had were well educated, dedicated, and effective. I especially remember Professor Joe Smart for English and Professors Allen Sweeney and Allen Vickers for mathematics. There were no Advanced Placement courses per se, but the content of my classes was well beyond what I had been exposed to in high school. For example, my calculus class included Differential Equations that were part of my first plebe math class at the Naval Academy.

On June 1st I graduated, ranked #6 in a graduating class of 72 and was one of the sixteen that graduated CUM LAUDE. I was now 18 years old, the age of most of my classmates, more mature - I assume - and the year away from home had helped prepare me for the Naval Academy.

Several years after I had retired from the Navy, it was suggested by a USNA official that I consider applying for the position of Director of Admissions at the Naval Academy that was soon to become vacant. I visited the Academy Admissions Office to get more information about the position and get updated on current admission standards and requirements. During my visit I asked to see the paperwork from a recent application. Privacy concerns prevented that, however I was offered a look at my file. Mostly out of curiosity I accepted the offer and began sifting through all the paperwork that was in my file. I came upon a letter with the Tabor Academy logo at the top, and remembered that among the application requirements was a letter of recommendation from one's school superintendent or headmaster. The letter in my file, on embossed, Tabor letterhead paper, read:

TABOR ACADEMY, Marion Massachusetts

Superintendent,
US Naval Academy
Annapolis, MD

Re: Candidate Richard R. Pariseau
Although academically qualified, I do not recommend this candidate.
If accepted, I do not believe that he will graduate.
//s// James Wickenden
Headmaster

I was shocked and had to read it a second time to comprehend what it said. My next reaction was to silently thank the football program for my admission. They likely had not bothered to read all (the late arriving?) paperwork in my file and were satisfied (had made their decision?) after

I had passed the admission exams and physical. The letter also called to mind the warning I had received from Coach Luchini. His offer in case, "things go badly" gained new significance and I had to admit that I had naively underestimated his understanding of the politics, small mindedness, and vengefulness of Tabor Academy's hierarchy. I was also reminded that Jewish classmates living in Knowlton House felt that you could only be among the elite at Tabor if you were a white, Anglo-Saxon, protestant, (WASP.) Although I considered the social hierarchy among the students a joke, prejudice, was alive and well at Tabor.

The letter is all the more startling because I have two letters sent to my parents and signed by Mr. Wickenden. The first dated, March 17th, accompanied my grades for the winter term and include the words, "It has been a pleasure to have had him here . . . I think he has been a force for good within the school." Perhaps it was a form letter sent to all parents with identical wording? The second letter, dated June 22nd, three weeks after graduation, states, "It has been a real privilege and joy to have Richard with us. We wish him all possible luck in his career at Annapolis." Perhaps, as a respected School Headmaster told me after hearing about the letter to the Academy, "Maybe 'Wick' was just having a bad day when he wrote to the Academy!" In that case his letter dated June 22 may have been to appease his conscience. Alternatively he may have sincerely thought that I did not fit the Naval Academy model, but that's rather far fetched and without prior indication. I wish that I had found his letter to the Academy Admission Board before he died so that I could have confronted him with it. His letter has led to my instantaneous sorting of letters from Tabor Academy appealing for donations. They have gone directly from my mailbox to the trashcan. Recently, an individual (with ulterior motives) reminded me that Tabor did me a lot of good and that I should not let the actions of one individual prevent me from helping the school. It gave me pause and made me realize that vindictiveness should not be used as retaliation for vindictiveness. Although sorely tempted as a first step to simply open the letters before relegating them to the trashcan, I have begun responding with monetary support for the school.

I think it was 2009 when I received a letter from the school's headmaster, Jay Stroud, informing me that Tabor Academy would be celebrating Mrs. Wickenden's 95th birthday. She and I had had a wonderful conversation during the reunion that I attended in 2006 (the class of 1956's 50th) and I would have enjoyed telling her again how gracious I considered her to be, but I was unable to attend. She has since died. I wonder how much of my story she knew?

Coach Luchini, a wonderful man and emotional Italian, was obviously a good and loyal friend and I regret not having maintained better contact with him. I saw him only once as a midshipman and only sent him one or two letters early in my navy career before I heard that he had died. I consider him a good man and true friend.

CHAPTER 4

U.S. Naval Academy, Annapolis, MD.

The Road To Admission

"It would have approached nearer to the idea of
a miracle if Jonah had swallowed the whale."
Thomas Paine, 1737-1809

Uncle Joe, my father's youngest brother, was a navy pilot, loved the military, and was the first to suggest that I consider attending a military academy - West Point or Annapolis. He was not a Naval Academy graduate. He had gone to Amherst College in Massachusetts, joined the Navy Reserve Officer Training Program and went directly from college to flight training in Pensacola, Florida. I decided on Annapolis and Uncle Joe (Captain US Navy) was instrumental in helping me complete the admission process, apply for a nomination, get a military physical, and remain in contact with "Rip" Miller, the Academy's Director of Athletics.

Other than infrequent letters to the family from Uncle Joe where he praised the teamwork, honor, and sense of duty, of the wonderful people he worked with in the military, I knew nothing about military life. What he could tell us about his duty stations and exploits sounded interesting, but those revelations were few and far between. The idea of spending five years as a naval officer in exchange for attending the

Naval Academy I found very exciting. Additionally, and important in my mind, it would be a "free" education, because my parents would have no tuition expense.

During the winter of 1955, I was contacted by Elliot Rose, who was called a "bird dog" in his role as football player recruiter in the New England area. He invited Dad and me to join him, and the other football players in the area "that he had discovered," for dinner at the Boston Athletic Club, to meet Navy football coaches, talk about the Academy, and watch films. One film was a professionally made marketing movie about the Academy and the other was a highlight reel of Navy's past football season featuring two All - Americans; George Welsh at quarterback and Ron Beagle at end. The evening was clearly designed to convince the uncommitted. I met privately with Assistant Coach Dick Duden and plebe football coach, John "Bo" Coppedge at the conclusion of the formalities. A few days later I received a very positive, personal letter from Coach Coppedge.

Each Senator and Representative is allowed five midshipmen at the Academy at one time and for each vacancy he may nominate a principal and five alternates. A provision known as Public Law 586 allows the Academy to fill a class (including unfilled congressional quotas) by including "outstanding and fully qualified, competitive, congressional alternates who would not otherwise be admitted." I had essentially been told, by the Director of Athletics and football coaches that if I was fully qualified (i.e., passed the entrance examination, physical examination, and aptitude test) and designated an alternate, that I would be admitted. (Not surprisingly, the major sport coaches are apparently allowed to recommend qualified individuals for appointments under Public Law 586.) As recommended by the Academy's Process for Admission Brochure, I had applied for an appointment to my Congressman Joseph Martin, Jr. and both Massachusetts Senators: Leverett Saltonstall and John F. Kennedy.

July 11, 1955. A letter from Congressman Martin authorized me to take the competitive examination for a congressional nomination at Hope High School in Providence, RI. Not to be confused with or considered a substitute for the Naval Academy Entrance Examination held the following March if one received a nomination.

November 1955. A letter from Senator Kennedy directed and authorized me take the physical exam at the Chelsea Naval Hospital in Chelsea, MA.

January 4, 1956. A letter from Congressman Martin informed me that I had been designated his Third Alternate for a nomination. One of the nominees ahead of me for a congressional appointment was R.A.K. Taylor, from New Bedford, MA who was completing his second year of study at Rensselaer Polytechnic Institute. He's a nice guy and classmate who retired as a Rear Admiral after 33 years in the Navy.

January 16, 1956. A letter from the Head, Naval Academy Admissions, directed me to report to the Secretary of the Board of Civil Service Examiners on March 28, 1956, in the Federal Building, in Providence, RI to begin a two and a half day, U.S. Naval Academy Entrance Examination. The Entrance Examination was held once per year on the fourth Wednesday of March, and consisted of the following: In the morning of the first day, the "Naval Academy Aptitude Test" and in the afternoon, "English." On the second day it was "Plane Geometry" in the morning and "Algebra" in the afternoon. On the morning of the third day, "United States History." (Three years later the Academy began using the College Boards instead of their own Entrance Examination.)

May 29, 1956. A letter from, E. E. "Rip" Miller, Director of Athletics at the Naval Academy, provided welcomed encouragement, "I personally and confidentially wish to advise you that by all indications you will be officially selected as a qualified alternate to enter the Naval Academy this summer. . . . with this information, please work out your plans accordingly, . . ." (i.e., I know we are late telling you about acceptance for admission, but please hang in there and don't accept an offer of admission from another college!)

June 1, 1956. I graduated from Tabor Academy.

June 25, 1956. A Western Union telegram from US Government Bureau of Personnel, read, "As a scholastically and physically qualified candidate for midshipman you are authorized to report two July AM to

Superintendent Naval Academy Annapolis, MD for admission under the Act of 30 June 1950."

July 1, 1956. With wishes for success and tears of goodbye, from Mom and Dad, I boarded a morning train in Providence, RI that was headed south to Washington, DC.

July 2, 1956. Induction Day. Midshipmen in the class of 1960 were sworn in and took the oath of allegiance. I officially became a midshipman in the U.S. Navy.

My Life as a Midshipman
"Universities are full of knowledge; the freshmen bring a little in and the seniors take none away, and knowledge accumulates."
Abbott Lawrence Lowell, 1856-1943

As a plebe in the class of 1960 I was one of 1,005 competitive, athletically capable, and relatively intelligent, males. (Women were not admitted to the military academies until 1976.) According to our "class portrait," 56% of us had graduated in the top 10% of their high school class and 89% were in the top third. Ninety percent had earned a varsity sports letter and 67% had been a varsity sport, team captain. Sixty one percent were members of the National Honor Society. A little less than 10% of applicants were admitted. Four years later, 797 of the 1,005 admitted (79%) graduated.

After being sworn in as Midshipmen, U.S. Navy, we were issued all the clothing and uniforms we would need and told to mail all our civilian clothes back home. Plebes were not allowed to have civilian clothes. We then lined up at the barbershop in the basement of Bancroft Hall for "military" haircuts. While waiting in line I heard a barber ask one of my new classmates, who had thick curly hair and heavy sideburns, "Do you want to keep your sideburns?" We were momentarily amazed at the question and watched as our classmate nodded in the affirmative. The barber shaved the sideburns off with his clippers then told my classmate,

"Hold out your hands. Here are your sideburns." I must have happened so often the other barbers only smiled in amusement.

The Naval Academy has a beautiful chapel and all midshipmen were required to attend a religious service every Sunday. Bancroft Hall, the world's largest dormitory, houses all midshipman, and has a mess hall that serves the entire 3600 man brigade, in one sitting, three times each day.

Plebe summer was spent learning to march, handle weapons, sail small boats, memorizing the regulations and traditions of the Academy, and getting prepared for the return of the upperclassmen in September. We were taken across the Severn River to the Naval Station firing range to be trained in the M-16 rifle and the 45 mm pistol. (Qualification ratings were: Qualified, Marksman, and Expert.) I "Qualified" with the rifle and earned an Expert Medal with the pistol. Many classmates (hunters?) earned Expert Medals on both weapons. Those who did not qualify repeated the training until they succeeded - a standard practice for all requirements at the Academy.

Dreaded by many plebes were the two swimming tests. The first was swimming 100 yards, any stroke, without stopping, i.e., within some time limit that I do not recall. The second involved jumping from the 10 meter board wearing navy white works, removing the trousers in the water, tying the leg holes shut, swinging the trousers overhead to collect air, and using the trousers as a flotation device for 30 minutes. For someone who spent summers at Cape Cod, neither test was difficult, but as I watched some classmates almost drown during one test or the other I realized that I had classmates who had never been swimming. These poor chaps ended up on the "sub squad" ("sub" as in "underwater body" rather than surface swimmer) and had to report to the pool for training during sports period every day until they passed the tests.

We heard and routinely observed that competition was the order of the day, every day, not only in athletics, but in everything. Many of us were from small town, middle class families, who needed a scholarship to attend college, realized this was a one-time opportunity, and that failure was not an option. The rest had their own motivation or were overly competitive by nature. The Academy encouraged such competition by publishing or otherwise making it generally known where everyone ranked in each academic course, military aptitude, leadership, and physical education.

An early plebe summer briefing by a doctor from the Academy's hospital encouraged us to make it known if we were ill or had gotten hurt and not to let our competitive urges keep us from getting help. The doctor acknowledged that it was unusual advice, but he considered it necessary ever since he had examined a midshipman and told the individual, "You have a fever."

"How high?" asked the midshipman?

I told him, "101.5"

And he wanted to know, "What's the world record?"

Joe Tranchini, a very successful classmate, football teammate, and career Navy pilot was so sure he would not be going to college that he signed up for "Auto Shop" his first high school semester and anticipated making lots of money in the local steel mill. (A Guidance Counselor got him into a college prep. curriculum – just in case.) He says that when he was invited to meet the Navy coaches on one of their recruiting trips, it was at a fairly swanky downtown hotel for lunch. Ordering from a menu in a fancy restaurant was a new experience and not certain who was paying for the meal, he ordered the least expensive and only recognizable item on the menu, a Salisbury steak. One of the coaches told him, "Salisbury steak! Boy, where I come from that's called a hamburger. Get yourself a real steak."

Many years after graduating, a Naval Officer who had been working in the Admissions Office on Induction Day in July 1956, told me a story about another of my classmates. During a quick trip back to his office the Director of Admissions, found a young man sitting in his reception room with an old battered suitcase. When asked by the Director, "What are you doing here young man?"

The answer was, "I passed all the exams and the physical, but couldn't get a political appointment. I took the train here from Oregon hoping that someone who had an appointment would not show up and that you might find a place for me."

The Director found a place for my unknown classmate. He fit the motivated and competitive type of individual the Academy is looking to admit. The individual who relayed the story to me said that he had to promise to keep it all a secret for as long as he worked at the Academy to avoid the Director's Office being filled by young men every year on Induction Day.

The plebe class is the 4th Class (4/C), the sophomores are the 3rd Class (3/C), the juniors are the 2nd Class (2/C), and the seniors are the 1st Class (1/C). The Brigade of midshipmen is composed of six Battalions each with four Companies. There was competition among the battalions and companies in athletics, academics, and military performance, e.g., marching precision during parades.

The daily schedule was the same for all midshipmen.

6:15 AM	Reveille
6:45 AM	Breakfast
7:15 - 7:45 AM	Clean the Room
7:45 - 11:45 AM	Classes
12:05 PM	Noon Meal
12:55 - 4:00 PM	Classes
4:30 - 6:00 PM	Sports Practice (Intramural's for the slide rule lovers.)
6:45 PM	Evening Meal
8:40 - 10:15 PM	Study
10:20 PM	Taps and Lights Out

(Yes, we used slide rules. This was before desk-top computers.)

Midshipmen live by published standards for personal appearance, manners, room cleanliness, and military bearing. Much of it remains with us beyond graduation as my wife, Becky, made clear during a dinner party conversation on the subject of courtship, when she revealed, "After Dick's first trip to Kansas to meet and spend the day with my parents, my mother commented to me that she had seen Dick opening doors for me, assisting me get seated at the table, and helping put on my coat, and that, 'He must really like you.' I had to tell her that it meant nothing, because he had gone to the Naval Academy and did that for everyone."

On the other hand, some of the requirements are easily ignored once a midshipman leaves Bancroft Hall. For example, from EXECUTIVE FORM 57, dated 5-18-55, "Standards of Personal Appearance and Room Cleanliness to be met by all Midshipman" here's a sample of living conditions that might not be strictly maintained after graduation.

Rooms. Interior of room, including bulkheads, transoms, door framing, pipes, baseboards, closet and shower is to be free from spots, dust, cobwebs and dirt. Bulkheads and decks shall be scrubbed when necessary. Decks must be clean and spotless. Photographs shall not be kept on tables or bookshelves by other than First Class who may keep one framed photograph on table or desk. Other classes shall keep photos on second shelf of locker.

Desk. Desk lamps are not authorized unless prescribed by a Medical Officer and approved by the Commandant. One ashtray, of regulation size and shape, may be kept on each desk, centered above the blotting paper.

Closet. Clothing on closet hangers will be arranged in the following order, starting inboard or away from the door, each man's clothing separated: rain capes, overcoats, reefers, service khaki, service blue, all clothing facing towards closet door or to the left.

Lockers. All clothing in lockers shall be folded as shown on the diagrams and stowed on the shelf and in the location indicated.

Plebe "hazing" by the upper class was suppose to teach us to be aware of current events, how to do research in the library, and time management, as well as weed out the unsuited. It was primarily done by the 2/C, because the 1/C was thinking about graduation and the 3/C was still in a fog from their plebe year. Every room did get a newspaper delivered to the door each morning and being aware of what was going on meant that by breakfast plebes should be able to answer routine questions posed by upperclassmen, "What movies are playing in the two theaters in town?" "Tell me all about the Baltimore Orioles baseball game last night." "What are the front page headlines?" "What will the weather be for Saturday's game?"

Midshipmen ate meals at tables for twelve, homogeneous by Company, and populated by three midshipmen from each class (4/C, 3/C, 2/C, 1/C.) Plebes sat at attention and were questioned during meals. Some questions had stock answers that plebes were to have memorized. For example, if someone wanted to know how much milk was left in the steel pitcher on the table he could ask a plebe, "How's the cow?" and expect to hear, "Sir, she walks, she talks, she's full of chalk. The lacteal fluid extracted from the female of the bovine species is highly prolific to the (approximate number of glasses of milk remaining in the pitcher) nth degree!"

In all cases if a plebe did not know the answer to a question, the proper (and only) response was, "I'll find out, sir." and had until the next meal to get the answer. The questions were supposed to teach us how to perform library research, but the librarians were merciful, had heard most of the questions before and often told us where to look, or helped us find the answer. Some of the questions I was asked and a couple of facts that I learned during my plebe year include: "How many cases of walnuts went down with the Lusitania?" (8,000 cases.) "What was Anne Oakley's real name?" (Phoebe Annie Oakley Mozee.) "Who was the first man to swim the Panama Canal and how much toll did he pay?" (Mr. Halliburton. He paid 38 cents.) The Panama Canal is south and east of Florida. (It really is. Check it out.) Guessing was not an option and could result in a "Come round" just like other infractions such as wearing shoes that needed polishing.

"Midshipman 4/C Richard Pariseau"
(Personal Photo)

A "Come around" was an order to report to that upperclassman's room at a specific time of his choosing and could include a dress requirement. For example, "Come around 20 minutes before breakfast wearing ten sweat suits." In other cases, the punishment was meted out after you arrived. "Sweating a penny to the wall" entailed standing at attention facing a wall and holding a penny against the wall with your nose until you had perspired sufficiently that the penny remained stuck against the wall when you stepped back. Stepping back prematurely or not making it stick quickly enough was cause for further action. "Swimming to Baltimore" was also interesting! In this case, you climbed up to the transom over the door, balanced on your stomach and swung your arms and kicked your feet as though swimming (all without losing your balance and falling to the floor), until a drop of sweat fell from your forehead to the floor - and you had arrived in Baltimore. Alternatively, a "come around" could go on for days or weeks at a time. At one time the three of us in our room were given a "come around" for having something (?) out of place in our room, with the order, "We like to sleep in a cold room with a window open, but want it warm when we get up. One of you will enter our room each morning 30 minutes before reveille, shut the window and open the valve to the radiator, without waking us up." That went on for almost three weeks until they found a room that was less squared away than ours. Physical hazing is no longer practiced and the explanation is that the Academy's entrance program selects the very best and there is no need for a 2/C midshipman to identify an individual he thinks is unsuitable and to attempt to get a resignation through hazing. There are still vigorous demands on plebes, but they are now focused on team building and mutual support. (For example, a group of six might be required to carry an old, heavy, wooden, rowboat across a field, launch it in the Severn River, row half-a-mile up the river to a disembarkation point, and haul the boat out of the water. Each group is timed and the slowest team must repeat the exercise.)

As a midshipman we all took the same courses, except for language, and we were placed in one of the 24 Companies according to the language we were taking. Thus classmates in a Company could be made to march to classes as a group since we were all going to the same classroom. We were given a written quiz, in each subject, at the end of each week and failing a quiz could mean mandatory extra instruction in that subject in lieu of sports practice. The standard excuse was, "What wasn't covered in class was covered on the quiz." But it was embarrassing and did not please the coaches when you did not show up at practice.

As a courtesy, but worth little in my case, we were asked which language we wanted to take. In fact most of us were simply placed in a class because of the language we had taken in high school, others - the really smart guys - may have been "requested" to take Russian, or some other undersubscribed language. I requested Spanish. I had taken two years of Spanish in high school and I didn't want to go through basic French for the third time. I was directed to take French, because I was a football player and I should not take on any unnecessary work. I was assigned to the 1st Company along with 47 other plebes taking French, (36 of us graduated.) True to form I was bored with basic French, didn't turn in all my written assignments, and didn't get good grades in French. Eventually, after almost two full years of sitting through French classes, I was tested and qualified as a Naval translator in French. At graduation I applied for an Olmsted Award, which offered two years of graduate school in a foreign country in a foreign language. My application was one of ten approved by the Superintendent of the Academy and forwarded to the Chief of Naval Personnel. Three applicants had studied Russian, three French, two German, and two Spanish. (General George Olmsted, West Point '22, believed that, "Great leaders must be educated broadly.") Two classmates were selected, Mark Golden (Spanish) and RAK Taylor – remember the guy from New Bedford, MA who got Congressman Martin's appointment ahead of me? – He was selected in French. I've often wondered how much weight the selection committee put in our grades in French class (mine were not good), but I could speak, write, and understand the language. Perhaps I would have won if I had shined instead of getting bored - would' a, could' a, should' a?

The 1st Company resided in the forward most wing of Bancroft Hall looking out at the statue of Tecumseh from his port side. My roommates all four years were Tom Hyde and Joe Rosengren. Tom and I were assigned as roommates during plebe summer along with Ed Killinger. Tom arrived two days late because when he finally heard about his appointment he was participating in the 1956 Summer Olympic trials at Lake Onondaga, NY as an oarsman on a four-man scull. Tom and I both went to the 1st Company; Ed took a different language and went somewhere else. We invited Joe Rosengren, who hailed from Hagerstown, Maryland, to join us in our three-man room. One year, when we had a large, four-man room, with an alcove, Bill Griffin joined us. Tom's sweetheart from high school, Anne, – with who he remains happily married – attended the nearby Mary Washington College and Joe's high school sweetheart, Betty, – with whom he remains happily married – went to Nursing School in Baltimore, MD. Both provided me with an assortment of blind dates with beautiful, well educated, women for four years.

Tom had gone to high school in Northern Virginia and had been recruited as a football end. He had a dark complexion - from some Cherokee ancestral blood - and was about my size, 6' 1" tall and 186 pounds. Our 1/C year, we both stuffed ourselves with mashed potatoes and milkshakes trying, unsuccessfully, to be listed in the football program at 190 pounds.

Two months of each summer are used to give midshipmen practical and real world experience in the Navy and Marine Corps. The third month of summer is vacation. The summer after plebe year is spent on aboard a warship. The following summer is an introduction to the Marine Corps (a month at the Amphibious Warfare Center in Little Creek, VA) and naval aviation (a month at the Naval Air Station, Pensacola, FL.) The third summer was again spent aboard a warship.

Following Plebe year I joined a large group of classmates aboard the battleship, USS Iowa (BB 61) heading for Rio de Janeiro, Brazil. The Iowa had a wooden main deck that became the midshipmen's duty - under the supervision of a Chief Petty Officer – to keep clean and polished. The deck was washed and scrubbed daily and holystoned weekly. The procedure called holystoning involved lining up shoulder-to-shoulder across the deck with a short, wooden pole that fit into a depression in the top of a soft, sandstone brick. In unison we responded to the Chief's commands to move the brick and advance, "Left – Right – Left – Right. Small step forward. Left – Right – Lefty - Right – Small step forward." Repeated all the way down the deck. In addition to cleaning and polishing, holystoning "whitened" the wood. (A good thing.)

On the way to Brazil we crossed the Equator and a pollywog to shellback initiation took place. There were many sailors in addition to the midshipmen who were pollywogs. Each of us pollywogs received a formal Subpoena and Summons requiring our appearance before Neptunus Rex. It was signed by Davy Jones, the Royal Scribe. Mine is dated June 26, 1957 and listed my specific Charges as: (1) Breathing near a Shellback. (2) Failure to jump overboard when word was passed to dump all trash and garbage. (3) Drooling at the movies. (4) Masquerading as a sailor. Failure to appear promised swift and painful action.

When called by name to appear on deck we were directed to a queue waiting to crawl, on hands and knees, through a small canvas tunnel, about 20 yards long, stretched out across a hot, metal deck. The tunnel was filled with all the garbage from the day's breakfast and lunch. We were crowded into the tunnel with our head inches from the butt of the sailor ahead of us. If someone got sick from the smelly, hot, confined quarters . . . well, use your imagination.

Exiting the tunnel we were allowed to ascent the platform where King Neptune sat overlooking a six foot square, canvas sided pool, about four feet deep, that had been build on deck. We were told to kneel and kiss King Neptune's belly. Did I mention that Neptunus Rex was the biggest, fattest, Shellback sailor aboard ship, weighed about 320 pounds and had body hair that would have make a black bear jealous? As soon as "the kiss" was completed to the satisfaction of the King's two royal "Servants of the Sea," they each stepped forward, grabbed an arm and with their other hand on your shoulder, pushed you over backwards into the pool. Did I mention that the pool was filled with approximately 50% seawater and 50% dirty, used, crude oil? Large cans of Borax, cakes of lava soap, and an array of various size, stiff bristled, scrub brushes were available at the entrance to the nearest large shower room. There use was not mandatory but extremely necessary. When there is a possibility of crossing the equator aboard a Navy ship, always carry your Shellback card.

Liberty in Rio de Janeiro was worth the wait. There may have been a minimum age for buying drinks, but "Cubra Libras" (rum and coca cola) were always available. That's because in many bars and restaurants, a bottle of rum sat on each table along with the salt and pepper. The rum was free; you only had to purchase the coca cola.

The midshipmen were invited to participate in sporting events and attend a dance at the Rio Yacht Club that I fondly remember. It was a formal affair to which we wore our dress uniforms. There were many young ladies our age, a dance band, and some older women. A classmate and I met two charming ladies who were good friends and had arrived together. They were both pretty and more importantly, spoke a little English. Before the party ended we invited them to join us the next evening for dinner. They discussed the offer and decided to accept since they would be together and if we would go to their favorite restaurant. We were assured that it was not exceptionally expensive, that it was easy to get to from the ship, that they would make the reservation, and that since we did not have a car, they would meet us at the restaurant. We readily agreed. All we needed to do was a little research to find a disco club near the restaurant where we could take them after dinner. And that proved to be easy. We arrived on time and in anticipation of a wonderful evening. They arrived fashionably late and immediately introduced us to their mothers who would be dining at the adjacent table. Apparently a common tradition in the predominantly Catholic, South American countries, but it caught us by surprise. You cannot imagine how having your date's mother at the next table can dampen one's enthusiasm. By the way, they went home with their mothers after dinner. Later, the two of us midshipmen, alone at the nearby disco, drinking free rum with a little coca cola, decided that those "older women" we had observed at the dance were all chaperones. We also concluded that experiences similar to ours at dinner could have resulted in the beginning of mother-in-law jokes.

The next summer, at Pensacola, many classmates were convinced that navy air was the way to go. The pilots lived, or at least represented, the flamboyant, exciting, appealing life style of drinking, girls, and reckless independence. I was interested, but not passionate about flying, and did not try to select navy air as my career path after graduation. Landing on an aircraft carrier at night in a rolling sea, distinguishes navy from air force pilots, and to survive as a navy pilot, one had to be passionate about flying airplanes. That summer we met women that had experienced a navy pilot's passion for flying and were quick to reveal that they knew their date with a navy pilot was half over when he said, "That's enough about me; let's talk about airplanes."

My third summer was spent aboard the destroyer, USS Sperry, in the Mediterranean Sea and adjacent beach towns in Spain and France. This was a splendid summer. The flotilla which Sperry was part of, had left Norfolk, VA before classes ended so I flew to the Azores on a Navy plane to meet her. An early Mediterranean port stop for the flotilla was Marseille, France. The destroyers were lined up at appropriate intervals behind the flagship, a Guided Missile Cruiser, to follow her safely into the harbor to the pier. We received word that the pilot sent to the flagship spoke no English and that if anyone could speak French, please contact the Admiral. I volunteered and had a ride in a launch over to the flagship. I met the Admiral and the pilot and we led the procession of ships into the harbor. One of the sections in the language course book use at the Academy was called "Naval Terminology." It went through the dialogue that could be expected during eight or ten common naval evolutions. One evolution was, "Bringing a ship alongside a pier." The author deserved a medal because I could have opened the book and read the responses to the pilot's comments, orders, and questions. It was all in the book and the event went beautifully. Three days later when we began making preparations to go to sea for some exercises with French warships, I was summoned to the Admiral's quarters. He told me that the French Navy had given him a car and chauffer (a young seaman in the French Navy) and that he wanted me to go on ahead with the car and driver to Nice, Cannes, and Toulon to prepare (translate into English) transportation schedules and fares, maps of the towns, lists of events during the ship's visit, recommended places to visit and how to get there, important and emergency telephone numbers, etc. Besides developing a love for the French Riviera, all I will say about that summer is that I'm glad that Maurice and I lost touch when the summer ended because either one of us could have threatened the other with blackmail.

Academically, I maintained "A"s and "B"s without too much effort. I even made the Superintendent's List (all "A"s) at least once. (I found a letter among my parent's archives from the Academic Dean that said, "The following named midshipmen were inadvertently left off the Superintendent's List for the fall semester," and my name was among those listed.

My last two years, I was able to travel home a week early over Christmas break as a member of the Academy's Operation Information group by arranging to speak to at least three, home town area high schools or organizations, and promoting the Academy and the naval service. My core group was Attleboro and Tolman high schools, and Tabor Academy.

First Class year I was the 1st Company Commander for one semester. Among other duties, I lead the Company onto the parade field accompanied by the announcement, "Entering the parade ground is the 1st Company led by midshipman Richard Pariseau of Attleboro, Massachusetts." The other 23 companies followed us. It would have pleased my family if they could have seen and heard that in person or seen it on TV, as the midshipmen marched into Philadelphia stadium for the Army - Navy game, but being with the football team was better.

The graduation festival lasted a week, occurred in early June and was affectionately called June Week. In 1960 it lasted from Saturday, June 4th until Thursday, June 8th. On Saturday, Army played Navy in each varsity, spring sport. The location rotated each year with approximately half being played at each Academy. After church on Sunday there was a Popular Music Concert and the Superintendent's Garden Party for the graduating class. Monday was the Baccalaureate, the Superintendent's Dress Parade at Warden Field and the Awarding of Commendations, and that night, the "N" Dance for Varsity "N" winners. If your team defeated Army, the "N" came with a star. At the Superintendent's Dress Parade, I received a Superintendent's Letter of Commendation as one of twenty-one midshipmen in the graduating class, selected for, "Having contributed most by their officer like qualities and positive character to the development of naval spirit and loyalty within the brigade."

"Midshipman Pariseau Receiving Letter of Commendation from
Admiral C. L. Melson USN, Superintendant, U. S. Naval Academy"
(Official US Navy Photograph)
(Release date June 3, 1960)

On Tuesday of June Week there was a presentation of Prizes and
Athletic Awards in the Field House, and an afternoon Dress Parade
and presentation of the Color Girl. The girlfriend of the Company
Commander whose Company wins the overall, annual competition
(marching, academic, leadership, military, etc.) becomes the Color Girl
and the winning Company is known as the Color Company until the
next June Week ceremony. The Color Girl and her beau were also

honored at the Farewell Ball that evening. Wednesday, June 8th, at 11:00 we mustered in the Field House, heard a few speeches, then threw our caps in the air and graduated.

A Bachelor of Science degree in Engineering was awarded at graduation. I graduated 234th in the class. That's the top third of the graduates and the top quarter of the initial plebe class. Not great, but better than classmates whom I have heard proudly recite their class standing at graduation as, "In the top half of the bottom ten percent." When pushed to identify the engineering discipline of our degree, most of us have said Electrical Engineering. Probably because it was one of the most difficult fields, or because we seem to spend a lot of time in the electrical laboratory, or because it's where we witnessed the occasional excitement of an electrical flash that singed a classmate's eyebrows or created a momentary "fireball" that opened breaker and darkened several academic buildings.

A midshipman was paid $111.15 per month - most of which went to repay the cost of the uniforms that we had been issued, text books, haircuts, laundry, and income tax. At graduation we were commissioned either as an Ensign in the Navy or a Second Lieutenant in the Marine Corps, and our base pay doubled to $222.30 per month or a hefty $2,667.60 per annum.

Plebe Summer Athletics
"He flung himself upon his horse
and rode madly off in all directions."
Stephen Leacock 1869 - 1944

Plebe summer at the Naval Academy is the period from the first week of July, when the plebes report, until early September, when the rest of the brigade returns from summer vacation and cruises. Without the upper class present to criticize and penalize performance - or lack of performance - plebes learn to salute and march, are shown how to fold and where, on which shelf, to stow each of their uniform/clothing items, learn the names of the monuments on campus, attend some indoctrination classes, and begin getting into physical shape. In addition to daily calisthenics and running the obstacle course, we were informed that playing a sport during plebe summer was mandatory. I was looking forward to trying out for the plebe football and basketball teams, but neither was included on the long list of those available during plebe summer. I had noticed with some envy that gymnasts typically had good upper body strength that would be useful in any sport and the hourglass shape that girls would surely notice, so I decided to give it a try. Within two days I knew that I had made a very bad decision. I could not climb the heavy rope hanging from a gym rafter and ring the bell at the top. It was not that my time to the top wasn't competitive; I literally could not climb the rope. After falling off the pommel horse each time I tried the most basic mounting technique and then witnessing a classmate, who had made a relatively spectacular mount, slip and fall with one leg on each side of the horse, I decided that it was time to try a different sport. I must have been standing in the gym like a lost sheep when I was approached by a short, round faced, gentlemen wearing a navy tee shirt and sporting a whistle hanging from a navy blue cord around his neck. He introduced himself to me as "Bildy" Bilderback, the plebe lacrosse coach. He knew that I had played lacrosse at Tabor Academy and asked if I would be interested in playing this summer with the guys that would become the plebe team. His timing was perfect and I accepted.

I had held a lacrosse stick for the first time at Tabor Academy and had minimal ball handling skills, but they were an improvement over my gymnastic skills.

The next day I joined my plebe classmates playing lacrosse at Hospital Point, an area behind the Academy's hospital that was reclaimed from the Severn River by dumping soil there when dredging the river. It expanded the Academy's grounds and was a nice grassy area, large enough for two adjacent lacrosse fields.

Lacrosse pads in 1956 consisted of arm pads, hockey gloves, and a thin leather helmet with a narrow, circular, horizontal bar at the level of one's teeth and a convex vertical bar up the center from the horizontal bar to the front of the helmet. We had jogged from the locker room in Dahlgren Hall to the field at Hospital Point, done calisthenics, run some passing and ground ball drills, and coach was orchestrating a half field scrimmage. I had observed for a while and then joined a few players playing catch along the sideline, when Coach Bilderback called my name.

"Put on one of those red pullovers the defense is wearing," he said and blew his whistle to stop play. He told the offense to start again from midfield, on his whistle, with the ball in the possession of the center midfielder. While the players were repositioned he called a player off the field and told me, "Go in at midfield and guard that guy with the ball."

I took my position a few feet in front of the player with the ball and noted that he was right handed, about my height and weight, with heavy, thick, black eyebrows; a square protruding jaw, and large, dark, intense eyes. To this day he remains the most intimidating looking individual that I have ever seen in a helmet.

Coach blew his whistle, my opponent moved towards the goal, and I retreated slowly, poke checking at his stick and staying between him and the goal. Instead of keeping his stick behind him, he moved it out to his right side seeming to offer me a good chance to hit it and dislodge the ball. I poked at his stick, but didn't commit to a big swing and possible momentary loss of balance. Since I didn't fall for his trick, he executed what I later learned was a face dodge. With the stick and ball in his right hand, he brought the stick across the front of his body, right between the two of us, intending to dip his right shoulder to the left to protect the ball and to run past me. An elegant move that I had not seen before and whose beauty I did not appreciate. All I saw was the ball and his stick passing between us, right in front of my face, and I was quick enough to get a good swing at it. Unfortunately, I was not quick enough to hit either the stick or the ball. I did however, hit my opponent in the face and reshaped his helmet's convex vertical, metal face guard into a concave shape that now rested against and conformed to the shape of his nose. He called me a son-of-a-bitch, took a step backwards, and threw the ball at my groin. It hit me on the thigh. I was sorry that I had accidentally hurt him, but I did not consider his deliberate attempt to hurt me an acceptable response. I dropped my stick, charged and tackled him. We were both on the ground trying to punch each other when we were finally separated by teammates. At the retelling of this incident, a teammate added, "Yeah, and coach saw no urgency in breaking up the fight. All coach did was smile."

My opponent that day was Karl "Rip" Rippelmeyer, a heavily recruited high school lacrosse and soccer star from Towson High School in the Baltimore, MD area. I made the plebe lacrosse team as a midfielder, Rip and I became friends, and we played together for four years. We began with an undefeated plebe season.

Navy Football
"I do not mind lying, but I hate inaccuracies."
Samuel Butler 1862 - 1902

Yes, we wore helmets in those days, but without facemasks, until some helmets arrived with a bar across the front to protect the teeth. A team could only substitute one player after a change of possession unless a time out was called; therefore most of us played both offense and defense. The one substitution that was allowed usually resulted in a defensive back going in for the quarterback when the team went on defense and reversing the exchange when the team went back on offense. The varsity traveling squad consisted of only 38 players – three teams (33) and five substitutes.

Plebe (4/C) Year Football (1956)

Over 100 plebes reported for the first football practice. We were told that there were only 88 uniforms so we would be doing calisthenics, running, and general drills to get into shape until there were only 88 remaining. The coach's policy was that no one would be cut. (In our 50th Anniversary Yearbook, two classmates mentioned plebe football in their Story Exchange. Gene Chancy claimed, "About 300 plebes were at the first practice," and John Michalski said, "240 plebes tried out for the team." Suffice it to say that there were enough of us to make it competitive!)

The fourth day of practice we had uniforms and were told, for the first time, to report to different coaches depending on what position we played. That was when I discovered that I was one of thirteen that had played quarterback in high school. By the time the plebe football team picture was taken we were down to ten quarterbacks. Of the ten, four left sometime before graduation, two (Tom Doherty & Mike Midas) went on to star for Navy's 150 pound, Sprint Football Team, Jim Tenbrook ended up playing fullback, I was a halfback, and Joe Tranchini and Jim Maxfield remained our two quarterbacks.

My best as a plebe was 5th team quarterback. I never got to play in a game, but I made the plebe training table. The football team ate their meals together, at reserved tables, in Bancroft Hall. The rest of the brigade ate at the same time, at assigned Company tables. One of the worst parts of plebe year occurred at meals - sitting on the edge of your seat, looking straight ahead, eating a "square meal," responding to questions from upper classmen, getting questions to be answered by the next meal, and getting "Come arounds." The plebe football team had training tables, 12 plebe football players per table, no upperclassmen and thus no plebe hazing. I don't remember how many plebe training table seats there were, the list changed and was posted weekly. Football practices, especially the contact drills, were especially competitive because it likely meant whether or not you sat at the training table. I sat at the plebe training table every day, for the entire season.

So why did I continue playing after plebe year? Well, there was no positive reason and it was not fun, but there were two self-imposed guilt reasons and the Aquarian desire to please others. Dad was a football coach and I thought he would be happy if I played. He had never said he wanted me to play and I don't think he would have done anything but support me if I stopped playing, but I felt like I owed it to him. I also felt an obligation to play since the football coaches were responsible for my admission. I had been told more than once during the admission process, " Once you are a midshipman you will have no obligation to play football." However, I would have felt some guilt if I had stopped playing.

3/C Year Football (1957) & The Cotton Bowl

I was moved to fullback the next year and got as high as third team. Most of the season I was on the team that ran the opponents plays against the first team every week. We were called *"poolies,"* because we had the same amount of respect and mimicked the slave labor done by coolies. Navy's 1957 team was very good and being a *poolie* did not enhance physical longevity. The team was ranked in the top ten in the country most of the year, lost only one game, beat Army 14 - 0, and accepted an invitation to play Rice in Dallas, TX in the Cotton Bowl, on New Years Day.

My Bancroft Hall roommate, Tom Hyde, who was a third team end, and I roomed together in Dallas. The team was treated very well in Texas. We were given Stetson cowboy hats and the Marching Kilgore (College) Rangerettes met us on the field a few days before the game for a "photo op." I didn't expect to play in the game so I inquired of the girls, "What's going on New Years Eve that we could attend?" The back room in the Bucket of Blood Saloon was mentioned more than once, so that's where I planned to celebrate the beginning of the New Year. Following a persuasive discussion with Tom about how much time he expected to play in the game, how much fun New Years Eve could be in Dallas, and how some of the Rangerettes would probably be at the Bucket of Blood Saloon, he agreed to join me. After the coaches came by for a bed check we exited via our window and climbed down five flights of fire escape. The Saloon was crowded and the mood festive when we arrived. The bar floor was covered with shells from the baskets of peanuts that were everywhere and behind the curtain at the end of the bar there was dancing to a small band. We had a wonderful time and by the time we returned to the hotel we were confident the coaches would all be asleep so we used the front door of the hotel. (I learned later, that the Bucket of Blood Saloon was one of Jack Ruby's bars. For young readers - in ancient history, Jack Ruby shot and killed Lee Harvey Oswald who was accused of assassinating President John F. Kennedy.)

Navy beat Rice on New Year's Day 20 - 7 and ended the season ranked in the top five. I did not get in the game, but did climb the side of the stadium on my way out to tear down and take home the Cotton Bowl banner. Today it adorns a wall in my poker room.

2/C Year Football (1958)

Still a fullback, I didn't play even one down on offense, but routinely substituted for the quarterback on defense and played cornerback. Other than returning punts, my one and only highlight for the season was intercepting a pass and returning it for a touchdown against the University of Maryland, at night under the lights, in Baltimore Colt stadium. According to the Baltimore Sun, "**. . . further demoralization came for the Terps after they stopped a Navy threat on the 16 yard line. On first down MD tried to pass but Dick Pariseau raced up from the secondary, picked it off and chugged 23 yards for a tally.**"

We used the Baltimore Colts' dressing room when we played in their stadium. They were National Football League Champions in 1958 (Colts 23, NY Giant 17 in Overtime) and in 1959 (Colts 31, NY Giants 16.) We used lockers with large name plates identifying current team players that included: Jonny Unitas, Raymond Berry, Alan Ameche, Art Donovan, Gene "Big Daddy" Lipscomb, Lenny Moore, Gino Marchetti, and Jim Parker. The Colts' were a powerhouse and most of the names mentioned can be found in the Pro-Football Hall of Fame.

Navy finished the season with a 6 - 3 record that included a 22 - 6 loss to Army.

1/C Year Football (1959)

It began with a coaching change in the spring. Wayne Hardin replaced Eddie Erdelatz. Long time head football coach Eddie Erdelatz insisted on and had been getting perks for the football team. We, the team, would occasionally get bussed to Baltimore on a Sunday afternoon to watch Johnny Unitas and his Baltimore Colts play. A new administration of military leadership demanded changes and soon after completion of spring practice for the 1959 season, coach Erdelatz was fired or resigned; we heard it both ways.

During our final spring practice scrimmage, Coach Erdelatz let me play the entire first half and then leave to play in a lacrosse game. For two years I had been referred to as, "the best lacrosse player on the football team." That was changing since I had a scored two TDs during the first half of the spring scrimmage, but that afternoon, without having practiced with the lacrosse team, I went and scored two goals against Washington College. Oh well!

Wayne Hardin, who had been the backfield coach for four years and was only 32 years old, became the head coach. He became a great coach and was inducted into the College Football Hall of Fame in 2013, but his first year as head coach was a learning year. He took his 22 best players and divided us into two (equally balanced?) teams, which he planned to alternate midway through each quarter, i.e., at 7 and 1/2 minute intervals. To avoid the terms, 1st team and 2nd team, he named the teams, the "Torpedoes" and the "Missiles." The time to change teams always seemed to occur at inopportune times e.g., in middle of a drive or momentum shift. It was commonly accepted among the players that the team that started the game was the 1st team, but in reality players never quite knew where they stood. It was not a good system, Coach Hardin has since admitted as much to a classmate, and he abandoned it after the season.

Joe Tranchini, a mobile, option quarterback, who was the starting quarterback during Navy's 1958 football season, led the Torpedoes. The Missiles were led by Jim Maxfield, a pocket passer who, after graduating from Los Angeles High School, spent a year at Pasadena City College where he broke season records for most touchdown passes, most passes completed, and most yards gained passing. I was on Jim Maxfield's team – not surprisingly I was Navy's leading pass receiver at the end of the year.

"Navy Football Squad 1959"
(Official Navy Photo)
#11 Maxfield, #12 Spooner, #15 Dietz, #16
Tranchini, #21 Pritchard, #24 Honeywell,
#27 Bellino, #30 Tenbrook, #33 McKeown, #36
McConnell, #38 Matalavage, #40 Correll,
#44 Zenyuh, #47 Pariseau, #48 Hardison, #49 Brandquist,
#52 Visted, #54 Dunn, #56 Mouyard,
#60 Gansz, #61 Solak, #62 Hewitt, #63 Polumbo,
#64 Lucci, #66 Blockinger, #67 Falconer,
#68 Michalski, #69 Thomas, #70 Butsko, #71
Boyer, # 72 Boecker, #74 O'Donnell,
#75 Driscoll, #76 Urchel, #77 Huffman, #78 Tash,
#80 Albershart, #81 Hyde, #82 Luper,
#84 Balish, #86 Schriefer, #87 Mankowich, #88 Dattilo, #89 Bezek.

NAVY OPENS ITS SEASON AT BOSTON COLLEGE

The starting backfield for Navy was Joe Bellino of Winchester, MA at left halfback, Dick Pariseau of Attleboro, MA at right halfback, Jim Maxfield of Los Angeles, CA at quarterback, and Joe Matalavage of Mahonoy City, PA at fullback. Massachusetts provided half of Navy's backfield and a lot of fans had mixed feelings about which team they wanted to win the game.

Boston newspapers reported that the two New England boys had a stellar day. Bellino gained 115 yards on eight carries. Pariseau scored on a dive play up the middle from seven yards out during the first period. Later, with five tacklers within 10 yards, Pariseau ignored his fair catch option, fielded a punt on his 20-yard line and returned it 80 yards for a touchdown. He returned a second punt for 35-yards, a kickoff for 18-yards, and was a standout pass defender against the Eagles.

A full page color photo by John Zimmerman, of Dick Pariseau carrying the football down the left sideline, became the Sports Illustrated "Color Photo of the Week" in their September 28, 1959 issue. The accompanying article included, " **. . . here, star of the day Dick Pariseau (47) . . . after a good gain."**

The final score was Navy 24 – Boston College 8.

"PARISEAU LEADS NATION"

NCAA statistics released the next week and reported in several newspapers indicated that, **"Navy halfback, Dick Pariseau, is the nation's leader in punt return yardage, with 115 yards after returning two punts – one an 80-yard return for a TD against Boston College."**

I was very impressed to be leading the nation in anything!

NAVY OPENS NEW STADIUM WITH 29 – 2 WIN

Navy inaugurated its Navy Marine Corps Memorial Stadium with a 29 - 2 win over William & Mary. Navy gained 289 yards rushing while holding William & Mary to 101 yards of total offense.

At a cost of three million dollars, the stadium was built with private funds donated by alumni, armed forces personnel, and the public.

Even after what I considered a stellar performance against Boston College the previous week, I did not get to start the game. The Torpedoes started the game – as first team?

NAVY VS. SMU

The game was played in the Cotton Bowl Stadium in Dallas, TX. Southern Methodist University was quarterbacked by Don Meredith and was ranked 4th in the Associated Press pre-season poll. Navy rotated teams in the middle of each period; it did not work. Navy outplayed SMU in every category except the score: first downs 22 - 12, rushing yardage 190 - 124, passing yardage 125 - 84. Tied 7 - 7 at the half and trailing 13 - 7 in the fourth quarter, Navy got to SMU's 3, 22, and 7-yard line without scoring. In the last minutes of the game, Navy got to the SMU 17 yard line when on fourth down, and 48 seconds left on the clock, SMU intercepted a pass on their 4-yard line and returned it 96 yards for TD. Final score was Navy 7 SMU 20.

Jim Maxfield found that I could get open on a 7 – 10 yard turn in, fan route, if he threw the pass before I turned. In the huddle after the first completion, Jim said, "Keep running the same pattern and I'm going to keep throwing to you until you drop one." One Dallas newspaper's lengthy game report included, " . . . **Maxfield moved Navy quickly down the field to the SMU 10 yard line with seven consecutive passes, five to Pariseau including three in a row of 9, 7, and 9 yards.**" I don't know if we fumbled, were intercepted, or the "other team" came in and we lost our momentum, but it did not say that Navy scored.

SYRACUSE ROUTS NAVY 32 - 6

It was the Shriner's Oyster Bowl game in Norfolk, VA. Syracuse sophomore, Ernie Davis, touted as the next Jim Brown, led the Orangemen. Navy was intercepted four times, completed only 10 of 28 passes and had to punt five times. (While still at Syracuse, Ernie Davis was diagnosed with leukemia and was never able to play professional football. There is a movie about his brief life.)

MIAMI 23 NAVY 8

The game was played in the Orange Bowl, at night, with a temperature of 81 degrees and 85% humidity. Navy lost its third in a row. It was Miami's skilled players not the weather that beat Navy. Quarterback Fran Curci and center Jim Otto led the Miami Hurricanes.

PENN TIES NAVY WITH LAST MINUTE KICK 22 - 22

Navy again outplayed an opponent, (first downs 21 - 10, rushing yardage 191 - 71, passing yardage 163 - 128), but had four passes intercepted and lost three fumbles. Down by 22 – 19, before a home team crowd, with 1 minute and 46 seconds left in the game, Penn kicked a 24-yard field goal to tie the score.

NEXT WAS NOTRE DAME AT SOUTH BEND

There was a tradition that after practice on Mondays, the team would take a bus across the yard to the N-Room at the boathouse. Crew shells were stored on the first floor of the boathouse with access to the Severn River. The entire second floor was the N-Room where a plaque for each varsity sport, every year, listed the varsity N winners. If your team beat Army you received an N*. The N-Room also accommodated special events. Monday evenings during football season the football team had a T-bone steak and baked potato dinner in the N-Room and then listened to the scouting report on the team we would be facing the next Saturday. Steve Belichick, our defensive backfield coach was also our scout. Instead of coming to our game he – and his young son Bill, currently head coach of the New England Patriots - would go watch the team we would play the next week. The Monday night before we faced a strong Notre Dame team led by quarterback George Izo, in South Bend, Belichick gave us his scouting report. According to Jim Dunn, our team captain, Belichick concluded by saying, "If we play to 150 percent of our ability and they play to 50 percent of their ability they are still going to kick our butts, so relax and play a miracle."

IRISH DEFEAT NAVY IN FINAL MINUTE

Navy could pass against Notre Dame, but couldn't move the ball on the ground. The number of pass completions by Jim Maxfield (18 in 30 attempts) matched the Naval Academy record set by George Welsh in 1955 against Army and his 290 passing yards broke the Academy record of 285 yards set by Welsh against Penn State in 1955. Notre Dame's size let them bull their way over Navy and run for 258 yards.

Navy took the lead 19 -14 on a 6-yard touchdown pass from Maxfield to Pariseau. Notre Dame's next scoring threat ended when Pariseau intercepted a George Izo pass at the Navy 7-yard line and returned it to the Notre Dame 47-yard line. That led to a Navy field goal and a Navy 22 – 14 lead. Notre Dame climaxed a 48-yard drive with a touchdown and a pass for a two-point conversion to tie the game at 22 with seven minutes remaining. Neither team could pose a viable final threat and with 32 seconds left Notre Dame's Monty Stickles kicked a 43 yard, field goal to win 25 – 22.

(Tradition, to insure contrasting uniforms, is that the home team wears "dark," school colored uniforms and the visitors wear white uniforms. The game was played at Notre Dame in South Bend, IN and I remember being disappointed that Notre Dame's home color jerseys were blue. I had anticipated that the "Fighting Irish" would wear green jerseys. When they had visited Navy the previous year they had worn the visitors white jerseys and without the benefit of color television I assumed the "Irish" would be in green. Could it have been a concession to Notre Dame's abundance of Polish and Italian players?)

NAVY BEATS MARYLAND 22 - 14

Navy spotted Maryland a 14 - 0 lead in the first period and did not score until the second half. It was an important victory because it was Navy's last football game against Maryland for a very long time.

In the 1950s, the University of Maryland students and athletes had the reputation of being a bunch of redneck ruffians. Midshipmen marching through the tunnel under the stands at Baltimore Colt Stadium before a football game would get cups and buckets of water

(?) dumped down onto them. During lacrosse games at Maryland's Byrd Stadium we had to keep our helmets on while sitting on the bench because the students would throw oranges and other fruit at us along with an occasional beer bottle. About 9 PM the night before the MD game, our study time was interrupted by a Bancroft Hall announcement that went something like, "Our two person security force has reported that several U. of Maryland students and supporters have climbed the wall and forced their way through the main gate. Some are carrying buckets of paint. Plebes in the first and second Battalions (That occupy the front wings of Bancroft Hall surrounding the main entrance, Liberty Bell, statue of Tecumseh, and with direct access to the Chapel, yard monuments, the museum, and academic buildings.) are hereby excused from study time and authorized to assist the security force in protecting the Academy's monuments and grounds. Do not leave the Academy grounds and do not kill anyone." The stampede was awesome and the upper class crowded the windows hoping to see the action. It was too dark to see much, but the reports the next morning were fun to hear and most of the plebes were told to "carry on" and eat breakfast without bracing up as a reward for their after hours work. No red paint was observed or reported on any Academy monument, building, or structure.

NAVY 16 GEORGE WASHINGTON 8.

It was the second game in Navy Marine Corps Stadium and was played in the mud after a week of rain. For Navy it was a long day of frustration, miss-firing offense, and bad breaks against a fired up team that had one win and eight losses.

ARMY VS. NAVY, THE SETTING

Like Navy's Wayne Hardin, Army's Dale Hall was a rookie head coach having replaced the retired Red Blake. Both coaches had replaced long term coaching icons and it was said that even if both teams had gone undefeated the credit would have gone to their predecessors. Red Blake left his successor the principal ingredients of his unbeaten '58 team including All-American halfback, Bob Anderson; quarterback, Joe Caldwell, a record setting passer, and Bill Carpenter, the fabled Lonely End. He had instituted the Lonely End formation in 1958 to spread the defenses and make running room for his two All American backs, Pete Dawkins and Bob Anderson. Future All American, (1959) Bill Carpenter was their Lonely End. The Lonely End never went into the huddle. He lined up four yards inside the out-of-bounds line, and was a decoy, blocker, or receiver. His pass routes were: quick pass (automatic if the defensive back gave him any room), a diagonal across the middle, a straight path down the sideline, a hook pass, and a hook and go. Army used an orderly, rectangular huddle with the end facing the Lonely End open so that Carpenter could look into the huddle. The rumor was that the placement of the quarterback's feet signaled the play to Carpenter. (I never found out for certain.) With quarterback, Joe Caldwell passing to Carpenter, Army ended up as the nation's number one passing team during their undefeated '58 season. By the end of the season opponents were putting one-and-a half or two men on Carpenter. No other team was using such a wide receiver setup and Coach Hall used it again for the 1959 season.

Coach Hardin's strategy was to concentrate on defense to stop Army's offense. He decided to have Pariseau cover Army's Lonely End wherever he went on the field and that a third halfback would replace the fullback, full time. On change of possession - only one substitution was allowed - a fourth halfback would relieve the quarterback when Navy went on defense. With three halfbacks on offense, Hardin decided that Pariseau, the team's leading pass receiver, would become a wide receiver, the fullback position behind the quarterback would remain vacant, and Bellino and Brandquist would line up in normal halfback positions.

During practice the week before the game Pariseau was given a few snaps at quarterback and told that if the team got caught on offense without a quarterback, he should play quarterback, call an end sweep to the short side of the field, and get out of bounds, so a quarterback could enter the game. His brief practice at quarterback was not in vain, the situation actually occurred, and Pariseau had to play one snap at quarterback against Army.

It was the 60th time that the game would be played in the hallowed rubble known as Philadelphia Stadium. The New York Herald Tribune predicted, "It's Army with ease" but at game time Las Vegas though it would be a closer game and had Army favored to win by 7 points.

ARMY VS. NAVY, THE GAME

The game was played on November 29, 1959. It was a cloudy and misty day. Philadelphia Stadium was packed to capacity with 100,000 fans.

Navy won the coin toss and elected to receive. Dick Pariseau returned the opening kickoff 35 yards and began lining up as a wide receiver on offense. On the third play of the game, a pitch-out to Bellino that looked like an end sweep became a halfback pass to Pariseau who was open several yards behind Army's defense back Bob Anderson. The pass was just off his fingertips he bobbled it, lost his balance, and fell into the end zone without the ball. With the Army defense suddenly concerned about a Navy aerial attack they shifted over to cover Dick Pariseau, "Navy's lonely end." Bellino went 25 yards for his first TD and 46 yards for his second, with less than 10 minutes gone in the first period.

On defense, Dick Pariseau, who is about as big as Carpenter and has deceptive speed, neutralized Army's Caldwell to Carpenter passing attack. Army's quarterback, Joe Caldwell completed only one pass in the first half and finished with 7 completions in 27 attempts. Pariseau intercepted one of Caldwell's passes intended for Carpenter later in the game. Army eventually was so frustrated that Carpenter gave up his lonely end position and began lining up as a tight end.

On two occasions when Navy stalled, Pariseau, who played 58 minutes of the 60-minute game, punted them out of trouble. Joe Bellino scored three of the six Navy touchdowns and was voted the outstanding player of the game.

The final score of 43 − 12 was the highest winning point total in the 70-year history of the series.

NAVY INDIVIDUAL STATISTICS, 1959 FOOTBALL SEASON

(Recall that except for the Army game we were each playing only half-a-game as the Missiles and Torpedoes substituted.)

Pass Receiving	No.	Yards
Dick Pariseau, hb	20	228 yards
George Bezek, e	16	198 yards
Tom Albershart, e	14	163 yards

Punting	No.	Yards	Ave.
Dick Pariseau, hb	13	496	38.2
Joe Tranchini, qb	7	265	37.8

Punt Returns	No.	Yards	Ave.
Joe Bellino, hb	6	123	20.5
Dick Pariseau, hb	4	113	28.2

Interceptions	No.
Dick Pariseau, hb	3
Joe Bellino, hb	3

"Middie Grid Star Home"
(The Pawtucket Times, December 31,1959)
(No Photo Credit listed in newspaper)
(Used with Permission of The Times)

North vs. South All Star Football Game

The North vs. South All-Star game was played in the Orange Bowl, in Miami, FL. The game was hosted by the MAHI Shriners and net proceeds went to Shriner Hospitals for Crippled Children.

My invitation letter, to play for the South Team, included the following information: A round trip plane ticket from the Annapolis area to Miami, FL. would be provided. I should arrive in Miami on December 19th, practice would start on the 20th, and I could return home on the 28th.

I would receive $6.00 per day for laundry, a sports jacket with a North vs. South All-Star patch on the pocket, a wristwatch, and $100 cash. The Oldsmobile Company would furnish a convertible, with a large magnetic door emblem that advertised the driver as a North vs. South All-Star player, for my use while in Miami.

I should have Navy's Sports Publicity Department send three photographs and a biographical sketch.

"Dick Pariseau, Navy Halfback"
(Naval Academy Public Relations Photo)
(Stu Whelan Photographer)

And finally, "We shall meet you on arrival. Please bring your football shoes, headgear, and bathing trunks."

Who could refuse such an offer? However, when it sounds too good to be true, be careful. I took a copy of the invitation to Captain A. Coward USN the Head of the USNA Athletic Association, to insure that the money would not give me a "professional" standing and keep me from playing lacrosse in the spring. He read the letter, made some calls, and finally assured me that I could go because, "All the money, including the $100 is for expenses."

We were required to appear, two at a time, on a live, Miami, TV sports program. We went as a team to visit the children at the local Shriner Hospital. It was wonderfully impossible to drive to a sports bar in our convertibles while wearing our jacket and avoid individuals who wanted to buy us drinks and talk football.

Practices were mostly "photo ops." We learned three running plays that we could run to the right or to the left, and about five pass plays. The game itself was obviously going to be all about individual effort, rather than a team effort, and I have since avoided watching All-Star games. Despite the shortcomings, the game was fun. I got to play defensive safety in a zone defense and intercepted a pass.

North won the game 21 - 17. Army's QB, Joe Caldwell, was MVP. Operating behind a big offensive line he passed to his lonely end, Bill Carpenter, and Iowa's Curt Merz and Joe Horn, completing 12 passes in 18 attempts.

We were assigned two to a room and I roomed with Jim Otto the center from University of Miami. He became famous wearing the number 00 (double zero) during a long stint as center for the Oakland Raiders and as an All-Pro. I had the pleasure of spending some time with him only once while he was with the Raiders. We met for drinks at a San Diego hotel out near the stadium when I was a naval officer aboard a destroyer in San Diego and he had just played against the San Diego Chargers.

Unsung Heroes of The Service Classic

Among the 144 pages of the 1978 Army vs. Navy football game program is a thirty-one-page story titled, Unsung Heroes of The Service Classic. It was written by Jack Clary, a sports journalist, who has written several sports books, including one on the history and highlights of the Army - Navy games. The story in the program describes the roles played by unsung heroes over the 88 years of Army - Navy football rivalry. (The games were ordered stopped for a few years by the War and Navy

Departments after the 1893 game when high-ranking officers from each service got carried away discussing the merits of their team and ended up challenging each other to a duel.)

In the 1958 game, Army halfback, Bob Anderson was the unsung hero. He was supposed to play a supporting role to the other halfback, Pete Dawkins, and their "Lonely End," Bill Carpenter. Army coach Red Blaik had remodeled his offense to spread out the defense and give Pete Dawkins room to run, by creating the famed "Lonely End" position for All-American Bill Carpenter. Carpenter remained spread near a sideline and never entered the offensive huddle, getting his signals instead from watching the foot pattern of quarterback Joe Caldwell before he stooped to call the plays. During the 1958 game, Dick Pariseau covered the "Lonesome End" one-on-one wherever he went on the field. Pete Dawkins won the Heisman trophy that year, but Navy was stacked to stop him and Bob Anderson's running carried the day, Army 22, Navy 6.

According to the article in the football program, the year after Bob Anderson's superb game against Navy, "the tables were turned by Navy halfback, Dick Pariseau, the 1959 unsung hero, when it was Navy 43 Army 12."

Army–Navy Football Program, December 1978, <u>Unsung Heroes of The Service Classic</u> by Jack Clary. Quoted with permission.

"In a sense, Pariseau and Anderson had much in common. Both played with an acknowledged backfield star who captured most of the team's attention . . . Anderson with Dawkins and Pariseau with Joe Bellino, who like Dawkins also would be a Heisman Trophy winner. Navy's hopes for beating Army rested on the legs of Bellino. The Cadets, with Anderson, Carpenter, and Caldwell back for another year, had a strong passing game and were solid favorites.

To spread Army's defense and allow running room for Bellino, Coach Hardin adopted Army's lonesome end idea and had Dick Pariseau, Navy's leading pass receiver, split out to the sideline on every offensive play. The first time Navy had the ball a halfback pass from Bellino was just off Pariseau's fingertips in the end zone. From that moment, though, Army's defense became unnerved because it had to worry about more than

Bellino's running. Loosened up, Bellino found the cracks and openings he needed and became the first Navy player to score three touchdowns in one game. Pariseau again covered Bill Carpenter, Army's Lonesome End, and was on the field for the entire game.

Pariseau, though victimized in part by Carpenter for a touchdown, stole one in the third quarter on Army's 25-yard line to set up another Navy score. Pariseau's ability to check Carpenter played a major role in defusing a very strong Army pass offense that the Army Coach later admitted was the Cadets only hope to match Bellino."

I wrote to Jack Clary after reading his article. I thanked him for his kind words and commended him on a very interesting and informative article. I also said that I thought he was mistaken about Carpenter catching a pass for a touchdown against me in that game. I certainly didn't remember such a play!

His response arrived in a 9" x 12" manila envelope. No note or letter, simply a photograph of Bill Carpenter crossing the goal line and Navy's #47 (that was me) chasing about two steps behind him.

I responded by thanking him for the photograph and commenting that, "I guess I quickly forgot my mistake rather than let it bother me, 'cause, even with the photograph I don't remember that play."

And thus it came to pass . . .

Thirty-five years later, in 2013, while doing research for this book, I found newspaper reports that late in the game Army abandoned their Lonesome End formation and reverted to a standard offensive formation to try to close the score. The Navy coaches must have called off my one-on-one defense of Carpenter when he lined up as a tight end and I went back to being the right defensive halfback, because I also discovered a photo sequence that showed Carpenter catching a pass in front of Ronnie Brandquist, Navy's #49, who was playing left halfback, running through his attempt at a tackle and heading for the end zone as I chased from the opposite side of the field. It was reported as a 30 yard pass play for a touchdown. From the photo sequence it appears that Carpenter caught the ball at the Navy 10-yard line and ran it in for a touchdown. The last photo in the sequence was the one that Jack Clary had sent me. If I had seen these photos before I wrote Jack Clary, I could have told him my memory was not so bad after all! (Army's earlier score was a 12-yard run by Anderson.)

Navy-Marine Corp Memorial Stadium

The stadium, build exclusively with private funds, was always intended to be a memorial to the individuals in the Navy and Marine Corps who have served and will serve to protect our country. It is a two tiered stadium and on the front of each level is listed, in large letters, the names of the battles fought by the Navy and Marine Corps, (e.g., Coral Sea, Midway, Inchon, Belleau Wood, Leyte Gulf, etc.) It is truly a beautiful memorial, but can be confusing to some visiting team players who are accustomed to playing in stadiums whose facade lists the years of championships won, retired jersey numbers, or the names of past, all-star players from that school. I cannot verify the authenticity of the following story, but this is how I heard it.

After warming up on the field before the opening kickoff, the visiting team, as is customary, directed their players back to the dressing room for last minute instructions. A coach, thinking he was the last man off the field, happen to notice one of his 296 pound, 6' 5" tall players still standing in the middle of the field looking up into the stands. The coach ran over to him and asked, "What are you doing? Get to the dressing room."

"Well coach you told us that Navy didn't have a great record so far this season, but I've got to tell ya," pointing to the stadium facades, " They play a hell of a schedule. Look at that, Normandy, Iwo Jima, North Africa, Guadalcanal, . . ."

Navy-Marine Corps Memorial Stadium's 50th Anniversary

Navy planned a large celebration for the first home game of the 2009 season. It would be the 50th Anniversary (1959 – 2009) of the first game played in the stadium. A football game/memorial program - that eventually consisted of 231 pages - was being prepared and would contain the history and renovation details of the stadium, highlights of games played in the stadium, Navy football hero profiles, facts about the Academy, future schedules, . . . and the team rosters for the game. I was unexpectedly contacted by Navy's Athletic Department and asked for a comment on, "What it felt like to score the first points in the new stadium?"

I don't remember the sequence of scoring during that inaugural game, but I had to suggested to the caller, that the headline be changed to, "The first points scored by Navy in the stadium." I explained that if I was party to the first points scored it would have been, on 4th down, with the ball on our 1-yard line, William & Mary blocked my punt attempt from the end zone and scored two points for a safety. (From the 1-yard line a punter can only be 11 yards behind the center rather than the traditional 15 yards.) I reminded the caller of the 29 - 2 final score and apologized for not scoring any points for Navy that day. I gave them Joe Bellino's telephone number. I didn't know if Joe Bellino had scored Navy's first points in the stadium, but it reads better than Pariseau having a punt blocked! (It was the only punt I had blocked in my football career.)

The story, published in the program reads in part, ". . .**Joe Bellino scored the first points in stadium history on a 53 yard touchdown run . . .**"

I've not seen the actual sequence of scores, but since the Navy Athletic Department chose to call me first, I assume that after the first score in the new stadium the scoreboard read Navy 0 William & Mary 2. Therefore, I have responded positively to the occasional question about, "being intimately responsible for the first points scored in Navy-Marine Corps Memorial Stadium," but am quick to deny scoring Navy's first points!

My Basketball Disappointment

"One of the commonest ailments of the present
day is premature formation of opinion."
Frank McKinney Hubbard 1868 - 1930

On the Monday after our final Saturday afternoon plebe football game, several of us - I seem to recall eight - football players went to the plebe basketball coach and asked for a chance to tryout for the team. We had all played in high school or Prep. School and many of us had achieved recognition and honors. As examples, Tom Hyde was All-State (VA), Don Boecker and George Bezek, (captain of the basketball team) both starred at Columbian Prep., Al Blockinger started for four years at Bethel (PA) High School, and Jim Tenbrook played for Wyoming Seminary. The coach sent us to an unused court, augmented our group by two of his players, sent an assistant to watch us, and told us to play half-court 5 vs. 5. There wasn't much finesse coming from those of us who had just left the football field and no one was calling fouls. Our shooting was somewhere between poor and ugly, and after a very brief workout the coach came over to announce that, "I cannot use any of you. Thanks for coming. Good by."

I understand now probably better than then, that the coach had recruited his own players, that the team had already been practicing for several weeks, and that the coach may not have wanted to deal with two sport athletes, but we were pissed and believed that we had not been given a fair chance to make the team. We watched the team practice for several minutes without being overly impressed and began talking about forming our own team and challenging the plebe team to a game. We made vague plans to meet again, but before I could get involved further, lacrosse coach Bilderback invited me to play "winter lacrosse."

Winter lacrosse meant no coaches, just players getting together for drills. We played outside when weather permitted; otherwise I played in a squash court in McDonough Hall that was no longer used since courts were built in the new field house. I used the abandoned squash court to practice throwing and catching without wasting time retrieving an errant ball. I played a good bit of "squash court lacrosse" that winter, mostly shooting - overhand, underhand, sidearm, and backward over-the-shoulder - at the doorknob and trying to catch the return. Shooting was easy, trying to catch the rebounds coming off four walls and the overhead, required a helmet and a heavy pair of sweats to minimize the number of circular, red, welts that my body was accumulating.

It paid dividends for me in lacrosse and I must reluctantly agree that it was probably for the best however, while at the Academy, I did not have a lot of respect for the basketball coach, attended only a very few basketball games during my years at the Academy, and never believed the basketball team was exceptionally good or that all the players were better than I would have been.

"Bildy" Bilderback, Navy Lacrosse Coach
"People seldom improve if they have
no model but themselves to copy."
Issac Goldberg 1887 - 1938

Coach Willis "Bildy" Bilderback was a soft spoken and unimpressive looking gentleman. About 5' 9" tall, he was forgetful, superstitious and a bundle of nerves. But, he understood the game of lacrosse, was a teacher, and developed tactics to maximize the capabilities of his players. Coaching at the Naval Academy he would only be able to recruit a limited number of good high school lacrosse players, but he had access to a lot of good athletes who had played several sports in high school and who would be in excellent physical shape.

Relative to today, the ball was frequently on the ground in the 1960s, partly because there were fewer players who had begun playing lacrosse at an early age and partly because the rules have changed. In 1960, when someone had possession of the ball you could do most anything to take it from him. As long as you hit his stick at the same time, you could hit him with your stick anywhere between his shoulders and knees - hitting him in the head resulted in a one-minute penalty. You could also hit him with a body block and you could leave your feet to do it, as long as it was not from behind or below the knees. And you could give an opponent your best body block if they were within 15 feet of a loose ball, i.e., if the ball was on the ground. Additionally, midfielders had to be capable and aerobically conditioned to play both defense and offense because substitutions could only occur during a time out or penalty situation.

He insisted that we be proficient at scooping up ground balls, have at least two players after every ground ball, knock people down to put the ball on the ground, and be able to run, run, run. He especially encouraged football players to play lacrosse. During his tenure it was routine to have several defensemen and a couple of midfielders who also played on Navy's football team. These players set the tone for Navy's, "knock 'em down and run, run, run" style of play. When I was playing, it was common for two Navy players simultaneously converging on a loose ball, to both shout, "I'll get the player. You get the ball."

During Coach Bilderback's fourteen seasons as Navy's head coach, 1959 - 1972, he had a record of 117 wins, 18 losses, and 2 ties. That's a win rate of 85 percent. From 1960 -70 he led Navy to at least a share of nine National Championships including eight in a row between 1960 and 1967. In the annals of college lacrosse the 1960s are referred to as, "Navy's Decade of Dominance." Like most great coaches he developed his strategy and tactics to maximizing the strengths of his players and take advantage of the rules of the game. He successfully recruited a few high school lacrosse players who were proficient at scoring goals, encouraged individuals he had available at the Academy to play lacrosse, and became a master at developing athletes into lacrosse players. My lacrosse initiation and experience at Tabor Academy under Coach Trautman fit perfectly in his scheme.

A Teaching Lesson
"Very simple ideas lie within reach only of complex minds."
Oliver Goldsmith 1728 - 1774

One day at practice midway through my 3rd Class (sophomore) year at the Academy, Coach "Bildy" came over to me, pointed to assistant coach, Buster Phipps, who was standing near a wooden wall that was part of the obstacle course on the adjacent field and said, "Dick, go over there and see coach Phipps."

I ran over to him, "Coach told me to come over here and see you."

"Yes. I just want to play catch with you for a minute. Stay here in front of the wall." he said while backing up to get about ten yards away from me.

He raised his stick and threw me the ball. It was a nice pass, shoulder high, to my right side. I returned the ball trying to mimic his pass location since I had no idea what he expected of me. He threw the ball to me again, shoulder high, to my left side. An easy backhanded catch. I returned it to him in a similar location. His next pass was a bit high and a little harder, but easy to catch. Again I returned a similar pass. The next pass he messed up; it bounced about a foot in front of me and skidded past me to the wall behind me. I retrieved the ball and threw him a nice pass, shoulder high to his stick side. His return was to my off-stick side and again bounced about a foot in front of me. I hit it with my stick while trying to catch it, but again it went by me and back to the wall. While retrieving the ball, I'm trying to figure out what's going on, but have no idea. Assuming that my passes were not good enough, I throw it back so that he did not have to move his stick to catch it. A perfect pass. His return pass hit the ground about three feet in front of me and bounced up towards my head. I instinctively moved my head, but missed the ball with my stick and the ball again went back to the wall. As I turned to go after the ball, he said, "That's enough. Leave it there and come over here."

When I got to him he asked, "How do you like playing catch with me?"

"Honestly Coach, not very much." I replied.

"Hard to stop those bounce shots isn't it?"

"Yes sir. Even when I began to expect them."

"You have a good hard shot and we want you to take more shots from out in the midfield. Remember this little drill we just went through and think what kind of shots the goalie hopes you don't take."

From that day on, my shots, both during practice and in games consisted almost exclusively of overhand bounce shots that I could eventually make stay low after hitting the ground or bounce high and just under the net. Not surprisingly, over 90% of my goals were bounce shots both at the Academy and later when playing Club Lacrosse. It was a wonderful teaching lesson that was impossible to forget and classic Coach Bilderback coaching.

Postscript: After playing club lacrosse and having many discussions with goalies about what kind of shots were hardest to stop I concluded that they unanimously disliked, "High to low" (an overhead release, "high," that bounced at their feet, "low") or "Low to high" (an underhand release from ground level, "low," that ended up just under the top of the net "high.")

Navy's 1960 Lacrosse Season
"God is always on the side which has the best coach."
Henry Brougham 1778 - 1868

The USNA Class of 1960's lacrosse legacy began with an undefeated plebe season and ended with a National Championship and the beginning of the "Golden Age" of Navy Lacrosse.

The NCAA Lacrosse Tournament did not begin until 1971. In the 1960s there were only about ten major lacrosse schools, everyone tried to play each other, and the US Intercollegiate Lacrosse Association declared the team with the best record National Champion.

Our season began in early March with games in Annapolis against Yale (not yet a lacrosse elite) and the Marine Corps team from Quantico, Virginia (that had several Navy, West Point, and other college graduates who had played lacrosse before joining the Marine Corps.) We won both games. On April 2nd we rode a bus to New Jersey for our first real test, in a game against Rutgers. My father and his brother, Gig, drove down from Attleboro to watch us beat a reputable Rutgers University team 15 to 2.

On our bus ride back to Annapolis we made a pit stop where, among the tourist souvenir items offered for sale, were straw hats with a narrow, straw brim. One teammate tried one on, thought it looked cool, made a purchase, and began wearing it around the store. A second teammate bought one and a Sharpie permanent marker and wrote our game scores on his hat. That was it. Everyone on the team had to have one and we wore them on every game trip, i.e., whenever we were away from the Academy and naval officers who might give demerits for being out of uniform - navy blue uniform, white shirt, black tie, and straw hat. (Men's hats were popular, fashionable, and a sign of distinction in those days. Men wore hats everywhere. Not ball caps, but real hats, e.g., banded fedoras, felt pork-pie hats, linen flat caps. The fashion had begun to wane and then got a big boost in 1960 when President J. F. Kennedy went hatless at his inauguration.)

Coach Bilderback developed a third midfield to enhance his "hit and run, run, run," style of play, and they got a lot of playing time as we built up big leads in our early games. Our attack men, three player from the Baltimore area, were our primary scorers: Karl Rippelmeyer, 1st Team All American; Hank Chiles, 3rd Team All American and an eventual 4 Star Admiral, and Tom Mitchell, a sophomore and two years later a 1st Team All American. I was the center midfielder and face-off man. Don Chinn and Jack Prudhome (a Navy fighter pilot who was killed in Vietnam) played the wings on the first midfield. The midfielder's scored a lot of goals on fast breaks, especially late in the game. I never found my playing time limited with three midfields because I was part of the Extra-man Offense (when the opponent was playing one man down because they had a player in the penalty box), the Extra-man Defense (when we were playing one man down), and often sent in to face off after a goal by either team.

We played a back and forth game against Maryland at Byrd Stadium coming out the winner by one goal, after being down by five goals early in the third period. Later we upset pre-season favorite Johns Hopkins on their Homewood Field when our run and hit style overwhelmed their deliberate, precision offense. With only the Army-Navy game, to be played at West Point, remaining, both Army and Navy were undefeated and the winner would become the National Champions. With two weeks before the Army game, Coach Bilderback scheduled a game for the open Saturday against the perennial, powerhouse Mt. Washington Lacrosse Club which routinely fielded 8 or 10 college All Americans from the Baltimore area. We played club style lacrosse, on a properly lined field instead of in a stadium, with families on blankets and folding chairs along the sidelines, eating, drinking, cheering, and critiquing every play. The Mt. Washington Lacrosse Club beat us 11 to 7.

"Lacrosse Team Leader – Captain Dick Pariseau"
(Navy Academy Public Relations Photograph)
(Stu Whelan photographer)

Traveling to West Point our record was:

Navy 26	Yale 6
Navy 16	The Quantico Marines 3
Navy 15	Rutgers 2 (at Rutgers)
Navy 17	Penn State 3
Navy 19	Washington College 0
Navy 16	Princeton 5
Navy 9	Virginia 2
Navy 15	Maryland 14 (at Maryland's Byrd Stadium)
Navy 19	Duke 5
Navy 15	Johns Hopkins 7 (at Homewood Field)
Navy 10	Baltimore University 3
Navy 7	Mt. Washington Lacrosse Club 11

Army had been scoring double digit wins, had beaten Maryland 17 - 6, and lost, only to the Mt. Washington Lacrosse Club, by one goal (8 to 7) in the first game of their season. Army had not played Johns Hopkins, but was favored to beat Navy. Army had been at least co-champions the past two years while Navy kept having trouble getting past traditional lacrosse powers Johns Hopkins and Maryland. Army also had the 6'1" Baltimore schooled, Bob Miser, touted as the best attack man in the nation and Bill Carpenter – Army's football lonesome end – who was being mentioned as the best defenseman playing college lacrosse.

On the bus ride to West Point we were a confident team. We were wearing our straw hats, mine and several others, embellished with each of our game scores. Since Marylanders consider lacrosse the State sport, Baltimore the crucible of the game's stars, and football a good off-season conditioning sport for lacrosse, we were not surprised that a very large contingent of team supporters, driving vans and personal automobiles, were following the team bus. It was the beginning of June Week (graduation week) and three teammates had their dates in one of the cars following our bus to West Point. Larry Dunne's date had a pet monkey that she had taken along for the ride. During our pit stop, Larry snuck the monkey onto our bus and another teammate bought a wig for our bald assistant coach, Buster Phipps. When we disembarked at West Point we must have appeared foolishly overconfident. We were in our midshipman uniforms except for wearing our straw hats, Coach Phipps was wearing his wig, and the first player off the bus had a little monkey sitting on his shoulder.

If the rumors are believed, even our coaches were confident. The Navy coaches, it is rumored, spent the night before the game drinking boilermakers in the cocktail lounge of West Point's Thayer hotel, telling stories of how the Navy team not only embraced Coach Bilderback's, "Run, run, run" strategy but now thought hitting and running were fun. At one point when attention waned, or patrons in the lounge tired of hearing how Navy was going to run Army into the ground, Coach Phipps, wearing the wig we had purchased for him, apparently threw a firecracker under one of the tables.

By 10:00 AM game time on Saturday morning the crowd was estimated at 5,500. Unlike in football where team benches are on opposite sides of the field, lacrosse is like basketball (both teams on same side) and ice hockey (teams separated by a penalty box and scorer's table.) Consequently, with open seating, the West Point band was directly behind the Army team, and the Navy supporters – including the monkey – were directly behind our bench and adjacent to the Army contingent. It seemed that the monkey objected to the noise from the West Point band and whenever the band began to play the monkey would turn towards them and with teeth bared, loudly, screech, "Ei! ei! ei! ei!" The screeching was impossible to ignore and during warm-up several Navy players offered interpretation of what the little monkey was telling the band and Army supporters to do.

Navy scored first on a goal by Rippelmeyer and he and Miser began trading goals. Goals seemed to come in bunches for both teams. Army scored three goals in less than two minutes to take the halftime lead 5 – 3.

In the second half it became a battle of conditioning between hustling, hard-hitting midfields bent on getting the ball to their attack men and that's when Navy's run, run, run approach paid dividends. Miser and Rippelmeyer were often double-teamed, but Navy's other two attack men, Hank Chiles and Tom Mitchell could also score and did. Miser was bottled up and Navy's midfields, maintaining a scorching paced, began getting all the loose balls and controlling the game. In the first half, Army had twenty-four shots; in the second half they were limited to eight. During one stretch in the fourth quarter, Navy scored seven goals before Army could get another one.

Navy won going away by a score of 10 – 7 and took the lacrosse title back to Maryland. It was Navy's sixth lacrosse title and the first since 1954.

The game was highlighted by Ray Cave in the June 13, 1960 issue of Sports Illustrated Magazine. The article, titled, *New Scalping For Old Army* is available on the Internet at

http://sportsillustrted.cnn.com/vault/article/magazine/ MAG1134483/1/index.htm

The Sports Illustrated article concluded with the story of a Baltimore, MD matron who had driven to West Point for the game and was sitting in front of an Army officer. Each time Navy began moving the ball she would stand up and cheer. And the Army officer in his starched uniform would politely say, "Madam, please sit down." The woman eventually announced to her friends, "You know, they don't deserve lacrosse up here."

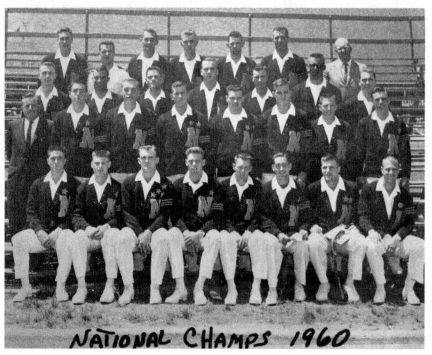

Navy's 1960 National Championship Lacrosse Team.
(Left to right) 1st Row: Fitzpatrick, Fraser, Rippelmeyer, Mitchell,
Byrne, Reeves, Pariseau, & Chiles. 2nd Row: Head Coach Bill
Bilderback, Chinn, Vinje, Prudhomme, Hewitt, Ryder, Quarterman,
& Williams. 3rd Row: Manager Mel Sollberger, Hill, Reich, Huffman,
Kisiel, Metzler, & Hastie. 4th Row: Dunne, Allegretti, Krulisch,
Inderlied, Shupe Schriefer, & Assistant Coach Lou Phipps, Jr.
(Official Navy Photo)
(Naval Academy Public Relations Photo)
(Stu Whelan Photographer)

Lacrosse Honors

"Success covers a multitude of blunders."
George Bernard Shaw 1856 - 1950

From the State's seven colleges that play lacrosse, three Navy player were unanimous First Team selections to the All-Maryland Team: Karl Rippelmeyer (Attack), Dick Pariseau (Midfield), and Neil Reich (Defense.) Hank Chiles (Attack) was selected on the second team.

On Tuesday of June Week at the Presentation of Prizes and Awards ceremony, I was awarded the Stuart Oxnard Miller Memorial Lacrosse Cup, presented, "To the midshipman who has contributed the most to the success of the team."

Karl Rippelmeyer and I were selected as First Team All Americans and we both played in the 19th Annual North vs. South All Star game at Holy Cross College in Worcester, MA on June 11, 1960. I wish to thank Navy's 1960 Lacrosse Team for giving me all the lacrosse honors that I received. It was truly a team effort for which I received recognition.

"Dick Pariseau, Navy, First Team All American" (Official Navy Photo)
(Naval Academy Public Relations Photo)
(Stu Whelan Photographer)

The 1960 All American First Team

Attack: Robert Miser, Army
                           Karl Rippelmeyer, Navy
                           Howard Albrecht, Baltimore

Midfield: Richard Pariseau, Navy
                           Herman Eubanks, Jr., Army
                           David Dresser, Cornell

Defense: William Carpenter, Army
                           John MacNealey III, Johns Hopkins
                           Jack Horton Jr., Princeton

Goal: Roos Nippard, Baltimore

Navy won the Wingate Trophy, presented annually to the National Champions. The trophy was presented on December 10, 1960, at the Hotel Manhattan in New York City, at the 78th Annual U.S. Intercollegiate Lacrosse Association Dinner, honoring the All American Team. Members of the All American team were invited to bring their father to the Award presentation and dinner. A newly commissioned Ensign, I flew to New York from San Diego, CA and I was very proud to have my Dad drive from Attleboro, MA to join me. The guest speaker was Reverend Robert "Bob" Richards, Olympic Pole Vault Champion 1952 and 1956.

In 2007 I was honored to write a letter supporting Rippelmeyer's nomination for induction into the National Lacrosse Hall of Fame and in 2008 to attend his well-deserved induction.

The Lacrosse Shot

"Gossip is what no one claims to like - but everyone enjoys."
Joseph Conrad 1857 - 1924

During a snowy winter day in 2006, I was performing an archival dig in a musty basement closet looking for something I'd misplaced. You know, archival dig, as in finding one or more boxes that you've been moving from house to house for over 25 years, but haven't opened since the initial packing, and you have no idea what's inside. In one of the boxes, as I fingered old pictures, papers, maps, and mementos that must have seemed important at the time they were stored, I discovered it. A rolled up poster held in its cylindrical form by a red rubber band that had lost all its flexibility and disintegrated when I tried to remove it. Not what I was searching for, but intriguing. Its faded look, musty odor, and tears visible along its edges suggested the poster's age. Without a clue to its content, I carefully unrolled it on a large nearby table being careful to avoid further damage. It was an 18" x 24" hand drawn and hand lettered poster that depicted a cartoonish facsimile of an Oscar Statue with the grim face and flapping ears of Alfred E. Neumann of Mad Magazine fame, wearing briefs that suggested hernia support. The hand printed words read, "Motion Picture Industry Award for Best Shot of The Year, to Dick Pariseau, NAVY LAX, 16 May 1960." I had only a vague recollection of informally receiving the poster from a classmate and no recall of the event depicted.

That spring, the Naval Academy completed the Bilderback-Moore Lacrosse Hall of Fame as an extension to the Navy Marine Corps stadium where football and lacrosse games are played. It's a beautiful building named in honor of two, very successful, Navy lacrosse coaches. Graduates who had played for these coaches were invited to a pre-opening party and tour of this splendid facility. The first several hours were spent viewing and reminiscing over the multitude of trophies, old uniforms and equipment, photos, and listening to a prognosis of the upcoming season by the current coach. When the event schedule called for cocktails and hors d'oeuvre, I joined nine teammates at a large round table, bathed in the sun, overlooking the stadium field. During a lull in the conversation, I mentioned my new discovery as I carefully unrolled the poster on the table and asked, "Do any of you recall what this is about?"

Surprisingly, to me at least, some of them claimed to recall the incident and began an animated, group retelling of the story. The primary story teller - of the moment - was constantly interrupted by teammates interjecting additional facts (exaggerations?) and frequently replaced by another teammate who claimed more specific recall as the tale unfolded. After much backslapping and laughing, that drew quite a large additional crowd, the following, according to my teammates, is what occurred and led to the drawing of the poster.

By the middle of May our lax team had won all ten of its games including an upset of Johns Hopkins a few days earlier. We had a game left against Baltimore U. and a showdown against undefeated West Point. On this sunny, warm, May 16th, coach Bilderback interrupted practice to say that Sports Illustrated, Inc. was making a documentary video on college lacrosse and they wanted to record video of our offensive team in action. He directed the first team offense, three attack-men and three midfielders, to proceed to the other end of the stadium field and, "Do what the guys from Sports Illustrated want."

At the far end of the field a platform had been erected above and behind the goal. It was occupied by the Director and a cameraman. The cameraman stood behind a shoulder high podium with his camera positioned on top to record the action taking place around the goal. The midfielders were instructed by the director to pass the ball two or three times among themselves, then pass the ball to an attack-man behind the goal, and set a screen for the closest midfielder who would cut across the front of the goal for a pass from the attack-man and a quick shot into the goal. It was basic lacrosse offense 101. We did as directed several times with either the right or left midfielder getting the shot. After each shot the director asked for, "One more time, please." After, a dozen or thirty takes, (the number recollected varied among the group) a teammate, now becoming the primary storyteller, said he came to me and requested, "Dick, you have to go tell Coach we've had enough of this. We have to get back to practice."

"That's right," another added and that's when you told the attackmen, "This time, after the midfielder cuts in front of the goal, pass the ball back to me and I will take the shot from out in the midfield."

Another storyteller continued, "The director said, 'Go.' the passes were made and you took a long, hard, underhand shot from out in the midfield. The shot hit the director where his legs came together. He fell to his knees on the platform with a thud, a gasp of air, and bulging eyes."

"Yes," another player added, "and while the speechless director remained on his knees staring out into space, some of us saw him make an arm movement that we interpreted as a goodbye wave and that the drill was over.' You must have seen it too Dick, because you quickly led us back up the field to practice."

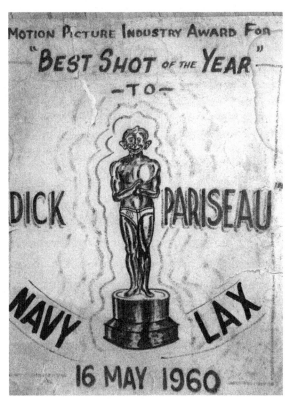

"Best Shot of the Year"
(Drawing by Steve Scheffer USNA '60, Editor of "The Log."
And given to the author.)

"I had remained with the practice squad and didn't see the shot," said another in the group, "but I remember that when you all returned you told the coach, 'We're all finished coach. One of the guys from Sports Illustrated is not feeling well."

I honestly don't recall the shot, but I know that I would not have aimed at an individual. Perhaps I believed that a shot over their head would sent a message or that the large podium that hid the cameraman and held the video camera would make a nice target and a ball hitting it would sent a message? The actual shot must have been one of those, "bad shot, but good result."

My memory stimulated, I remembered that a classmate, Steve Scheffer, had given me the poster. He had been in the stands covering the Sports Illustrated filming event for *The Log*, the Naval Academy school newspaper. He had drawn up the poster for submission with his article, "The Shot" but said he no longer needed the poster because his article did not pass editorial acceptability by the Navy brass and would not be published.

Forty-six years after the event my memory has faded, I still don't remember the shot, but who can argue with teammates who are willing to describe you as their hero. I have no doubt that the event occurred exactly as their combined recollection described and neither should anyone reading this tale.

I sent a photo of the drawing to Steve Scheffer, but he recalled neither the incident nor the drawing. That's not surprising because he was sitting in the stands and was not privy to the on-field discussion leading to the shot. In all likelihood, he simply saw the result of the shot, drew the cartoon, and made up the scenario that was not published. Additionally, when I contacted him, he may have had other things on his mind. He was in NY City, President of Film Programming, Video & Enterprises for Time Warner, responsible for buying all the movies for HBO and CINEMAX, and at the moment was overseeing distribution of the HBO original programming of "Band of Brothers," "Sex in the City," and "The Sopranos." You're excused Steve!

Team Captain & Leadership
"We had deep depth."
Yogi Berra 1925 - 2014

I am extremely proud to have been elected by teammates as Captain of the Naval Academy Lacrosse Team in 1960 and to have been awarded the Stuart Oxnard Miller Lacrosse Cup as, "The individual who contributed the most to the success of the team." And even though I had been designated an Honorable Mention All American as a junior, I was clearly not the best player on the team.

"Presentation of the Stuart Oxnard Miller
Lacrosse Cup to Midshipman Pariseau"
(Official US Navy Photo)

I tried to understand why my teammates had voted me team captain and occasionally wondered whether or not I was worthy. I always played and practiced at full speed, but there has to be more to leadership than that? When I played in the annual North vs. South Lacrosse All Star game I saw many midfielders whom I thought were better players than I, but I had been selected as First Team All American. I had been told that leadership was an issue, but I didn't understand what that meant until a couple of events occurred much later.

The first was at an awards banquet hosted by the Baltimore Athletic Club in the mid 1970s. Art Donovan, the Baltimore Colts' Hall of Fame and All-Pro defensive tackle who had become a professional raconteur was the Master of Ceremonies, and recently retired Coach Bilderback was the guest speaker. I was a young Navy Lieutenant Commander at the time, stationed in the Northern Virginia area and had been invited to attend by Coach Bilderback, who had been requested to invite someone who had played for him and who would be willing to make some very brief remarks - if invited to do so. When the Coach finished his talk someone asked him, "Your first National Championship Team in 1960, when did you decide they would be a very good team?"

He answered with the following story. "I had been with Navy's 1960 lacrosse team the whole way. I was the plebe coach when they were plebes, the assistant varsity coach under Dinty Moore when they were sophomores and their junior year was my first year as head coach. In 1960 they were seniors and I had a year as head coach under my belt.

Two day before our first game, we were finishing our last, long, hard practice. I told Dick, the team captain, - sitting right over here - to take the team to Hospital Point and "Run the hill ten times." Hospital Point is about half-a-mile from our practice field along the seawall and across a walking bridge. The hill was about twenty-five feet higher than the fields reclaimed from the Severn River with dredged landfill. The Academy's hospital was located at the top of the hill. We didn't practice in the stadium so there were no steps to run. Our drill was to pick up a ground ball, run up the hill, pass the ball to a teammate, run across the top of the hill, receive a pass, and run back down the hill while cradling the ball. While the team jogged over, I would either drive over and be standing at the top of the hill when they arrived or just wait for them to return. On this occasion I was trying to determine if we were too tense, over-thinking the first game, or if some other Academy requirement had taken their mind off the game so I drove over and parked out of sight among a group of cars, but close enough to watch them run the hill. When I counted Dick running the team up the hill twelve times, I knew he had something else on his mind and I was afraid my concerns might be justified. When they finished at the hill and began their return jog to the locker room, I drove back to greet them.

I called Dick over and asked, "How did it go at the hill?"

"It went well coach. I think we are ready for the game on Saturday."

"How many times did I tell you to run the hill?" I asked him.

"Ten times, coach."

" How many times did you and the team run it?" I asked thinking that I could loosen him up by kidding him about not being able to count.

"Twelve times coach. Ten for you and two for the team in the fourth quarter."

All I could say was, "Oh . . . OK . . . Go take your shower." That's when I knew that this team was going to be able to run with anybody and would be very hard to beat.

And about the rumor that the night before every game at Navy I would leave the sprinklers on all night to soften the field and keep the grass moist so that missed passes would not roll out of bounds and stop the action, let me say that I never personally turned on those sprinklers."

The second event occurred about ten years later, during half time of a Navy lacrosse game at the Navy Marine Memorial stadium. Navy had not played well in the first half, had gotten a couple of bad breaks, and was down by three goals. I was with a group of ex-Navy lacrosse players from a variety of years enjoying a hot dog and beverage at the north end of the stadium. We were discussing the game and Navy's play thus far.

Someone offered, " I hope Navy doesn't get discouraged. They could still win this game."

To which someone in the group, whom I did not recognize, pointed to me and said, "They would win if Dick Pariseau was their captain."

It was instantly obvious that the comment was a total surprise to me and the group looked from me back to the speaker for an explanation. The speaker continued, "I was a sophomore when Dick was captain in 1960. For our home game against Virginia, coach let four of us sophomores who were playing on the JV team, dress for the game. We didn't expect to play, but it was nice being on the field, in game uniform, with the team. Some of you probably know what I mean?"

Several heads nodded and the group continued to look expectantly for the rest of the story. "Virginia was playing us tough, their goalie was red hot and we were ahead by only one goal when we went into the dressing room at half time. In my opinion it was anyone's game. Whichever team got some momentum or a lucky break could win it."

"Yeah. I remember that game. It was a great game." came a comment from someone in the group.

"Well, when coach finished talking to us and making a few adjustments, he told Dick to take the team back out on field for the second half. Dick went to the door, turned to face the team and said, 'If any one here doesn't believe we're going to win this game, don't come out for the second half.' He then reached back pushed the door open, stepped to one side so he was blocking half the exit, and stared at us. He scared the shit out of me. I didn't want to stay in the locker room, but I wasn't convinced that we were going to win. Someone made the first move to the door; I think it was Hank Chiles. He tapped his stick against Dick's while looking him in the eye and said, 'We're going to win.' And went out onto the field. Others lined up and began the procedure. Look him in the eye, tap sticks or give him a high five, convince him that you mean it when you say the words, and he would let you squeeze by and go back out onto the field. I sat there stunned and mesmerized. But, as I watched the guys go by Dick and out the door, I became a believer. I was one of the last to leave the locker room, but by the time I got to the door I was so pumped up that I had no trouble looking him in the eye and saying, 'We're going to win.' with the utmost of confidence.

"Well, since you went undefeated you obviously won, but what was the final score?" someone asked.

"Yeah. What was the second half like?" Interjected another.

Several final scores and second half scenarios were offered, but no one really remembered. The consensus, before we disbanded to return to our seats, was that Navy had owned the second half and won by five or six goals.

I had no recollection of the incident, but that night I looked through some Navy lacrosse game clippings and found that on April 23, 1960 we had a very difficult time with Virginia.

Navy won 9 -2 but it was not pretty. Virginia came with a record of only one win and three losses, and we might have been looking ahead to our game against Maryland at College Park the next week. We let Virginia get 27 shots – more than any team had against us in the previous six games. Rippelmeyer could add only one goal and one assist to his team leading 13 goals and 16 assists. Fortunately it was a 90-degree day and we wore out the Virginia midfields. Seven different Navy players scored goals with Tom Inderlied and I leading the midfielder scoring with two goals each. Coach Bilderback must have been livid after the game when he found out we took 59 shots to get 9 goals. We had been getting between 15 and 26 goals per game with an 18 goal average. I could not find a half-time score but the heat and our running style of play must have made the second half better than the first, at least for Navy! Perhaps during half-time, I was more concerned about the game outcome than the Coach or was he counting on me to do something?

After these two episodes I felt better about my contribution to the team and can now appreciate that the best player does not always make the best team captain.

Cape Cod Sushi

"We go by the majority vote, and if the majority
are insane, the sane must go to the hospital."
Horace Mann 1796 - 1859

During my summers at Cape Cod, I had two buddies; Fred Young from Larchmont, NY and Buzz Shaw from western Mass. For several summers we worked together for the town of Dennis paving roads, repairing bridges, raking hay from alongside roadways, and cutting trees. Trying to "stay in shape for sports." It's a guy thing. Nights we chased the parties together.

One summer Fred got a job with the Dennis Port police as a summer cop, in police uniform, directing traffic at the three-way intersection in the center of town. That was a great summer. Buzz and I, still working for the town of Dennis, would take our lunch hour at the corner where Fred was directing traffic and when a car with young women came by, he would stop them, briefly look them over, and if "suitable," would tell them to pull ever to the side of the road. Buzz and I would then try to get some names and contact numbers, or tell them where the parties were going to be that night and hope to see them again later. If they seemed nervous, we would tell them that we would take care of whatever problem had caused the policeman to stop them. If that didn't work we'd wave Fred over. If we walked away before he arrived he'd know they were not receptive and mention some traffic transgression he suspected. If they were friendly, but unsure of our ability to "handle the cop," we would stay around and Fred would tell them it was a joke and assure them that they were the only car that he had pulled over all summer. Good friends, always looking for fun, and easy company.

The first summer that I brought George Mahelona with me to the Cape he made a lasting impression on my friends. George was an Academy classmate and genuine friend. He was from Hawaii, dark skinned, fun loving, smart, and a bit over the top with partying. The last being a trait that I've found to be relatively common among children whose father was a minister. He was a submarine supply officer and during his tour at

Supply Officers School in the early 1960s, in segregated Athens, GA he was denied entry to establishments that did not allow blacks.

I had not hesitate to introduced George to Fred Young and Buzz Shaw, the four of us had attended a couple of parties together, and we were enjoying the summer. One morning the four of us rented a small boat with an outboard motor from a marina on Bass River. We were going out to Target Rock to go fishing. Fishing around Target Rock was a summer ritual because you were sure to catch some flounders, scup, blowfish, eels, or even a small sand shark. We had four fishing poles, a pound of cleaned, frozen squid for bait, and some beer. Squid was the preferred bait on Cape Cod. Sea worms, minnow, and clams were good, but difficult to keep on the hook when bottom fishing while drifting in a boat. It was a warm, June day with a pleasant sea breeze, and light waves. Target Rock is plainly visible from the mouth of the river and George, being our guest, was given the helm and the wide seat in the rear of the boat with the beer and the bait. We were enjoying some beer and telling stories during our twenty-five minute boat ride out the river and to Target Rock. As we approached the fishing area we began preparing our fishing poles and when Fred went to get the bait, he found George eating it as an hors d'oeuvre with his beer. Sushi was not popular in the 1960s and squid, unlike in Hawaii, was used only for bait in New England. The story was retold many times that summer and if George was present he simply shrugged his shoulders, 'cause it wasn't a big deal.

My buddies no longer remember George's name, but even today, if I see them at the Cape, or we speak on the telephone they always ask, "Do you still see that cannibal you brought to the Cape that summer?"

Reader's Digest
"There are very few good judges of humor, and they don't agree."
Josh Billings (pseudonym of Henry Wheeler Shaw) 1818 - 1885

The first payment I received for an original submission, published in a national magazine, was from Reader's Digest in 1963. It was published in the "Humor in Uniform" section of the magazine. I received a check for $70.00

We were studying electrical power generation and learning the relationships between Power (P), Voltage (V), Current (I) and Resistance (R). Our end of the week quiz was approaching and Tom, my roommate was having some difficulty with the relationships. Here's my story.

"In preparation for a quiz at the U.S. Naval Academy, my roommate, who was having trouble with electrical formulas, was advised by a classmate to memorize just one important equation from which many others could be derived. The key to memorizing it was the jingle: "Twinkle, twinkle, little star, POWER EQUALS I SQUARED R." (P = I² R)

When the results of the test were posted, he could not believe his failing grade. He had solved each problem with the magic formula -- "Little star up in the sky, POWER EQUALS R SQUARED I." (P = R² I)

Hall of Fame Awards
"A bare assertion is not necessarily the naked truth."
George D. Prentice 1802 - 1870

US Naval Academy *(1960)*

By virtue of being selected as a 1st Team All American in Lacrosse, I was automatically in the Academy's Hall of Fame. My lacrosse photo is displayed, alongside other Academy graduates with similar honors, in the second floor corridor surrounding the natatorium.

Attleboro Area Football Hall of Fame (1980)

Annually a committee selects individuals from Attleboro, North Attleboro, and Bishop Feehan high schools for induction into the "Attleboro Area - Football Hall of Fame." I was honored to be inducted in November of 1980. Rollie Kerkhoff, our fullback, had been inducted a few years earlier. I joined my Dad and his brothers, Joe and Gig as the 4th Pariseau member.

Attleboro High School Athletic Hall of Fame (1995)

In March of 1995, I was honored to be selected for the Attleboro High School Athletic Hall of Fame. The program for the banquet and induction ceremony states:

"The Attleboro High School Athletic Hall of Fame recognizes the contributions of both men and women as builders and participants in athletics as an integral part of the education program of Attleboro High School. Eligibility is based primarily on the athletic prowess of the individual and includes consideration of personal integrity, high standards of sportsmanship and good character."

Ronnie Boivin, my long time friend, classmate, and teammate was my presenter.

When we cleaned out our parent's house after their death, my brother, sisters, and I divided up the several boxes of letters, newspapers, magazines, and family clippings, that families with attic storage space collect. Searching for facts relating to this book, I have recently looked through all the boxes that I "inherited." In one box I found an article from the Sun Chronicle (the combined Attleboro Sun and North Attleboro Chronicle) that I had never seen before and that took me by surprise. It was in the Sports section, dated Friday, March 17, 1995, written by Peter Gobis - a man whom I now consider to be profoundly knowledgeable. Under the heading, **"Hall Adding Eight"** he began the article with, **"Perhaps the greatest athlete of all-time from Attleboro High School, Dick Pariseau, an All-American selection in lacrosse at the U.S. Naval Academy, is one of the new eight inductees into the AHS Athletic Hall of Fame."** On a future trip to Attleboro, I must try to meet Mr. Gobis and thank him for his opinion.

RICHARD R. PARISEAU

A Small Gesture Can Make a Big Impression
"Be nice to people on your way up because
you'll meet them on your way down."
Wilson Mizner 1876 - 1933

Football fans were poring out of the stands onto the field to congratulate us when the final whistle blew and we had beaten Army in 1959. I remember a small boy coming up to me and asking if he could have my chinstrap as a souvenir. I didn't consider it much of a souvenir, but I had nothing better to offer, so I gave it to him. It turned out that the boy's Dad was a friend of my father and a teaching/coaching colleague in Pawtucket, RI. I had told my Dad he could invite anyone he knew to the Navy football dinner reception later that evening and the young boy and his parents attended. When I saw that the youngster was carrying his prize chinstrap in his hand I thought I could improve on his memento. I found a pen, autographed the chin strap then walked the boy around the dinning room introducing him to players and having them sign the chin strap. Joe Bellino, always gracious and indulgent, was one of the signators. A small gesture on my part for an enthusiastic young boy.

The young boy's name was Jim Donaldson and he became the sports editor for the Providence Journal Newspaper, in Providence, Rhode Island. Thirty-six years after we met, an upcoming Army vs. Navy game, reminded him of our meeting and he wrote a very flattering article about our first meeting. He even took time to track me down and favor me with a telephone call. My small gesture had made an impression.

Here is the beginning of the lengthy article by Jim Donaldson that appeared in the Providence Journal newspaper on Saturday, December 2, 1995. The article is headlined, "Pariseau played tough against Army, Admiral" and is reproduced with permission.

Pariseau played tough against Army, Admiral, by Jim Donaldson
The chinstrap, made of leather, sits on my desk, as it has for years and years. The signatures on it, written in pen have faded. The memories have not.

It was 36 years ago that I was given that chinstrap, on the field at Municipal Stadium, in Philadelphia, moments after Navy had beaten Army, 43 - 12.

It was 1959, and I was 8 years old. My mother and father and I had gone to the game to watch Dick Pariseau, a senior from Attleboro, Mass., whose father Rollie and uncle "Gig" coached football at Tolman High in Pawtucket.

A letterman as a sophomore and junior, Dick was a first-class midshipman that year, playing in his last game for the Naval Academy, and final Army-Navy game.

He played almost every minute of it. There was limited substitution in those days - unlike today, when entire teams seem to go in and out on almost every down.

Dick Pariseau played 58 minutes that afternoon against Army. He played halfback alongside Heisman Trophy winner, Joe Bellino on offense, and, on defense, he covered Army's famous "Lonesome End" - All-American Bill Carpenter.

When it was over, we went down on the field, and shook hand, and he unsnapped the chinstrap from his helmet and gave it to me.

I brought it with me that night, to a dinner and reception for the players' families and friends at a downtown hotel. Dick signed the chin strap for me, then took me from table to table, and had several of his teammates sign it too.

I think about that game every year, when Army and Navy play. But, until this week, I never thought to call Pariseau.

"You probably don't remember . . . 'I began when I reached him in Arlington, Va. "I certainly do," he said.

Which really wasn't all that surprising because, if you've ever seen an Army-Navy game - certainly if you've ever played in one - it's something you never forget.

When Pariseau played, Army and Navy were national powers. The Cadets had been ranked third in the country in '58 when Pete Dawkins won the Heisman Trophy. Navy, sparked by Bellino, was fourth in 1960, *and second in 1963 when Roger Staubach quarterbacked the Mids to a national championship showdown with Texas in the Cotton Bowl.*

Sports Injuries

"He is remarkably well, considering that he has
been remarkably well for so many years."
Sydney Smith 1771 – 1845

I was fortunate to have avoided serious injury while playing sports. I only remember two injuries, a severe thigh bruise or "Charlie horse," and a dislocated shoulder. The first is memorable to me for the way it was cured and the second because it sometimes limits the mobility of my left arm. Both occurred during lacrosse games.

A mid-season, Charlie horse from getting hit with a lacrosse stick during a game had me limping badly and missing practice, as late as Wednesday between Saturday games. A Naval Academy equipment manager, know only as "Tiny," inquired about my recovery process and the approaching game. He was a middle-aged, black man whom I had been seeing in the football and lacrosse locker room for four years, but with whom I had never had a lengthy conversation. When I told him that I was not recovering very quickly and that I was concerned about being able to play in our next game he offered to help. He said that if I were willing, he would try to massage the injury and reduce the swelling, pain, and stiffness. After practice on Wednesday he massaged my thigh. He used no lineament, but I remember his hands were hot right from the beginning and after he had only rubbed them briefly together. There was no immediate relief, although the massage felt good. That night at bedtime the swelling and stiffness seemed to have been reduced. Thursday morning I could walk without pain or limping, and the swelling was almost completely gone. By Friday I could run at almost full speed. Saturday I played in the game as though I had never been injured. In addition to thanking Tiny profusely and often, I inquired about his magic touch. He said that he seldom if ever tried to use it, but when motivated it usually worked. It was an amazing experience. I don't know if he inherited or was taught his secret and magic touch, but I do know that he helped me tremendously. I never heard another player talk about Tiny's amazing ability.

Very near the end of our season ending lacrosse game at West Point I dislocated my shoulder. The ball was free in front of our net and as I stretched to cover it with my stick an Army player took a big swinging with his stick trying to knock it into our goal. His stick hit my left shoulder while my arm was fully extended and my arm popped out of its shoulder socket joint. My subsequent movement put it immediately back into place. They didn't score and the game ended before I had to pass or catch the ball. After the game, Red Romo, our trainer only had to put my arm in a sling to rest it. I went to the North vs. South All Star game a few weeks later, but could not face off and only made a token appearance during the game. The shoulder did "pop out" a couple of times when I lunged forward with a poke check during a Club Lacrosse game, but other than being weaker than the right shoulder, it has been of minimal bother. All in all I consider myself to have been very fortunate with respect to sports injuries.

CHAPTER 5

Surface Warfare Officer

Operational Experience

"Don't believe the world owes you a living; the
world owes you nothing - it was here first."
Robert Jones Burdette 1844 - 1914

My service and ship selection from the Academy was the destroyer
USS Richard S. Edwards DD-950, home-ported in San Diego, CA.
I was not enthusiastic about the Marine Corps, submarines, or naval
air and selected a destroyer because, we had been told, "one gets more
responsibility quickly on a small ship." San Diego was appealing because
I thought living on the "left coast," in the land of fruits and nuts would
be an adventure. The bottom line however, is that I did not know what I
wanted to do, had no "sponsor" who had tried to sell me on a particular
career path, and had five years of obligated service to decide my future.

The ship was a general-purpose destroyer, built by Puget Sound
Bridge & Dredging Company. The ship honored Admiral Richard
Stanislaus Edwards USN and was commissioned in February 1959.
When I arrived on board she was only 17 months old, the kinks had
been worked out, and she was proud and fast. She had been nicknamed
the "Ready Eddie."

I was assigned as the (Gun) Fire Control & Anti-Submarine Warfare
Officer and inherited an enthusiastic, intelligent, squared-away group of
sailors. My Division included three Torpedo men, seven Fire Control

Technicians, and nine Sonar men. They were all about my age except for their leader, Sonar man, Master Chief Petty Officer Armstrong. Chief Armstrong was a quiet, professional, and respected gentleman. We worked together very nicely. I listened to what he had to say and followed his recommendations, and he kept me out of (shipboard) trouble. Several of the sailors in the Division have had remarkable and very successful civilian careers and attribute it to the leadership and guidance of Master Chief Armstrong.

When I reported aboard, I was an Ensign with one month of longevity and that made me "George," the most junior officer in the wardroom. With that title came collateral duties as projectionist for the wardroom movie every evening after dinner, and Special Services Officer for the ship with responsibility for sports teams, movies, parties, games, and special events, i.e., "crew morale & entertainment." The ship was scheduled to leave on a six-month deployment to the Western Pacific (WEST PAC) three months after my arrival.

At "Officers Call" in the wardroom, one morning about three weeks before we deployed to WEST PAC, while I, as George was selecting and collecting movies for the trip; arranging cribbage, pinochle, and backgammon (acey-deucy in the navy) tournaments, the Captain mentioned that too many sailors were being brought back to the ship by the shore patrol for fighting while ashore, and that we should control our men. As Special Services Officer, responsible for crew entertainment, I suggested that we could build a temporary boxing ring on the main deck when needed, advertise a boxing smoker for the middle of our transit to Japan and that in addition to volunteers who wanted to box, anyone returned to the ship by the shore patrol for fighting, was automatically added to the list of boxers. I was given permission to proceed. By the time we left San Diego, I had two pair of oversized boxing gloves, and enough volunteers and "shore patrol delivered, bar brawlers" for four or five matches . . . if I could match people up by height and weight. The event was being routinely discussed and anticipated by the crew and I was feeling rather proud of my idea for a boxing smoker. Our first port heading west was Hawaii and that's when potential disaster occurred.

During our over-night stop in Oahu a young seaman in the deck division was delivered to the ship by a pair of Marine Corps Military Police. According to the report, "The sailor had become a problem when the bartender in a downtown Honolulu bar refused to serve him further because he was drunk. When the Shore Patrol arrived he refused to leave with them and attacked them both." The young sailor was about 5' 7" tall and 155 pounds.

When I read the Shore Patrol report, I recognized the sailor's name and knew he was young and from Tennessee, because I had been the Duty Officer in San Diego when the telegram from the Red Cross arrived requesting that he be given leave and allowed to return home because his father had died in an accident. (The truck his father was driving went off a mountain road and into some trees while being chased by Revenue Agents.)

The next morning, by the time we had put to sea and Diamond Head was falling below the horizon, I was armed with the fact that this individual had quite a reputation for bar fighting and a documented record of previous Military Police reports that began in the shipyard while the ship was being built. I found him with several of his shipmates stowing the mooring lines we had use while in port and approached him with confidence that he would agree to be in the boxing smoker. This sailor obviously liked to fight and seemed unconcerned about the several reddish, bumps on his forehead and top of his head that looked like they came from a sap. He passively agreed to fight in the boxing smoker with a nod of his head, but quickly added, so that his shipmates and the Chief Bosun-mate would hear, "And I want to fight you." I understood the regulation forbidding fraternization between officers and crew, but even though boxing didn't sound like fraternizing, I understood that I needed some guidance. I responded, "We'll see." and left to visit the Captain.

Commander H.E. Thornhill Jr. USN was a skilled and seasoned commanding officer and a cool guy. He was professional without being up tight. He played in poker games with his officers in the wardroom on Saturday nights when we were at sea and occasionally hosted games at his home when we were in San Diego. Realizing that the proposed boxing match would be entertaining if controlled and done for fun, he asked how I felt about it?

I was confident of my Academy boxing training that consisted of four, 1-hour PT boxing lessons followed by two rounds in the ring against a classmate. For my fight in the ring, I was paired against my roommate, Tom Hyde. We had agreed to demonstrate the techniques we had been shown without making much contact. (We were probably the first to ever think of doing that, right?) Our plan lasted until one of us caught a jab in the nose - getting hit in the nose always hurt - which resulted in the brain forgetting all the techniques we'd been taught and the two of us simply standing in place swinging at one another.

I responded, "Well Captain, with my Academy training, plus my height and size advantage, (5" in height and 35 pounds) I think I could last the two, 2-minute rounds, without getting hurt or hurting him." We agreed that it could be fun and it became the "Main Event" of the boxing smoker. (For those with military experience, I understand that a commanding officer would be relieved of command for allowing such an event today, but, hey, this was 55 years ago, before "political correctness" forbid personal enthusiasm, initiative, and fun.)

The first four matches went well, no one got hurt and there was a lot of cheering and unsolicited advice to the two fighters. For the final match and main event, I came out on deck and entered the ring wearing a Shore Patrol tee shirt, a black Shore Patrol armband, and a fore-and-aft cap with a Marine Corps insignia. (Sometimes "trash talk" and psychological warfare can be effective?) I could tell that my opponent was not amused when he came charging across the ring at the sound of the opening round bell. He swung wildly and often, and at one point I was reminded of Don Quixote fighting a windmill. "Defense" did not appear to be a word in his vocabulary. I jabbed a lot and kept "dancing" out of his reach. We hit each other enough times to keep the crew cheering and hollering like banshees, but doing little damage. At the end of our fight, after we had removed the gloves, he was quick to come to my corner and extend his right hand. The crew was still yelling as we shook hands and my opponent, with a smirk on his face and a twinkle in his eyes said, "You're an OK guy - for an officer?"

I qualified as an Officer of the Deck (OOD) and stood watches on the bridge. Chief Armstrong (he was not yet a Master Chief) joined me as Junior Officer of the Deck (JOOD.) During our transit we practiced ship handling while learning about surface warfare; anti-aircraft combat; convoy protection, submarine hunting, and dropping depth charges. The Task Force making the WEST PAC trip consisted of four or five destroyers, a guided missile cruiser and the aircraft carrier, the Bonhomme Richard, affectionately called the "Bonnie Dick." During recent correspondence, Master Chief Armstrong, (Yes, he is retired, but Mr. does not sound appropriate) revealed that he, "Remembered and relished the days when he and I were OOD and JOOD on the bridge." Always able to deliver praise without contributing to overconfidence, he continued with, "You keeping station in your head through triangulation and the morning the Captain came to the bridge and said that he had had a dream that you had wrecked his ship!"

Destroyers are the greyhounds of the fleet and when orders are given for a formation or course change we had been trained to show a "puff of black smoke" as the ship went to "Full Speed" and an immediate, and discernible change of heading as the helmsman responded to the order for "Left/Right Full Rudder." The Officer of the deck is usually standing within 15 feet of the helmsman and the Engine Order Telegraph and we practice executing orders quickly and smartly. And then we were assigned "plane guard duty." When an aircraft carrier is conducting flight operations, a destroyer is positioned in its wake and relatively close behind the carrier. That destroyer is responsible for providing immediate assistance if an aircraft goes in the water and its role is called, plane guard duty. When the carrier changed course and speed, to head into the wind at full speed for launching or recovering aircraft, for example, it would alert the ships in the flotilla of its intensions and then execute the command. This was usually done with flag-hoist or flashing light to avoid the possible interception of voice transmissions. Two of us newly qualified OODs were having trouble smartly, relocating behind the carrier when it changed course and speed when we were assigned to the plane guard station. We would often end up on its beam before it came to its new heading. During a routine high-line exchange with the carrier (we were always getting fuel, provisions, parts, or exchanging movies) the two of us were high-lined to the carrier for a day to observe how they operated and become better able to maneuver our ship. The first maneuver I observed was an ordered course change of 65 degrees and a speed increase from 10 to 25 knots. When the carrier ordered the change executed, the carrier OOD spoke to the helmsman, who was located about 20 feet away behind an 8" steel wall, via a voice tube, and ordered, "Left, half-a-degree rudder."

The helmsman didn't hear the order and replied, "Repeat, Sir."

The OOD repeated the order and the rudder was moved very slightly - I assumed - because movement of the ship, if any, was so slight that I could not detect it. The speed increase was performed more rapidly, but the carrier was so large that no perceptible speed increase was detected for several minutes. Without more speed, the heading change was painfully slow. Meanwhile the destroyer was at the newly ordered speed and could have circled the carrier. The lessons were unmistakable and when we told our shipmates what we had learned we summarized it as, "There is more than one way to execute an order. Slowly on time or rapidly after a delay." and "Expectations can differ depending on who gives the order. That is when the captain says change course and speed (Full rudder and puff of black smoke) vs. when the carrier executes a change order." We were both glad to be high-lined back to our destroyer.

Liberty in the Philippine Islands, Japan and Hong Kong was fascinating and provocative. Saki, chopsticks, communal hot baths, pachinko machines, and "pushers" at train stations in Tokyo, Japan, were all culturally new and exciting. It was a wonderful experience and I could not get enough of it.

The problem was the boredom of day after day at sea with negligible variety. While at sea, the most enjoyable part of my day was teaching algebra to four of my men who wanted to go to college.

There were four bachelor, junior officers in the wardroom, Mike Freeman, Jim Izard (USNA '58), Jack Bradshaw, and I. During deployment and in San Diego we were a team - on liberty, in rented apartments, at Officer Club happy hours, Friday night dances, and Sunday bull fights in Tijuana with our boda bags full of "vino rojo." We were referred to by the rest of the wardroom as the "Unholy Four." About the only entertaining thing I did without them was play poker in the card rooms in downtown San Diego.

My two-year tour on the "Ready Eddie" was enjoyable, but my excitement did not come from ship handling and the prospect of a 20-year career in destroyers did not fascinate me.

Back in San Diego during the fall of 1961, crewmembers wanted to enter an 8-man, flag, football team in the 11th Naval District's Destroyer Conference. Captain Thornhill promised support with late afternoon time off for practice and I joined eleven enlisted sailors to form the team. I got to be quarterback because, depending whom you asked, I was the best passer, or I was in charge, or it was my football. These were good athletes who had played sports before and not simply someone wanting to get a couple of early afternoons away from the ship. There were five, good size, hard-nosed sailors that wanted to be lineman, a pair of 6'3" basketball players and three speedy runners/pass receivers. (One of the linemen, Wesley Schmaltz, went on to play football at U. of Minnesota.) We were all 18 - 24 years old, became a team, went undefeated with a 7 - 0 record, and had a wonderful time scoring 199 points and allowing opponents only 25. As Destroyer Conference Champions we were invited to play in the 11th Naval District play-offs. We beat the Marine Corps Team from the Marine Corp Recruit Depot in the 1st round then lost to Naval Air Station Team from Miramar, CA. in the 2nd round.

The next spring, the ship left San Diego for an overhaul in Long Beach, CA. One beautiful, sunny, California morning, I heard on the ship's announcing system, that my presence was requested in the crew's mess. When I arrived, the collected group of sailors were standing around a mess table and reading something that was spread out on a mess table. One of men who had been a leader on the ship's flag football team, saw me arrive, requested that the sailors make a small space for me to stand at the table, and pointing to the opened copy of the Long

Beach Naval Station's paper, the _Seahorse_ announced, "We have to play these guys."

I saw a photo of ten men wearing burgundy colored, sweat suits with "Cowell" printed, in large, white, letters across the chest. Beneath the photo, The _Seahorse_ proclaimed that the "Untouchables" from the destroyer USS Cowell were living up to their flag football reputation. They had met all comers and defeated them all. They were currently champions of Destroyer Squadron 19's flag football league, having routinely beaten teams by scores of 68 - 0 and 44 - 0. They recently played the Long Beach Naval Station's Surface Craft team and beat them 48 - 6. They had issued an invitation to play all comers, but could not find anyone willing play them. Oh boy! I felt the assembled group's competitive adrenaline coming my way!

It was not long before we sent a naval message that read:

Drafted by: R. Pariseau
From: USS Richard S. Edwards (DD-950)
To: USS Cowell (DD-547)
INFO: (1) Special Services Naval Station Long Beach.
        (2) Editor, "The SEAHORSE"

1. Our Flag Football Team Would Like An Opportunity To "Touch" The Cowell Untouchables.
2. Am Available Anytime. Dry Dock #3 Long Beach Naval Shipyard.

The return message said, "Accept With Pleasure Your Challenge To Try And Touch Us. Rep. Will Contact You."

The _Seahorse_ promoted the event, Special Services provided referees, and the Saturday morning contest drew a small audience. The Edwards was able to touch the Cowell Untouchable. The final score was 6 – 0. It was a grudge match that turned into a defensive battle with a host of penalties. The Edwards scored the winning touchdown on its opening drive on a quarterback sneak from seven yards out. The linemen called our touchdown play in the huddle. They said they wanted to trap the defenseman who was giving us trouble up the middle and told me to take the ball under center, drop back three yards as if to pass, then run straight up the middle. It was a classic quarterback draw. It worked so well that I had to leap over the defenseman who had gotten the trap block. He was on the ground, on his back. He must have learned a lesson because it only worked once. We got close to their end zone on three other occasions, but could not score. We shut down their offense and they could never get anything going. It was one of those flag football games where there is a very fine line between touch and tackle.

On the "Ready Eddie" we also had a very good basketball team. We tied the destroyer, USS Bausell (DD-845) for the 11th Naval District Destroyer League Championship. We had handed the Bausell its first and only defeat, earlier in the season and played a playoff game for the championship in San Diego. We lost to the Bausell 43 – 39. They ended the season with a 10 -1 record and it was their second straight year as 11th Naval District Destroyer League champions. The Bausell left San Diego to have some repair work done at the Puget Sound Naval Shipyard and won the Puget Sound Naval Shipyard Basketball League Championship with a 16-0 record."

Staff Experience
"Except for the Flood, nothing was
ever as bad as reported."
Edgar W. Howe 1853 - 1896

My second duty station, not anything that I had envisioned, was as Aide and Flag Lieutenant to Rear Admiral R.C. Johnson, USN, who was Commander Cruiser - Destroyer Flotilla 11. The Admiral's staff was aboard the cruiser USS Los Angeles, stationed in Long Beach, CA. I reported aboard in May 1962. As an admiral's aide, my job was political rather than operational. I was his secretary, arranging his schedule, drafting correspondence, and accompanying him to most military events. Mostly I learned by making a mistake the first time. Like the first time he hosted some public relations people at a lunch in Los Angeles and he brought me along. When lunch ended everyone left except me and the check. I didn't know that I was supposed to pay the check and get reimbursed later by the Admiral. My fiscal policy in those days was cash. Bi-weekly pay was given in cash by the ship's dispersing officer, poker in the casinos in Gardena, CA was an all cash affair, and money didn't last long enough to have a saving account. I did not have enough cash to pay the bill; I did not own or at least was not carrying a credit card, and the bill would have overdrawn my account anyway. So what to do? Well, I took the check to the Admiral and as surreptitiously and inconspicuously as possible, gave it to him and told him that he'd forgotten to pay the bill. Right, I took a lot of sh_ t on the ride back to the ship as I expected. I was not told how I should have handled the situation, only that I should carry more cash in the future.

In June, the Admiral's son, who had just completed his third year of college somewhere in the mid-west, came to visit his family for a vacation. Early on a Friday, afternoon, I received an uncommon task from the Admiral. "My son has been here a week. He doesn't know anyone, is bored, and has just been hanging around our apartment. Would you help him find something to do this weekend?" His son and I had met when the Admiral's family had come aboard ship for lunch, we had gotten along well enough and he seemed like a pretty good guy. I called him and we made plans. Since this was an official duty assignment, at least in my mind, I did not hesitate to call the Naval Station and tell them that the Admiral wanted to use their boat to go deep-sea fishing on Saturday and that he would appreciate it if they had it rigged with four fishing poles and some lures for trolling. I called two women, schoolteacher friends of the "Unholy Four" and invited them to go deep-sea fishing. The four of us may have caught some fish? We did drink a lot of gin & tonic, had dinner at a beach restaurant, and went clubbing that night. Sunday morning the Admiral found his son and me sleeping on the living room floor of his apartment. After waking us the Admiral gave us the silent treatment. His wife was more gracious and cooked us breakfast. The breakfast of bacon, eggs, and pancakes was tasty (and rewarding?) so I figured that I was getting a handle on this staff stuff.

I only lasted as Flag Lieutenant and Aide until December, a total of seven months, but not for the reason you may suspect! Actually, I was getting along rather well with the Admiral, his staff, and the crew of the cruiser Los Angeles. It was Admiral Rickover who ended my career as a staff officer.

"Lieutenant Junior Grade R. Pariseau USN
Flag Lieutenant & Aide, CRUDESFLOT 11"
(Official US Navy Photo)

CHAPTER 6

Nuclear Power Training

The Admiral Rickover Interview
"It takes a lot of things to prove you are smart,
but only one thing to prove you are ignorant."
Don Herold 1889 - 1966

Admiral Rickover was typical of the unpopular, single minded, effective but hated leaders that accomplish great things. At about 5'-5" tall and 150 pounds he deserved his napoleon complex. He cursed, dressed sloppily, often in an unpressed business suit, and with single mindedness, pushed the nuclear power program through the Navy bureaucracy and Congress. As a member of both the Atomic Energy Commission and the Naval Nuclear Reactor Program he recognized that the "buck" stopped with him. He accepted that fact and insisted that the best, brightest, and most dedicated people - whom he personally chose, surround him.

And he was effective. When the nuclear powered submarine Thresher was lost during a deep dive after an overhaul, he discovered that the flooding had begun in the seawater flushing line to a toilet. Further investigation led him to believe that shipyard workers, supervisors, and managers were attentive to "things nuclear," but less so to more common systems. So he decided to improve all work and management responsibility. Forever after, when a nuclear powered submarine had work done by a shipyard or submarine tender, the ship would have a logbook at the brow and every workman, supervisor, and manager that came aboard to perform, check, or verify work was required to sign the log. When they signed the log they were informed that every name in the log would be included in a random drawing and that ten names, randomly selected would join the crew on the deep dive following completion of the work. For the first time, supervisors were visiting and calling to insure that work was being done correctly, properly tested, and if anything else was needed.

As one of the Admiral's chief engineers, we were required to report every issue, problem, and incident - however minor - in writing to him along with the cause, recommended long-term solution, and what had been done to prevent recurrence. And he read every one, because if he had a question he would call the ship to ask you for clarification. My chief engineer tour was in Hawaii and Guam and because of the time difference to Washington, DC I received several calls in the middle of the night from "the Admiral" who wanted to discuss something I had written to him or to pass along a change he was making. As far as he was concerned we were next-door, at his beckoned call, and responsible to him. But, all this I learned later. At this point in my story, the Admiral was a humorless, irascible, legend about whom I had only heard rumors.

When I received "the Message", I was Aide and Flag Lieutenant to Rear Admiral R.C. Johnson USN, Commander of Cruiser - Destroyer Division 11. The message to me was from the Bureau of Personnel (BUPERS) soliciting volunteers for nuclear training and was dated, July 3, 1962. The message read, *"The high priority requirement for nuclear trained officers continues. A review of your official record indicates you have the potential qualifications to succeed in this highly important program. Reply by message whether or not you volunteer for this program. If affirmative, you may anticipate orders to Washington DC on July 27, 1962 for interview by Vice Admiral Rickover and final determination of selection for nuclear training."*

Consultation with senior officers and Admiral Johnson convinced me that nuclear power was the future of the navy and that I should, "At least, go talk to the man." I replied to the message in the affirmative and received order for two days of interviews beginning July 27th, at Naval Reactors Division of Atomic Energy Commission, Main Navy Building, Washington, DC.

Senior naval officers that I knew were very willing to help me prepare for my Admiral Rickover interview. They told me how I should expect the Admiral to act and to prepare answers for questions he was rumored to ask frequently. Among the several questions I was warned about and that I should be prepared to answer, was, "What was the title of the last book you read? Who wrote it and why did he write it? Why did you read it and what did you learn from it? Yes. Advanced preparation would be very useful, especially since I had only been reading recreational fiction, and that only infrequently, and none of the novels, whose author's name I could not even remember, would impress the Admiral.

Most of what I knew about Admiral Rickover's way of thinking was from the stories after he had come to the Academy to speak to a select group of classmates three months before we graduated. He had apparent told them, "You should each be taking at least one correspondence course in math or physics because you have too much free time. If you want to get into my nuclear power program you should improve your class standing by 5 - 10 places before graduating. You should stay in your room and study on weekends instead of going out or going to church." When he was reminded that all midshipmen were required to attend a church service on Sunday, he rudely responded, "Well, goddamn it. Then take a book to church."

The actual Admiral Rickover interview process consisted of a series of four, one-on-one interviews. The first three were lengthy, detailed and technical with engineers, nuclear physicists, reactor designers, or shielding experts, from his staff. At a final meeting with the Admiral himself you were told whether or not you were accepted into his program. By the time you got to see the Admiral he had the reports from your interviews with his staff, and knew if he wanted you or not. Meetings with the Admiral were typically brief, frequently lasting less than two minutes if he liked the reports from your interviews and simply wanted to put a face with your name. Occasionally, if he didn't like your answer to one of his questions you could be sent from his office to stand in the hallway by his door to reconsider your answer. Waiting time outside his door varied, some claimed to have stood there for over an hour before being summoned back into his office. He asked one individual to postpone his upcoming marriage for one year until after nuclear power training, because he would not have time to learn nuclear power and how to be a husband at the same time. When the individual paused before answering, Rickover sent him out to stand in the hall and consider his answer. It was not unusual for several candidates to be standing side-by-side along the wall, outside his door. When Admiral Rickover was undecided about an individual, his interview lasted longer.

My first three interviews went marginally well. I sensed that I was asked several questions to which I was not expected to know the answer so they could evaluate my inductive reasoning. On the other hand, perhaps I was supposed to know the answer to all the questions?

For example, "What's the muzzle velocity of an M-1 rifle?"

"I don't know sir."

"Give me an estimate. Is it closer to 500 feet per second, 2,000 feet per second or 5,000 feet per second?"

Apparently I should have known that, but I had to guess.

When I was invited to see the Admiral, I assume that I had mixed reviews from my three interviews, because we were together for tens of minutes, while he made up his mind. I had been warned that I would be sitting in front of his desk, in a wooden chair whose legs had been cut so that my chin would be marginally higher than his desktop. He wanted to be looking down at his candidates during the interview. They didn't warn me that the front legs would be shorter than the rear legs so that relaxing meant sliding out of the chair. I was also forewarned that there would be someone, a senior naval officer in my case, standing behind my chair to prevent anyone from attempting to "attack" the Admiral in response to his verbal provocations. I must admit that if I had my heart set on getting into his program, I probably would never have made it.

"So you're the idiot who majored in sports at the Academy. I assume you now realize how stupid that was and if you had it to do over again, you would study more and not play sports?" was how he greeted me.

I think I tilted my head in disbelief at the question and responded, " No sir. I only had that one chance to play collegiate sports, but if I missed something academically I can buy a book and read about it."

Pounding a fist on his desk he told me, "You are more stupid than I thought. You're a god damn imbecile."

I assumed no answer was required so I remained silent.

After what I considered a rather lengthy pause, he asked, " So what did you learn from all that football?"

"Well, I learned to be a team player, to never quit, to be a leader, and . . ."

At which point I was interrupted with, "Bullshit. I'm a better leader than you and the only sport I play is to push my plate away at the table. And you know that guy Napoleon; he was a Frenchman like you? Well he was beaten at Waterloo by the Duke of Wellington who was a great leader and the only sport he ever played was to jump a ditch one day."

Not knowing what to say I again remained silent, but might have had a smirk on my face.

"So big leader, what would you do if you were on liberty, in uniform, in a foreign country, and saw a woman in uniform that was drunk, staggering down the road?"

"I would help her off the road, away from peering eyes, sit her down, and contact the shore patrol to take care of her."

"Goddammit, there is no shore patrol. What are you going to do?"

"The primary issue is that you don't want her to embarrass the uniform so I would get her out of the middle of the street. Secondly, I don't want her to get hurt so I would try to sit her down somewhere, out of site."

"Oh, you stupid bastard." Pointing at the aiguillette I was wearing as Aide & Flag Lieutenant, he abruptly changed the subject again. "Why did you accept a worthless staff job? You should be learning about propulsion or gunnery systems."

"I did not have much choice Admiral. It was not a position that I requested."

"So, how much overweight are you?"

"I am ten pounds heavier than when I left the Academy, Admiral."

"So how long would it take an athlete like you to lose ten pounds?"

"About five weeks, Admiral."

And it was at this point, I realized later, when the Admiral proved he was smarter than I was. From our conversation he must have realized how I would react if he told me that I could not do something, so he said, somewhat in disgust, "Well. I don't think you could pass my program even if you were accepted." (Dangle the bait.)

"I know I could pass your program Admiral." (Outsmart the fish.)

"Well I am going to give you a chance." (Set the hook.) "Now get the hell out of here." (Don't give him time to realize what just happened!) Smart man this Admiral.

As I left the Admiral's office, not totally sure of what had transpired, his secretary was waiting with a letter that she wanted me to sign. It was dated July 28, 1962 and read:

Vice Admiral H.G. Rickover, USN
U.S. Atomic Energy Commission
Washington 25, DC

Dear Admiral Rickover:

"I hereby spontaneously volunteer to lose ten (10) pounds by September 8, 1962. I further volunteer not to regain the weight lost.

I will notify you when I have lost the specified number of pounds.

Very respectfully,

Richard R. Pariseau
LTJG, USN

I signed the paper and wondered who else was listening to these interviews?

The saddest part was that most of the individuals that had been turned down, and there were several, wanted the program above all else and were devastated by the rejection. I did lose the weight and on September 2, 1962, I sent him a one-sentence letter, "I have lost ten (10) pounds and will not regain lost weight." I guess he was testing me by offering a way out if I had failed to write the letter. Whatever his motives, he was obviously much smarter than I at getting his way.

Nuclear Power Training
"That must be wonderful; I don't understand it at all."
Moliere 1622 - 1673

I reported to the Commanding Officer Nuclear Power School, Mare Island, in the town of Vallejo, CA. located northwest of San Francisco, on January 1, 1963. Nuclear power training consisted of six months of classroom study followed by six months at a nuclear prototype. Classes were on the second floor of an undecorated, dingy, wooden, typical military building on the Naval Station Mare Island. Classes were 55 minutes long, five days per week, from 7:30 AM until 4 PM. Admiral Rickover had concluded that instead of having his students change classrooms after each class it would be more efficient to keep the students in one room and rotate the professors. In so doing we only needed five minutes between classes, instead of ten minutes. (Thus 55 minute classes instead of 50-minute classes.) We each had a large desk with an attached bookshelf for our textbooks, notes, and lunch - if we wanted to eat during our 20-minute noontime break. If you did not bring a lunch, there was a vending machine with soda, chips, and candy bars a few buildings away.

There were nine courses, we had to pass each one individually and pass a five-hour comprehensive examination at the end. The nine were: Mathematics (Differential & Integral Calculus), Advanced Nuclear

Physics, Electrical Engineering, Nuclear Chemistry, Heat Transfer & Fluid Flow, Shielding & Radiation Control, Reactor Metallurgy, Reactor Operations & Casualty Control, and something referred to on the class grading summary as, "PlCh & CS." I have no idea what that was!

Nuclear Power School has frequently been advertised and referred to as equivalent to getting a Masters Degree in six months.

Although expected of us, most of us were not willing to spend every minute of our time studying. I lived in an apartment in the small town of Vallejo with three classmates. We were assigned weekend homework, but we were inclined to do it as a group and share the results.

My time away from the books was more a respite from engineering formulae, than an exciting adventure. One enjoyable weekend break, in May 1963, I went to the local movie theater to see, "Doctor No," the first of the James Bond films. The one-hour drive to San Francisco was popular along with touring the nearby Napa Valley vineyard tasting rooms. The Naval Station scheduled their volleyball tournament games in the early evening, after our classes had ended, so a group of us, mostly USNA grads, formed a team and entered the tournament. Having been warned that a previous student had been thrown out of the nuclear power training program for playing on a sports team, we called ourselves, "the Smith Brothers" and signed up as Dick Smith, Bill Smith, Charlie Smith, Carl Smith, et. al. We won the trophy. Unfortunately, the USNA graduates did better at volleyball than in class.

"Mare Island Naval Shipyard Volleyball Champions"
Left to right, kneeling, Jim Kinney '60, Charlie Lyman
'61, Dick Pariseau '60, (?), Bill Dick '61.
Standing, Pete Bowman, Carl Schubert, Jerry
Cooper '60, (?), Bud Pezet '60, (?)
(Personal photo)

About a month before completing our studies at Mare Island, a naval officer visited us to solicit volunteers for submarine service. We knew this was very important because they let him interrupt class to speak to us for about twenty minutes. His story about the excitement of being aboard a submarine was moderately compelling, but when he mentioned that one received an additional $200 per month hazardous duty pay, Bud Pezet and I, both bachelors and in need of additional money, raised our hand and volunteered for submarine duty.

By the end of the course, two who started the course had failed and had been sent back to the fleet, but whose counting? Twenty-eight graduated. A grade of 2.5, in each individual course and cumulatively including the 20 questions, five-hour, comprehensive written examination, was passing. There were eight of us from the Academy in the class, five of us from the class of '60 and three from the class of '61. Ranked by class standing after six months of nuclear power training, the bottom six included five, from USNA '60 and one from USNA '61. The bottom six students in descending order of glorious, academic performance, and their weighted average grades, were: Jimmy Wilson 2.90, Jim Kinney 2.89, Bud Pezet 2.88, Bill Dick (USNA '61) 2.87, Jerry Cooper 2.80, and at the bottom of the class, "c'est moi" with a 2.78. (We did better in volleyball than academics and perhaps Admiral Rickover had reason to tell midshipmen they should study on Sundays even if it meant bringing a textbook to church.) The top two graduates were probably Ensigns, right out of Cal. Tech. or MIT who majored in nuclear physics and did not play volleyball?

We graduated and left Nuclear Power School on June 21,1963 with orders to report to U.S. Naval Nuclear Power Training Unit, (NPTU) Idaho Falls, Idaho for training at the S1W site. There are two training reactors in the desert in Arco, Idaho: S1W (S1 = submarine prototype #1, W = built and operated by Westinghouse) and A1W (an aircraft carrier prototype built and operated by Westinghouse.)

Despite some low marks at Mare Island, we were such a premium commodity that our orders forbid us to ride more than three to a car while on leave and traveling to Idaho. I traveled between duty stations via Greeley, Colorado to be Best Man at Bill and Linda Dick's wedding on June 29th. I also had the privilege of recently attending their 50th wedding anniversary in Moraga, California.

I reported to NPTU on July 15, 1963. The nuclear site in Arco is in the middle of a desert inhabited only by herds of antelope. Hunters ignored the antelope because the hunters could not be certain that the animals had never tasted contaminated effluent. There were no military facilities; students were expected to rent apartments in Pocatello or Idaho Falls. It was a bus ride of approximately one hour to the test site from either city. There was minimal parking at the test site and bussing was mandatory if there was snow on the ground, because a student had frozen to death when his car got stuck in the snow on the way to the site. Four of us chose to rent an apartment in Idaho Falls during our stay from July 1963 until January 1964.

Studying and working at the reactor plant was just as intense as the classroom phase. We each had a bunk at the site and were encouraged to remain there to study, trace systems, observe normal operation, and witness proper recovery procedure from scheduled, induced casualties and failures. The plant was operated 24/7 and events were scheduled largely at the convenience and discretion of the Westinghouse engineers running the plant. In the classroom we had learned that there was a pump in the reactor cooling line, now we were expected to find that pump, determine pump specifics (e.g., power supply, flow rate, pipe diameter, pump speed, etc.), pump performance (e.g., What happens to reactor temperature if the pump fails? Where's the back up? What fail-safe action will automatically occur in case of failure? What's the recovery procedure?), and pump system (e.g., Where can the pump be manually isolated? What type of valve isolates the pump?) We were expected to spend at least eight hours at the site when "on duty." Our schedule was four days of duty then a day off, followed by ten days of duty and three days off.

Once the heavy snow fell, three days were plenty of time to drive to Sun Valley for great skiing. During the fall and early snow, my time off was spent in the woods with a bow and arrow. I was not interested in killing any animals, and wouldn't know how to dress it out if I did kill one, but I was interested in trying to get close enough to a deer to get a shot with a bow and arrow. Bow and arrow deer season began three weeks before rifles were allowed so I went early in the season while the woods were relatively safe. I purchased a hunting bow – shorter than a target bow for carrying through the woods and with a higher draw weight – mine had a 65-pound draw. I carried a quiver of arrows consisting of two razor tips (in case I ran into a bear or large cat) and ten blunts. Blunts have a hard, bulbous, rubber tip for hunting birds and small game. I intended to used my blunts to hit a deer. It would satisfy my hunting goal without harming the deer. I only saw one deer during my early morning excursions into groves of aspen trees and it left the scene before I could draw my bow.

Beginning at the half waypoint, the 14th week, we began getting three hour, oral exams every five weeks, in addition to written exams. The written exams were given weekly and were typically 120 multiple-choice questions with a grading system that penalized guessing. Correct answers were worth 1 point. Wrong answers were minus 2 points. Questions left blank were minus 1 point. It was the first time I had ever experienced a grading scheme that could result in a test score that was a negative number!

The oral exams were given by six examiners from the group of plant supervisor, Westinghouse engineers, system managers, and plant qualified navy representatives. The setting was a long table with the student alone at one end. The first oral at the 14-week, half waypoint, was crucial for continuing in the program. A passing grade was 65, excellent was 80. I got a 71. My three roommates got 69, 77 and "a failing grade." Two days after failing his oral exam, our roommate left with orders to a ship in Charleston, SC and we were short one roommate. Discussion among the students did reveal that the students doing the best had oral exams that 90% of us could have passed and that the bottom third had orals that only the top 10% might have been able to answer easily. Life is just not fair!

Five weeks later, at the 19th week (three quarter point in the course) we had a second oral. The chaff was still being weeded out and the low performers pressured. I was among a few who were told that we were "weak" and would have to re-take the oral. I passed the re-exam.

The final assessment was a ten-hour written examination and a third oral examination. Understandably, I was delighted when I passed and the ordeal ended. Memorable, non-academic, highlights were limited to some unsuccessful deer hunting with a bow & arrow, and three day skiing trips to Sun Valley. I left Idaho on January 15, 1964 with my skies on the roof rack of my car and a mapped route to Submarine School in New London, CT that went through numerous ski areas in Utah and Colorado.

CHAPTER 7

Submarine Life and Adventures

Submarine School

"We make more enemies by what we
say than friends by what we do."
John Churton Collins 1848 - 1908

I remember that we were called "sub'mariners" and "submarine'rs" equally and arbitrarily. My dictionary said, "sub-ma-ri-ner" offering little help. One day we were informed that we would forever after refer to ourselves and insist on being called "submarine'rs." It did not matter why, we simply followed orders however, a rumor did blossom. The story was that the order had come from Admiral Rickover's office in response to someone in Congress referring, during a heated argument with the Admiral, to his personally selected "sub'mariners" as below par (sub), sailors (mariners.) It no longer mattered what was correct; we were submarine'rs.

Submarine School was an eight-hour workday without homework. Much of it was in trainers where we could practice submarine evolutions such as diving, surfacing, casualty control, and making a torpedo attack. After nuclear power training, it was almost a vacation. I say almost because one of my classmates from nuclear power school failed a mid-course examination on submarine diesel propulsion systems, had orders to Admiral Rickover's office in Washington, DC within hours, and was gone from Submarine School within two days

I got involved with the Groton Archers. They had a wonderful, fourteen target, course in the woods near the Submarine Base. Target range varied from fifteen to sixty yards according to National Archery Association rules. At close range the target was a tiny bulls-eye but as the shooting distance increased the target size increased and became squirrels, rabbits, pumas, deer, and bears. Four arrows were shot at each target and scores were recorded. With Dad's help, I purchased a target bow (longer than a hunting bow) with a lighter, 40-pound draw, because the course required shooting 56 arrows. (Four arrows at each of 14 targets.) Dad helped me by introducing me to the owner of the sporting goods shop where Tolman High bought their sports equipment and I was treated very well! I was cutting wooden and aluminum shafts to fit my draw, burning and gluing turkey feathers to the shafts, and applying nocks to make my own arrows. My first duty station after Submarine School was in New London, CT and I remained very active in the club. As a bare bow archer I did get offended as scores became the overriding issue and archers began attaching telescopic devices and target aiming devices to their bows, and using compound bows with pulleys to get increased draw power with minimal effort (and thus be able to aim directly at the bulls-eye rather than necessarily account for an arrow's significant drop in altitude at longer ranges.) Years later, when I was living in Virginia and unable to find a nearby archery club, I gave my bows and arrow making paraphernalia to the son of a SEAL that I had befriended – but that's another story!

We did spend two days training at sea on an old diesel powered submarine during submarine school. I remember the intense smell of diesel oil, that many systems dripped water when we were submerged, and that I was thankful that I would only be going to sea on nuclear powered submarines. (By 1963 we were only building nuclear powered submarines.) The 1981 movie, <u>Das Boot</u>, is not an exaggeration of life aboard a diesel-powered submarine during WW II.

Claustrophobia

"It takes less time to do a thing right
than to explain why you did it wrong."
Henry Wadsworth Longfellow 1807 - 1882

In my experience, when non-military people in a social setting learn that I have been on a submarine an early question is, "How did you know that you were not claustrophobic?" My answer is that the submarine community found out for me, before I ever went aboard a submarine.

All potential submariners attended Submarine School in New London, CT. For officers, the school lasted six months. Courses included the design, function, and operation of a submarine and its systems: diving, surfacing, propulsion, electrical, flushing, ballast, fresh water, etc. - and emergency escape training. In case of an accident that required escaping from a submarine that could not surface, submarines have an escape trunk. Nuclear submarine because of their length and larger crew size had one forward and one aft. The escape trunks can also be used for submerged launch and recovery of Navy Seal Teams. The escape trunk is a cylinder, wide enough to hold several men jammed tightly together, with a hatch on the bottom, inside the submarine, and a hatch on the deck, outside the submarine. Valves for flooding, draining, and high-pressure air complete the escape system.

Escape training occurred early in the submarine school curriculum. There are two submarine escape training tanks, one at the Submarine Base Pearl Harbor, HI and one at Submarine Base New London, CT where the Submarine School in located. There is one located on each coast to facilitate periodic requalification. They are painted white, look like silos, and contain a 50-foot column of water. They are used for escape training and for testing new equipment and escape techniques. There is an elevator, not much larger than an escape trunk that operates between the top pool deck and the bottom of the water column. The day of our training during submarine school we gathered inside the tower on the pool deck, wearing our bathing suits, to receive instructions on how to make a buoyant ascent. We understood that we would ride the elevator to the bottom of the tower and make a free (without equipment) ascent. At the top of the tank we met the Dive Master, a Senior Chief Petty Officer wearing a pair of kaki shorts and sleeveless tee shirt. He was of average height with impressive muscular definition, had a tattoo of a mermaid partially hidden by dark hair on his right forearm, and exuded the confidence of one who was expert at his craft. He began our briefing with, "The air in your lungs will take you rapidly to the surface, and thus it's called a buoyant ascent. The air in your lungs will also expand two and one half times during the 50-foot ascent so you must continually exhale to avoid your lungs exploding. You will exhale by continuously and loudly hollering 'Ho Ho Ho' during your ascent. You will have sufficient air to exhale all the way up and you must resist the impulse to stop exhaling because of fear that you will run out of air. For the non-believers, there will be scuba divers stationed at several depths and unless they hear you shouting and see air bubbles coming out of your mouth they will stop your ascent and pull you into an air lock. If that happens you can start the drill over on another day. During your ascent, clasp your hands together and extend them over your head. During an actual escape this will help you avoid hitting your head on debris that may be present on the surface."

We were then directed to follow an instructor, introduced only as a Navy Petty Officer qualified in both scuba and hard-hat diving. He led us to the elevator (simulated escape trunk) and invited all of us to join him inside. We were jammed in the elevator so tightly that it was difficult to raise an arm - maximum number of escapees per event or a claustrophobia test? The instructor closed the door, pushed the lowest "floor button" and we descended to ground level. The instructor continued our education. "Atmospheric pressure at sea level, is 14.7 pounds per square inch (psi.)" (In seawater the pressure increases by one atmosphere every 33 feet of depth. At a depth of 66 feet the pressure is $2 \times 14.7 = 29.4$ psi.) "Here at the bottom of the escape tank the pressure against the outside of the door is 37 psi. I am going to increase the pressure in the escape trunk (elevator) until the pressure on both sides of the escape hatch (door) are equalize and we will be able to open the escape hatch into the tank with minimal effort. I will first open a water flood valve and fill this escape trunk until the water is at chin level." I think we all glanced at the instructor to insure that we were standing, on tiptoes if necessary, with our chin at a higher level that his. That's also when I became acutely aware that the top of the escape trunk (elevator) was only about five inches above my head and about an inch above the tallest man's head. The instructor toggled a switch and we heard the swoosh as cold water rapidly engulfed us and rose quickly over our knees, waist, chest, neck, . . . and finally stopped just as I was preparing to hold my breath.

"Nice huh! Tilt your head back and breath air from the bubble at the top of the tank," he instructed, "and try to relax. Raise your hand if you have a problem." Yeah. Like we could free our arm enough to raise a hand! No one in the group panicked or wanted out, but this was it. The point when you knew for certain whether or not you were claustrophobic. In a submarine or anywhere else I can think of, short of a terrible catastrophe, we would never again be in such a confined space with a threat of drowning.

After a pause - it seemed like many, many minutes - to see if we were all breathing, we were packed too tightly for anyone to fall down even if they passed out, the instructor continued, "I will now open the high pressure air valve and equalize the pressure between us and the bottom of the tower. It will only take a second. Try to swallow and equalize the pressure in your ears as it increases so that you don't rupture your eardrums."

A brief blast of cold air, caused eardrums to "pop" (the space was flooded with water first in order to conserve high pressure air.) "Now that we have equalized the pressure between the escape trunk (elevator) and bottom of the escape tank, we can easily open the door into the bottom of the tank." The instructor informed us as he did precisely that. "Now, one at a time, on my command, take a full breath of air, bend down and exit the escape trunk with your hands on the top of the hatch to hold yourself down and avoid banging your head because you are very buoyant. The air in your lungs is acting like an inflated life vest and wants to get to the surface. Once outside the trunk begin hollering, 'Ho, Ho, Ho,' and see the air bubbles in front of your face before letting go and beginning your ascent."

The ascent lasted only seconds and at the surface we popped half a body length out of the water. They had it right. It worked as advertised and there was plenty of air in our lungs to exhale all the way to the surface. Upon completion of the exercise, I knew, among other things, that I was not going to have claustrophobia aboard a submarine.

Submarine Duty
"One half the troubles of this life can be traced to saying 'yes' too quickly, and not saying 'no' soon enough."
Josh Billings (pseudonym for Henry W. Shaw) 1818 - 1885

In military parlance, submarine types are referred to by their acronym with "SS" the designation for a submarine. Add an "N" if it is nuclear powered and add a "B" if it carries ballistic missiles. Thus an "SS" would be a WWII type conventional, torpedo carrying, attack class submarine, of which there were a few remaining in the late 1960s. An "SSN" is a torpedo carrying, nuclear powered, attack class submarine; and an "SSBN" is a nuclear powered, torpedo carrying, ballistic missile class submarine that carries 18 - 24 ballistic missiles in permanent, vertical, launch tubes. The first ballistic missile submarine was built by cutting an SSN in half just behind its sail, adding the missile compartment, and welding the sections together. The missile tubes, large diameter cylinders inside the submarine, extend the full height of the submarine in two horizontal rows. They occupy "the missile compartment" which is affectionately referred to as "Sherwood forest." Submarines were traditionally named after species of fish (Haddock, Tautog, Pollack, etc.) until SSBNs were build and were named after U.S. Presidents (Washington, Adams, Jefferson, etc.) Since the end of the Cold War the ballistic launch tubes of several SSBNs have been converted to carry and launch cruise missiles. Some new submarines have unique capabilities, e.g., carry swimmer delivery vehicles for use by SEAL Teams. Politics, congressional funding support requirements, and political correctness, have resulted in submarine now being named after cities, states, and people. (Fish and deceased US presidents don't vote!)

During the Cold War with the Soviet Union, SSBNs were a key component of the nuclear triad - aircraft with nuclear bombs, land based missiles, and sea launched missiles - that assured nuclear retaliation if the United States was attacked. During deployment SSBNs were tasked to maintain continuous, electronic reception capability (to receive a launch order), remain within range of its targets, and remain undetected, even by friendly forces. To maximize time within target range each SSBN had two crews (Blue and Gold), operating on 90-day cycles. The submarine remained forward deployed to minimize transit time. To begin a deployment cycle, crews on SSBNs home-ported in New London flew to Holy Loch, Scotland, crews from Charleston flew to Rota, Spain, and crews from Pearl Harbor flew to Guam in the Marianna Islands. For three days crewmen would meet with their counter-part to learn what needed repair, replacement, or attention. The crew completing patrol would then fly home and the relieving crew would spend the next 24 days preparing the ship for patrol. Patrol length was approximately 60 days, limited only by how long the crew could remain in reasonable spirits.

To remain undetected there were no routine communications transmissions of any kind. Each member of the crew could receive three messages, called "family grams," per patrol. A family gram was limited to fifteen words including the addressee's name and sender's name. The primary function of family grams was to reassure the man on patrol that all was well at home and to maintain morale. Family grams were reviewed to insure that the meaning and intent was clear, would not cause the recipient to worry, and if the message gave the appearance of code, extreme frivolousness, or risqué material it would not be accepted for transmission. Birth notifications, illness, death, and other emergencies warranted a priority message, usually drafted by the squadron chaplain, and did not count against the three-message limit.

Food aboard a submarine is excellent, except that fresh fruit and vegetables do not remain eatable for very long. Meals are typically served every six hours, when the watch changes: breakfast at 6 AM, lunch at noon, dinner at 6 PM, and soup & sandwiches at midnight. In addition to standing watches, sailors remain occupied learning the requirements and training for a watch station with increased responsibility, studying for advancement in rate exams, and studying to qualify in submarines and wear the coveted pin, a pair of dolphins. One movie per day is carried and shown after dinner. The ship has a small library, two stationary bicycles, a few rubber coated free weights, playing cards and backgammon boards are available, but time is primarily spent on watch, studying, or working.

My first submarine was the Thomas Jefferson SSBN 618, home-ported in New London, CT. She was 410 feet long and the 10th SSBN built. I was assigned as Reactor Control Division Officer and in addition to managing the Division, was expected to complete my Submarine Qualification Notebook, earn my dolphins, and prepare to return to Washington, DC to take the chief engineer's exam by the end of my two-year tour.

After a patrol, an SSBN crew can take up to 30 days of unused vacation before spending the remainder of their off-crew time running the ship's office (for both crews) and taking training classes. After two of our patrols, a shipmate and I, both bachelors, remained in Scotland instead of flying back to New London, CT and spent our 30 days leave in the United Kingdom, France, Spain, and Germany. Europe is always enjoyable.

My second submarine tour was as Chief Engineer aboard the Ulysses S. Grant (SSBN-631), home-ported in Pearl Harbor, Hawaii. My third submarine tour was as Executive Officer aboard the John Adams (SSBN-620) in Pearl Harbor, Hawaii.

During one patrol the ship's doctor and I conducted an experiment to determine how much cardio stamina was lost during 60 days underwater in a submarine. Eleven crewmen and I were timed in a mile and a half run before we left on patrol and again upon our return.

The results were statistically insignificant because only four of us could finish the run after the patrol. The results did suggest that cardio health could be impacted (motivation may have been a factor after patrol) and caused me to promote a stationary bicycle competition on the subsequent patrol. I traced a circular coast-to-coast route on a map of the USA with frequent mileage markers and posted it alongside a wall chart where an individual could keep track of his daily and summary mileage pedaled on a stationary bike. Some crewmen had spectacular numbers and I created letters of commendation for various levels of achievement. The Captain signed the letters and made the presentations with fanfare, during our Blue Crew-Gold Crew change of command. The Squadron Commander even congratulated the top distance riders. It was interesting, provided some stress relief, and may have had some health benefit.

Patrols also provided an opportunity to experiment with facial hair. I tried various combinations of beards and mustaches. Here are two variations. What do you think?

"With a mustache."

(Personal photo)

"Add a Beard."

(Personal Photo)

Roaches. On a Submarine?

"In all matters of opinion, our adversaries are insane."
Mark Twain 1835 - 1910

On my first submarine, the USS Thomas Jefferson (SSBN 618), I was the most junior officer and thus had collateral duty as the Recreation Officer (again!) The primary duty of a submarine recreation officer was to insure that the ship left for patrol with 60 personally selected movies (one per night); to accept all criticism about the quality, theme, or entertainment value of every movie, and to run the reel to reel movie projector in the wardroom each evening. The recreation officer was also responsible for insuring that the small library was well stocked, insuring that the ship's two stationary bicycles were in good working order, and that the ship carried several decks of playing cards, dice, and backgammon boards for acey-ducey. (In acey-ducey the blots are not prepositioned around the board as they are in traditional backgammon, but are brought onto the board one at a time with a roll of the dice.)

It was my third patrol and we were proceeding submerged from Holy Loch, Scotland to our patrol area. I had my Submarine Qualification notebook and was following a high pressure air line into the torpedo room while learning the intimate details of the ships torpedo launch system when I recognized the voice of a torpedo man 2nd Class and heard, "Look at him go. He must be the fastest thing on six legs."

"Well now. What's going on here?"

"Oh. Good evening, Lieutenant. We're watching our cockroach run. He's really fast. We found him in Storeroom #3 this afternoon. The cooks found the first one a couple of days ago. We keep ours in this jar right now."

"Does the Doctor know that our submarine has roaches?"

"Yes sir. He was informed. Said the storerooms would be fumigated after patrol."

"Do you know what happened? How we got roaches?" I asked confident of an answer because there were few secrets on a submarine during patrol.

"Chief Barker said that some of the provisions arrived late and instead of opening all the boxes on the pier and only carrying the cans aboard ship, they carried a few unopened boxes aboard. He thinks there were some roaches inside the boxes."

Further inquiry revealed that several others roaches had been captured and that a verbal competition was developing among the different Divisions relative to which had the largest roach, which had built the best cage/home for their new pet, and whose roach was the fastest.

The Supply Officer was concerned with containing the roaches to the single storeroom, where there were only canned goods, by keeping the hatch shut and did not like the idea of sailors keeping any as pets. I went by Storeroom #3, noticed what appeared to be roach capture related activity and had an idea. I penned a proposed entry for the next day's, Plan of the Day (POD) that I thought might solve the roach problem and went to see the Executive Officer who is the person responsible for publishing the daily POD.

The next day's POD included the following note:

The Thomas Jefferson Roach Race Open will be held before the movie, two weeks from today. The track will consist of a starting circle six inches in diameter around which a four-foot circle will be drawn. Contestants will run individually, one-at-a-time, and be timed from when they cross the inner circle until they cross the outer circle. Entrance fee is 75 cents per contestant. Prizes: $5 winner, $3 second place, $2 third place. By order of the Medical Department a $1 fine will be assessed any owner whose entry escapes after the race. Alternatively, for a fee of 25 cents the Corpsman will insure the demise of a roach as it crosses the finish line. All money collected will go to the ship's fund. No roaches may be kept as pets after the races.

As recreation officer for a crew of 130 sailors at sea for 60 days, I assumed every opportunity for entertainment should be grasped!

Three days later, at lunch, the Captain said, " You certainly started something with your roach races. The Supply Officer says he has trouble getting into Storeroom #3 to get canned goods, because there are always a couple of sailors inside, on their knees, with flashlights and jars trying to catch a roach."

"I know Captain. It was like that this morning when I was there."

"What were you doing there this morning?"

"Well Captain, five dollars is five dollars."

"Oh no; not you too."

"Well not yet anyway. I haven't been able to catch one yet."

As the recognized Roach Race Coordinator I was the one approached by the crew on all related matters. I was shown several elaborate cages that were constructed to house a contestant until the race. One that was especially regal, was made of transparent plastic, had two stories with stairs, a room full of food and a room with an overturned jar cap full of water for drinking (or swimming?) I was also kept appraised of feeding problems, training regimes, etc., and would post "noteworthy" information on the mess deck, bulletin board.

> *Bulletin: Roaches apparently prefer Pream* (a dry, powdered, cream substitute for coffee that was popular in 1960s) *to other foods, but it is too rich for them. It makes them run around like crazy for about 20 minutes then stop and refuse to run again.*
>
> *Bulletin: If you have any of the library book on "Insects," the encyclopedia Volume VI, Q - S, or tore out the page on roaches from the dictionary, please return same to the library.*
>
> *Bulletin: Roaches will not eat chocolate bits, but peanut butter has proven to be a favorable menu.*
>
> *Bulletin: Two deaths have been reported from roaches drowning in their drinking water.*
>
> *Bulletin: Rumor is that male cockroaches run faster than females. How their sex was determined was not revealed.*
>
> *Bulletin: The Missile department reports that their starvation training diet was succeeding nicely, but carried too far. Their roach died last night.*

Bulletin: Training theories involving lack of sex and an overabundance of sex have proven inconclusive. (Sex determination remains classified information.)

The day of the races the mess deck was a beehive of activity, excitement, and anticipation. Attendance was at a maximum and the sailors who had anticipated the rush and arrived early were being crowded to the edge of the track, wedged against the judge's table, and stepped on by two individuals passing among the crowd selling small bags of popcorn, with profit going to the ship's fund. The spectacle began with a parade of proud owners and trainers flaunting their flashy, emblematic colors in the form of vests and headbands made from material carefully selected from the ship's supply of cleaning rags. Among the parade of contestants being formality introduced were roaches whose name and reputation had become well known aboard ship. There was *Shooting Star* from the Communications Division, who reportedly started so fast that all four of his legs left the ground; *Footprint*, from the Electrical Division, whose speed and power could only be kept under control if his feet were moistened to keep him from slipping, and *Cosmo*, from the Atmosphere Control Division, whose velocity could only be measured in light years per microsecond. On the heels of these great contestants came the medical department's contribution. Corpsman 1/C Harrison, 215 pound executioner, his bare chest covered in dark hair, wearing a black hood with jagged slits from which cold eyes peered, and carrying the 15 pound sledge hammer he would use to liquidate contestants as they crossed the finish line - if their owner had paid for the service of course.

At the rear of the procession a mourning party from the Navigation Department carried a little wooden casket on a black pillow. This was *Whirl A Roach*, whose fame had spread from bow to stern before he met his death the day before the race. A respectful silence allowed his trainer to describe how on his fateful day, "*Whirl A Roach* had just completed a wonderful training run and was heading for a crack under a navigation cabinet. Hurrying to prevent his escape I pounced with my trapping cover, but misjudged the distance and cut off his head." Moving to the rear of the mess deck, the sympathetic audience watched as the valiant racer was buried at sea by being jettisoned out the Trash Disposal Unit.

During the races the sailors aboard the "T.J." saw some of the finest racing roaches in the world. Each racer's name and course completion time was recorded on a blackboard, and their run announced in real time over the ship's entertainment system by the Executive Officer. (Not all roaches ran in a straight line and with spectators crowding the finish line the end of the race often proved hilarious.) No roaches escaped after their race. The winner was a diminutive roach without a name, listed simply as Boat Roach #16 and entered by the Missile Division. A tidy sum from the races, popcorn sales, and efficient roach annihilation by the executioner, corpsman, was added to the ship's fund. It was an entertaining evening, gave the sailors something new to discuss, and brought a happy crew closer to the end of patrol. It also solved a potential problem, because three days before the races, the Supply Officer reported that no roaches could be found in any of his storerooms. (We did however submit a work order to fumigate the storerooms after our patrol!)

First Marriage
"The man who lives by himself and for himself is
apt to be corrupted by the company he keeps."
Charles H. Parkhurst 1842 - 1933

While stationed in New London, CT during Submarine School and my first submarine tour aboard the USS Thomas Jefferson (SSBN 618) four of us bachelor rented a large, four bedroom, house in Gales Ferry, CT about five miles from the Submarine Base. Three of us were USNA classmates and recent Lieutenants: Bud Pezet, George Mahelona, and me. Our fourth roommate was Gib Smith, USNA '58. We were all assigned to ballistic missile submarines with three month cycles so at least one of us was usually at sea. We had calling cards made that said, "THE LIEUTENANTS" followed by our names, address, and telephone number. We thought that we were pretty cool. George was a submarine Supply Officer so our condiments, (e.g., mustard, mayo, and ketchup) were in gallon jars and we usually had lots of good food in the refrigerator. Together we maintained a well stocked bar. With a fireplace in the first floor living room and a second fireplace in the oversized downstairs recreation room, we frequently hosted the party. Our recreation room was the hiding place for Christmas toys and gifts purchased by married shipmates and neighbors so Christmas Eve there was always a "toy assembly" and wrapping party. Men assembling toys with a drink in one hand and advise from shipmates did not promote the reading of assembly instructions. I recall the assembly of a new bicycle for a neighbor's young daughter that had beautiful, large white handle grips, with molded finger impressions, and long protruding pink and white leather tassels. Anxious to see how they looked "a helper" slid them into place and gleefully showed the rest of the attendees how beautiful they looked. Many man-hours and innovative techniques were devoted to removing one of the handle bar grips so that the handlebar could be inserted into the bicycle's mainframe. Someone even read the instructions and pointed out the warning, in bright red letters, that said, "Do not install the handle grips before inserting the handlebar into the mainframe."

Periodically, if we did not have plans for the weekend we would leave as early as possible on Friday afternoon and drive to New York City. The USO was on Broadway, one block from Times Square and they had made spectacular arrangements for active duty military personnel. They received unsold tickets to plays, movies, sporting events, etc. on Fridays and list them on a large board. Beginning at 4 PM military personnel could get a numbered card from a USO volunteer that would indicate the order in which to line up at 7 PM to select up to two free tickets from those remaining on the board. We would go to the USO as close to 4 PM as possible to get a low number then have roughly three hours to get a date. The Cattleman's Restaurant and Cherry's Cocktail Lounge were nearby, and had great happy hours, (drinks were half price and there were wall to wall women - - with a few competing males mixed in.) After an evening of entertainment, a Broadway show, and at least the telephone number of a beautiful woman, we would drive back to New London, CT about two hours away.

One Friday afternoon, five days before leaving for Holy Loch, Scotland and another three months deployment aboard the USS Thomas Jefferson, I made the New York City trip, alone. I arrived in time to get a numbered card in the teens, anything under 40 was usually good, and went to happy hour to find a date. I drank and chatted up girls until the last minute before admitting that I had struck out. I returned to the USO to get a single theater or sporting event ticket, but arrived after my number had already been called. There was still a long line and nothing of interest to me would be left if I went to the end. So, with a false sense of entitlement (from alcohol?), I asked to see "the manager." A well dressed woman (she was a volunteer and had come directly from work) with blond hair came to hear my complaint. Her name was Evelyn Gathy.

"Yes. I knew the rules."

"Yes. I was reminded to stay close by and return before 7 PM."

So what did I want? "Well, since I was going to sea in defense of our country in five days and could get killed, you should come and have a drink with me!"

"No. I cannot do that. And beside you're probably married."

"No I'm not. I'll prove it to you." I said as I began looking through the cards and pieces of paper in my wallet. I discovered that it is impossible to find proof that one is not married, because it's trying to prove a negative. Consequently she would not even tell me what time she would close up the USO and leave so I could walk her to her metro station. I did get her address. Driving back home I realized that I had not made a great impression and that she probably gave me her address out of curiosity and to possibly get a letter from Scotland. Perhaps she was a stamp collector? She later admitted to have given me her address to get rid of me! I did send her a letter from Scotland in which I asked her for a date for the Army - Navy game that was going to be played at New York Giant stadium in the Meadowland.

Three months later, back in New London, I called her. No, she didn't care for football and had never been to a football game, but "heard" that I had played football for Navy. No date for the Army-Navy game, but she would go out with me for dinner. She gave me the address of the apartment where she lived with her parents. When I rang the bell at her home, her younger brother quickly opened the door. He wanted to talk about football and Notre Dame. He was an avid Notre Dame fan, listened to every game, knew all the players by name, kept a ND scrapbook, could recite year-by-year team statistics and records, and recognized my name from the Navy-ND game three years earlier. After seeing my name on the return address label on my letter, he had convinced his sister to go out with, "this guy she didn't remember," so he could meet me and talk about the ND game. Getting a date by impressing a girl's younger brother was a first for me.

We dated during my three months of normal life, until my next submarine deployment. My next three months in New London included a trip to Washington, DC where I passed the Chief Engineers Examination and received orders to become Chief Engineer of the USS U.S. Grant in Pearl Harbor, seven weeks later. We had known each other less than one year, including a couple of 90 day deployments, but we were in love and I proposed that we get married. In retrospect it was more like a combination proposal and threat. "If we want to be together we should get married, because if I go to Hawaii as a bachelor it's unlikely that we will ever get back together." Is that romantic, or what?

With only weeks to prepare, my folks drove to New York and I arranged a dinner so the parents' could meet, and we got married in the Chapel on the Thames on the Submarine Base in New London, CT because it was half way between New York and Massachusetts. A Saturday, morning wedding, on July 6, 1966, a reception at the Holiday Inn just outside the Base, cut the cake then rush to the airport in a cab for a flight to Hawaii. I left my credit card with my brother Bob, so he and George Mahelona could keep the reception party going. I received a variety of credit card bills from establishments within 30 miles of New London, one of the bridesmaids still has a burn scar on her calf from contact with a hot exhaust pipe while riding behind the driver on a motorcycle, and another didn't get back to work in New York until Tuesday. After several requests for details about what went on after we left, all I was ever told is, "It was a lengthy and exciting reception. Too bad you missed most of it."

Evelyn was a gracious and generous woman who enjoyed entertaining and beginning with her work at the USO, was quick to support the military. She loved animals, doing volunteer work, and was a voracious reader, especially of modern history. We had a wonderful life during our 30 years of marriage. We had a son, born at the Fort Ord, U. S. Army Hospital in Monterey, CA six weeks premature. His name was Rhett Richard Pariseau. He died of respiratory failure after spending the four days of his life in the intensive care unit.

Evelyn was diagnosed with "cancer of unknown origin" and died in Arlington, VA Hospice Center on February 28, 1997, five week after the cancer diagnosis.

Chief Engineer
"What I have been taught, I have forgotten;
what I know. I have guessed."
Charles Maurice deTalleyrand 1756 - 1838

For two years I was Chief Engineer on the USS U.S. Grant (SSBN 631) home ported in Pearl Harbor, HI and operating out of Apra Harbor, Guam. As chief engineer I was responsible for the ship's electrical, steam, and nuclear reactor systems, making fresh water, and controlling the temperature and atmosphere inside the submarine. (We burned carbon monoxide to form carbon dioxide, which was collected in a charcoal scrubber and pumped overboard. Exposed to 1050 volts of direct current, pure water disassociates into its hydrogen and oxygen components. The hydrogen is pumped overboard and the oxygen is used to maintain a proper atmosphere in the submarine. All without coming to the surface.) Typically there were five or six officers and 30 - 35 sailors working for the chief engineer.

Annually the engineering department of every operational nuclear submarine was given a three day, Operational Reactor Safeguards Exam (ORSE.) Admiral Rickover arrived with an entourage of engineers from his staff and the Atomic Energy Commission to give the exam. They were tasked with guaranteeing the safe operation of the nuclear power plant. Engineering department personnel were orally quizzed during one-on-one sessions, radiation control records were examined, administrative obligations were verified, and the physical plant was closely examined for cleanliness and operability. On the third day the ship went to sea and submerged to demonstrate operation, casualty control, and recovery. With the approval and advanced knowledge of the commanding officer and chief engineer, the Admirals staff would initiate plant casualties that required the watch standers to recognize the problem, take corrective action, and return the power plant to normal operating conditions. The casualties were significant and at least one would cause the nuclear reactor's fail-safe system to shut it down. The commanding officer and chief engineer were not allowed to reveal or assist in the drill. We were informed only because the ship and power plant were our responsibility and if things went badly or got out of hand it was our duty to save the power plant/ship. When an operating reactor shuts down, the ship's batteries provided emergency electrical power that is sufficient to identify and repair the problem, if done quickly, and to initiate a single attempt to restart the reactor i.e., withdraw the reactor control rods to produce controlled heat and steam. If recovery is delayed, or a glitch occurs in the multiple, sequential, steps in the reactor restart procedure, the ship must go "to the surface" to obtain the air required to run the a diesel generator and provide electrical power. Minor discrepancies or problems in any part of the ORSE required documented corrections and a plan to prevent recurrence. More serious discrepancies or problems had to be corrected before going to sea and a delayed departure disrupted the ballistic missile submarine rotation schedule. Severe problems or anticipated lengthy operational delays would cause the commanding officer and/or chief engineer to be relieved for cause, i.e., fired. My engineering department successfully completed two ORSEs.

On a typical day underway, on watch in the engineering department would be the Engineering Officer of the Watch (EOOW) in the control room seated behind three individuals who controlled: electrical power, the reactor plant, and the steam (propulsion) system. In each engineering compartments there would be an individual standing watch to start, stop, and monitor running equipment; take and record hourly readings of operating equipment, (e.g., temperature, flow rate, etc.), to respond to commands from the control room, and be available in case of a problem. Ideally there would be three people qualified for each watch station and rotation was six hours "on watch" and twelve hours "off." Admiral Rickover's directives encouraged the EOOW to periodically leave the control room and walk through the engineering spaces to check on the watch standers, observe the status of equipment, and check the logbooks. (Yes. data reading were taken and recorded manually, in those days.) Equipment failures were usually preceded with an increase in noise and/or operating temperature. I got in the habit of listening carefully as I stood by a piece of running equipment and placing my hand, palm down, on the equipment until it got to hot and I had to remove my hand. I would count the seconds while my hand was touching the equipment and check the equipment temperature with a contact thermometer and the equipment's temperature gauge if there was one. Eventually I could walk through the engineering spaces, feeling the operating equipment with my hand, know whether or not it was running normally, and estimating its operating temperature with some accuracy. When I conducted a final watch station qualification with my men, I would discuss listening and feeling the running equipment for early detection of a potential problem and challenge them to tell the temperature of the equipment by how long they could touch it. The idea caught on. When my officers and chief petty officers conducted qualifications they would pose similar questions, engineering department sailors were challenging one another on their ability to estimate an equipment's temperature by feeling it, and I even observed a machinist-mate demonstrating his temperature estimating capability to a torpedo-man. It became obvious that compartment walk throughs had become somewhat exciting rather than a chore, were occurring at least as frequently as necessary, were now quickly and efficiently performed, and that engineering plant problems should be detected early.

I felt rewarded when I overheard a watch-stander who was being relieved; tell his replacement, "Everything is normal. The #2 seawater pump is running a little hot, by two seconds on my touch. The gauges are within normal operating range. I checked with the navigation department and found out that we have been heading south for the past eleven hours and seawater temperature has increased about six degrees since my previous watch. We are still heading south into warmer water so you should detect a change also."

I wish I could report that the little mannerism was responsible for early detection of a potential problem, but alas, it did not happen. Perhaps that was because we did not have any problems? It did make learning fun and seemed to work.

I left the ship with a Letter of Commendation from Commander Submarine Squadron 15 for, "Outstanding performance of duty as Chief Engineer aboard a nuclear powered submarine during deployments of great national importance . . ."

Admiral Rickover did keep track of his engineers. The first congratulation I received when I was promoted to Lieutenant Commander was a personal letter from the Admiral. It was addressed to me at Naval Postgraduate School and said, "I am pleased to see your name on the selection list for promotion to Lieutenant Commander. Best of Luck." The letter was dated 28 October 1968; promotion did not occur until 1 May 1969.

Naval Postgraduate School, Monterey, CA.

"He who devotes sixteen hours a day to hard study may
become as wise at sixty as he thought himself at twenty."
Mary Wilson Little 1880 -1952

Monterey, CA is a beautiful city on Monterey Bay where the monarch butterflies gather during their annual north-south migration, and the foghorn in adjacent Pacific Grove frequently provides evening musicality. The Navy Postgraduate School occupies an old resort with elaborate Spanish style architecture, flowered grounds with multiple walking paths, and roaming peacocks.

I attended for two years while acquiring a Masters Degree in Operations Research & Systems Analysis, (ORSA or more commonly OR.) Classmates were from all the services and had arrived from a variety of tours. Ed Scholes, now a retired Army General, had arrived directly from a second tour in Vietnam. It took him months to calm down and fully concentrate on his studies. We did a lot of studying together, especially early on, and became very good friends. The curriculum was superb and the professors knowledgeable, understanding, and eager to help. My assessment of a "superb curriculum" is based on my application to Stanford for a Doctorate in OR immediately after completing the Naval PG Program. I was informed that I had already taken every course they offered, but that I could take the required number of semester hours, pay the tuition, and get the Doctorate degree if I desired.

We lived in Pacific Grove, three blocks north of Monterey Bay and six blocks east of Cannery Row of Steinbeck fame. In the late 60s, women were burning their bras, the hippy movement was in full swing, pot smoking was popular, the Haight - Ashbury district of San Francisco made the news every day, and Cannery Row was a pleasant, often visited, mini-hippie area of boutiques, cafes, bars, and restaurants.

I took a $200 per month pay cut to go to PG school, because I was no longer eligible for submarine "Hazardous Duty" pay. So, I responded to a newspaper advertisement for evening work as a "bouncer" at the Monterey library. The librarians were all women and they wanted a male to stop "young adults" from smoking a joint in an isolated corner of the library, help them lock up at night, and walk them to their car. When I got the job, I was assured that I'd be able to spend most of my time studying, but in reality I found it necessary to make frequent tours of the facility to chase out the pot smokers and occasional hippies who were sleeping on the floor.

Throughout my school years, my grades had always been "A"s and "B"s, and I had been satisfied. I studied, but took time for other activities. Along with three colleagues, who were not getting all "A"s and having their names published on the Dean's List, I was being chastised by several wives for having my evening job and like their husband not being able to make the Dean's List. One of my male colleagues reminded us that the last time we had spent a weekend in San Francisco we had past a sign advertising "Topless Shoeshines." He proposed that if we got all "A"s next semester and made the Dean's List, we should be taken to San Francisco and allowed to frequent that establishment. The women agreed - without even asking for a "reward" if we did not make the Dean's List. Two of us made the List. Calendars were cleared and grand preparations were made for a trip to San Francisco. Our preparation and planning included consideration of further dirtying our dirtiest shoes so it would take a longer time to shine them? The big day finally arrived, the weather was grand, the ride north was pleasant, and the establishment was no longer there! What a bummer. Making the Dean's List for nothing. Did the ladies know something they have never told us?

"Four Pitch" Softball

To minimize the time it took to play a softball game, yet have all the excitement and competition, we played "Four Pitch." I had not heard of it before going to NPGS, and found it to be a great game. One variation made the game exciting and a seven-inning game last about one hour. The team at bat supplied its own pitcher. The pitcher must pitch from the pitcher's mound, but could pitch overhand, underhand, fast or slow. The variation and key to the games appeal and speed was that the pitcher could only throw four pitches to a batter. If the fourth pitch was not hit or was hit foul, the batter was out. For the team in the field, the individual who would normally have been the pitching could play anywhere in the infield, outfield, or on the base path. It was speed softball and without arguments over balls and strikes, and four pitches per batter. We could complete a game in an hour. Great fun. I'm surprised I never found it being played elsewhere.

Monterey Adult Flag Football League

Another diversion from studies was the town's flag football league. I played on the team called, "Navy School." We had some very good athletes, but the competition was remarkably good, and most games were as close to being tackle without pads as to flag football. During the 1969 season, the teams in the league, in addition to the Navy School were: the Elks, PG&E, the Garbage men, La Cantina at the Mission Inn, Roscelli's, and the Prison (a minimum security prison, of course, but they could only play "home" games.)

Our opponents and game scores were:

Navy School	16	La Cantina	0
Navy School	24	Roscelli's	0
Navy School	19	Elks	14
Navy School	18	PG&E	19 (We missed three PATs)
Navy School	25	The Prison	14
Navy School	29	PG&E	28
Navy School	14	Garbage men	18
Navy School	30	La Cantina	6

Season ends with Navy School and Elks both with a 6 - 2 record. The League declared a one game playoff.

According to the League flyer summarizing the season, "With the Elks leading the Navy School 15 - 14 with six seconds left in the game, a 60 yard pass from Ruth to Paddock won the game for the Navy School,

21 - 15." I no longer remember anyone named Ruth or Paddock. They were in a curriculum other than OR.

The school got the trophy. We had lots of fun.

Duplicate Bridge

We lived in a duplex house with a very old couple, named Bolschweiler, occupying the other half. When you are 25 years old anyone 55 or over is very old. After a number of evenings playing bridge, men against the women, Mr. B convinced me that he and I should try duplicate bridge. There were weekly games at several local hotels and clubs, in addition to frequent tournaments. We played basic Goren and agreed not to be critical of each other's performance. We played quite a few times during my two years in Monterey, but one night was special. It happened when we earned Masters points from the American Contract Bridge League. The Rating Point Certificate that I've had with me since 10/9/69 indicates there were 9 tables and I earned 0.23 Masters Points. It does not say whether we came in 1st, 2nd, or 3rd - and I do not recall - but the certificate does remind players that, " To record your certificate on your life time record, send them to the above address in lots equal to 100 Rating Points or more." I did not bother registering for a lifetime record or sending in my prized certificate. I simply framed it and at one point, it was mounted on the wall of my den, above my PhD Diploma.

Anchor Submerged

Jack McNish had been the Executive Officer on the USS Grant SSBN 631 when I was the Chief Engineer and we had become friends. He visited briefly one evening while I was in Monterey. He was the Commanding Officer of a renovated and specially outfitted submarine from Mare Island Naval Shipyard when he visited me. He could not tell me much about his submarine or his next mission, only that he was here in the calm waters of Monterey Bay to practice and verify the feasibility of anchoring a submarine while it remained submerged. A strange requirement at the time, but later was part of one of the biggest intelligence coups of all time, tapping the underwater cable in the Sea of Okhotsk that carried information between the Soviet fleets in Petropavlovsk on the Kamchatka Peninsula and Vladivostok on the mainland.

To learn about that operation and what our submarines were doing during the Cold War, read the book, <u>Blind Man's Bluff</u>: <u>The Untold Story of American Submarine Espionage,</u> by Sherry Sontag and Christopher Drew. Much of what is in the book was so highly classified when it was ongoing that you could only speak of it in a security vault. When I read the book I had trouble believing how much information had been declassified. It's a good read and exciting story. In this "bare all" story of my life I must reveal that I had an additional surprise when I began reading the book. The book had been recommended to me simply by the title, "Blind Man's Bluff." I ordered the book and until it arrived and I began reading it, I thought it was a book about playing poker!

Club Lacrosse

While at Monterey, Al Ryder, a class '60 lacrosse teammate and first-string defenseman, contacted me. He was playing for the San Francisco Lacrosse Club and invited me to join them. I played two or three games, but it was a long ride to the games and I couldn't attend practices. There were a couple of Navy lacrosse players attending the school (Bobby Sutton and Joe Stewart) so I spoke to them about forming our own team. The school had jerseys from when they had a football team and one of the clubs from the San Francisco area agreed to play us in Monterey if we played them in San Francisco. Our team picture has nineteen players and we played two games.

After our brief two game season, I was contacted by Ed Gibbons, Captain of Navy's 1959 lacrosse team, and invited to join the 1st Marine Division Lacrosse Team stationed at Camp Pendleton, CA. The marines who played lacrosse had started the season playing for the Clairmont Club of Los Angeles and won the championship of the California Lacrosse Association. They were reorganizing, augmenting, and practicing as a team representing the 1st Marine Division. They had home-and-home games scheduled against the California All Stars followed by a weekend trip to Colorado to play the two strongest teams in the Rocky Mountain area, the undefeated Air Force Academy on Saturday and the Denver Lacrosse Club on Sunday. Of course I'd play. It would be an honor to represent the Marine Corps and what a team I would be joining. It was loaded with outstanding college players. Pete Powell (Princeton) and Walt Schmidt (Rutgers) led the attack. Bill Walters and Tom Towers (both Princeton), Ed Gibbons, Don Chinn, and I (three Navy first team players) played midfield. Dave Collard (Princeton) and Dave Traynor (Holy Cross) anchored the defense and Harry Bowdoin was in the goal. Besides, I owed Ed Gibbons a favor. He was not only Navy's team captain my junior year, but had made Honorable Mention All American as a junior and was having a good senior year when I broke his leg with a body block going after a loose ball during practice while scrimmaging. I always felt badly about that.

We played and the game scores for the 1st Marine Division's inaugural season were:

1st Marine Division 14	California All Stars 5
1st Marine Division 25	California All Stars 2
1st Marine Division 12	Air Force Academy 8
1st Marine Division 13	Denver Lax Club 3

The Air Force Academy was good. Score by quarters was Marines 2-1 after the first period, 5-5 at the half, and 7-6 after the third quarter. I am surprised they are not and never have been on the national lacrosse scene.

Monterey PG School Graduation

Yes. I did a lot of studying. I did get my Masters of Science Degree and I was not at the bottom of the class. I arrived at the school in July 1968 and graduated September 30, 1970.

Following two tours aboard SSBNs I had requested an SSN tour, but . . . for the needs of the service . . . my orders were to become

Executive Officer of the USS John Adams (SSBN 620) home ported in Pearl Harbor, Hawaii. I was to report after completing a seven week Command Weapons Course in Dam Neck, Virginia.

Open Door Policy
"Why they call a fellow who keeps losing
all the time a good sport gets me."
Frank McKinney Hubbard 1868 - 1930

It was my second ballistic missile submarine patrol as Executive Officer (XO) aboard the John Adams (SSBN 620) with Captain Ken Loposer USN as Commanding Officer. The ship's homeport was Pearl Harbor and we were operating out of Apra Harbor, Guam. Ken and I got along well, enjoyed working together, and were known to have a drink together while on liberty. As the ship's XO, I had normal daytime working hours, when administrative and personnel issues usually occurred. Since I was up and awake during the daytime, the Captain formally made me the Command Duty Officer during the day. He slept during the day and he took over at night. As Command Duty Officer I made operational and navigational decisions that affected the ship. We were a good team, had a great crew, were winning performance awards, and had a wonderful relationship with the crew. The XO on an SSBN has a private stateroom with a single bed, a shower and head (toilet for the landlubbers), and a fold-down desk that made it an office as well as a stateroom. It was known that, " I had an open door policy and that I would be available to talk with anyone in the crew anytime."

One afternoon, a few weeks into patrol, I returned to my stateroom to find that, the door that I had left closed, was now missing. I decided to take a walk around the ship looking for clues, like Spenser and Hawk would do in a Robert Parker novel!

I encountered a few sailors who were "on the inside" and knew what had occurred. They smiled when they saw me and asked if they could help me find something. (Was that a clue or what?) I made it known that I was looking for my door in case it had wandered off on its own, because otherwise, "There would be serious repercussions!" I received no help and my threat went unheeded.

After the crew had eaten dinner and gathered for the movie in the crew's mess - and I still did not have a stateroom door - I decided it was time for serious repercussions. I quietly went to the forward crews head with a wrench, removed the six toilet seats and hid them in an overhead compartment - all without being detected. When the movie ended and the crew went to perform personal necessities, there was quite a commotion. I was not visited and no trade offer appeared to be forthcoming.

The next morning when I returned to my stateroom from breakfast, my mattress was gone. Within the next hour the Chief of the Boat, the most senior enlisted man onboard, visited me. "Heh Chief. What's up?"

"I don't know what you are going to do next, but I'm here to make a trade and to protect a couple of pranksters."

"Well I am delighted to do some trading, but I don't understand what you mean about protecting a couple of guys?"

"It's a couple of new guys testing your reputation. Someone went by your stateroom; saw the door shut, took your "open door" policy literally and thought it would be funny if your door went missing. Many in the crew were upset that they messed with you in the first place, now everyone using the forward head is angry at these guys, and before you retaliate again I want to keep these guys from getting hurt by their shipmates."

"Sounds good Chief. Here's the deal. I will tell you where the toilet seats are; you get someone to reinstall them. My door gets re-hung, my mattress returned, and my bed made. I don't care to know who the culprits were. I assume you will take care of them. Do we have a deal?"

"Yes, Sir. We have a deal."

"By the way Chief, I actually thought the missing door was pretty funny and the Captain was laughing at my predicament. So take it easy on these guys."

"I will. And you should know that you will get the crew's full attention if you ever mention 'severe repercussions' again."

I spent some time back aft in the engineering spaces away from my stateroom while the changes went on up forward. That was the end of it. It wasn't mentioned again aboard ship - but probably retold ashore and in bars - and I never had to use severe repercussions with the crew again!

"Severe Repercussions"
(Personal photo)

Final Patrols

"A variety of nothing is better than a monotony of something."
Josh Billings (pseudonym for Henry W. Shaw) 1818 - 1885

After my third patrol as XO, I received a Letter of Commendation from Commander in Chief Pacific Fleet for, "Outstanding performance of duty as Executive Officer during three strategic patrols . . . ." More rewarding was when two senior leaders in the crew, a Machinist Mate (MM) and a Radioman (RM) – who were to be promoted and transferred before our next deployment – asked to meet privately and personally with Captain Loposer and me. At the meeting they gave us each a signed statement dated 12 December 1971 that read:

To: Commanding Officer, A. K. Loposer
        Executive Officer, R. R. Pariseau
        USS John Adams SSBN 620 (Gold Crew)

Gentlemen:

Speaking as men to men, it has been our pleasure to serve in your command. We feel you have earned and deserve the best the Navy has to offer. We believe everyone on board has strived to their utmost in helping you achieve your task and lighten your burden of responsibilities that go with command and the training of an SSBN to be constantly ready to perform our assigned task and fulfill our responsibilities to our country. As we leave your command permit us to take this opportunity to wish you both smooth sailing and the best of luck to the best "CO and XO" in the business.

Very Respectfully
Your Shipmates
//s// MM1 (SS) W.T. Brickey and RM1 (SS) D.L. Richie

That patrol was however, my eleventh, 60 day, submerged patrol, aboard an SSBN and I had had enough of the patrol boredom. With its sophisticated acoustic detection system and traveling quietly at slow speeds an SSBN can detect a contact at very long range. When policy is to remain at least ten miles from any contact to avoid being detected, the routine does not get very exciting. The Navy's vision for my future would be qualification for command, and one or possibly two tours, eight more patrols, as commanding officer of an SSBN. I wrote a letter stating that I was no longer a volunteer for submarine duty and that I wanted to change my designator to naval intelligence. I showed the letter to the ship's Captain, Ken Loposer, who warned me that submitting such a letter would guarantee that I was never promoted again. I was not convinced because my record was great, but even if he was right, I wanted some other duty. He then asked if I would delay sending the letter because he was due to be relieved and it was unlikely that the Navy would let both the Commanding Officer and the Executive Officer leave at the same time. He was on his second tour as SSBN commanding officer, had at least five more patrol than I did, and he had given me maximum responsibility while sharing the role as Command Duty Officer. As a faithful subordinate and friend, I agreed to make a patrol with whoever relieved him as commanding officer. I did not submit the letter until he had been relieved, the off-crew was over and we were departing on the next patrol.

The patrol was terrible. The new Commanding Officer was up tight, by the book, and risk averse to the exclusion of all else. His new policies included: Saturday mornings everyone not standing watch was to get up for field day (house cleaning.) The low-level background music normally heard in the ship's office and navigation compartment was no longer allowed because it could be distracting. I had approved the idea that if at least three sailors wanted to show a second movie after the scheduled evening movie, it was allowed as long as it was a previously shown movie not a new one that had not yet been scheduled. I though it was reasonable in case someone was on watch or otherwise working when the movie was originally shown and it had been an ongoing routine during the last two patrols. The new commanding officer disapproved and forbid any second movies. It was not a wise move to alienate the crew, but a series of these petty changes intended to improve the crew's performance had done just that.

It is routine before departing for patrol, to go to sea to test all the equipment, especially any that has been repaired or replaced and to conduct a torpedo attack. The new commanding officer was conducting a basic torpedo attack against a non-maneuvering surface vessel. The approach had gone smoothly and we were almost at the firing point when I noticed that the torpedo had not been warmed up. Rather than mention the fact to the Commanding Officer and embarrass him for his oversight, I went to the torpedo room to find out why the torpedo men had not taken the action on their own (like they would have done the last two patrols.) The three torpedo men were sitting together, chatting, and casually monitoring the communications among the torpedo approach team.

"What's going on?" I asked.

"Nothing Sir. No problem were are ready to respond."

"But the torpedo has not been warmed up and you can hear the reports of the range to the target, so you know we are getting ready to shoot."

"Yes Sir. We are just waiting for the Captain to tell us to warm up the torpedo. He has his own ideas about everything and we don't want to do anything that he wouldn't like."

"Call the control room and recommend warming up the torpedo just like you would have done in the past."

"Yes. Sir. But it is not like the past."

They were correct; it was not like the past. The patrol was more than simply boring, it was terrible because the crew was not happy and it showed in less than stellar performance.

During the patrol I received a message reply to my letter that essentially said, "You volunteer in, not out."

Towards the end of patrol I was notified that I was among those designated, Qualified for Command. Command is the dream of most military officers and is awarded stingily. It would have been nice, but to me it was not worth four or even eight more SSBN patrols. My response, that I did not want command, could not be ignored and was probably considered treason. When patrol ended and we returned to Guam, letters notifying me that, I was no longer qualified in submarines and no longer qualified as a nuclear engineer, were waiting.

I returned to Ford Island with the crew, but was immediately transferred to the Submarine Force Pacific's Intelligence Command, briefing SSN crews until travel funds became available and I could move to Navy Field Operational Intelligence Office at Fort Meade, MD.

I was giving a mission briefing to the senior officers of an SSN that had recently completed a shipyard overhaul. Its mission would be to trail a Soviet SSBN from Russia across the Pacific Ocean to its patrol area off the West Coast of the USA. We wanted to know what route they were taking because they had begun to avoid detection by our fixed acoustic systems in the Hawaiian Island area. The SSN's Commanding Officer requested some personnel assistance because his crew had been in the shipyard and not operated for quite some time and several new officers had reported aboard. I was asked to make the trip as Special Assistant to the Commanding Officer for Intelligence. I called attention to the fact that I was no longer qualified in submarines or nuclear power, but told that would be remedied. Messages re-qualifying me in submarines and nuclear power were received. I made the trip, but we did not detect the next Soviet SSBN leaving port to cross the Pacific. Back in Hawaii, before leaving for Maryland, messages did inform me that I was no longer qualified for submarine duty or nuclear power. I consider the episode a bit self-serving of the submarine force and the Navy, but only to be expected. And the submarine force would make me feel that way at least one more time!

I eventually received orders and reported to the Navy Field Operational Intelligence Command, tenants in the National Security Agency (NSA) building on Fort Meade, MD in July 1973.

During my military career I made twelve, 60 day submerged patrols aboard SSBNs (12 x 60 = 720 days), one 60-day patrol aboard an SSN (= 60 days), and 24 days of sea trials and deep dives (= 24 days) for a total of 804 days submerged aboard nuclear powered submarines. Or, more effortlessly assimilated, that's two years, two months, and 14 days, spent submerged aboard a nuclear powered submarine!

Adrenaline Moments

"A good scare is worth more to a man than good advice."
Edgar W. Howe 1853 - 1937

It was not all boredom aboard a submarine during the Cold War; there were occasional operational moments of significant excitement. Some exciting moments that I experienced include a flooding casualty while submerged at deep depth, a Soviet submarine torpedo firing incident, and a brief excursion under the polar ice cap.

Flooding in the Engine Room

Seawater is used for many purposed aboard a submarine. Uses include flushing water for the heads (toilets), liquid to be evaporated to produce fresh water for drinking and cooking, and cooling water for a wide variety of systems. When sea water is used for cooling another liquid, one liquid is usually circulated through a series of tubes inside a large cylindrical container while the other liquid flows around the outside of the tubes causing the heat exchange.

The distance from Guam, where the Polaris Submarine Blue-Gold crew exchange took place, to a patrol area with missiles targeted for the Soviet Union, could be 2,000 to 3,000 miles. The transit for an SSN between Hawaii and Petropavlosk or Vladivostok, the two main Soviet submarine bases in the Pacific, could be over 4,000 miles. Submarine transits are completed submerged and deep, to avoid the noise from propeller cavitation. Such transits take several days.

During one such transit, an announcement declared, "Flooding in the lower level engine room." I was chief engineer and arrived at the scene shortly after an engine room watch stander who was trying to climb down the ladder into the lower level engine room. The spray from the incoming seawater was denying visibility. It was as if you were in a closet and had a fire hose, fully opened, spraying against the wall. The incoming seawater was stopped by the Engineering Duty Officer using the remote control toggle switches available in the control room. Simultaneously, the Officer of the Deck proceeded towards the surface decreasing depth and water pressure. The excitement was relatively brief, but memorable. The "flooding" was coming from a two inch hole in the bottom of a cooling tank where a drain plug had corroded and failed.

Bronze is made from a combination of tin and copper and is resistant to seawater corrosion. Brass is a combination of copper and zinc in varying ratios and is corrosive in seawater. When a brass plug is exposed to seawater, the zinc can corrode leaving a copper shell that retains its shape, but has little strength. Visual discrimination between the two is not obvious. From equipment records we determined that during routine cleaning, inspection, and preventive maintenance, an individual from the submarine tender repair department had inadvertently installed the brass plug in the seawater cooling system. (Isn't it always someone else's fault?)

At sea level the atmospheric pressure is 14.7 pounds per square inch. Submerging in seawater, the pressure increases by one atmosphere (14.7 psi.) for every 33 feet. At a depth of 33 feet it is two atmospheres or 29.4 psi. (14.7 x 2), at a depth of 66 feet it is three atmospheres or 44.1 psi. (14.7 x 3), at a depth of 660 feet it is 20 atmospheres or 294 psi. (14.7 x 20.) Nuclear powered submarines can operate and transit at depths below 660 feet. The pressure behind the stream of water coming out of the two-inch hole was in excess of 300 pounds per square inch and thus ricocheted off the bulkheads (walls) with sufficient force to fill the compartment with dense spray and prevent visibility.

The pressure on a submerged submarine hull routinely causes groans and squeaks as depth is changed. To visually demonstrate the pressure changes on the hull to a novice a string can be stretched taut across a compartment and attached to each bulkhead. As the submarine's depth is increased the string will slacken astonishingly and the significance of external hull pressures in the 200-400 psi. range will not be forgotten.

"Torpedo in the water."

When we were tasked with following a Soviet ballistic missile submarine across the Pacific Ocean to determine their new route that was avoiding our underwater acoustic detection systems off Hawaii we proceeded to a position outside their harbor and waited.

Historically, when the Soviets began building nuclear powered submarines, the primary nuclear weapons threat to their country were airplanes flying from US aircraft carriers with nuclear bombs. They designed and built their submarine to be fast and capable of intercepting and attacking an aircraft carrier. The US designed its submarines to be quiet and capable of detecting and attacking Soviet submarines. The US focus on being quiet allowed US submarines to trail the much noisier Soviet submarines. To counter the possibility of being covertly trailed Soviet submarines would occasionally reverse course and increase speed back down their track hoping that a trailing submarine would be detected when it increased speed and move off the track to avoid a collision. We called the maneuver a "Crazy Ivan." More recently the Soviets had begun to send a very capable Victor Class SSN along with their SSBN to insure that the SSBN was not being trailed.

One morning after a number of uneventful days of harbor surveillance we detected an SSBN exiting the harbor. Unfortunately a Victor Class SSN was exiting a few hundred yards behind it. As we waited the submarines cleared the harbor and then the SSBN turned north and the SSN turned south. We maneuvered quietly in behind the SSBN hoping that it was going on patrol and that this was going to be our lucky day. The Soviet SSBN was in her home waters and making no attempt to remain quiet. We were following her from well over a mile away and everything was going smoothly until SONAR reported, "Target is turning to starboard."

We stopped and listened, anxious to determine what the SSBN was doing.

SONAR reported, "Target has reversed course and is coming towards us. It could be a Crazy Ivan, except that the target has not increased speed."

We increased depth and slowly moved off the track to avoid a collision in case the SSBN continued down its new course. After several minutes SONAR reported, "Torpedo in the water." We knew that the Soviets could be very aggressive and we were close to their shore, perhaps they had detected us and were attacking? With the torpedo masking our noise we increased speed, moved further off the track, and began a downward spiral to avoid a homing torpedo. The only remaining anti-torpedo device at our disposal was launching decoys, a submarine's last resort because it confirms the submarine's presence.

The torpedo passed overhead and a safe distance away from us. We waited, detected no further aggressive action and came to periscope depth to observe the surface activity and listen to voice transmissions. A torpedo retriever was being directed to recover the torpedo now bobbing at the surface and the Victor Class SSN was reporting that the SSBN had calculated a perfect attack solution because the torpedo had passed directly beneath the targeted Victor. The two Soviet submarines had open the distance, both reversed course, and the SSN had played target for the SSBN's submerged, torpedo attack. We just happened to be between the two contestants!

Both Soviet submarines returned to port. We changed our shorts and resumed our port surveillance.

Under Polar Ice

At the conclusion of a patrol instead of returning to port, we were diverted to collect some data under the edge of the polar ice cap.

Sunlight penetrates seawater to depth of about one hundred feet and with a periscope above that depth sea life can be observed. In addition to the propeller cavitation noise from surface ship traffic, a submerged submarine can detect the noise from surface waves, rain, thunder and lightning strikes, and biologics. Some biologic noise, from the crackling (like frying bacon) of shrimp beds to the cries and low frequency moans of whales, is routinely present and detected by a submerged submarine's sonar system. In sum, the underwater environment is relatively noisy.

Near the edge of the polar ice cap, a dense assortment of various size ice burgs and burger bits collide with one another and with the polar ice cap, due to wind and wave action. Transiting under this area, the noise can be deafening.

Once under the stationary ice cap, it is dark because sunlight cannot penetrate the ice, and it is eerily quiet. There are no surface waves or wind to hear, there is no surface ship traffic, and there are virtually no biologics. The acoustic variation and abruptness is remarkable. Since a submarine cannot surface easily from beneath the ice, fire replaces flooding as the worst potential casualty. Because a fire can quickly deplete the air/oxygen in the submarine and without the ability to surface and replenish the onboard atmosphere, a fire can be deadly. No smoking was allowed and the atmospheric oxygen level in the submarine was decreased to 18 percent. (Normal oxygen level is between 21 – 18% with 17% the minimum allowed.) Simultaneously, the cold, water temperature allows cooling water flow rates to be reduced in heat exchangers and with the submarine at relatively shallow depths the seawater pressure is reduced in case of a flooding casualty.

We gathered the necessary data with minimal excursion under the ice cap and returned to port. It was a rather brief but memorable experience.

Sea Duty Incompatibility
"There are fools everywhere, even in asylums."
George Bernard Shaw 1856 - 1950

In retrospect, I was a mismatch as a sea going naval officer. Operating at sea whether on a ship or on a submarine was not as satisfying to me as it is to many others. It was not the job so much as the long periods of sameness without alternative stimulation and change. It was less of an issue aboard a surface ship because they occasionally made worldwide port visits to show the flag, but the proficiency of a nuclear submarine crew, the technological sophistication of the vessel, and the inherent danger of operating submerged were also intoxicating. Some people can embrace as sufficient, the danger, thrill, technological sophistication, and camaraderie of being at sea, but with little or no diversions from duty for months at a time, I was always seeking ways to avoid being bored. I needed more frequent excitement even if only the availability of sports or the routinely available diversions during shore duty tours. When I found reading books, playing in card tournaments, and maximizing occasional opportunities such as boxing smokers and roach races were not enough to keep me from getting bored, I tried taking correspondence courses. Beginning on the Richard S. Edwards and continuing through my chief engineer and executive officer tours I always went to sea with at least one correspondence course to complete. I began by completing courses from the Naval Correspondence Course Center (Introduction To Space Technology, Naval Operational Tactics, Fundamentals of Naval Intelligence, General Oceanography, and Oceanography in Anti-Submarine Operations) mixed in courses from the U.S. Armed Forces Institute (Introduction to Real Estate, Criminology, Personnel Management, Plumbing, Disaster Control, International Law, The Economics of Defense, and Russian History) and progressed to a Personal Income Tax Course from the Tax Education Institute (that qualified me to be a Paid Preparer of Individual Income Tax Forms), a Counter-Insurgency Course from the Naval War College in Newport, RI, and a Fiction Writing Course from the Famous Writers School in Westport, CT that required 30 - 40 written submissions and allowed three years to complete.

In addition to helping me cope with the boredom of sea duty, the fiction writing course encouraged me to retain, "Write a Novel" on my Bucket List and the Tax Course convinced me that the best, most efficient way to minimize one's income tax is to own a business. When I returned to homeport after completing the tax course I contacted a colleague who was selling Amway and asked if I could join his group. Accustomed to giving presentations to unsuspecting friends and acquaintances under disguised invitations, he was in awe of someone who actually wanted to join. Owning a business remains good tax advice.

The education derived from the courses not withstanding, taking correspondence courses to cope with large stretches of boring work is neither very effective nor efficient. At sea, aboard ship, I was a round peg in a square hole.

CHAPTER 8

Naval Intelligence Command

Navy Field Operational Intelligence Office
"We learn from history that we do not learn from history."
Georg Wilhelm Friedrich Hegel 1770 - 1831

I was not a good engineer and never enjoyed building, operating, or repairing machinery. I was a successful engineer, including four patrols as the Chief Engineer on a nuclear powered submarine, because I was a leader who treated his men with respect and routinely evidenced my trust in them, a teacher who worked at stroking their inquisitiveness and making learning fun, and an administrator who paid attention to details.

I was however, a very good analyst. In the world of operational intelligence, system analysis and evaluation, and analysis of enemy tactics and operational capabilities, I found my passion and proved my worth. As a military officer my opportunities in this regard occurred during my two final tours of duty.

In the 1970s, the US Intelligence organization was divided according to assets. The Defense Intelligence Agency (DIA) controlled the camera equipped satellites and spy plane operations. DIA produced photographic intelligence called PHOTINT. The National Security Agency (NSA) was responsible for communication and signal intercept and their intelligence products were called COMINT and SIGINT (communications intelligence and signals intelligence.) The Central Intelligence Agency (CIA) controlled the spies and had the responsibility for human intelligence - HUMINT. Each service (Army, Navy, and Air Force) had organizations that collated the information from these agencies to satisfy their particular requirements.

From 1973 - 1977, I was the Director of Soviet Anti-Submarine & Undersea Warfare at the Naval Operational Intelligence Office (NFOIO) within the Naval Intelligence Command. NFOIO was a tenant of the National Security Agency at Fort Meade, MD. As Director I was responsible for the production of original, in depth analysis, from all source intelligence, dealing with submarine and anti-submarine operations of the Soviet navy. Operational areas of analysis included strategic capability, tactical doctrine, national goals, and command organizations. A companion organization, the Naval Intelligence Support Center (NISC) in Suitland, MD, performed technical analysis of Soviet systems and platforms to determine characteristics and inherent capabilities so that NFOIO could assess, recognize, and forecast operational use, tactics, and operational capability.

My tour of duty at NFOIO was especially exciting because the Soviets were changing their operational procedures, incorporating new tactics, testing radically different sensors (with a concentration on non-acoustic submarine detectors,) constructing new classes of submarines, and operating in new areas e.g., their ballistic missile submarines under the polar ice cap. The concern was that the Soviet's had made a significant technological leap in the area of submarine warfare, especially detection, and that they were now aware that we were routinely following their ballistic missile submarines while they were on patrol. We were trying to understand and counter whatever was driving the changes we were observing. About ten years later we would discover that the changes were the result of intelligence the Soviets were receiving from spies, namely John Anthony Walker and his spy ring. Even later, after the collapse of the Soviet Union I learned of the connection between Walker's actions and the Pueblo Affair.

During this same period the Chinese launched a nuclear powered submarine with missiles in the conning tower and the Peoples Republic of China (PRC) Navy was added to our analytical responsibility as a country of interest.

Our studies were routinely classified Top Secret Codeword including the title. Titles were often classified to avoid revealing our areas of interest and concern.

Spies

"Trust everybody, but cut the cards."
Finley Peter Dunne 1867 - 1936

John Walker, convicted of spying for the Soviet Union from 1968 - 1985, had been a Navy Chief Warrant Officer, whose specialty was communications. He had been stationed aboard a nuclear powered, ballistic missile submarine and at the Atlantic Fleet's Submarine Communications Center. He had access to the navy's encryption codes, the location of U.S. underwater surveillance systems, and knowledge of submarine operational procedures, patrol locations, and top secret submarine weapons and sensor data. He told the Soviets that we were tracking their submarines and later, after they acquired the hardware to go with the codes Walker gave them, were able to copy and read - among other communications - coded U.S. submarine patrol highlight reports. Submarine highlights reports are transmitted at the end of a mission, but before returning to homeport, and might have included, " . . . and we trailed him from __to __, at a depth of __, speed of __, . . .") that must have caused a panic and the initiative for the changes that we were observing.

Walker recruited his brother Arthur who was a retired Navy Lieutenant Commander working as a military contractor, his son, Michael an active duty seaman, and Senior Chief Radioman Jerry Whitworth. The amount of data and codes Walker gave the Soviets was massive. A Soviet KGB defector, Vitaly Yurchenko, is reported to have said that while John Walker was operating, "If there had been a war we (the Soviet Union) would have won."

He admitted that he had done it for money. In a plea bargain he was offered a life sentence in lieu of execution in exchange for full disclosure of what data and codes he had given the Soviets (so we could assess what was compromised and what needed to be changed) and for testifying against Whitworth, et al. All members of his spy ring received life sentences (e.g., Whitworth was sentenced to 365 years in prison and fined) except his son Michael who had played a minor role and as part of the plea bargain was sentenced to only 25 years.

After divorcing his wife, Walker further angered her by refusing to pay alimony and trying to recruit their daughter into his operation. He was caught when his wife retaliated by reporting his spying activities to the FBI. John Walker died in a federal prison in North Carolina on August 28, 2014; he was 77 years old.

The USS Pueblo
"Men occasionally stumble over the truth, but most of them pick themselves up and hurry off as if nothing happened."
Winston Churchill 1874 - 1965

After receiving the top secret communication codes from Walker the Soviets desperately wanted the communications hardware to go with it. To avoid suspicion by stealing or capturing a platform that had one onboard, the Soviets offered North Korea a large sum of money (some estimates are several million) to get one. The plan was for the North Koreans to capture the USS Pueblo that was quietly and harmlessly steaming about sixteen miles off the coast of North Korea. The Pueblo was an old ship, commissioned in 1944 as a light cargo ship and currently designated as a Technical Research Ship. We, the Soviets, and the North Koreans, knew that it was a communications collection vessel and that it likely contained classified codes and communication hardware. North Korean patrol boats, claiming that the Pueblo had been within their 12-mile territorial waters, captured the Pueblo. Captain Bucher USN, the ship's captain initially refused to surrender and tried to escape. The North Koreans fired on the Pueblo wounding the Captain and two sailors and threatened to sink the ship if it did not surrender. After stalling as long as possible while burning and shredding the communications codes, classified documents, publications, and correspondence, - and reporting that action to his US command organization - Captain Bucher surrendered his ship. The crew was held captive in North Korean POW camps from January to December 1968. The U.S. Navy and Department of Defense did not realize the gravity of the situation because the important classified documents had been reported destroyed and no one suspected that the prize was a piece of hardware. It was also the middle of the Vietnam War and the Tet Offensive had begun so U.S. military focus was elsewhere. After the release of the 82 man Pueblo crew, Captain Bucher was allowed to spend time at the Naval Postgraduate School in Monterey, CA recovering from his ordeal and documenting in writing the details of the Pueblo event and subsequent captivity. It was my time at the School (1968 - 1970) and Captain Bucher was frequently seen at a desk in the school library. Military personnel at the School regarded him with mixed emotions. He had saved the lives of his crew, but had surrendered his ship - clearly a no win situation.

"Open Water"
'It's what a fellow thinks he knows that hurts him."
Frank McKinney Hubbard 1868 - 1930

The position title, Director of Soviet Submarine & Anti-Submarine Warfare, correctly revealed that the Soviet Union was our only enemy with nuclear powered submarines, submarine launched missiles, and the capability to threaten US submarines. During my tour of duty the Chinese (Peoples Republic of China/PRC) Navy launched a nuclear submarine with two missiles in its sail and test fired a ballistic missile into the South China Sea. In response, I was directed to add the Chinese submarine force to our plate of analytical responsibilities.

To begin a file, I asked colleagues at the National Security Agency (NSA), the Central Intelligence Agency (CIA), and the Defense Intelligence Agency (DIA) what they had on the Chinese submarine force organization and headquarters location. The NSA reported the submarine headquarters as the land based location from which the majority of the intercepted submarine communications and signal intelligence originated. The DIA reported the headquarters location as the harbor area where submarines were seen most often in overhead photographs when they were not at sea. It was not at the same location NSA had reported. From information gleaned from informants and spies the CIA reported a third location as the Chinese submarine headquarters. The truth was that the US Intelligence Community did not know where the Chinese submarine headquarters was located.

Intelligence reports on the Chinese military in general and their navy in particular seemed to confirm the common opinion that the Chinese were not logical. One of the current topics of interest was ownership of the Paracell and Spratly Islands --- whose ownership was claimed by Japan, the Philippines, Vietnam, and China. The motivation for ownership was the strategic location of the islands in the South China Sea and their proximity to a potential undersea source of oil. The claims were based on historical precedence, past occupation, and proximity of the islands to the mainland, i.e., within territorial waters. The Chinese had been trying to exploit undersea oil deposits in the Yellow Sea and South China Sea. One report indicated that they had drilled to a depth that indicated a sophisticated capability, but when a leak developed they plugged it with a mixture of straw, mud, and fertilizer (dung.) Another reinforcement of the common belief that we did not understand the Chinese because they were not logical. Classified intelligence reports constantly contained such dichotomies and we were making little headway towards understanding China's plans for their nuclear submarines and ballistic missiles. Actually, we were getting more and more confused from the conflicting data.

In the 1970s, communication intercepts deemed to have real time value were collected by human operators who wore a headset and sat at a desk with a keyboard for typing. They were linguistic interpreters who translated what they heard and typed it in English. It was also assumed that someone with a sensory impairment (visual) would have an enhanced capability in a compensatory sense (hearing). If you were visually impaired, fluent in one or more foreign languages and could type, NSA offered a very nice career opportunity. The largest concentration of Seeing Eye dogs I have ever seen was in the NSA cafeteria at lunchtime. To encourage personnel to learn a new language or improve their foreign language fluency, NSA offered free, evening courses in a variety of languages at various proficiency levels. I decided that perhaps if I learned some Chinese I would be better able to interpret the available Chinese intelligence data.

I began a Level I Chinese language course taught by a portly, mustached, and well-dressed individual named, Mr. Wu. The course began in the traditional fashion, learning some vocabulary and basic phrases, e.g., "Good morning." " Where can I find . . .?" Within a couple of weeks, we were introduced to idioms and what I call "ganged words."

"The Chinese language includes two common words put together to form a new, third word." Explained Mr. Wu. "For example, we have the word 'open,' the word 'water,' and a third word, 'open-water'. What do you think open-water means?" he asked, gesturing to invite any student to answer.

Answers were plentiful, but generally related to: The ocean? The mouth of a large river? Any large body of water? The sea?

Shaking his head and smiling, (he had probably asked this same question before and knew the answers he would get,) he responded "No," to each answer and after a pause, said, "It means steam. When water opens you get steam."

That was my epiphany. I had learned a valuable lesson, more than I had hoped to get from the course, and I realized that I would learn nothing more of value in understanding Chinese intelligence reports.

The next morning I wrote a memo, via the chain of command, to the Director of Naval Intelligence. In the memo I relayed the above story and stated as my conclusion: The Chinese are not illogical, but their eastern logic is totally different than our western logic. The Submarine Warfare Division will never be able to anticipate Chinese submarine developments and intentions without someone raised and schooled in eastern logic on its team. If we try to forecast Chinese submarine developments and intentions using what we believe might be eastern logic, most conclusions will not only be incorrect, but many will sound absurd.

We did not get an Eastern-thinking analyst before I received orders to a new duty station. There may not have been one in the system with a sufficiently high level of security clearance to work with us. We did not make much progress anticipating Chinese developments either!

"CANUKUS"

"It is not necessary to understand things
in order to argue about them."
Caron deBeaumarchais 1732 - 1799

In the mid 1970s the Soviet Union had begun construction of a very large nuclear powered submarine at a shipyard known for innovative submarine designs. Not only was the hull larger than any previous submarine, but the hull penetrations for the ballistic missiles appeared to be larger than necessary for any missile in their inventory. We had been photographing the submarine construction using the SR-71 Blackbird spy plane flying at 85,00 feet and the early, Key Hole spy satellite photography system. There was no way of determining the precise diameter of the missile tubes from the photographs because there was nothing in the photographs whose dimension was known. (This was prior to real time links for video download and steerable satellites. These were actual pictures that had to be developed and analyzed at a light-table.) The larger diameter missile tube was troublesome because without it the missile's increased range or payload could not be estimated. Knowing the missiles range and where the submarine conducted its patrols would provide estimates of its target package, or knowing its target package the submarine's patrol area could be estimated. Thus the new submarine's missile tube diameter was a red-hot issue.

CANUKUS was the acronym for the annual meeting of a small, select group of naval intelligence specialists, with very high level and compartmented security clearances, from Canada (CAN), the United Kingdom (UK), and the United States (US). We met for a week once per year and the meeting was hosted on a rotating basis among the three participating countries. The host country, using inputs for topics from each country prepared a schedule of topics to be discussed and arrange for briefers. It was in fact an international, intelligence exchange.

In May of 1976 the British hosted the conference and we met at the British Ministry of Defence, in London, England. One very important topic was the new Soviet submarine and the size of its missile tubes. Analysts from DIA showed the most recent overhead photographs of the submarine being built and various agencies and individuals were scheduled to provide their best estimate of the missile tube size and the basis for their estimate.

The late 1970s was before the digital age and briefers using visual aids used viewgraphs, (pictures and text on clear plastic sheets) and an overhead projector. At informal briefings the overhead projector would be located at the front of the room and the briefer would change his/her own viewgraphs. At formal briefings and conferences the viewgraphs were given to a non-participating individual, located in a small, darkened room separated from the conference room by a one-way glass window and containing an overhead projector. In response to the briefer's command the individual in the projection room would manually change the viewgraph.

It was noon on the third day of the conference and we had just adjourned for lunch. The weather had been warm and sunny, unusual anytime in England, and the room temperature beers, "pints", served in British pubs had always been much to my liking. I had given my briefing on the previous day and while delivering my viewgraphs to the projection room had noticed a large, soft, leather chair in the room. Since I had renewed British and Canadian friendships late into the night/morning and consumed a "couple of pints", I had visions of a quick lunch and a nap in the projection room. I entered the projection room and asked the Royal Navy Intelligence Specialist 2nd Class, "Will you be leaving this room unlocked during the lunch break?"

"Yes sir. I will put the viewgraphs that have been given me in a safe. The room will be unlocked and empty."

"Looks like a comfortable place for a brief nap after a long night." I said, pointing to the brown, overstuffed chair. "Don't be surprised if you find me here when you return."

"No problem sir. I guess everyone is having a good time at the conference. Will you be discussing the new submarine's missile tube size all week?" he inquired.

"It will consume much of the agenda and as you've heard, there are a lot of different estimates on the diameter."

"Yes sir. I've noticed. I was just wondering if you were going to wait until the end of the week to reveal its exact size?"

With undisguised surprise and some guilt, since I had been enjoying myself much too much at the conference, I asked, " What do you mean? All we have are estimates. Each organization believes their estimate is the best, but none stand out above the rest."

"Well sir, I could tell you the diameter of the missile tube and thought perhaps you were just having some fun estimating the diameter until the end of the conference."

I asked, "How he would do that?" and he showed me!

As we were reconvening for the afternoon session, I told the British Navy Captain who was the conference host and moderator, that some new and exciting information had become available and that we should begin the session with a guest speaker. After revealing "the secret" to him, I had his concurrence and the Royal Navy Intelligence Specialist

2nd Class, (whose name, unfortunately, I no longer recall) was introduced as the first afternoon speaker.

"Good afternoon," he began, "while changing viewgraphs this morning I noticed one photograph at the end of a sequence as the satellite passed over the submarine that was shown only briefly because the submarine was only partly visible. That photograph is now on the screen. I call your attention to the very top, right, corner where there is an empty field with a football goal. That's soccer for you Yanks. The Russians love their football and the goal is most likely built to international standards of 2.44 meters high and 7.32 meters wide. (8' x 24') With those dimension as reference the diameter of the missile tubes can be determined."

Pencils and paper rattled as calculations were begun and shouts for copies of the photograph were heard, but mostly people were staring at the speaker with their jaw at half-mast until someone began clapping and everyone joined in. He was right. The missile tube calculations based on mensuration from the soccer goal proved to be accurate and patrol areas and target packages for the new Soviet ballistic missile submarine were estimated before the submarine was launched.

Recalling the event, two lessons come to mind. First, never be afraid to admit that everyone knows something that you do not know and no matter how well educated you may be, it usually pays to listen. Second, no experience, education, or adventure is ever wasted, because "cross-training" may unexpectedly provide the answer to an unrelated problem.

Studies, Lectures & Briefings
"We are all geniuses up to the age of ten."
Aldous Huxley 1894 - 1963

Some of the studies I authored during my three years at NFOIO, that had unclassified titles include:
"Soviet Submarine Tactics"
"The Soviet Strategic Naval Posture"

"Soviet Submarine Anti-Convoy and Anti-Surface Ship Capability & Tactics"

"The Soviet *Victor* Class SSN: Its Role and Mission"

"The Phenomenon of Bioluminescence and Submarine Detection"

"The Soviet Submarine Launched Ballistic Missile Threat"

"Soviet Naval Strategic Command, Control, and Communications"

"The Operational History of China's *Golf* Class Submarine"

"The Personnel Lift Capability of the Amphibious Forces of the PRC Navy"

"Chinese (PRC) Submarine Tactics"

"PRC Naval Command, Control & Communications System and Organization"

"The Implications of Chinese Naval AID to Other Countries"

"PRC Fuel Oil Replenishment Capability in Spratly Islands & South China Sea"

"China and the Question of Sovereignty Over Islands in the South China Sea"

"PRC Motivation for the Development of the Islands in the South China Sea"

The studies relating to the Islands of the South China Sea were completed in the late 1970s. Since 2012 ownership of the islands in the South China Sea has again become a hotly contested issue between, China, Japan, and the Philippines. The capability for recovering the undersea oil has been added to the importance of the Islands' strategic geographical location.

Letters of appreciation were sent to me via Naval Intelligence Command from the following organizations/individuals after I had provided a requested naval intelligence briefing. The National Cryptologic School; Military Strategy Class at Marine Corps' Command & Staff College, Quantico, VA; Assistant Secretary of Navy for Research & Development; Defense Intelligence Agency; Naval Undersea Warfare Center, Newport, RI; Naval Post Graduate School, Monterey, CA; and Admiral S. Turner USN.

CHAPTER 9

Submarine Research

Office Of Naval Research

"Work is a form of nervousness."
Don Herold 1889 - 1966

From NFOIO I was ordered to report as Director of Advanced Submarine Technology at the Office of Naval Research (ONR), in Arlington, VA. It was not the job that I wanted.

In preparation for a government change due to the election of a new president I gave several naval intelligence briefings to a presidential transition team headed by Dr. Pat Parker from Naval Postgraduate School, Monterey, CA. Several months later and shortly before I was due to be relieved at NFOIO, Dr. Parker called me and revealed that he was organizing a new graduate level curriculum at NPGS called National Security Affairs and wanted to know if I would be interested in being the Director. I enthusiastically replied in the affirmative, but cautioned him that I still held a Submariners designation not an Intelligence designation and that the submarine community may not let me go. He told me that he had been assured by individuals at the highest level of the Department of Defense that, he could have whomever he wanted as director, and therefore, could arrange my orders.

When I received orders to ONR, rather than the Naval Postgraduate School, I contacted Dr. Parker who told me he tried everything he could but that the submarine community would not release me. I called

Admiral Robert Long USN, the Vice Chief of Naval Operations for Submarine Warfare and arranged for a personal, private meeting with him at his pentagon office. I pleaded my case. 1st: The submarine community promised that I would never get another promotion because I refused a submarine command (when my name appeared as an officer eligible for promotion, the submarine representative on the promotion board would declare, "We don't want him promoted." and my record would not even get opened for review.) 2nd: Since the submarine community does not appreciate what I can do and since I will be retiring at first opportunity, in three years, the opportunity at NPGS could result in a career teaching at the school.

Admiral Long responded quite clearly. 1st: I would be going to ONR. 2nd: There was a need for someone with nuclear submarine experience to canvas emerging technologies and initiate new research programs that would have submarine applications. 3rd: For the first time, the director of ONR would be a submariner and I would have a large budget to accomplish my tasks.

I sometimes wonder what my life would have been like if I had been an instructor and program director at NPGS, but Admiral Long was true to his word about the new director and my budget, and - in hindsight - everything worked out fine at ONR.

As program manager and technical director of a systems oriented approach to improved submarine performance, I was responsible for programs involving all facets of submarine performance including energy conversion, unique (non-acoustic) sensors, drag reduction techniques, communication, navigation, automation, detection and detection avoidance.

While at ONR I was an active member of several national and Department of Defense (DoD) panels and advisory groups: The National Academy of Science's *Space Panel* that met to study and recommend naval applications for space technology. The Naval Research Advisory Committee's *Mid-Depth Sea Technology Panel* that examined the potential for sea floor exploitation using emerging technologies and the strategic implications of such exploitation. A Senior Advisory Panel for a unique technology program involving non-acoustic submarine detection, under the direction of the Director of Naval Warfare. And a member of the Naval Strategic Study Group at the Center for Strategic & International Studies.

Why a PhD?

"A great many people think they are thinking when
they are merely rearranging their prejudices."
William James 1842 - 1910

As head of a naval intelligence group and later, directing submarine research and development programs, I had occasion to routinely brief Flag Officers, prestigious committees, and high-powered groups. I frequently got the impression that what I had to say was tainted in the mind of the audience, because I was a lowly Lieutenant Commander (LCDR.) For example, after finding correlation between Soviet "Bear" Anti-Submarine aircraft flights to the choke points at the Greenland-Iceland-UK gap and the transit of US ballistic missile submarines, I briefed a collection of senior intelligence officers, submarine officers, and government civilians at the office of the Director of Naval Intelligence. The data negated a coincidence between the aircraft flights and submarine transits, proposed some hypotheses that might explain the events, and identified our intended course of action. A mole was not one of our hypotheses (See Walker- Wentworth), but several potential explanations were of grave concern. After the briefing, the audience huddled briefly before telling me, "Leave all you data, notes, and presentation here with us. We will take it from here and there is no need for you to pursue this any further." I got the feeling that they agreed that the evidence was important, but that a LCDR couldn't possibly be smart enough to solve the problem, avoid a political confrontation, and prevent any leaks. Later, while at ONR and seeking funding for a new or developing project, I was occasionally denied funding, not because it was a bad idea or low priority, but because, "You're just an engineer and you don't understand bottom line requirements and financing."

I was aware that I had earned GI Bill educational benefits and decided that getting a PhD - in any subject - and becoming Doctor instead of LCDR would make me credible to audiences that should hear about the work I was presenting. The University of Maryland was closer to Ft. Meade, but only George Washington University allowed for courses leading to a PhD to be taken at night. They also had a program whereby older applicants, with significant work experience, could develop a personal program plan. I developed a personal plan for the School of Government and Business Administration to get a PhD in International Business. I was able to validate the language requirement with some technical publication translations (French to English and English to French) and all the quantitative courses by passing the final exams from a previous semester in the classes I wanted to validate in the Computer Science (Operations Research) Department. Thus my classes to fulfill the 42-semester hour requirement were almost exclusively, "listen" courses. (In my mind there are two kinds of courses, "Do" and "Listen." "Do" courses require problem solving homework to understand the concepts, e.g., Statistics. "Listen" coursed only require reading the text or attending the lecture to understand the material. For example, if you hear, "Don't try to sell half-gallon bottles of juice or milk in Japan, because their refrigerators are too compact to accommodate them." OK you've got it. No homework required.) My major difficulties were the papers and reports that required visiting, interviewing, or touring a business to understand and appreciate how they operated, - my days were taken at work and my courses were at night.

The announcement of Final Acceptance of my dissertation, "Stock Market States: A New Approach to Investment Timing for the Average Investor," was in June 1980. I went on stage to receive my diploma on February 16, 1981.

Adjunct Professor

"The vanity of teaching doth often tempt a
man to forget that he is a blockhead."
George Savile, Marquis of Halifax 1633 - 1695

I became an adjunct professor somewhat by embarrassment. When I approached the first professor that I hoped would be one of the required six professors on my dissertation committee, he asked, "Why do you want to get a PhD?" I was reluctant to tell him the real reason and paused before answering.

He made it easy for me, "It's not that hard a question. People want a PhD either to teach or do research."

"Yes sir. That's it. I want to teach." And that became "my final answer!"

It was not long after my graduation that I was asked to teach Statistics at the George Washington University. For individuals who are not in a mathematical or engineering curriculum (e.g., seeking a Masters Degree in Business Administration) statistics is only taken because it is required for the degree. It is not a course professors are lining up to teach to MBA students because those students all know they will hate it, that it will be difficult (i.e., they will have homework problems to solve), and they have usually saved it until their final semester hoping the requirement would go away because one's final semester should be easy. A bit of a dichotomy there! Of course, I didn't know all this at the time, thought it would be fun, and readily agreed.

In an attempt to make the Statistics course palatable I began saving articles from newspapers, magazines, and other publications that were misrepresentations of statistics, misleading mathematical manipulations, biased data collection, or spin. I opened each course by showing this data to demonstrate the importance of recognizing the importance and proper use of statistics. I collected sufficient data to develop and teach a course with seven, one and one-half hour sessions titled, *"Figures Can Lie: Separating Numerical and Statistical Facts from Fiction."*

I eventually got involved teaching at night as an adjunct professor for the Florida Institute of Technology (FIT.) The school began with an innovative niche and I'm happy to say that they have succeeded. FIT was founded in 1958 by J.P. Keuper PhD, to offer continuing educational opportunities to scientists, engineers, and technicians who were working at the Kennedy Space Center in Melbourne, FL. Both faculty and students worked on the space program during the day and studied in the classroom at night. The school grew quickly and the military became a major consumer. The agreement between the military and FIT was: FIT would provide accredited professors, teach graduate courses, only teach at night, and confer a Masters Degree upon completion of a curriculum. The military command would provide the classroom and students would be military personnel and Department of Defense civilian employees. It was wonderful because all the students wanted to learn and real world problems could be introduced. During my years teaching as an adjunct professor with FIT, I taught at the Army's Defense Logistics Agency at Fort Belvoir, VA, at the Naval Air Test Station Patuxent, MD, at the Marine Corp Base Quantico, VA, and at the Army Engineering Research & Development Center in Alexandria, VA.

Primarily, I taught the quantitative courses: Probability, Statistics, Decision Theory, and Systems Analysis, but occasionally a business course such as: Managerial Economics, Business Policy Formulation, or Organization & Management of Marketing. I found the real world problems introduced by students exhilarating and teaching student who are eager to learn, to be refreshing. I am convinced that teaching and coaching are in my family genes. My father was a math teacher and coach, his brother, Gig, was a history teacher and coach, my brother, Bob was a math teacher, my sister, Joan was a Physical Education teacher, and at least three cousins with Pariseau genes are teachers.

Today, Florida Institute of Technology is a large college. Still located outside the main gate to the Kennedy Space Center in Melbourne, Fl, it now teaches both graduate and undergraduate courses, has a campus and supports athletic teams.

What's in a Name?

"Every man is a damn fool for at least five minutes every
day; wisdom consists in not exceeding the limit."
Elbert Hubbard 1856 - 1915

My given name is Richard. I was named after my French-Canadian grandmother whose maiden name was Delina Richard. In French-Canada and to all ice hockey fans, it is pronounced "Ree - shard" as with the Hall of Fame hockey player, Maurice "the Rocket" Richard. Born and raised in southeastern Massachusetts, my name was pronounced in standard American English. I did not learn of this ancestral connection until I was in college, but I don't think it would have made a difference.

During my high school years in Attleboro, MA, I was an above average athlete and honor student. In a small town like Attleboro, with a population that avidly supports its high school teams, that meant you "got ink" in the *Attleboro Sun,* the local newspaper. It was fine being called "Richie" by my family and high school friends, but as I got older and saw my name in print, "Richie" seemed childish. I was not alone with what I considered the childish name since I had teammates named Ronnie, Bernie and Eddie, but that didn't help me accept the name "Richie." In my limited experience, as a 17 year old, small town, high school senior, being called by the formal names Richard, Bernard, Ronald, or Edward would only be encouraged by the very wealthy or those with self-impressive ancestry and a roman numeral after their name who wanted to impress their fellow country club members. So, my dilemma was that I though being caller "Richard" was pretentious, but I did not want to go into business or middle age and still be called "Richie." The opportunity for a trial name change occurred after graduation from Attleboro High School when I reported to Tabor Academy and met new people. I introduced myself to everyone I met as "Dick." The name worked for me and after my year at Tabor I reported to the US Naval Academy in Annapolis as Dick Pariseau. My high school friends, now in their seventh decade, are still called Ronnie and Bernie, so either they didn't feel as I did about their name being childish or they did not have a convenient and "acceptable" nickname they could use?

I was always pleased to read my name and be called "Dick" not "Richie." When I go back home my siblings try to call me "Dick," but are much more comfortable with "Rich" or "Richie." I know it is from habit and I go along when I'm with them or call them on the telephone. So, everyone aside from my family, high school classmates, and people in Attleboro, MA knows me as "Dick". When in Attleboro, I expect it and acknowledge without comment however, I do introduce myself to new people as "Dick." The name change was a good choice for me although one particular name related incident does stand out.

It took me five years of night classes, research, and dissertation writing at the George Washington University to get my PhD in Business. In the propitious month of June 1980 my PhD dissertation was approved and I retired from the navy. My last three years in the Navy I served as the Director of Advanced Submarine Technology at the Office of Naval Research. Ruby, the charming and very efficient secretary that I inherited with the position, referred to me as "Dr. Pariseau" even though I was still taking classes and working on a dissertation. Soon she had most people I dealt with at work calling me Dr. Pariseau. The exception was David Herrington, a close friend, and member of our monthly poker group who had worked with me during my tour with Naval Intelligence. He would call me at the office, identify himself to Ruby, and ask to speak to Dr. Dick. Each time, Ruby, terribly proper and modest, whose upper body garment was always buttoned to the throat, would correct him and request that he be more respectful. David, always a comedian, didn't change. Eventually, Ruby told me of David's disrespect and said that I should talk to him about it because he was not listening to her. I did. I told David that Ruby was a jewel, I did not want to lose her, and to please stop asking to speak to Dr. Dick. As with any good male friend, he changed his way at my request. The next time he called, he identified himself and told Ruby that he wanted to speak to the "Dick Doctor."

She was both flustered and angry when she told me, "David, that awful friend of yours, is on the line and wants to speak with you."

I asked David what had transpired and I could not contain a hearty and noisy laugh when he told me. I'm sure Ruby heard me laugh and I suspect my reputation was tarnished in her eyes.

Not long after that telephone call, David came by in person, met Ruby for the first time, brought her some flowers, and spent some time with her before coming to my office. He's tall, handsome, witty, and can be impeccably mannered and charming when it suits his purpose. He won her over and they became friends. Ruby even loosened up a bit after her encounters with David. During the following Christmas holiday season, her liberation was evident as we exchanged token gifts at the office Christmas party. With only mild embarrassment she gave me and watched me unwrap what even today, is my favorite coffee mug. Bright yellow with large black lettering it states, "TRUST ME. I'M A DOCTOR."

Don't underestimate the importance of a young person's environment and that includes its impact on one's name. While gaining self confidence it helps to have a name that one is at least comfortable with if not proud to have. If that's not the case, make one up or give yourself a nickname. I think it helped me.

Doctor Dick and Ruby after Dick's "private,"
Navy Commendation Medal Award Ceremony. (See "Titanium")
(Personal Photo)

Titanium

"To know what everybody else knows is to know nothing."
Remy deGourmont 1858 - 1915

There were intelligence indications in communications intercepted by the National Security Agency (NSA) that the Soviets were interested in building titanium hull submarines. Metallurgists in the USA said it could not be done because when titanium is welded the oxygen in the atmosphere weakens the weld. The largest titanium parts being produced in the USA were the leading edge of airplane wings because, it was claimed, that was the largest size component that could be economically welded in a controlled, oxygen free, environment.

Maintaining liaison with friends in naval intelligence I discovered, in a classified album with the title, "Unknown & Unexplained Photos" an overhead photograph of a large hangar with tens of large tubes extending beneath the closed doors. I described what I had seen to several PhD researchers, without disclosing my source, and asked what they thought it could be and/or could it be an attempt to maintain an atmosphere such as nitrogen, in a very large building? The most positive answers contained words such as, "perhaps," maybe," "very inefficient," and "possible but unlikely." The Defense Intelligence Agency (DIA) was able to geo-locate where the picture was taken. Naval intelligence recognized that the location was on the outskirts of a shipyard in Northwestern Russia that had man-made channels to the Kara Sea near Novaya Zemlya and was known to be a site of innovative submarine research. A colleague at the Central Intelligence Agency (CIA) was informed of what was known and I asked him if he had anything to add. Several months later I was invited by my CIA colleague, to look at pieces of titanium, that I was told, "were recovered from a dumpster near the building with the large tubes running under the doors." One rectangular titanium piece, about 8" x 10" in size, had numbers engraved on it indicating that it was intended for use on a submarine. Another piece of titanium appeared to be someone's unsuccessfully attempt to carve a smoking pipe with the head of a fisherman as the bowl. However unsuccessful the attempt to carve a face out of titanium, it was clear that the Soviets were comfortable working with titanium and apparently way ahead of the USA in the use and fabrication of the metal.

I received an award for my contribution to discovering the Soviet's use of titanium for a submarine hull, in one of those classified ceremonies that could not, at the time, be revealed and where the attached letter was sufficiently innocuous to permit denial of the reason for the award. In my case it read, " . . . awarded a Navy Commendation Medal by the Secretary of the Navy . . . for personally gathering and evaluating technical intelligence data to provide a unique and heretofore unapparent characterization of a future Soviet threat." But that's only the beginning of the story!

Why a Titanium Submarine?

Just because they could, why would they? In a quest to determine why the Soviets might want to build titanium hull submarines, I developed the following hypotheses (Ho):

Ho #1. Since titanium is stronger than steel, perhaps the Soviets want a deeper diving submarine without changing submarine volume or displacement? Analysis: Going deeper would put them in the "deep sound channel" where acoustic noise propagates even longer distances and since we were already tracking their relatively noisy submarines their situation would worsen. Additionally, when I queried individuals in the US submarine community I found that they had no desire or intention of operating deeper, and they were not impressed by titanium's additional strength relative to steel.

Ho #2. The additional strength of a titanium hull could make a submarine better equipped to patrol in the arctic and under the arctic ice cap. Analysis: The Soviets had sent at least one ballistic missile submarine under the arctic ice cap and the assumption was that they would operate close to a polenia (break/opening in the arctic ice cap) and that a missile launched through a polenia would survive. It was known that because the Soviets were adjacent to the arctic ice, they routinely and extensively studied and operated in that environment therefore; it was easy to hypothesize that they might have identified and mapped the location of several useful polenias. However, as US arctic mapping increased it became apparent that polenias were unstable, i.e., routinely opened, closed, changed size, or relocated. Furthermore they were not areas of "clean water" and the floating ice chunks commonly present would likely destroy the body of a missile launched from beneath it.

Ho #3. Titanium is lighter than steel therefore, they could theoretically increase missile weight without increasing sail-away weight. <u>Analysis</u>: Why not simply continue to build longer and broader submarine - with current material as they had been doing - to accommodate more missile tubes? They could also increase the number of targeted missiles by deploying more submarines. The desire for more targeted missiles - how many is sufficient? - did not seem to justify the risk of a new and unproven submarine hull material?

Ho #4. Titanium is non-magnetic and if the Soviets had made a significant advancement in magnetic anomaly detection (MAD) devices, they may want to protect their submarines from such a capability? <u>Analysis</u>: This could be promising, but inquiries did not reveal any evidence that Soviet aircraft that routinely carry MAD equipment were operating differently or reporting more submarine contacts.

Ho #5. Because US submarines were quieter than Soviet submarine we would normally get the first torpedo shot in an encounter. If the Soviet submarine turned and exited the area to avoid the torpedo, upon his return the US submarine would again originate detection and get another "first" shot. If however, realizing this scenario, the Soviet's were concentrating on active torpedo decoys and radical maneuvers to avoid a torpedo and intended to close the distance to the US submarine so that both submarines would have acoustic contact, the Soviet submarine's maneuverability advantage and a stronger titanium hull that would increase survivability from the nearby explosion of a torpedo could provide the Soviet's with an advantage in case of a "dog fight" or close combat. <u>Analysis</u>: Not a popular hypothesis among the US submarine community.

None of the hypotheses were satisfying, nor did I receive useful feedback from readers of my report.

MIT Summer Study

If the Soviets did build a "titanium submarine" what would its basic characteristics be and where would the titanium be used?

In 1979, I was one of forty five individuals who agreed to attend a "Professional Summer at MIT" studying, *Submarine Design Trends*, (code name for Titanium Submarine Study, to avoid displaying an interest in titanium for submarines.) Among the attendees were individuals from several codes within the Naval Sea Systems Command (NAVSEA), from naval shipyards (Norfolk, Mare Island, New London-Groton, Newport News, Portsmouth, and Charleston), Naval Ships R&D Centers (Carderock, MD, Portsmouth, VA, Bethesda, MD.), Naval Underwater Systems Center (NUSC), intelligence commands (NISC, CIA, and DIA), from the offices of the Under Secretary of Defense for Naval and Tactical Warfare. We were under the direction and guidance of Harry A. Jackson, P.E. Captain USN (Retired) who was renown for his submarine design and development work. After receiving classroom lectures on submarine design criteria, measures, and constraints (e.g., sizing, weight, buoyancy, propulsion, speed, and internal arrangement) and completing reading assignments (e.g., single versus multiple propeller trade-offs, various arrangements of main ballast tanks, deck and sail options) he assigned us to one of seven submarine design group. He had chosen the groups to distribute the areas of expertise so that we could learn from one another. Each group was given different design requirements. I was in the group that was required to design a submarine using the maximum amount of titanium - i.e., for the hull, equipment, sensors, screws, etc.

The result from our group was a submarine that was volume limited and that would not submerge without 204 tons of lead ballast to compensate for the light weight of the titanium. No design using titanium was spectacular in its performance and a satisfying assumption of Soviet intentions.

The question remained a burr in the back of my mind and it would be fifteen more years before I found an answer to my dilemma.

Wye Woods Center

In June 1994, several years after the collapse of the Soviet Union, I was invited to participate in the week long, Joint US - Russian Conference on Coastal Anti-Submarine Warfare. The conference was held at The Aspen Institute's Wye Woods Center, in Queenstown, MD and jointly sponsored by The Research Center of Geopolitics and Security Problems of the Russian Academy of Natural Sciences and US Defense Group Incorporated. The Aspen Institute is an international, independent, non-profit organization supported by foundation grants, and contributions. The Wye Woods Center is a fenced, conference center of rustic cedar-shingled lodges, deep in the woods, on the banks of the Wye River, on Maryland's Eastern shore. The center includes a dining hall, conference building, swimming pool, fitness center, and a large outdoor area with footpaths and rest areas with benches. In addition to the invitation, the price of admission included a written paper, on an approved topic, to be presented at the conference.

Of the 21 people in the Russian delegation, 16 were admirals or captains and two were generals. Most were retired with submarine and intelligence (KGB) experience. The others were senior, technical, sensor specialists. It was our understanding that the Russians were trying to preserve their Navy by demonstrating a feasibility of jointly operating with the US Navy and, desperate for cash after the collapse of the Soviet Union, were willing to "sell" sensor technology that might have commercial applications in America.

The 15 members of the US delegation had backgrounds similar to the Russians. Mostly retired navy captains and admiral, plus senior civilians analysts, all of who had submarine and or intelligence experience. I suspect that the "US Defense Group" was incorporated to avoid identification of the US funding source. We were informed that the US agenda was to gather intelligence, especially about Soviet/Russian submarine operations and non-acoustic sensors.

Rudolph Aleksandrovich Golosov

Vice Admiral Golosov, a senior member of the Soviet delegation, was born in 1927 and retired from the navy in 1990. He had served on submarines, commanded a flotilla of "atomic" submarines, was Chief of Staff of the Pacific Fleet, and, at the time of our meeting, was professor in the strategy department at the General Staff Academy. We met unofficially during a lunch break while walking a footpath along the Wye River. I found our conversation very interesting and we spoke together privately on several occasions. The Admiral told me that he had never been to the USA before this visit, but had seen the coast from a submarine periscope. It also became obvious that he hated the Germans with a passion when he told me the story of the hardships he and his classmates had endured after being taken out of school as youngsters and put on a train heading east because the Germans were invading Russia.

Each attendee had been required to provide a minimal amount of background information to justify their participation in the conference. Everything I knew about Admiral Golosov's career was what I had read (and he had provided) in the brief biographical information section of the conference notes. During our conversations it became increasingly clear that he knew every submarine I had served aboard, that I had worked for naval intelligence at NFOIO, as a "researcher" at ONR, and had published several articles in the Naval Institute Proceedings. None of that was in my conference biography. The KGB's files must be incredible and nothing is apparently too trivial to note?

In response to my questions concerning reports and the widely held belief that Soviet submarines, and other platforms, had frequent maintenance problems, he revealed that they were not maintenance problem, but philosophical issues. As he explained it to me, "In America you test a system over and over and over again before you put it to sea. You don't have many problem, but it take years to get a new system or platform in the fleet. In Russia we put a system on a ship as soon as possible and expect to fix and change it as necessary while using it. You called it a maintenance problem. We call it efficient use of new technology." His explanation reminded me that a report from someone who had visited the office of Admiral Gorshkov, the Admiral of the Fleet of Soviet Union, had included the observation that the Admiral had a sign above his desk that read, *"PERFECTION IS THE ENEMY OF GOOD ENOUGH."*

Different philosophies and traditions can explain a lot. I would never again equate a Soviet "maintenance problem" with shabby production, design, or development.

I broached my titanium conundrum and asked if he could help me understand what was going on. He smiled when I outlined my several hypotheses relative to why the Soviets wanted a titanium submarine and replied, "You analyze too much. We are very simple people. I was director of the shipyard where we were developing the titanium capability. I was directed to build the fastest submarine in the world. The only way to do that was to build a submarine with two complete, nuclear reactor plants. Because of the weight of the reactors we had to build the hull of titanium."

I recalled US submarine patrol reports of a very high-speed Soviet submarine doing speed trials. His story made sense. I believe he was telling me the truth!

"The Hunt For Red October"
"Three may keep a secret if two of them are dead."
Benjamin Franklin 1706 - 1790

Quiet propulsion techniques, technologies, and research were a high priority during my time at the Office of Naval Research. Among the research programs that I was monitoring and funding were two that involved quiet propulsion. One had a longitudinal centerline opening the entire length of a submarine with a flexible wall of magnetic fluid that could be made to ripple by a moving magnetic field and move water from the bow to a stern exit. It was a peristaltic pump trying to mimic the way one's intestines moves waste (quietly) through the body.

The other involved a series of hydraulic systems that "pumped" water to propel a submarine without using a screw.

Improved navigation, both method and accuracy, was also a high priority. A submarine that was required to raise an antenna above the surface of the ocean risked being detected and the longer it had to remain in that condition the higher the risk. The Global Positioning System, GPS, was in its infancy and coverage in forward, deployed, submarine operating areas was limited. Naval navigational satellites (NAVSAT) could be used, but they passed within range of a patrolling submarine infrequently and briefly, therefore submarine maneuvers to periscope depth for antenna exposure had to timed to their arrival. We were aware that an enemy could concentrate its search along the satellite's track to enhance the probability of detecting a submarine updating its navigational position. LORAN (**Lo**ng **Ra**nge **N**avigation) involved low frequency radio transmissions from known locations of land based sites and the time difference between receipt of signal from a pair of transmitters provided a navigational aide, but of limited accuracy. It also required the submarine to operate at shallow depth. A new method of navigation was of great interest. Ballistic missile submarines were also being used to target enemy land-based missiles, including those in bunkered silos, in the hope of destroying them before they could be launched, in case of war. To destroy bunkered missiles required a precise hit that was beyond the capability of ballistic missile submarine in the late 1970s. Among the accuracy improvement program requirements was the stated need for better submarine navigation. (As an aside: A ballistic missile is launch to arrive a specific point in space at a precise altitude and speed, cease powered flight and free-fall to the target. Potential targeting errors are: target location, launch location, and incorrect point in space, speed, or altitude at powered flight cut off. A major study, several years later, revealed that the only real error was that the submarine didn't know where it was when launch occurred. It was a submarine navigation problem, not a missile problem.) The ocean floor is contoured similar to the face of the earth with mountains, valley, hills, and holes. Ships had been outfitted with sonar for bottom contour mapping and it was hoped that by overlaying a map taken by the submarine in real time over the map provided of the area from prior mapping that the submarine's location could be precisely located – without having to raise an antenna. Research and development work was also being done to improve the capability and applicability of a high frequency, upward looking sonar being used to detect and avoid downward protruding ice pinnacles when operating a submarine under the arctic ice.

The Office of Naval Research was not the only organization looking for answers to these issues and much of the research was classified in the 1970s when Tom Clancy decided to publish his first book, <u>The Hunt for Red October.</u> The book assumed that quiet propulsion without using screws, the capability to navigate while remaining submerged, and to avoid pillars and pinnacles while maneuvering at high speed, had reached fruition and were routinely employed. I was concerned that several of my classified research programs had been compromised. The navy was concerned where Tom Clancy had gotten his ideas and data, and wanted to stop publication of the book. At a meeting of opposing attorneys, a standoff occurred when the navy was asked, "Tell us what is classified and we will give you the source." And the navy's reply was, "We cannot tell you what's classified, that would be divulging classified information."

Meanwhile the navy was looking into potential leaks. A submarine intelligence specialist with terminal cancer was investigated with the idea that passing information to Clancy could have been his "swan song." That proved not to be the case. An individual at the Defense Advanced Research Project Agency (DARPA), who had been turned down on two occasions by Admiral Rickover when he attempted to become a nuclear submariner, was investigated. He admitted to reading the book after it was finished when he was asked only to review the naval and submarine terminology for accuracy. No other leads prove fruitful. Tom Clancy was a great novelist. The navy decided that perhaps the book would provide useful advertisement for the navy in general and the submarine force in particular. The Naval Institute published the book as its first book of fiction. When it was made into a movie, the navy made a submarine available for some below deck photography and for photographing a submarine surfacing at high speed following an emergency, main ballast, blow. Both the book and the movie were exciting and a great success. The navy received good publicity from both.

Unrelated to publication of his book, I have had the opportunity of meeting Tom Clancy. I also had occasion to be seated next to and converse with his first wife, Wanda. She is a wonderful, gracious, kind, and unassuming woman. She confirmed that Tom had written the book while employed as an insurance salesman and that it had been written at their kitchen table.

CHAPTER 10

My Civilian Career

What I Wanted and What I Got

"The best you get is an even break."
Franklin Pierce Adams 1881 - 1960

I was anxious to retire from the navy and was looking forward to June 1980 when I would have completed my 20 years of service. I decided that I'd had enough military, intelligence, government, and defense work, and I wanted a career in a civilian field. Two very exciting opportunities came to my attention during the three months before my retirement.

The first was a job advertisement from Bausch & Lomb, an international, optical goods company headquartered in Rochester, NY. The company produced the first optical quality glass made in America, developed groundbreaking sunglasses for the military, created the lenses used on cameras that took the first satellite pictures of the moon, and in 1971 was the first to introduce soft contact lenses. The largest producer of eye care products, they were seeking a manager for their Paris office. The job qualifications included a doctorate degree in business and bi-lingual in French and English. I had my doctorate in International Business and had been certified as a translator in French while at the Naval Academy. I sent in a resume, disguising my military background as all ex-military personnel seeking civilian employment are advised to do. I received an interview call from Paris that was going extremely well until the other party insisted on knowing the name of the organization where I had developed my management and leadership ideas. The interviewer had the commonly accepted impression that a military person, use to giving orders and having them obeyed, could not manage, lead, or otherwise interact with civilians. That was the end of my interview and contact with the company. And it would have been such a wonderful fit!

The second was a solicitation from the United States Agency for International Development, (USAID.) The Agency was created by President John F. Kennedy in 1961 as the federal government agency with primary responsibility for administering civilian foreign aid and whose mission was to extend a helping hand to people living overseas and struggling for a better life in a free and democratic country. The solicitation specifically wanted someone to be the AID advocate for the Aswan Dam project in Egypt. Duties included frequent visits to the site to insure that the project was and remained realistic, on track and within budget, and to update, brief, and justify continued project expenditure to USAID decision makers in Washington, DC. The job description requirement was for frequent overseas travel, engineering and management experience. I submitted an appropriate resume and was interviewed by a committee at USAID in Washington, DC. The interview progressed nicely until one individual made the point that the majority of my engineering experience was with nuclear power plants and declared that I was over qualified because no AID project would include a nuclear reactor. Such a shame to have so many small-minded government employees.

While looking for non-defense employment, I was being courted by companies that I had funded or worked with during my tour at ONR. I needed a job, the offers were very appealing, and I succumbed.

From retirement in July 1980 until October 1982, I was Senior Program Manager and Director of Washington, DC Operations for Systems Control Technology, (SCT). The company's headquarters was in Palo Alto, CA adjacent to Stanford University and was one of the two elite operations research companies in the US. It was staffed with operations research graduates from Stanford and competed head-to-head on all contracts that required operational research expertise with The Analytic Science Corporation (TASC), headquartered in Massachusetts and staffed with operations research graduates from MIT. Twenty six months after joining SCT, I was denied entrance to an intelligence agency for a meeting where I was to report my progress on an analytical contract that they were funding. I was told that my clearance had been downgraded from Top Secret to British Reciprocal Confidential. After several conversations with Palo Alto headquarters it was determined that the problem occurred when SCT sold a "small division of the company" to British Petroleum that wanted to develop their own satellite system to provide navigation to their fleet of oil tankers. The SCT negotiator apparently did not realize that the Washington office was under that division. My situation with SCT was resolved when they told me, "Leave SCT and start your own corporation. SCT will transfer all your classified contracts to your new corporation and all income from the contract will be your. Our only concern is that SCT avoid litigation." Since I was the principal investigator on the contracts, the government had no objection. Thus, within a few days, I became president of *Submarine Consultants Inc.*" and had my own company and a contract base already in place.

As president of a small company (that does not have a marketing department) you are responsible for getting new contracts, i.e., marketing. I enjoyed doing the analysis, but not the marketing. I acquired a few more contracts for analysis that I could personally accomplish and teamed with a couple of associates who brought in their own contracts. Eventually I tired of the marketing, completed all our contracts, and found employment with other companies. First I worked for Harold Rosenbaum Associates (HRA), later with Ervin Kapos Associates Inc. (KAI) and finally with Advanced Marine Enterprises (AME). In between those jobs, I formed and sold another company, (Global Associates) and worked as a private consultant. I found consulting work disturbingly disconnected, i.e., market to get work, spend full time doing the work because the client always needs it yesterday and you are the only worker, deliver the product and have nothing to do, begin marketing again, repeat. My niche, which I eventually discovered, was to be an employee with a company that needed an operations research department (even if I was its only member) and was willing to let me perform consulting work, on my own time, if there was no conflict of interest. As an employee I had a steady pay check, holidays off, paid vacation, insurance, etc., but could charge exorbitant amounts to other clients as a consultant. I had such an arrangement with Advanced Marine Enterprises until my final and complete retirement. It was a win-win situation and an enjoyable arrangement.

I retired from the naval service with a Meritorious Service Medal from the Secretary of the Navy and continued work as an operations research analyst solving military rather than civilian problems.

What is Operations Research?

"The trouble with most folks isn't so much their
ignorance, as knowing so many things that ain't so."
Josh Billings (pseudonym for Henry W. Shaw) 1818 - 1885

Operations Research (OR) has been called black magic because verbal descriptions are typically ambiguous and applicable tools cover the broad range from linear programming and risk analysis to stochastic modeling and probability theory. Furthermore, since the title does not lend itself to meaningful literal translation, here are some examples, a bit of history, and an explanation of some of the OR studies and analysis that I conducted.

The name *operations research* came into prominence during WW II when diverse groups began working successfully together to solve wartime operational problems. One of the earliest and most famous groups was British. It was headed by the distinguished physicist, P.M.S. Blackett and consisted of physiologists, mathematical physicists, mathematicians, an astro-physicist, a general physicist, an army officer, and a surveyor. Later the U.S. established its first operations research group of mathematicians, statisticians, probability theorists, and computer experts. Possibly because operations research began in England, the British love and still use the term, while Americans frequently substitute the term *management science*. A more descriptive term would be *decision analysis*, because the fundamental thrust of operations research is to facilitate decision making under conditions of uncertainty.

Operations researchers believe in the legitimacy of physical phenomena, mathematical concepts, and statistical theories, and will develop quantitative data to facilitate decision-making. Their process involves formulating the problem, building a model, identifying measures, performing analysis, and presenting findings.

Problem Definition & Selection of Measures

An early World War II task was to reduce the significant number of B-17 aircraft losses to German anti-aircraft fire being experienced during bombing runs from England. Prior to the OR team's involvement, the solution was to carefully map the weapon fragment holes on each aircraft that returned from the continent in order to identify where aircraft should receive shielding. Upon assuming the task, the OR team pointed out that the study did not provide useful answers, because they were working the wrong problem. Since all the aircraft being mapped had safely returned, they did not represent the problem; those that should be mapped were on the bottom of the English Channel. Unfortunately, history does not identify the OR solution.

Selecting proper measures for evaluation remains a problem. Recently a sports reporter criticized the performance of a defensive halfback who had been a first round draft choice three years earlier. The reporter quoted data that showed the number of interceptions by the player had been declining - six in his rookie year, two the next year, and none in his third year - therefore the player was slowing down and/ or pass receivers had learned how to beat him and he should be replaced. This was not a valid measure of the player's performance because it did not consider opportunities. In his rookie year opponents challenged him and the next year they gave him a modicum of respect. Near the end of the third year a coach from an opposing team was asked about the player's lack of interceptions. He replied, "He's not making interceptions because he's so good we don't even throw the ball to whoever he's guarding. We look elsewhere and challenge less capable players." It's important to study the right problem using valid measures.

A Strategy for Drug Supply Reduction

The drug supply trade is an amorphous system of linked activities that loosely connects growers and processors with petty dealers working the streets in America's cities and towns. Some parts of the system are more vulnerable or more disruptive than others, but the potential for success must also be considered when assessing how particular technologies and strategies may impact the counter-drug mission.

We attacked this problem by first establishing a hierarchical decomposition of the drug supply system because this would allow numerical values to be assessed. The decomposition began at the system level where we identified the drug supply sequence as: PRODUCTION, WHOLESALE, RETAIL, and CAPITAL. At the function level, PRODUCTION can be decomposed into **grow, harvest,** and **process**; WHOLESALE can be decomposed into **transport** and **storage**; RETAIL can be decomposed into **distribution** and **sale;** and CAPITAL can be decomposed into **reinvest, launder,** or **bank.** The operational level describes the action taken to avoid detection, arrest, seizure, or harm, (**counter-detection, counter-identification,** and **counter-action**.) Pair wise comparisons were made within the same level of the hierarchy and "Importance" was defined as the product of <u>system focus</u> (social, political, and legal considerations); <u>functional vulnerability</u> (susceptibility to catastrophic damage or loss of profit); and <u>operational weakness</u> (capability of being disrupted). Once "Importance" was calculated the impact of various technologies could be assessed. The analytical results clearly identified CAPITAL (reinvestment, laundering and banking of the drug money) as the most important and sensitive area to attack.

The study's usefulness and effectiveness was never determined because the politics of financial privacy considerations "prevented" the client from implementing the study's recommendations.

Resource Consolidation and Relocation

In preparation for input to the Congressional Defense Base Closure and Realignment Commission the Navy desired an assessment of their aircraft carrier and air wing facilities in San Francisco-Alameda, CA vs. Seattle-Everett, WA and if consolidation was required where it should be located. A quantitative assessment of each area was determined based on the following variables: The cost and availability of individual skill and team training, at-sea unit and battle group training, operational readiness, and quality of life. The analysis of quality of life assessed the availability and/or cost of: health care, housing, living, weather/climate, employment outlook (for spouses and dependents), education, transportation, recreation and the arts, and safety. The analysis showed a decisive advantage for carrier basing in the San Francisco-Alameda area. The study's recommendation was implemented.

Selecting Warship Design and Capabilities

The Navy desired a quantitative process that would allow it to develop and evaluate alternative warship designs. It's a classic operations research problem.

The process we developed combined a top-down, requirements pull, and a bottom-up, technology push. Requirements pull originated from high level pronouncements of national objectives, Department of Defense missions, Navy requirements and Mission Needs Statements. The bottom-up process focused on the available technologies that could be combined into systems to eventually build the platform. In addition to developing platform options, the process had to facilitate the accurate assessment of each option relative to operational needs. This was done by ensuring that each measure used to discriminate among platform options was explicitly represented as an input/output factor in the warfare-battle force modeling and simulation that would be used to evaluate the platforms. Critical platform variables and their sensitivity were addressed. The critical system characteristics selected were: speed, range, payload, sensor performance, weapon range, lethality, acquisition cost, operational & support cost. Sensitivity was addressed by developing an acceptable range (i.e., minimum number and overkill maximum) for each characteristic, on the margin. These were: Minimum requirements? Relative importance? How much is enough? The marginal value of increasing capability, i.e., cost-benefit? A minimum amount of risk analysis was also performed at various levels. At the earliest level there is technological risk (the likelihood of being able to make the system work), later there is manufacturing risk (that the system can be produced at all, or at an affordable price) and finally there is operational risk (that the system is installed, but the operators choose not to use it because it is too difficult, too different, or too hard to maintain.)

The variables used for assessment and decision making are called measures. Despite routinely being called "measures of effectiveness" regardless of their application proper description and usage was important in this project and the following example was included as explanation.

The utility assessment of a system, platform, or concept has several steps in the process of its development. It can first be defined as a "thing." As a thing it has a behavior or activity that is natural and independent of the task or mission to be performed. Examples of behavior measures are the container capacity of sealift ship or the roll & pitch expected of a ship design in various sea states. An example of a "thing's" activity is the transmission capacity in bits per second of a communication system. These are Measures of Activity or Measures of Behavior.

When a "thing" that has a natural behavior is applied to a task, the important measure becomes one of performance. Now the "thing" has a capability relative to a specific task in a specific environment. For example, the capability of a ship to perform helicopter operations or mine laying under various geophysical environments are examples of Measures of Performance.

Notice that the "opposition" is benign; it is Mother Nature rather than an enemy.

As the task becomes part of a mission, the "thing's" capabilities and employment become important relative to the specific mission, specific enemy, and specific scenario. Now the critical measuring characteristic must be evaluated relative to its performance against a malicious and aggressive enemy. These assessment characteristics are Measures of Effectiveness. Effectiveness only applies when consideration is given to the application of something in the face of an enemy that is trying to deny its fulfillment of an objective. An example is the probability of killing a specific type of aircraft, in a specific geographical location, in a specific geophysical and geopolitical environment.

Finally, the measure of effectiveness must be assessed relative to its impact on the outcome. For example, the ability to shoot down a specific type of aircraft, regardless of how effectively it is done, may have zero impact on the outcome of a mine-laying operation. Thus, the final measure is how well or badly something contributes to a favorable mission outcome. This Measure of Outcome or Measure of Utility reflects how the "thing" impacts the outcome of the battle or war.

Once we designed this process it was used by the Navy to select design and capability alternatives for the Surface Combatant of the 21st Century.

In Summary

If the examples I've given created more confusion than clarification, simply understand operations research as a process that uses quantitative techniques to solve everyday problems. Once the problem is clearly and correctly defined, a model selected, and measures identified, the quantitative analysis may be simple arithmetic.

A list of my publications, conference papers, and contract reports is contained in Appendix A.

Overseas Travel

"In America there are two classes of
travel – first class, and with children."
Robert Benchley 1889-1945

Some contracts were exciting both because of the task and because they involved overseas travel. Two examples took me to Brazil and Turkey.

Rio de Janeiro, Brazil - CASNAV

For three consecutive years, under contract to the Brazilian Navy, I spent several weeks in Rio de Janeiro lecturing and working with Brazilian analysts at their *Centro De Analises de Sistemas Navais* (CASNAV) - their Center for Naval Analysis. In the mornings I would lecture on the application of Operations Research and Cost Benefit techniques to real problems, and the development of Tactical Analysis and Evaluation techniques for assessing the operational effectiveness of new technologies, tactics, and systems. In the afternoons, I would join them working on a current problem - when security classification issues allowed. (They considered Argentina a potential threat and routinely used Argentina's naval force level as the enemy force level. Cuba was the rogue country that might act foolishly with its military.) I knew that I had been accepted when I was invited to join the boys during lunch break (from 12 noon - 2 PM) for a "sand check." We walked about 100 meters to a small hut on the beach, ordered lunch with a caipirinha, sat at an outside table, and waited. They eventually revealed that a new, young, secretary had been hired and, assuming that she would join the other girls sunbathing at the beach over lunch, wanted to see what she looked like in her Brazilian, mini bikini, - "the sand check." (A caipirinha is a Brazilian drink made with crushed mint leaves, powered sugar, the juice of a lime, and rum.)

My host and the team leader was Gustavo Benttenmuller. He invited me to parties and dinners at his home and we remain good friends. He is currently the Director of Science, Technology, Innovation, and Strategic Technology Planning at CASNAV.

I returned to Rio a fourth time, strictly for pleasure during Carnival, called Mardi Gras in most other places. My colleagues help me make hotel reservations and get tickets to the Samba School Parade, and evening balls. The main event, the Samba School Parade occurs after dark on Saturday and Sunday nights when 300 - 600 members from each of the "best" 14 (of the 26) samba schools parade, march, sing, and samba down a one mile long road (parade ground) sided with bleachers full of jumping, caparenia drinking, singing spectators, and a panel of government appointed judges. Each school has 50 minutes on the one-mile long parade ground to demonstrate its talents with floats, samba dancers, musicians, percussionists, and costumed marchers. The winning school is "king" for the year with enormous prestige and market presence. The four lowest scoring schools are replaced the next year by the four best from the "junior parade" of the non-qualifying samba schools that occurs on Monday.

There are also street parades in the suburbs and at the beaches. The most famous are the "Banda de Ipanema" about 15,000 strong that parades through the streets and along the boardwalk of Ipanema stopping at bars along the way, and the "Banda de Ferreira" that does the same along Copacabana beach. Smaller parades, some spontaneous others advertised in newspapers and hotel flyers, occur all week long. The locals understand that the roads along parade routes, even though unidentified before the parade begins, will be closed to vehicle traffic and that the public transportation schedule will be seriously disrupted. Consequently, many companies and government organizations close during the festival and the people that I had met who lived in the city, all admitted to leaving during Carnival.

NATO Conference - Turkey

Under contract to the Secretary of Defense for Plans & Policy, I acted as session chairman of the NATO conference in Istanbul, Turkey on "The Soviet Threat in the Eastern Mediterranean." Panel members included past and present U.S., NATO, and Turkish ambassadors, senior military officers and political decision makers, and foreign policy institute directors from most NATO countries. After the conference, our host extended an invitation to spend four additional days touring their country. I was one of six that accepted the invitation. I found Turkey to be exotic, friendly, modern, replete with magnificent historical sites, and a place that I would enjoy revisiting. On the other hand, I did decline an invitation to have a massage from a 330 pound, bare-chested, mustached, Turkish giant, wearing an earring, and I found the cabaret belly dancers (based on a cabaret sample size of one and three solo dancers) to be older than my mother, overly garbed, lacking in sensuality, and plus-plus-plus in size. I did return home with five beautiful, Persian and Turkish carpets.

Naval Station New York – BRAC
"Politics is perhaps the only profession for
which no preparation is thought necessary."
Robert Louis Stevenson 1850 – 1894

The Naval Station New York (NSNY) is on Staten Island. It had been extensively upgraded to provide basing for the battleships brought back into service for gunfire support and shore bombardment in Vietnam. In 1993, we were no longer at war in Vietnam and NSNY was included on the list of bases recommended for closure by the Department of Defense's Base Realignment and Closure Commission (BRAC '93.)

Hired by a group representing NSNY to provide a rebuttal, I read the Commission's criteria and analytical methodology for selecting the bases to be closed. I found the methodology to be full of errors and inconsistencies, that there were critical faults in the survey questions and the analyses, and that the assessment value scale was defective.

Here are some specific errors that I found in the report.

Question Bias Error. Instead of evaluating a base's capability to berth different ship types by asking, "Can you berth cruisers? destroyers? auxiliaries?" they asked, "Do you provide berthing to cruisers? destroyers?

auxiliaries?" NSNY answered "NO" because, despite a capability to berth other ship types, only battleships had been sent there.

Defective Value Scales. The Evaluation Committee designated the Importance of each question by assigning it a "Band." Band 1 was most important, 2 was less important, and 3 was least important. The Analysis Team assigned military value scores to each question based on its "Band" with the following scheme:

Band	Range of Military Value Scores
1 (Most Important)	10 - 6
2 (Less Important)	7 - 3
3 (Least Important)	4 - 1

A fundamental, statistical blunder when a question of lesser importance can receive a higher value score than a more important question. A question in Band 2 (Less Important) with a Military Value Score of 7 would receive a higher score than a question in Band 1 (Most Important) with a Military Value Score of 6. A similar defect occurs in Band 3 where a Value Score of 4 can exceed the Value Score of 3 in a Band 2 question. Such scoring errors were plentiful in the actual base evaluations.

Badly Worded Questions. Inflated question values also resulted from badly worded questions.

Band	Question	Value Score
1	Is the average wait for housing 1 month or less?	10
1	Is the average wait for housing 6 months or less?	6

The intended relative value is 10/6 = 1.67. Because of question wording if the answer to the first question is "Yes" it is automatically the answer to the second question resulting in an actual relative value of 16/6 = 2.67. The second question should have been, "Is the average wait for housing greater than 1 month but less than 6 months?"

Solving the Wrong Problem. Questions that focused on solving the wrong problem were also common. For example, "Is the base less than 10 miles from open ocean?" attempted to value the importance of response time. Distance is not the only variable in response time, nor necessarily the most important. Previously a retired, Coast Guard, Rear Admiral testifying before the Commission on behalf of Naval Station Mobile Bay argued the advantage of Mobile's 400' & 600' wide channels vis-à-vis Pascagoula, Mississippi's, 350' wide channel despite the fact that Mobile is 27 miles further from the ocean. Staten Island is only 12 miles from the open ocean, its channel is 2,000' wide, and based upon my conversation with pilots at Staten Island, if no ships are anchored in the vicinity of the channel, a warship could exit at flank speed. If ships are at anchor in the vicinity, a five-minute warning/alert must be given before going to flank speed. Clearly, ships can exit quickly from Staten Island, and the fact that it gets a zero military value score because it is two miles further inland than the arbitrarily chosen and irrelevant distance of ten miles, highlights the case that the question focused on the wrong problem.

Staten Island was also punished because of unreasonable questions that again focused on the wrong issue. "Do you have on-base college level education?" misses the point. NSNY answered "No" without the opportunity to explain that there are 35 colleges within 30 miles of the naval station and that at least one college had requested an opportunity to conduct classes on the naval station, but the Navy had refused permission. The opportunity for pursuing a college education while stationed at NSNY is among the very best (the real issue) but NSNY was given a zero value score because the question focused on the wrong problem.

Visit the Scene. No member of the Evaluation Committee or Analysis Team visited NSNY. A visit may have eliminated some of my documented 20 pages of problems with the analysis, methodology, value scales, and question wording. I was embarrassed for the Navy and before testifying revealed my findings to some friends who were still on active duty. They told me to go ahead and testify. There was nothing they could do about the problems, because it was now a congressional issue.

My Testimony

I testified before the Department of Defense Base Closure and Realignment Commission in New York arguing against the proposed closing of Naval Station New York because the Commission's Analytical Methodology and Assessment of Military Value included serious errors, inconsistencies, and mistakes. My "Report of Findings" was delivered to New York Congresswoman Molinari and my formal testimony was covered on page 1 of *The Staten Island Advance*," on May 11, 1993.

The Staten Island Naval Station was closed despite my testimony. The Commission did however, reveal to me in private after my testimony, that, "The Navy and Congress (no jobs lost in my district) knew what bases they wanted to close but, as you made quite clear, they did a terrible job of trying to quantitatively justify their choices. Now that so many bases have already been closed and realigned we cannot change their methodology."

Welcome to the gelatinous, indolence of politics.

Professional Engineer

"Education is what remains when we
have forgotten all that we have been taught."
George Savile, Marquis of Halifax 1633 - 1695

My classmate, Al Bissell, whom I had invited to Rio de Janeiro for some lectures on "Explosives" mentioned that he had a lot of consulting work giving expert testimony in court cases, e.g., was the truck going too fast on the exit ramp or did it tip over because the curve is too tight? He said that if I would get my Professional Engineer (PE) license he would get me "Forensic Engineering" business. Two other PE certified, forensic engineering, USNA '60 classmates - whom I had not seen in years - vouched for my good character. To these two classmates who created and operate successful engineering companies, Michael Shanok, Forensic Engineering, Hamden, CT and Warren Hahn, Hahn Engineering, Tampa, FL., I owe a debt of gratitude. I documented my engineering experience on nuclear submarines and my engineering Research and Development experience while at the Office of Naval Research to avoid having to take the written PE examination. I went to Richmond, VA for a half day of oral questioning by five examiners as we sat around a large oval table. (Reminiscent of Nuclear Power School oral exams. Ugh!)

I passed the examination, paid my annual dues, told Al Bissell about my availability, and received no work. It turned out to be an exercise with zero payback. It did however, contribute to an elegant ten-year symmetry in my education: BS 1960, MS 1970, PhD 1980, and PE in 1990.

SEAL Team Six and Red Cell

"Every normal man must be tempted, at some time, to spit on his hands, hoist the black flag, and begin slitting throats."
H. L. Mencken 1880 - 1956

In 1980 the Navy decided that it needed a SEAL Team that was dedicated to counter terrorism. That Team became SEAL Team Six. Dick Marcinko was chosen to select team members, organize, train and lead SEAL Team Six. He did it by unceremoniously selecting the best from the SEAL Teams on both coasts. Although authorized and necessary, if this was to be the elite of the elite, he made some enemies of other Seal Team leaders. SEAL Team Six started with 75 enlisted men and 15 officers. Because their operations area was world wide and their very existence a secret, they were allowed to dress like civilian, blue collar workers. Dungarees and Tee shirts were popular and navy grooming standards did not apply. Long hair, ponytails, and beards were authorized and encouraged. They were given the best of equipment, a very large budget, trained hard and became the very best. They earned medals and had successes all over the world . . . none of which were made public.

In 1983, worldwide terrorist incidents were increasing and during SEAL Team Six's operations around U.S. embassies and naval bases they noticed a serious lack of security against terrorism. Directives to enhance security at naval bases and embassies were thought unnecessary and ignored by embassy personnel and base commanders. The Navy decided to demonstrate the security shortfalls by conducting training terrorist attacks against naval installations. The group of "terrorist" would be called Red Cell. Its existence and mission was classified Top Secret. Captain Dick Marcinko USN was directed to form, organize, and lead the group. He was authorized to select his 14 men (3 officers and 11 enlisted men) from SEAL Team Six. Again taking the most accomplished and decorated. The best of the very best.

Dick Marcinko himself was a highly decorated warrior, but a renegade. His attitude was and continued to be, the team was his family, it deserved to have the most advanced training and equipment, it would not fail, and screw the Navy if it got in the way. In his experience, the Navy was simply an obstacle to getting things done. You wanted something done, he'd get it done, but don't ask how. He began his career as a 17 year old enlisted sailor, became a SEAL and then went to Officer Candidate School in Newport, RI and became an officer. He was very, very good at what he did as a SEAL, trainer, and team leader, and there were a couple of Navy admirals who realized his ability. Those admirals chose him to create, organize and lead SEAL Team Six and Red Cell, and "protected" him within the naval establishment. Eventually, the admirals who supported him got transferred.

Red Cell created havoc within the Navy establishment when it began pointing out security problems. Despite security designed and put in place by the Naval Investigative Service (NIS), Red Cell claimed, after an "inspection" (an undetected sneak & peek) that security at Naval Base Naples, Italy, had some serious shortcomings. No one wanted to believe that so a weeklong exercise was conducted to resolve the issue. In addition to leaving "bombs" and infiltrating secure areas during the exercise, Red Cell kidnapped the Commanding Officer of the base, three different times. NIS was berated and Marcinko had more enemies.

At the Submarine Base New London, the Red Cell terrorists got aboard submarines to leave "bombs," and took civilian hostages. Red Cell's modus operandi was to call the base and using the name of a bogus terrorist group, announce an impending terrorist act. A favorite terrorist group name they enjoyed using was, "The Organization for the Ejaculation of Palestine" and a threat might be, "Release all my people or we will kill everyone in your commissary." Then Red Cell infiltrators would take over the base's short term housing building and the navy, poised at the commissary, would cry foul. The hostage takers would change clothes with the hostages making innocent people dress in black with hoods, have a colleague steal a Base ambulance or fire truck and come to the hostage site with the siren blasting, to pick up their colleagues (now dressed in civilian clothes.) If anyone caught on, they enjoyed escaping by driving the wrong way down one-way streets. The good guys hesitate to do that, so again it's not fair, yet embarrassing. Embarrassment meant more enemies for Marcinko.

At Point Magu in CA they spent several days at the local bars stealing ID cards and badges, and scraping base stickers off of cars to be used on their rental cars. If you held your finger over the photo you could even use a female's badge or ID card, and they did. With base access, some ingenuity, stealth, and guile they left a "bomb" on Air Force One after President Reagan arrived in California despite security by the Air Force and Secret Service. That created more enemies for Marcinko and cries that Red Cell was getting out of control.

Red Cell's champion and Marcinko's main protector, Admiral "Ace" Lyons USN, received orders taking him from the Pentagon to Hawaii. To provide a semblance of order (I assume) the departing Admiral gave Kapos Associates a contract that included having a civilian "report writer and umpire" tag along with Red Cell on their exercises. I was the lucky Kapos Associate employee chosen for the job. Hallelujah. Best job I ever had.

Once I had the job, I went to the Pentagon to meet Navy Captain Marcinko, introduce myself, and find out what was on the schedule. I found the small, hidden away office that SEAL Team Six was using in the Pentagon, knocked and entered. Marcinko was behind a desk shuffling papers and someone was looking through a grey metal, file cabinet off to the side. Dick Marcinko didn't look up as I walked to the front of his desk and said, "Hello Captain. I'm Dick Pariseau from Kapos associates, and . . ."

I was cut off by him saying, "Who the f _ _ _ cares?" without even looking up to acknowledge my presence. It was neither a good nor a bad start; it was simply Dick Marcinko. We became friends. An early task I received was to write a justification for why the 90 men in SEAL Team Six expended more ammunition last year than the entire Marine Corps and needed an equal amount for this year.

I traveled with Red Cell on selective self-training exercises in addition to their terrorist exercises against naval establishments. How good were the SEALs from Team Six and Red Cell? Let me tell you some things I personally observed. Upper body strength "requirement" was to bench press 400 pounds. At a driving and shooting facility in West Virginia we arrived after the Maryland State Police SWAT Team had used the firing range. Touring the range with Dick Marcinko, I noticed that the firing line with six shooting stations was set up only about 15 yards from the silhouette targets and said, " In assume that you will have your men firing from a longer range?"

He said, "No. We will start here."

The next morning the SEALs took to the firing range without moving the firing line. Weapons holstered, Marcinko gave the command, "Go" and started a stopwatch. Each SEAL turned and sprinted back about 50 yards to a grove of trees that had been enhanced with ropes hanging from limbs about 25 feet in the air. Climb to the top of the rope, fast "fall" back to the ground, sprint to the firing line and fire right handed then left handed, and don't be last or slow. Oh and by the way, a 3" x 5" white card had been placed on the forehead of the silhouette and that was the target. All shots were "double taps," i.e., two nearly instantaneous shots. After the first group of six fired, Marcinko gave me my assignment. He gave me a wooden pencil, explained that it was the same diameter as the rounds they were firing and told me that my job was to insure a two shot target kill. If the hole in the 3" x 5" card was a little larger than the pencil, i.e., I could wiggle the pencil slightly in the hole that was good. If it was a perfect fit perhaps the second bullet missed? Not a chance. The worse shots I measured all morning, with firings from different distances, shooting around the right then left side of barricades, etc. were two visible holes whose edges barely overlapped. Remember my first task about ammunition expenditure? Members of SEAL Team Six under Dick Marcinko were allotted 2,500 rounds per person per week, every week. He started Red Cell at 3,000 rounds per person per week, "to bring them up to speed."

I joined them driving cars in the woods on a race track cut out among the trees and learned how to maximize speed around corners, how to perform 180 degree course reversals, and how to avoid an ambush by enemy cars coming out of the woods and attempting to stop you. We drove at night, in a wooded area, not always bothering to remain on the racetrack, without lights, using night vision goggles. These guys had a lot of fun.

After our three days in the woods, Marcinko said the team was going climbing and invited me to join them. I asked where the mountains were and he said, "Not mountains; buildings in Norfolk, VA." I later asked one of the guys if they were really going to climbing buildings in Norfolk and he said, "Yes, and it's easy. Hard was when Marcinko made us parachute into the North Sea, at night, in the winter time, swim a mile or so, then climb a cold, frozen, deep sea, oil platform." And neither of them was kidding. A SEAL's physical ability is incredible, but their real strength is their mental toughness. Don't ever get in a fight with one because you can only win if you kill him. Otherwise he will keep coming after you without giving up, no matter what. With that attitude they can do "anything" and often do. The other interesting point is that the vast majority are not the biggest or tallest guys, most are quiet and reserved, and you would be hard pressed to identify an individual as a SEAL in a social setting.

Marcinko's downfall occurred at the Red Cell exercise at Seal Beach, CA. It's a weapons and nuclear storage facility. Remember, there are no uniforms and modified grooming standards were in effect. That meant cut, or don't cut, your hair, beard or mustache anyway you want, and wear civilian clothes that will let you blend in with the local civilian population. A few miles from the Naval Station, an advanced party had identified a "friendly bar" and a motel within a couple of blocks of the bar. A "friendly bar' usually serves some food and its owner is amenable to the following proposition from Marcinko. "I'll be here for a while with about a dozen guys. We will drink huge amounts of your beer and eat a lot of your food. If it gets rough and there is any breakage I will pay for it. Are you interested?"

In the Seal Beach case the owner said, "Yes. I'm interested. Who are you guys?"

Marcinko replied, "We're with the circus." And it was all set.

As an aside, in case you're ever with any of these guys around a pool table, dart board, or pinball machine where beers bottles can get mixed up on a crowded little table you should know two rules. First, beer is beer, doesn't matter too much if you pick up someone else's bottle by mistake. Second, all these guys chew tobacco and a beer bottle with a thumbnail tear down the middle of the label is a spit cup, don't drink from it.

Beginning the night before the exercise the owner began being thankful for his newfound customers as the team arrived at the bar from various locations and his wife stayed busy cooking food. At one point that night, a team member slurred the announcement that he was ready to go back to the motel and go to bed. No team member goes alone; pairs had left earlier, but this man was asking for a buddy. I had been ready to leave for quite a while and gladly volunteered. I was walking with a man who was about 5' 9" tall and 165 pounds. I had heard that he was a sniper and had gotten an award after remaining in position for over thirty hours to get a shot, and kill, a high ranking North Vietnamese Army General. Tonight he was drunk and staggering. I took his arm to keep him on the sidewalk. Half way to the motel we passed an automobile repair facility. A ten-foot high, chain link fence and two large mixed breed dogs that were loose inside the fence kept people out after closing time. As we began to walk by the dogs charged in our direction, barked aggressively, and leaped against the fence gate. I was glad the gate was solid and locked shut. My new buddy, stopped, took his arm from mine, and headed for the gate, declaring, "Wait. I have to go see the dogs." Oh shit. A very bad idea, but how do I stop him? Physical force was not an option; even drunk he could whip my butt and he was not listening to my pleas to keep walking towards the motel. He went to the chain link gate, mumbled something like, "Nice doggy" and squeezed his hand between the gates. The dogs sniffed his hand, stopped leaping on the fence, and barked only intermittently. After a brief few minutes he removed his hand and told me we could go. Pleased that we could continue our walk and that the dogs had not bitten him, I asked, "What was that all about?"

"Not long ago I was crawling to a target through a field. A guard dog found me and chewed on me for quite a long time. I just wanted to make sure that I had not become afraid of dogs."

There were three of us with Captain Marcinko the morning we went to the Seal Beach Naval Station, as scheduled, to brief the staff in an auditorium full of interested individuals who worked on the base. It was a routine during which Marcinko outline the goals of the exercise, the rules of engagement, and generally what to expect. When we arrived at the main gate and presented our military ID cards, we were denied entrance and the Security Officer was called. He revealed with much bravado that he had Los Angeles Police Department (LAPD) SWAT Team experience, that his base was totally secure, and that if any security breaches occurred they would be artificial and occur only because this was an exercise. He made us ride with him in a van with blacked out windows so that we could not view the inside of his base.

We avoided laughing and Marcinko didn't tell him that some of his men had been all over the base for a week, knew the combination or how to pick several important locks, and likely knew the base layout better than the Security Officer himself. Before letting Marcinko speak, the Security Officer took the stage to remind everyone that the base was secure, that this would be an exercise game and any problem would be game related not real world. We soon learned that others shared our opinion of the Security Officer. After Marcinko's briefing and before we were ushered out of the auditorium and off the base in the windowless van, the head of the Marine Corps Security Detachment (there were nuclear weapon storage sites on the base) approached us and when we were alone commented, "I understand that as part of these exercises you sometimes take a hostage."

Marcinko replied in the affirmative and added, "We want to see how the base operates when one of its leaders, the base commander or security officer, is missing."

"If you take our security officer, the Marines will send you a case of beer and another case for every day that you keep him." It sounded like both a request and a challenge, as I'm sure the Marine intended.

As terrorist events intensified, early in the exercise, the Security Officer locked down the base, which meant that all personnel assigned to the base remained on the base overnight and no access was allowed. Except of course for the Security Officer. He declared that he had an impenetrable security system in his house and a guard dog in his fenced yard so he was safe both on the base and at his house. A SEAL followed him home, poked around the house and yard that night, made friends with the dog and observed his morning routine. The following morning after the Security Officer entered his garage, and with one hand holding a mug of coffee and the other opening the driver's side car door, a SEAL dropped behind him from the rafters. With a weapon at his head and an arm tightly around his neck, the Security Officer was told, " This is an exercise. You are my prisoner. Just play along. Get in the car and drive. I will tell you where to go."

In the car the Security Officer attempted to open the glove compartment where he carried a weapon. The SEAL stopped him and asked him again to simply play the exercise. At a stop sign, still within the residential area, the Security Officer tried to reach a can of pepper spray that he carried hidden under his seat. That was enough, and the SEAL reportedly made him ride in the trunk of the car for the rest of the trip to the "safe house." Continuously unwilling to participate in the exercise and refusing to stop talking, threatening, and cursing he claimed that he was placed in a room with a headset taped to his head blaring hard rock music. A medical corpsman was continuously present at the safe house with the hostage. The Marines, true to their word, sent a daily case of beer.

At the conclusion of the exercise, mid-day on Friday, the Security Officer was unceremoniously "dumped" from a van at the main gate to the base.

The next morning, when we arrived for the out-briefing, to discuss security enhancement recommendations, and to answer all questions, the base Commanding Officer told Marcinko that the Security Officer was going to sue the Navy and the Base Commander because he had been physically abused - had his head held in a toilet bowl while it was flushed - and that he had suffered bruised ribs and other injuries. The Commanding Officer was upset and didn't know what to do. Marcinko asked for permission to speak to the Security Officer to dissuade him from filing a lawsuit. Marcinko spent about three minutes with the Security Officer and reported to the Commanding Officer that no lawsuit would be filed. When asked how he had convinced him to change his mind, Marcinko simply said, "I told him that I would kill him."

The Security Officer's wife eventually filed a lawsuit against the Navy claiming, "Injuries to her husband that prevented sexual performance." The Navy paid. It was the final exercise for Red Cell.

The Navy spent millions of dollars investigating Marcinko and trying to get him for overcharging for equipment while with SEAL Team Six and pocketing the additional money (there was no evidence), and then for conspiracy with an ex-SEAL Team Six sailor who confessed to taking some diving equipment home for personal use. It took two trials, but the Navy got a conviction despite the fact that the sailor who confessed to taking some equipment home admitted that it occurred after Marcinko had left SEAL Team Six. Marcinko was sentenced to 21 months in the Federal Correctional Institution, fined $10,000, and reduced in rank to Commander. While in prison he began writing his first two books, <u>Rogue Warrior, SEAL Team Six</u> and <u>Rogue Warrior, Red Cell</u>. I highly recommend them both if you don't mind reading the language he used every day. The books describe Marciko's background, training, tours in Vietnam, and intimate details of many of the operations of SEAL Team Six and Red Cell.

I was questioned by an agent from the Naval Investigative Service (NIS) about Marcinko's expenditures and use of government money. I was and remain firmly convinced that Marcinko might have been a little (lot?) aggressive, but he would not steal anything nor misappropriate funds for personal gain. I testified at the trial of Marcinko's deputy when the Navy tried to convict him. While in the witness stand at that trial, the prosecutor, holding notes ostensibly from the NIS agent who had interviewed me twice, tried to attribute damning comments, which I had not made, to me. After denying several of these fabricated comments, I pointed to the NIS agent sitting behind the prosecutor's table and called him a liar. The prosecutor had no further questions for me. What a farce!

My admiration for the Navy SEALs is unequalled.

Jury Duty
"A jury is a group of twelve people of average ignorance."
Herbert Spencer 1820 - 1903

I was summoned for jury duty for my very first time in August 1990. It was a capital murder case. I discovered that bad guys are not very smart, if accused keep your mouth shut until you have a lawyer, and a coin toss can have an influence on the outcome of a case.

On March 31, 1990 a woman riding her bicycle on an Arlington, VA bike path noticed an "unthreatening" man walking towards her. They made eye contact as they passed, then two or three seconds later the man pulled her off her bicycle from behind and dragged her to a ditch along the path. The man beat her in the face and head, always using one hand to keep her face turned towards the ground. He also managed to pull her pants part way down.

A man riding his bicycle along the same path saw the man "throw a punch towards the ground." He got off his bicycle and walked toward the man to investigate. When the attacker saw him coming, he grabbed the woman's purse and ran off. The police were called, searched the area for about one hour, but found no useful evidence.

Later that same night a woman was beaten, raped, and stabbed 21 times. The murder occurred within a few hundred yards of the earlier attack. The murdered woman was walking to a Metro station on her way to her 23rd birthday party. She was a recent Tufts University graduate and a paralegal. When she failed to arrive at her party, her friends searched for her without success. Her body was found the next morning in the stair well of a business next to the bike path. There were no suspects.

Five months later police were called to a bike path in Springfield, VA several miles west of Arlington, after two different women reported that a man had tried to attack them. When the police arrived they found Michael Satcher loitering along the bike path. He claimed that he had come to visit a friend that was not home so he had gone jogging. The police took him in for questioning.

During the ride to the police station, the officer driving the police van, in an effort to keep the prisoner sitting in the rear calm and avoid any trouble when they disembarked, turned and asked Satcher, "Hey. What's up?" Satcher responded, "They are trying to frame me for a rape and murder or something in Arlington." That was the first connection the police had between Satcher and the rape and murder that had occurred five months earlier.

The woman who was attacked earlier on the night of the murder described her attacker as a stocky, black male between 25 - 30 years old, about 5'9' or 5'10" tall, and weighing 190 - 200 pounds. The police sketch artist made a sketch from her description. The man who had run off the attacker gave a similar description and his sketch was almost identical to the woman's. When arrested Satcher was 5'6" tall and weighed 152 pounds.

An awl was found in the glove compartment of Satcher's car. It was clean, but based on the stab wounds, could have been the murder weapon. Satcher was working as a furniture mover, but despite a reputation for not missing work, had not reported for work the day of the murder.

This was early in DNA testing and Satcher voluntarily gave blood, saliva, and hair samples to the police. DNA from Satcher's blood, a blood type carried by 7% of the population, matched DNA from the semen sample taken from the body. The hair samples were inconclusive. The defense attorney had a different laboratory run DNA on Satcher's blood and found a 3% difference in two of the bands. (A national sampling protocol had not yet been established and each laboratory had their own protocol.) The government claimed Satcher's DNA match was unique by a ratio of one in 400 million. The defense argued that it was not reliable.

At a lineup before the trial, the woman who had survived the early attack in Arlington narrowed her attacker down to number two or number four. She picked number two because he looked "unthreatening" remembering the man she had passed on the bike path. Satcher was number four. The man who had run off the attacker could not positively identify anyone in the lineup; although he testified at the trial that he was "pretty sure" it was number four (Satcher.)

At the trial the woman positively identified Satcher. When asked by the prosecuting attorney, "What changed your mine?"

She replied, "I have been observing Satcher sitting at the defense table and as he left and entered the courtroom. I recognized his walk and the way he shrugs his shoulders while walking. I have no doubt that he's the person that attacked me."

The jury was composed of five women and seven men. When the trial ended the jurors were directed to retire and select a foreman. In a secret ballot, a male in the computer sales business and I each received six votes. He pulled a coin from his pocket and offered to flip for the position. I agreed, he flipped his coin, and I won. (This also could have had a major impact on the jury's final decision.) I thought it was a slam-dunk that Satcher was guilty and after letting everyone get a cup of coffee, I proposed a secret ballot vote. Much to my surprise, there were: ten "Guilty," two "Lets discuss the case," and one "Not Guilty." We discussed the case briefly until the afternoon ended and we were sequestered at a nearby hotel. A police guard spent the night outside our rooms.

The next day we debated the case for six hours without resolution, but we convinced the "undecided" that wanted to discuss the case. One was convinced when a juror demonstrated the maliciousness of the attack, by having me lie on the floor while he simulated stabbing me 21 times and making all the jurors count along with him. The other "undecided" did not like the fact that the woman had chosen someone else during the lineup, but was certain it was Satcher in court. I explained how at football and lacrosse practices with everyone wearing a helmet the covers the face, and lacking numbers on the jerseys, it is readily apparent who everyone is by the way they move. No one else had played either sport and could support me, but apparently I helped convince the last "undecided."

I proposed another vote. The result was eleven "Guilty" and one "Not Guilty." I was getting frustrated and declared that whoever though the defendant was "Not Guilty" should identify himself/herself, tell us what was bothering him/her, and argue to change our mind. The man who had received six votes for jury foremen identified himself. He said DNA was not yet proven and if it later turned out that we had convicted an innocent man he would not be able to get over it. (The coin flip could have made a difference?) I called a break and told everyone to get fresh coffee. During the break I gathered the women jurors and explained that in true scientific fashion I had been leading the discussion linearly, in a step-by-step manner, and realized that was not going to change this man's mind. I acknowledged that women are good at emotional arguments and suggested that they go talk to this guy or we would never get out of here. The women complied, one or two at a time, while the rest of us milled around taking an extended break. About 45 minutes later, the man asked me to take another vote. The result was unanimously, "Guilty." Back in the courtroom after submitting our decision, the jury was polled and everyone stood firm.

We were sequestered another night because in Virginia the jury recommends the sentence. The next morning, we all agreed that this man must never be released, but were informed by a woman juror who happened to be a law student, that a sentence of, "Life in prison" meant only that the convicted would spend 60% of his remaining life in prison before becoming eligible for parole. We did not have an option of "Life without parole." It was suggested that we recommend a sentence of 100 years to keep him in jail, but a note inquiry to the judge revealed that was not allowed because it would be cruel and unusual punishment. We finally agreed on the death sentence.

If Satcher had kept his mouth shut on the ride to the jail, if the coin had landed heads instead of tails, and if there had not been several women on the jury, I believe the outcome could have been different.

Michael Satcher has been executed for the murder of Ann Borgazani.

Pets I Have Known

All the animals except man know that the
principal business of life is to enjoy it."
Samuel Butler 1862 - 1947

KOA

Koa and I joined up in Hawaii. He was pup and his name means "warrior" in Hawaiian. I selected a boxer breed because that's the kind of dog I had when I was growing up. Koa loved to play with "balls" of every type. In Hawaii coconuts and mangoes from trees in my yard qualified when nothing more interesting was available. Mangoes, whose skin is reported to cause an allergic reaction in some people, caused his face to swell up and his eyes to be almost shut after playing ball with a freshly fallen mango. It became important that I beat him to that kind of ball.

He was two years old when he moved with me from Hawaii to Maryland. By then he was a solid, broad chested, male and a good watch dog. One night as our newly formed poker group was arriving, one player asked me why they call the breed "boxers"? I had played on the floor with Koa enough to know some of his moves so I told the inquisitive gentleman to get down on the floor on his hands and knees facing the dog. When they were in position, I said, "Now reach out with one hand to touch the dog's head." Wham! The dog's right paw whipped forward like a boxer's right hook, knocked the arm away and sent the man's glasses flying clear across the room. I was holding Koa by the collar so he didn't follow up by pouncing on the startled man. It was a beautiful demonstration.

My yard in Maryland was a fenced acre so there was a lot of room for Koa to run. There was a large German shepherd that would occasionally come by and the two dogs, one on each side of the fence, would race the north leg of the property while barking at each other. The problem was that when the fence made the 90-degree turn and headed east or west, Koa had to put on the breaks. He did this by spreading his rear legs slightly and squatting down. It was an athletic display that went awry one day and he dislocated his right rear leg at the hip.

The veterinarian operated and made repairs with rubber tubing. After several follow up visits the veterinarian proclaimed the leg totally healed, but Koa insisted on keeping it up by his stomach, refused to put any weight on it, and remained downs stairs when I went up to bed. The veterinarian would pull, push, and rotate the leg without Koa showing any discomfort, just to convince me that it was healed and as good as new. The veterinarian proclaimed that the dog remembered the pain and psychologically was afraid to use the leg. He suggested that if the dog was in the water and had to use the leg for swimming he might admit the absence of pain.

So, off to the Severn River I took him. I eventually found a small wooden pier just barely above the water line that extended about twenty feet out into the river. I lifted Koa gently and put him in the water at the end of the pier. It was about four or five feet deep and he sunk like a rock. Here's a dog that would leap off a diving board into the water, but would not use his once injured leg to save himself. Talk about stubborn! I had to jump into the water, fully clothed, to save him.

One evening, several days after the water rescue, Koa followed me up stairs as if the past months walking on three legs had never occurred. I don't know what happened, seems like he just got over it on his own time.

Koa moved with me a second time, this time from Odenton, Maryland to Springfield, Virginia.

He was a faithful companion and pet for almost eleven years.

PEEPERS

One Sunday morning in May, our neighbor's young children, returned from church and presented my wife with a birthday gift. It was in a small, brown, paper bag tied loosely at the top, with a narrow, red ribbon. Inside was a tiny, baby duck.

The young thirteen-year-old girl who had brought the gift was invited to pick a name for this new pet. Perhaps because it had not stopped peeping since being removed from the paper bag, she suggested that it be named, "Peepers."

We had no idea how to care for a baby duck or even what to feed it. Fortunately there was a Feed & Grain store in the area operated by Mormons that was open on Sundays. Off I went on a fact-finding mission.

"What do baby ducks eat?" I asked the salesman who offered assistance.

"Finely cracked corn." he responded with confidence.

"Great. I need a small bag for a baby duck."

"Sorry, but it only comes in 50 pound bags." He sounded apologetic and added, "If you only have a single chick I'll give you a handful of corn to last until it dies."

"What do you mean, until it dies?"

"These chicks are flock animals; they don't live long alone. All the chicks purchased as pets around Easter are probably dead by now."

"Well, how much company does it need? Will one more chick work?"

"Yes. One more is usually OK."

"All right, then let me buy another baby duck."

"We don't have any ducks, only chickens and turkeys."

"Will the duck know the difference?" I asked, fearing the answer.

"Nah. The chicks are all alike."

That's why I returned home with a 50-pound bag of finely cracked corn and a chicken chick.

While placing straw in the bottom of a shoebox and arranging a desk lamp to provide overnight warmth, I suggested that the girl's ten-year-old brother select a name for the chicken. The sermon at church earlier this morning obviously remained fresh in his mind; he suggested, "Moses." I proposed that we nickname him "Mo" so that he would not be expected to part any river waters and the naming was settled. We were now the proud, but less than confident owners of Peepers and Mo.

Our residence at the time was the fenced acre in Maryland ruled by Koa, but we had acquired a second dog. A small, eight-pound, female, mongrel with multicolored hair that looked like the TV dog, Bengie. We called her Meiling because of her long, scraggly, chin hairs that looked like a Chinaman's goatee. She had been thrown from a bridge into a stream, in a plastic bag with a young, male, black poodle. A jogger witnessed the event, saved the animals, and took them to our veterinarian. I was visiting with Koa while the veterinarian was still trying to find a home for the female. It was a sad story so I took her home.

Koa was tall enough to peer into the shoebox on my workbench and peepers imprinted on him. She both thought she was a dog and the pecking order in the yard as the chicks grew was Koa then Peepers. She would chase Meiling away to cuddle up next to Koa when he was lying on the ground and she followed him around the yard like an adoring little sister.

I assumed that ducks needed somewhere to swim so I bought a child's wading pool, dug a circular hole the diameter of the pool and to a depth that put the pool rim at ground level, and filled it with water. With pride in my new gift to Peepers, I placed her in the water. And she panicked! Peeps of contentment were replaced with loud squawks of panic while flapping her wings violently trying to get out of the water. She didn't sink; she just didn't know what was happening. I scooped her from the pool and put her on dry land. Another pet saved from "agua panica." Was this déjà vu or what?

However, there remained a problem. If mother ducks had to teach their young to swim, how was I going to do that? Pondering the problem while smoking a cigar, (cigars enhance the possibility of finding a solution to vexing problems) I had an idea. I emptied the pool, put Peepers in the dry bottom, got no reaction, so I slowly began refilling the pool with water from a hose. Soon she was calmly floating. Eventually the pool filled and she discovered that she could maneuver, and enter and exit the pool at will. How's that for a swimming teacher "mother?"

The two chicks stayed together and when Peepers went swimming, Mo would perch by the edge of the pool and observe. On two occasions I had to intervene when Meiling, innocently sniffing Mo, knocked him into the pool. Chicken feathers apparently have no oil and Mo did not float. My intervention was to race over and scoop Mo out of the pool before the occurrence of "death by drowning." In Mo's case memory of these murder attempts remained vivid. Mo grew up to be a 12 pound rooster and once aware of his four pound weight advantage over Meiling, planned revenge. Mo would casually and innocently peck away at the ground while edging over behind Meiling. Then in a sudden charge with wings flapping, Mo would leap onto Meiling's back and begin pecking the dog in the head. It was no contest; this was a large bird dedicated to vengeance and the number of attacks appeared to be endless. Our sympathy was with Meiling; so Mo had to go.

Despite being ornery, Mo was a pet so "disposal" required careful consideration. After telephone calls to several local chicken farmers I found one who sold eggs, not chickens, promised to give Mo a good home and not to have him as the main course at dinner. When I delivered Mo to his new home the owner looked appreciatively at Mo's size and confided to me, "I have only one rooster and almost 400 hens. Your pet will think he's in heaven. You have nothing to worry about." It sounded good to me!

When Koa ran after a thrown ball in the yard or ran along the fence barking at something of interest Peepers would follow as fast as she could waddle. Returning with a ball or changing direction along the fence Koa would jump, dodge, or simply run over her. Peepers had not learned to fly. What's a "mother" to do?

I pondered this situation unsuccessfully on several different occasions until I ran out of cigars. I was not about to jump out of a tree with her, and throwing her up in the air seemed neither kind nor practical. So Peepers never did learn to fly and continued to go tumbling when Koa reversed course and she hadn't caught up. Eventually I think her wings atrophied and she did not have sufficient wing strength to fly.

I once asked our veterinarian the life span of a duck? He confessed he didn't know because, "they are most often killed by a local cat." The smell of the dogs kept cats away from our yard and we did not have a problem. The dogs were housedogs and Peepers stayed in the yard alone except for exceptionally cold winter nights when we nested her in the garage.

Peepers was always in the way, whenever there was digging in the garden or yard. She especially enjoyed eating earthworms and would dive into a hole being shoveled when she saw one. During a visit, my Dad noticed that after handling her to lift her out of a hole she would immediately spread her wings and fluff her feathers. He reported that he had taught Peepers a trick. As we watched, he picked her up, held her for a moment, and put her back on the ground with the command, "Peepers. Make like an eagle." And peepers would spread and flutter her wings, "like an eagle." Not bad for a duck and it occasionally provided entertainment for a visiting child.

She also laid about five eggs per week. Duck eggs are larger than chicken eggs, have a stronger shell, and the yolk was more orange than yellow in those that I cracked open. If I found a nest with one or two eggs we would cook with them. If there were four or five we knew some were too old to use and simply removed them from the nest. When a nest was emptied, Peepers would build a new nest by forming a rounded depression in the ground in some protected area (e.g., under a fir tree) and seeding it with a smooth stone. She is totally responsible for providing me with these interesting bits of avian education that I am sharing with you.

Peepers was six years old, when we moved, with our three pets (Koa, Meiling, and Peepers) to the house in Springfield, VA with a small fenced yard. One day I returned home from work and could not find Peepers. She was gone. There was a K – 6 school up the street and I wondered if a child had seen her, opened the gate to play with her, and inadvertently let her loose. I sought help from the school's administration and was advised to make a flyer and offer a reward because; "These kids will do anything for money." Posters offering a reward were distributed and posted in the neighborhood but garnered no response.

Two weeks later, after we had given up hope, we received a call from a teenage boy wanting to know if we were the owners of "Disco Duck?" His description of the animal sounded like Peepers so we invited him to bring Disco Duck over for confirmation. When Disco Duck arrived and was released it immediately ran over to Koa and began bobbing up and down, and peeping with contentment.

The teenager said he was a student at George Mason University and saw the duck in the middle of the highway on his return from school one evening. He stopped and went to assist thinking it was wounded because it did not run or fly away. He took it home and kept it in a large cardboard box in his bedroom. He claimed that when he studied he played rather loud, disco, music and the duck would bob up and down in the box as though dancing to the disco music. Thus he called her Disco Duck. He had only recently heard about the reward poster, refused a reward, and seemed content to watch the duck and large boxer interact.

Eight years later I moved again, this time to Arlington, VA. I fenced the yard for Peepers and Meiling; Koa had died. Peepers eventually outlived Meiling and I worried about the lack of fresh canine smell keeping cats away, but never saw any cats near the yard. Peepers died in her 16th year. I found her lying peacefully in her nest one morning. There were no rumpled feathers or sign of a struggle and my conscience was eased when I concluded that she had died a natural and peaceful death. Peepers is buried in a flowered corner of my backyard and her resting site is prominently identified by a black slate marker with the name PEEPERS painted in large, block, letters above a duck footprint and the years 1974 – 1990.

Class President

"The average man's judgment is so poor,
he runs a risk every time he uses it."
Edgar W. Howe 1853 – 1937

The Naval Academy Class of 1960 elects Presidents for five-year terms. I had the position for two terms, from 1990 until 2000.

My initial platform, in 1990, was based on the fact that we were now in our fifties, had earned some money, tallied some experiences and it would be fun to assemble in a relatively small group so that there would be time to become reacquainted during leisurely, one-on-one, discussions, somewhere in the country other than Annapolis. I called them mini-reunions. Class homecoming reunions, held every five years in Annapolis, are massive affairs where there are so many people it is difficult to say more that "hello" before being interrupted. At a mini-reunion classmates should be able to spend time together updating their life story, reminiscing, and telling lies. By visiting different parts of the country there would be an opportunity to see classmates who don't always make it back to Annapolis for the conventional five-year reunions. I selected vacation locations where there were at least three or four classmates so they could help me with the organization, planning, lodging, and itinerary. My other constraint was that the mini-reunion should not be in the fall to avoid interfering with the Academy's annual homecoming and football game.

In 1990 our class published a second Yearbook called, "The First 30 Years." It was a major endeavor with many volunteers. The book has become a favorite and very useful document for becoming reacquainted, because each classmate was asked to describe his military career, civilian pursuits, and family life.

In June 1992, thirty-two of us met for a mini-reunion in Minneapolis, MN. Bill Griffin was the class resident in charge and who arranged for lodging at the Decathlon Club, a Mississippi River riverboat cruise, and formal dinner at the Interlachen Country Club. It was a wonderful vacation and successful reunion.

In June 1993, thirty-six of us vacationed, toured, and renewed friendships in Albuquerque and Santa Fe, NM. K.C. Jones was on-scene-commander in Albuquerque and Chuck Kiger handled Santa Fe. Nine classmates live in the area so, I assume, they had lots of help? We visited the Pueblo Cultural Center, the Atomic Museum, and rode the tram to Sandia Crest. In Santa Fe the highlights were the art galleries and native Indian craft stores.

In May 1994, Dave Schnegelberger arranged a reunion in Vail, Colorado. The outdoor, "chuck wagon" dinner was terrific, but taking the ski lift to the top of the mountain and riding down on a dirt bike was even more exhilarating than coming down on skis. It was necessary, at least for me, to brake almost the entire way down.

In the summer of 1995, we took advantage of having a classmate, Joel Febel, married to the U.S. Ambassador to Guatemala, Marilyn MacAfee, who was the sister of classmate Bob MacAfee. With specially arranged briefing at the Embassy, shopping trips arranged by the Ambassador, and a formal dinner at the Ambassador's residence, it is not exaggerating to say that we were royally treated. The visit to the ancient Mayan ruins at Tikal, in the middle of a tropical jungle, was also memorable.

By 1996 classmates with a particular interest began organizing mini-reunions as travel adventures such as a cruise to Alaska, a tour of Ireland, and a barge trip down the Rhone River in France. The mini-reunions continue to be a success and no longer the responsibility of a single individual.

The Outer Banks of North Carolina (OBX)

One event that began as a mini reunion for a week of golf in the Outer Banks of NC has taken on a life of its own. No longer just for golf, ten couples have been meeting for about eleven consecutive years in a three story, ten bedroom, beach house in Kill Devil Hill, NC. The house is one block west of the beach and two blocks east of the site of the Wright Brothers' museum and memorial where their first flight occurred. The event has morphed into a week of fine dining, drinking, hot tub soaking, skeet shooting, game playing, local touring, shopping, . . . and yes, golf. Rod and Paula Friedman are the organizers. Since a majority of the males were Navy pilots, Rod, a fellow submariner, frequently wears his ball cap that declares him a, "Bottom Gun." The only rule is that, "There are no rules." Couples sign up to prepare a main course, salad, hors d'ouvres, etc. for dinner. Breakfast and lunch are "selfies." One year we had a wine tasting to determine if the wine aficionados could tell the difference between a $4 and a $40 bottle of wine. Results were interesting! Traditionally wine is consumed with less fanfare since someone provided coasters that declared, **"WINE!**

How Classy People Get Shitfaced." One evening we go out to dinner at a fancy local restaurant. Golf remains popular and there are daily tee times for those interested. Recently a miniature golf tournament with cash prizes for lowest scores and most holes-in-one attracted twelve participants and may become an annual event.

One year, Bob Bell described his bare boat sailing experience in the British Virgin Islands and inquired if anyone was interested. (Bare boating means without a hired captain or crew. Someone in the party must have a resume/experience that convinces The Moorings that he/she knows how to sail and the rest of the party agrees to act as crew.) Each sailboat had four staterooms with private heads and showers. We invited some friends and chartered three boats to accommodate the twenty-four people that wanted to go. We had two experienced sailboat sailors and two Admirals who had commanded aircraft carriers. Their spectacular resumes filled with deeds of bravery, hours of fighter aircraft combat experience, performance awards, cooking and golfing skills, overwhelmed the performance evaluator at The Moorings and the two admirals were given a ship. Rod Friedman and I volunteered to be their crew. We motored just fine and won the egg-throwing contest when we passed alongside a vessel with water balloons going in opposite directions. We arrived safely and on time at every beach, snorkeling site, island, town, and floating bar. We were even able to briefly raise a sail on the sixth day. We had a grand time.

Retirement - Why Now?
"My father taught me to work; he did not teach me to love it."
Abraham Lincoln 1809 – 1865

Not retirement from the Navy, nor from analytical work, adjunct teaching, or consulting, but from "everything" as in, I finally decided that I could no longer waste my time making money!

My wife, Evelyn, died February 28, 1997. We would have been married 30 years in July. A woman who was never sick, she was diagnosed with cancer and died five weeks later. She went to several doctors each of whom told her she had the flu until one aspirated fluid from her lungs and detected cancer cells. The source of the cancer was never determined despite a multitude of tests and scans. The death certificate identifies the cause of death as, "cancer of unknown origin." Towards the end of her brief stay in hospice, she said to me, "Help me. I don't want to die."

Feeling helpless, I tried to think of ways to bring her peace. In case she thought she had not confessed all her sins I found a young priest who agreed to visit her and give her absolution and a blessing. I took pages of photographs from our photo albums and spent several hours reminding her, with photos, of all the places we had been, sites we had seen, events and parties we had attended. The next day I brought our address files and reminisced with her about each of our friends and the people we had met. I brought in her two dogs for a final face licking that always caused her to smile. Eventually the nurses told me that she was resting more peacefully, so I chose to believe that at least one of my efforts was a success. She is buried at Arlington National Cemetery with our son.

I did unexpectedly discover that the time I spent with her going over our photo albums and address files made me appreciate that we had had a wonderful life together, were well traveled, had lots of friends, and that I should have no guilt over having not done or provided something for her. It was a peaceful closure to our life together and she may have been intentionally doing that for me? The event did make me realize how fragile life can be and that time should not be wasted.

I continued working for almost a year after she died - as an employee at Advanced Marine, a consultant on the Chiles Commission, and an Adjunct professor at Florida Institute of Technology. With no one spending money I was able to pay off my three Virginia mortgages (Condo in McLean, house in Springfield, and home in Arlington) and add to my retirement accounts. By the end of 1997, I had given notice of retirement where appropriate and in January 1998, the month before my 60th birthday, I stopped wasting my time making money and began having fun.

CHAPTER 11

Mid-Life Bachelor Years

The Poker Group

"The gambling known as business looks with austere
disfavor upon the business known as gambling."
Ambrose Bierce 1842 - 1914

During one of my early poker playing visits to Las Vegas, I wanted to
buy a couple of new poker playing books. This was in the 1960s when
libraries and bookstores had very few poker books, and before poker
became popular with on-line betting and Indian casinos in the 1980s.
In the yellow pages of the Las Vegas telephone directory I found a full-
page advertisement for sport books that claimed to occupy an entire
city block. It was located in old town Las Vegas about ten miles north
of the Strip. With great anticipation, I took a cab from the Gold Coast
(my hotel-casino of choice during my poker trips to Las Vegas) to the
store. It was as large as advertised and I entered with anticipation. It
was cavernous inside, but there were no books. I could however, "make
book" on everything from horse racing to a cricket match between a
team from London, England and a team from Mumbai, India. That's
when I discovered the meaning of "sport book" in Las Vegas, the only
city in the USA where betting (especially on sporting events) was legal.
When such places are in casinos they are called sports bars. Indeed one
can buy a drink, have a seat at a table, place a bet on a large variety of
events, and watch the events unfold on one of the tens of televisions

mounted around the room. It was a very interesting and educational visit, but not a place to augment one's library holdings.

A friendly group of ex-military officers and analysts began having a monthly poker game in November 1980. The core group included Denny Harman, Bill Watkins, Bud Pezet, Jeff Bailey, Hal Martin, John Leahy, and yours truly. Before moving out of town Hal Martin played in 42 games and Jeff Bailey played in 82 games. John Leahy stayed for 41 games. The remainder of the core group continued playing for thirty-one years, until March 2011. I have record of hosting and playing in 162 games and the others in the core group played in at least 120 games. Bob Wilson joined us early and played in 69 games. Dave Herrington, Dick Buzzelli, and Mike Gawitt played in over 30 games, and Jim Maxfield, Tom Marti, Doug Johnston, Ken Loveland, and P. J. Kirkeguard played in over 20 games. My brother, Bob, sat in on at least twelve games. Another twelve players sat in on a few games. It was a friendly group with lots of laughs and good competition. They also "advised me" on some of my adventures.

We began with a rotating host, but traffic made it impossible to begin on time. I began hosted all the games because I lived within a mile of the Pentagon and Crystal City where most players worked. Players came directly from work and secretaries were told and appointment calendars noted a meeting of the Applied Probability Working Group. I provided food, beer, and soda, and we split the cost of the food. I kept a list of interested players, added new players at the bottom, and began calling from the top of the list until we had seven players for a game. Games were dealer's choice, but no wild card games were allowed. High–Low split pot games became a favorite. The maximum bet was two dollars.

In this book, I disparage members of the poker group by revealing several of their foolish ideas, actions, and suggestions – which I seem to have routinely accepted. As a result, I feel compelled to state that most of them were not Navy fighter pilots, but were actually rather well educated and successful. Many were on their second career after retiring from the military and at various times the group included: the Deputy

Director of Naval Intelligence, the Director of World Wide Sales for Sun Micro Systems, the Executive VP of the Center for Strategic & International Studies, a West Point golf coach, an attorney, the Director of Business Development at Oracle Corporation, a stage & screen actor, a software engineer working on the NASA Space Shuttle, a Deputy Assistant Secretary of the Navy, a published book author, and a Military Attaché to Moscow. It was an imaginative and motley group. I leave it to you to sort out who was who.

When I retired, I considered becoming a professional poker player. I enjoyed playing poker, had a 69% win rate in the local games, and held my own in the low stake games in the card rooms in San Diego (while on the Richard S. Edwards) in Gardena, CA, (while the Admiral's Aide in Long Beach, CA.) and more recently in Las Vegas and the Foxwood Casino in Connecticut. I calculated how much money I would need to rent a Las Vegas apartment and live while taking poker lessons from a professional and beginning to play seriously. I assumed a variety of winning percentages, table stakes, and living costs, and developed a business plan for myself. I found that it would require that I play at significantly higher stakes than I was use to playing and the swing between my bankroll's highs and lows would be more than I could tolerate comfortably. It was an interesting exercise that kept me from trying a third career that would have been high pressure, likely to eventually lead to boredom, and be unsuited for someone like me who hates to loose money. I would be devastated to lose thousands of dollars in a sitting even if I had won that much in a single sitting several times. With that attitude I would occasionally hesitate to call a very large bet even if the odds were slightly in my favor. Not a winning attitude for a professional poker player. So I remained completely retired and content with the friendly, monthly, poker game.

In July 2014 Denny Harman died after a battle with cancer. In addition to enjoying poker, Denny loved golf, lived in a house alongside his course and played almost every day. His Memorial Service, done beautifully and respectfully by his family, was held at his Golf Club. As part of the affair there was a "21 golf ball salute." The club granted permission to take over the first tee for twenty minutes. The first flight was eleven of Denny's golfing buddies and friends all in a line along the front of the tee box with a teed-up golf ball and a golf club. Denny's daughter gave the commands, "Ready, Aim, Fire" and eleven golf balls went flying down the fairway. Everyone brought their own favorite club or took one from Denny's golf bag consequently the balls went high, low, short, and long depending on the club used. It looked good. Actually it was rather spectacular. The second flight of ten other friends performed similarly. The golfers had been given the golf ball to hit; it had the picture of an eagle and Denny's name on it. After the second flight of balls had been hit, the daughter released the children down the fairway (clean-up crew) saying they would get $1 for each of the 21 balls they brought back. It was clever, unique, memorable, and fitting.

Retirement Does Not Equal Golf
"Men become old but they never become good."
Oscar Wilde 1856 - 1900

For many people, including my Virginia neighbors, retirement is synonymous with playing golf. For my first birthday in retirement (I was 59 years old), a neighbor gave me a free golf lesson with the head golf pro, Steve Tobash, at the prestigious Army - Navy Club in Arlington, VA where they played and were members.

I made a same day appointment on a relatively warm day not too long after my February birthday. I arrived on time and went to the pro shop to meet Mr. Tobash.

In response to my introducing myself, he nodded and then said, "Where's your collared shirt?"

"This is a sweat shirt; it's cold outside and I'm not here to play golf only for you to show me how to hit the ball on the driving range."

"You still need a collared shirt. There are several styles right behind you, go buy one."

I bought a shirt and went into the men's room to put it on. It's a nice shirt, worth about one-third of what I paid for it. Mr. Tobash was pleased with my new outfit and invited me to follow him through the back door of the clubhouse to the driving range.

"Where are your clubs?" He asked as we began our walk.

"I don't have any clubs. I've never played before. I thought you would lend me a club and show me how to hit a golf ball."

"No. You need your own clubs. Let's go back inside to my office and I'll see if I have a used set someone traded in for a new set, that you can buy."

Somehow I knew that he would find a set and he did. I don't recall what I paid for them, but clubs and a bag are not cheap and this "free lesson" was turning into the proverbial money pit.

He showed me the interlocking finger grip (it felt awkward) and then corrected my every swing saying, "You must shift your weigh forward." Apparently you cannot hit off your back foot like a baseball batter, hockey or lacrosse player." The swing he was looking for, whenever I was able to perform, felt unnatural. Fortunately for him, I think we spent most of my one-hour lesson buying a collared shirt and bag of golf clubs. Then he found out that I was not a member of the Club and therefore would not be taking further lessons from him. His enthusiasm waned, he tired of repeating the hundreds of thoughts that I must consider during my golf swing, and he declared the lesson completed.

I try to make my own swing corrections, am happy to shoot in the upper half of the 90s, and will never be good at golf. It is not a relaxing game for me, because I must think about rotating to the forward foot (and a few other things) at every shot and woe is me if I just relax and hit it easy 'cause that means off the back foot and the results are usually embarrassing. I try to play once or twice each year with some friends who struggle to break 100. By no means does retirement equal golf for me!

What retirement meant to me was the opportunity to take some courses, travel, and begin some adventures. In Virginia, if you are at least 60 years old and content to take a course without getting credit,

University courses are free. Among the first of the many courses I took at George Mason University were a couple of Behavior Analysis and Abnormal Psychology courses hoping to better understand some of my friends. At the Virginia Fencing Academy I learned Medieval Sword Fighting. Weapons included the two handed, 40" long, broadsword (a slashing weapon) and the equally long, but lighter, rapier (a thrusting weapon) that allowed carrying a 14" dagger in the off-hand to use for blocking, or stabbing in clinched. The school provided wooden weapons. No up and down the fencing carpet with electric contact detectors when you're Medieval sword fighting. This was freestyle sparring where only real contact counted. Wearing fencing headgear and a padded jacket it was fun chasing each other around the fencing room with little regard for what we had been taught. Perhaps that contributed to my less than perfect golf swing?

As far as travel and adventures are concerned, that's the rest of this story.

My Favorite Birthday Parties
"Boys will be boys, and so will a lot of middle-aged men."
Frank McKinney Hubbard 1868 - 1930

Lake Powell

I give credit to Dave Schnegelberger, USNA '60, for making me realize that the birthday party you will enjoy the most is the one you arrange. My education began with a letter from Dave (a bachelor at the time,) that read something like this:

I'm tired of having someone else plan my birthday party and inviting people that I don't even care to be with, so I am arranging my own party. I have reserved a houseboat at Lake Powell on the Colorado River for a week of cruising. (Lake Powell is on the Utah - Arizona border about 350 miles from Vail where Dave was living.) *The boat will sleep 12 . . . the first 12 that respond, in the affirmative, to this invitation. I will supply all the beer and cigars. We will equally split the other costs, e.g., food.*

273

Twelve guys made the trip including his co-pilot from Vietnam, his ex-brother-in-law whom he said he liked better than his sister, four USNA classmates, other friends and neighbors.

After we arrived and Dave checked-out the boat, we boarded, selected bunks, and gathered for assignments. Dave declared himself captain since he was responsible for the boat. He told his co-pilot that he would be the navigator. He then pointed to two of his remaining crew and announced, "You two fat guys go buy the food so we'll know that we will eat well. If you buy anything fancy make sure one of us knows how to cook it before you buy it." The rest of us had rotating duties, e.g., cook, dish washer, etc. His ex-brother-in-law had brought red, ball caps that he distributed while encouraging us to wear them so we could be found in case we fell overboard. We wore them all the time, and adopted the name, the Red Hats, (partly because that's how all the other boaters referred to our boat.)

We had a wonderful week full of adventures and I decided that self-directed birthday parties were great things.

Paintball Wars

My favorite birthday party was for my 60th birthday in February 1998. I arranged it. My invitation read as follows:

YOU'RE INVITED TO A PAINTBALL BIRTHDAY PARTY

For my birthday I have reserved the Hogback Mountain Sports Club's Paintball Fields, in Leesburg, VA. You are among the motley group of adventuresome cowboy and Indian wannabes invited to spend a day in the woods shooting paintballs at each other. Are you still young enough to play in the woods for a day?

GENERAL ITINERARY

Friday, February 6th, Afternoon: Out of area players arrive. I have three beds, two couches, and lots of floor space. Sleeping bags are welcome. Beds allocated on a first to respond basis.

Friday, February 6ᵗʰ, 1800: @ 2750 South Ives Street (that's where I live) beer, wine, booze, food, and cigars. Discus paintball rules, location of the course, divide into two teams, strategy sessions, jokes, (the last two may be identical!) make and pack food and drink for lunch in the field tomorrow. Cannot drink booze at paintball site until after the last paintball has been fired.

Saturday, February 7ᵗʰ, 0830: Depart 2750 South Ives to arrive at paintball course at 1000. Four courses are available and they are all ours. Each course/field is about 120 meters long and 100 meters wide. The courses and games that I observed were: Game #1 Course 1: In a relatively level, wooded area supplemented with fallen trees, bales of hay, and other stuff to hide behind each team had a flag, set atop a flag stand, near its end of the field. Objective is to capture the enemy's flag and carry it back to a position alongside your flag. Game #2 Course 2: In a valley between two wooded hillsides was a dry creek bed. Teams started from opposing hillsides with one flag placed in middle of creek bed, objective was to capture that flag and return it to your position. Game #3 Course 3: In a clearing in the midst of a heavily wooded area there was a two-story fort. The team in the fort had to protect a flag located in the clearing about 30 meters from the fort and 30 meters from the tree line. Game #4 Course 3: Repeat of last game with the teams reversing positions in the fort and protecting the flag. Game #5 Course 4 The terrain on this course was uneven and had been augmented with an abundance of tree stands and tree houses where someone could hide. Game #6 onward: Whatever we care to play on any course we want to use.

*   *We have the courses from 1000 – 1700, darkness, or exhaustion.*
*   *Each player gets a facemask with goggles, a paintball gun and 100 paintballs.*
*   *Extra paintballs cost $7 per 100. (Your only expense.)*
*   *The Sports Club provides an umpire. If you, or anything you're carrying, e.g., gun, are hit anywhere (leg, arm, foot) and the paint spot is at least the size of a thumb print, you are out of commission for the rest of that game and must exit the game area.*

* *Games appeared to last from 10 - 40 minutes depending on player aggressiveness and team strategy.*
* *Paint will wash off clothes. Camouflage color in February may be the color of mud or snow? It will most likely be damp.*
* *We will have access to a cabin with a fireplace for breaks, lunch, and to treat the wounded. Bring your own oxygen bottles and vitamins. We will use the cabin after the game for wrap-up comments from the umpire followed by player comments (lies), beers, and cigars.*
* *When I visited the site there were different groups on each course. One group went home at 1330. They were exhausted (perhaps we need more than two teams?) Then again they were old farts in the 30 - 45 age group and it was a coed group.*

Saturday, February 7ᵗʰ, Evening: *I have three showers and my hot tub will be ready for use. We will have whatever beer, booze, and cigars are left. Domino's Pizza knows my address.*

Please RSVP as soon as possible so I can finalize arrangements. Call me at work or at home and leave a message if I'm not available. Hope to see you in February.

Eighteen came to play, arriving from CA, NH, MA, SC, MD, and VA. We divided into two teams by selecting from 18, face down, playing card - 9 red suited cards and 9 black suited cards.

The photo of the eighteen participants was taken before the first game and before anyone got covered with paint and mud. The weather was cold and damp, but there was no snow.

"The Paintball Wars"
Left to right, front row, Bill Townsend, Tom Springer,
Ron Hinkel, Jim Knorr, Bob Pariseau.
Standing, Peter Cain, Bud Pezet, Gene Gardner, Mike
Salewske, Tom Solak, Dick Pariseau, Rich Haver, Jim Duffy,
Jim Duffy Jr., Chuck Woodworth, Mike Pariseau.
(Personal Photo)

We played from 10:00 AM until dark and played on every course. (We played the course with the fort twice, so each team could try to defend the fort. We timed how long the defense lasted so there would be a winner in each event.)

Bud Pezet was the only casualty. It occurred when, with utter disregard for his own survival, he abandoned the safety of a large oak tree and braving heavy enemy fire ran to capture the enemy 's flag. Racing back to his camp in a circuitous route like a ball carrier dodging tacklers on a football field and avoiding enemy fire coming from all directions, he took a header into the mud with a torn hamstring. In the heat of competition the enemy fire continued and he was hit several times and "killed" before he could get up or crawl to safety. The referee blew his whistle signaling a time out and two comrades helped Bud from the battlefield as he dragged his painful leg. His hamstring has healed, but his heroism will be remembered

The feedback was positive and complementary from all the participants. The only negative comments I received were from women who heard about the wonderful time we had and berated me for not making it a coed event. Several wives of participants strongly recommended that I "Do it again next year and include us."

Grand Canyon Rafting

The Red Hats met again in 2001 for a trip that began at the Bellagio in Las Vegas, then went to a campsite on the edge of the Grand Canyon, where we ate cowboy style over an open, outdoor fire and slept either in an old, log cabin bunkroom or on the floor of a Conestoga Wagon. The next day we took a helicopter ride to the bottom of the Canyon to meet our rafting guides. The helicopter ride was exciting because the pilot was a retired air force officer who tried to get one or more of his navy riders to barf by flying low over the canyon wall then dropping vertically as fast as possible until just above the river when he would change to a horizontal flight. No one got sick, but he did provide us with an exciting flight.

For the next three days we rafted about 100 miles of the Colorado River within the Grand Canyon. We slept on the ground alongside the River inside the Canyon. Our guides provided food. The sand we slept on was created by the water wearing away the stone face of the canyon and was extremely fine. That's not "fine" as in very good, but "fine" as in miniature or microscopic, because it got into everything: food, sleeping bags, bathing suits, eyes, ears, and sneakers. We returned to the Bellagio to gamble away any money we had left before returning home. Another interesting party although I do not recall whose birthday it was?

Porch of No Ambition

"More than one cigar at a time is excessive smoking."
Mark Twain 1835 - 1910

During time spent on my porch of no ambition, I have learned that age means nothing as long as you're old enough to know your limitations and young enough to continually try to exceed them. Fortunately I have several friends with similar outlooks, so my porch gets a lot of usage.

My porch of no ambition is a screened gazebo at the northwest end of my deck. It's well shaded by large oak trees and visually isolated on one side by an eight-foot high wooden fence about thirty feet away. On the other side, a four-foot high wooden fence is fronted with tall and dense holly trees and aromatic lilac and forsythia bushes. It is truly a quiet and inviting location, except for the noise a few weeks each year when the tall oaks bombard the gazebo's wooden shingle roof with acorns. Their sudden crack has interrupted some serious contemplation. My gazebo is stocked with comfortable all-weather chairs, and has a large, old, ornate, pitted-metal chandelier hanging from its ceiling. What more could one ask for?

The rules for using the porch of no ambition are essentially what is not allowed: no work, no television or electronic devices, and no reading material above the 8th grade level, i.e., a requirement for literature with more pictures than words, and then only allowed on limited occasions. It is primarily a place where one gathers with friends for drinking, cigar smoking, relaxing, and contemplating issues we think are important. It is called a "porch" of no ambition because Dave Schnegelberger, (of "Plan Your Own Birthday Party" fame) who introduced me to the concept had designated a second floor, screened porch on the rear of his house as his "porch of no ambition." The idea has spread and one friend has his porch of no ambition in his garage. Everyone male should have a "place of no ambition" somewhere.

You wonder about the chandelier in my porch of no ambition? Well, it has a story of its own. It arrived in a large unidentifiable box for a Yankee Swap Meet. That excuse for a Christmas season party when everyone must bring a wrapped item that will be exchanged for something else. Numbers are randomly drawn and the lowest number gets first choice from among the piled, but wrapped and thus unidentified items. A later number after making a selection may trade their item for anything already opened. The chandelier came with a couple that was redecorating their home.

A woman (with the initials JH) who later admitted she selected it because it was by far the largest box in the pile chose it early in the evening. (I thought women knew better?) It was out of style, made of brass now faded and slightly pitted, had five ornate arms that held small light bulbs, and had sufficient chain to be hung from a very high ceiling. After seeing what she had chosen, she tried to induce someone to trade for it by forcing her husband to tape a dollar bill to the chandelier after each selectee that opened an item she would prefer to have, failed to trade with her. No one opened a gift they thought was worse than the chandelier and wanted to trade despite the one-dollar bills that had been added to the offer.

When she left the party, instead of taking the chandelier home, as required by the party rules, she clandestinely left it in my garage. The following day while cleaning up from the party, I found it in my garage. Two days before trash pick up; I put the chandelier at the curb, on top of a trashcan full of party residue. The next morning, still a day before the trash was to be picked up, the chandelier was gone. That same morning I received a call from a wife thanking me for a fine party and inquiring if the chandelier was still available. She said that she was disappointed that she had not traded for it, replaced the five lights with candles and hung it on her porch. A nice idea, but unfortunately it was gone. A day later, trash day, a neighbor two houses away, called with thanks for the party and mentioned that the chandelier was now on top of his trash pile. We both concluded that a couple out for a walk, there are many walkers in my neighborhood, had taken it, reconsidered it while continuing their walk, and deposited it back on a trash can, two houses away. What a wonderful eventuality! I immediately went over, collected the chandelier, and hung it in my gazebo. (Guys do things like that!)

I neither changed the lights for candles nor informed the woman who gave me the idea for putting it on a porch. (She has since divorced and moved to Wisconsin so she will never know.) The chandelier has been put to good use on my porch of no ambition when darkness arrived before an assembly had concluded or when a late night cigar or drink seemed appropriate.

"My Gazebo/Porch of No Ambition."
(Personal Photo)

One routine gathering on my porch occurs before our monthly poker game. Even those players who are still working can usually arrive in time to contribute some wisdom, because the game is scheduled as a late-afternoon Applied Probability Workshop and whose boss would object to attendance at such an auspicious learning experience. Among the poker players there is no shortage of fertile minds and individuals who can assume a dissonant attitude when appropriate. I think they would all think it was cool to have a pet zebra named "Spot."

Veto of an issue proposed for discussion or a suggested solution to a question being pondered is typically done with abusive language, intelligence assassination, and unrestrained laughter. Competition is ever present and no quarter ever given. Some ideas and questions that have been vigorously discussed include:

"Why do the Flintstones, in their TV program, celebrate Christmas?" (Dumb writers and dumber viewers since Christ didn't arrive until after the Stone Age.)

"Who invented the two-seater outhouse?" (Several plausible and acceptable answers: Congress, the teacher left behind, a farmer with a very low tooth to cavity ratio, and a hillbilly who goes to family reunions to find a date.)

"Why are there no "B" size batteries? (Unsolved.)

On one occasion a poker player arrived after dining at a Chinese restaurant the night before and reported that two of the four fortune cookies had the same printed message and that none of the four were memorable. He challenged the group to come up with statements that would be instructive and memorable if found in a fortune cookie. A few of the many suggestions made that day that I can recall are: "Someone will steal your identity and your credit rating will improve." "In case of fire remain seated, stay calm, pay check, then run like hell." "You may get lucky tonight." "The best sermons are lived not preached." "You only think you can use chop sticks." "Excite your woman; compliment her on her shoes." "Spend a lot of money on booze, women, and poker; the rest just squander." "Improve your golf game by having a tailgate party before your next match." "It's more important to explore than to succeed." "Don't do anything stupid; we have politicians for that."

The boys are arriving. The porch of no ambition is filling up and I can smell cigar smoke. I just heard someone say, "The trouble with eating Italian food is that in five or six days you're hungry again." I wonder if that's open for discussion?

My Painting Adventures

"Give me chastity and self-restraint,
but do not give it to me yet."
Saint Augustine 354 - 430 AD

Eleven months after being widowed I decided it was time to bachelorize my home. It looked nice; my wife, a woman with great taste had been furnishing and decorating it for the eighteen years we had lived here in Arlington, VA. However, whereas women furnish and decorate for effect: "fashionable, welcoming, charming, cozy, and homey," men furnish and decorate simply for functionality. A consequence of this motivational dichotomy was that the elegant, white, wicker furniture in the sun room had to go (not comfortable) and all the furniture that might solicit from my poker buddies the question, "Is this an antique or can I sit on it?" had to go. And I wanted to rearrange furniture so that my poker table would occupy a place of prominence after having been in the lower level, recreation room for eighteen years. I hired an agency to conduct a weekend estate sale.

Among the items I collected and located for the sale were about a dozen paintings that had decorated the walls. Almost all had been purchased at charity art auctions for the local animal shelter, school, or church. The self-imposed obligation to buy at such an event resulted in purchases that, now that they were off the wall and piled on the floor in a corner, I appraised as "not so visually aesthetic" and in several cases, "not so difficult to paint." Having fully retired a few weeks earlier, I had some available time and decided that it would be a worthwhile and challenging goal to be able to paint a picture of which I was sufficiently proud that I would want to hang it on my wall. Yes, ignorance is bliss.

An engineer without training, or even much exposure to the visual arts, I systematically concluded that I must begin my foray into painting with a drawing course. Fortunately, Arlington County, Virginia offers a variety of courses and I was able to register for one that I considered both inexpensive and appropriate.

I was serious about learning to draw, so on the first day of class I arrived early and sat front row center in one of two chairs behind a large, fold-out table. I noted that the other six people in the class were all women. I attributed this to the fact that it was a daytime course on a weekday and that women were more likely to be free for the course than men and that the arts were likely more appealing to women than to "straight" men. As a new bachelor, I filed these "facts" away for future reference.

The woman who subsequently became my tablemate was tall, thin, and whom I assessed as being in her early forties, plus or minus twenty years. She had lackluster, straight brown hair that hung unimaginatively to her shoulders, wore large hoop earrings and a one-piece dress that hung loosely over her body all the way to the floor. She reminded me of the pot-smoking hippies that I use to see along Cannery Row in Monterey, California during the late 1960s.

The teacher entered, introduced herself to the class, summarized her bona fides, and said to the class, "I'd like each of you to tell me why you are taking this class and what you hope to learn from it?" She then quite naturally pointed to me, sitting in the first row directly in front of her, and told me to begin. I admitted to being a total novice and told my story about being underwhelmed over some of the painting I had acquired and my hope of someday creating a painting or drawing (I'm no dummy) that was worthy of hanging on my wall. She nodded, approvingly I thought, although it could have been condescending of this student without any experience who had the audacity to join her Drawing I Class.

She then turned to my tablemate, who quickly commanded my complete attention as she assertively revealed, "I'm having an affair with a guy who owns a Tattoo Parlor. I'm here to learn to draw tattoos". I can only assume that the teacher nodded approval, my mind was busy recognizing the fact that these people were unlike the engineers and mathematicians that I had spent my life dealing with and that this foray into the world of artists could really become an adventure. My tablemate continued as she raised the hem of her dress up to her knees, "And I've been practicing. I've drawn a chain bracelet around each of my ankles and some pictures on my calves." Her legs were shapely; "very good" in male parlance, and the ballpoint pen drawings she displayed raised my self-esteem. She needed this course worse than I did.

The stories told by the rest of the class paled in comparison. One woman had been painting landscapes and wanted to expand her repertoire. Another, the youngest of the class, was an art major at the local Community College and was taking the class because none were offered at the college during the summer semester. I don't recall any details about the other women nor why they were taking the class.

The teacher, with great elaboration and precision, stood an egg - hard boiled I presumed 'cause it stood rigidly erect on its end - on a table that was covered with a white cloth, shined a 1,000 watt spotlight on the egg and said, "I want you to draw the egg with your pencil and show at least six different shades from white to black". I had prepared for this class by reading the book, Drawing on the Right Side of the Brain by Betty Edwards. The book offered drawing hints, techniques, and tricks to help beginners and engineers. Those were the people who when told, for example, to draw the table shown in a picture, knew what a table looked like and were likely to simply draw a stick figure with four legs and a flat top, without even looking at the table in the picture. The shoe fit so I considered a trick from the book that I thought useful when I read it. The book recommended turning the figure upside down so the object became "unrecognizable" and then drawing what you saw with special emphasis on the negative space where there was an absence of figure. I tried to visualize the egg upside down, but that did not help much. Moreover, I saw white, gray, and black and didn't know what three other shades she was talking about. I figured they must be those fancy shades women talk about like taupe, mauve and chartreuse?

There was no peer review during any of the classes. I do not know how the rest of the class performed; I only saw my drawings and those of my tablemate. We were both awful. She was however, serious about learning to draw and continually reminded the instructor before each session, "Don't forget to show us how this lesson (e.g., perspective) applies to drawing tattoos."

After this introductory drawing course that convince me that I could not draw and did not have time to learn during this lifetime, I decided to bypass drawing and go directly to painting. I was still determined to complete a painting that I would like to hang on my wall. With thoughtful (naive?) analysis I concluded that landscape painting probably did not require drawing skills so, I decided that would be the focus of my adventure into the visual arts. Some mistakes are simply too much fun to make only once.

Not long thereafter, while scrolling through the TV channels searching for something interesting to watch while having lunch, I luckily stumbled upon one of interest from among the 300 plus TV options. The program was *"The Joy of Painting"* on WHUT/PBS DC. The painter was Bob Ross. I watched with increasing fascination as he completed a landscape painting during the thirty-minute program and made it look easy. While painting, he continually interspersed his painting instructions with statements such as," So you can't draw a straight line; well there aren't many straight lines in nature." "In my opinion too much drawing, of any type, can make your painting look tight and over-worked." "You're not too old, nor do you lack the talent to learn to paint." "Paint like a child without fear or reservation and realize that talent is nothing more than a pursued interest." This was my defining moment and Bob Ross became my hero.

The program was regularly scheduled, became my favorite, and I watched Bob Ross paint a different, landscape painting each week. I taped a few of the programs and soon began trying to copy his technique. Watch him paint a sky. Stop the tape and paint a sky. Restart the tape. Watch him paint a mountain. Stop the tape and paint a mountain. Restart the tape. Watch him . . . etc.

During the next year I purchased his book and decided to attend one of his five-day classes in New Smyrna Beach. Florida. Before driving from my home in Virginia to Florida, I called the school to confirm my enrollment and inquire about the talent level and composition of the class. I was told there would be sixteen students in the class, talent levels unknown but unimportant, and that four students would be males: Jim, Bob, Antoine, and me. Having a French Canadian ancestry, I mentioned that I would be especially interested in meeting Antoine, whom I assumed was a Frenchman and likely from the Bayou of Louisiana. Always accommodating, I was told by the class organizer that she would seat us next to each other. Antoine, it turned out, was a short, dark skinned, mustached, Hispanic, originally from Jamaica, now living in Key West, FL. He spelled his name and signed his painting, "Ant-Juan." The people who populate the arts have a unique style and are unlike those who populate nuclear powered submarines!

As we painted side-by-side, Ant-Juan never stopped talking. He revealed that cooking was his claim to fame in his neighborhood and that his piece de resistance was "beer butt chicken." He explained in excruciating detail how he would, " . . . heat the grill, put an opened can of beer in the center, 'sit' a chicken over the can of beer, and let it cook. The evaporating beer, continually basting and flavoring the bird always resulted in a tasty and moist chicken." Despite my promise to Ant-Juan, I confess that I have not tried his recipe. However, both before and since, I have successfully marinated chicken in beer.

I considered my first Bob Ross, landscape, oil painting class a success. I proudly decorated my wall with my "final exam" painting of snow-covered mountains, painted the afternoon of day five, without assistance or guidance, in less than three hours. (I still think it looks pretty good!)

I found painting to be fun and signed up for an Arlington County sponsored, painting class when I returned to Virginia. Most beginning level classes focus on still-life painting. My painting improved and I learned tricks to overcome my lack of drawing expertise. A 4"x4" piece of glass lined horizontally and vertically, and used to view the subject to be painted, made "drawing" on a canvas that was similarly lined, tolerable. Over the next three years, I took advantage of the painting courses available through Arlington County, made another visit to Bob Ross' class in Florida, and eventually began taking courses at George

Mason University. Painting I, wine bottles and apples. Painting II, cow skulls and draped cloth. And then, Painting III, Figurative Painting, where all the students were art majors except me of course.

The first day of my Figurative Painting class, I followed the lead of the other students in the third floor art studio at George Mason University and set up an easel in front of a couch placed casually on a raised platform. As the instructor, Professor Chawky Frenn, briefed us on his expectations with respect to composition, value, hue, and texture, a co-ed quietly entered the room, selected a text book from her backpack, took a seat on the edge of the platform, and began to read. When the instructor finished briefing us, he turned to the co-ed and said that she could get ready to pose. In a single graceful motion, she stood and raised her green and gold George Mason University Tee-shirt over her shoulder length, honey-brown hair. She then unzipped her low rise, stone-washed, dungarees while kicking the dark blue, well-worn mules from her feet. Her skimpy, black, Victoria Secret bra and black thong with narrow lace border joined her other garments at her feet on the floor. (And don't tell me that men don't notice what women are wearing!)

She proceeded to stretch out comfortably on the couch while the Instructor moved portable lighting to best highlight shadows and angles. While this was going on, most students, actually all except me, were putting paint on their pallet and selecting brushes. I was staring in disbelief with my jaw agape having assumed that if she were going to pose naked, as I had only hoped, she would have retired to a private place to disrobe and reappear in a robe. Trying to assume the nonchalance of the other students, I realized that it could be hard to paint this semester. Pun intended!

After about forty minutes of painting, the Instructor told the model she could get up and stretch. He then told us that at each break during the three-hour class, we would view and critique each other's painting, beginning with the easel located at far left edge of our semi-circle around the couch. After the first painting's critique, as I turned to proceed to the next easel, I gently bumped someone. I began to apologize while continuing to turn only to see that it was the model. Buck naked, she was standing among the students listening to the critiques and smiling at her likeness or the lack of same, on the canvas. She was even bare footed on the paint splattered studio floor. It seemed to me that I was the only one in the room that was embarrassed by her nakedness. Why was I born so long ago?

As the only "adult" in the class, I became and remain friends with the Instructor. Since the course was free for me, a senior Virginia resident, not taking the course for credit, I was invited to return if desired. The course required that for four and a half hours every Wednesday, for three months, I had to do a painting of a naked coed. It's not easy, but it's a step every serious artist must go through. Realizing my need for additional painting practice, I found it necessary to take the course three times. I remained to a degree uncomfortable over the casual striptease I witnessed each Wednesday afternoon, but I only missed one class. I missed a class on a hot and humid July day in Virginia after leaving a telephone message for Professor Frenn informing him that I was taking "a snow day." I had learned that the model was going to be a male.

My painting must have improved because the gentlemen in my monthly poker group began arriving early so they could preview my latest work and hear about my ever-increasing exposure to body art and body piercing.

One evening, while I was in my card room setting up poker chips for the night's game, several players were critiquing my latest painting. As usual they were also making fun of my admission of discomfort with the model's blatant disrobing and indifferent nakedness. Eventually, I heard them coming towards me while loudly and laughingly shouting, "Hey Dick, we have another adventure for you".

Apparently their conversation that I had missed went something like this:

Player #1 "Dick's paintings are getting better. In fact some are really good."

Player #2 "I agree, but he keeps saying the model's nakedness bothers him. He's got to get over that."

Player #3 "Perhaps he'd get over it if he spent time at a nudist camp?"

Player #2 "That would be cool. I've often wondered if it's true that the only people who are nudists are those you would not care to see naked."

Player #1 "Well, purely for the sake of his art perhaps he should . . ."

Players in Unison "Hey Dick, we have another adventure for you."

When I heard their suggestion I thought, "Why not? It might be useful to my painting hobby and it would certainly be an adventure".

But that's another story!

In Pursuit of Artistic Composure

"If it was the fashion to go naked,
the face would be hardly observed."
Mary Wortley Montagu 1689 - 1762

My poker buddies tried to convince me that they thought I should spend a weekend at a nudist camp purely to help me overcome my admitted nervousness while painting nude coeds in art class. Yeah. Right! I'm quite certain their suggestion was motivated by a combination of, "I dare you," and "I've often wondered what it would be like. Try it and tell us." Whatever their motivation, I decided that it was an exciting idea, certainly an adventure, and perhaps even useful in my pursuit of artistic composure. (Age does not always bring wisdom; sometimes age comes alone!)

I had realized that painting women, clothed or unclothed, was a subject I enjoyed. Furthermore, all my instructors have recommended that students paint real life objects and live models rather than from pictures or photographs. With real life objects and people, the color variations are accurate, the light source is distinct, and going from 3-dimensions to a 2-dimensional canvas was the best training. Using a photo or picture (2-dimensions to 2-dimensions) is considered cheating, except for professionals.

I mentioned the idea to my unmarried, dance friends, Stan Crockett and Bob Bell, when I saw them at the next singles dance. Stan, the bashful, gentleman responded, "I can't believe you are considering such a thing. Do you think they are any nudist camps in the Virginia-Carolina area?" Bob, the hunter whose favorite color is camouflage, thought it was a great idea and volunteered, "I'll even loan you my hi-tech binoculars and camera." As his hunting instincts led him towards a short, blond, woman standing by the dance floor, he turned to utter a final thought, "It's also probably a wonderful place to find a woman and develop a meaningful overnight relationship."

With all that support, I made plans to spend a weekend working on overcoming my shyness with nudity and pursue artistic composure. A little research revealed a lot of information and a subculture population of unimagined size with facilities in everyone's backyard. My first discovery was that nudist clubs are either "non-landed" or "landed." The former consist of people who get together at a residence or travel together to nude beaches or nudist resorts. Landed clubs own and operate a nudist resort and typically have cabins, townhouses, campgrounds, restaurants, swimming pools, tennis courts, and recreation centers. I discovered to my surprise, that in Virginia there are non-landed clubs in Vienna, Merrifield, Leesburg, and Oakton, and a large, landed club in Ivor. In Maryland there are non-landed clubs in Baltimore and Linthicum Heights, and landed clubs in Davidsonville and Hancock. Pennsylvania has four non-landed and five landed clubs, and West Virginia has a large, landed club just over the Virginia border in Paw Paw. Not surprisingly, there are more landed clubs in the warmer weather States, (e.g., 16 in FL and 15 in CA), but colder locations are not exempt, (e.g., 5 in MI, 2 in MN, 3 in WI, 2 in MA, 2 in KS, 2 in Manitoba, and 3 in Ontario.) There are also nude cruises and travel that can be booked through agencies such as Bare Necessities Tour & Travel. (I know you were curious and wanted to know about all this!) By now, I considered my weekend adventure at a landed club rather tame and my worst fear became seeing someone I recognized.

While trying to make a reservation, I discovered that most clubs are family/couples oriented and many do not welcome single males. In virtually all cases entry requires membership in the American Association of Nude Recreation (AANR) at $60 per year. So I joined. I was eventually able to reserve a camper hookup site, for my Roadtrek RV in the Chesapeake, VA area, at the White Tail resort in Ivor, VA. Hopefully a location far enough away from Arlington to avoid meeting anyone I knew yet within a reasonable driving distance. It was also close to Bill and Linda Townsend's residence and I made arrangements to spend the night before my adventure with them. We spent the evening trying to imagine what my weekend would be like and reading the "Standards of Conduct" that I had received from the resort:

* When nude always carry your own towel to sit on.

* First time visitors are allowed a limited adjustment time while remaining clothed however, all pools, saunas, and hot tubs are nude use only.

*No camera, camera phone, photographic or video devices of any kind are allowed and will be confiscated.

*Do not approach or play with any unfamiliar children if you're an adult.

* Most people will use a first name only; do not solicit personal information.

In sum, it appeared, and I was to confirm, that nudist clubs are very private and conservative places. Except for the nakedness of course!

The next morning, beginning about 7:30 AM, my friends began preparing me for my adventure with a Bloody Mary, followed by a vodka & cranberry juice mixture, and ending with coffee laced with brandy. I was eventually fed a spectacular brunch and sent on my way, a little tipsy, for a noontime check-in.

The people frequenting nudist camps are of all types, shapes, sizes and ages. Most of the adults were in the 35– 70 age group and without clothing, a college professor indistinguishable from a sales clerk. Above all, the living is easy. Get up, take a towel, and go to the pool. When hungry, go to the outdoor bank of three or four showers, take a quick shower - often next to a naked woman - take your towel and go to the dining room or the bar for lunch. I witnessed naked tennis and pool volleyball, and played in a single elimination cribbage tournament. One stage of the tournament was particularly distracting because my female opponent, a bit less than average height, sitting very close to the table on a folding chair that did not raise her much above the table top, and possessing an ample bosom that was sagging slightly with age . . . Well, perhaps you get the picture? I acclimated to her breast bumping the cribbage board as she played her cards, but wasn't certain how Miss Manners would have advised me to move my peg when her anatomy rested comfortably over the hole it was to occupy. But hey, I was there to get over it!

At a separate dining facility away from the pool area they advertised a dinner dance party for Saturday evening. I went early to inquire if the people would be attending and dancing while naked. The waitress I spoke to said, "Some will be clothed and some will be naked. Typically, those who have been here all summer get dressed for a change and those here for a week or weekend will come naked." It made sense to me and that's what apparently occurred although 90% of the people were naked. That evening I saw naked couples dancing together to all types of ballroom dances, from slow numbers to swing and Latin. It is easy to imagine a situation when dancing with a partner, both naked, could be especially exciting, but instead, as I watched that evening I was simply in awe.

Overall, I found the atmosphere within the resort "charged," but not overtly sexual and for me it was liberating, a good experience, and a revealing adventure. Ah, to what lengths the artistically handicapped will go in their search for artistic skill!

The sum of my artistic training has resulted in my painting attaining at least a level of "acceptability." I have been qualified to teach the Bob Ross painting technique in both Landscape and Wildlife, and I have conducted such painting sessions for friends on several occasions. Most of my paintings, over fifty, reside on the walls of my home, but

I have sold seven paintings to friends and collectors, and completed three commissioned works. The subject of my paintings include still life, landscapes/seascapes, figures, wildlife and Trompe L'oeil ("fool the eye.") I remain a hobby painter, but one day would like to have a showing of my work. It's on my Bucket List.

Dance Host

"Adam was human, he didn't want the apple for the
apple's sake; he wanted it because it was forbidden."
Mark Twain 1835 - 1910

The Dance Host Idea

I was introduced to the single dance scene by Bob Bell, a classmate who was widowed a year before I. He arranged for me to be routinely invited by three groups that hosted single dances. Of the three, the Cosmopolitans was the best.

Bob was short, compact, and muscular. Always remembering the joy of his early years in rural Pennsylvania, when queried about his favorite activities, he would invariably respond, "I like to kill things. I hunt and fish." Direct and plodding, he was equally convincing when sweet-talking the girls and having people believe him when he said he didn't know something. He was comfortably retired after years as a Navy helicopter pilot, a career as a United Airline pilot, and selling a lumber mill and construction business that he had developed. He occasionally worked as a fishing and hunting guide, and proudly identified his favorite color as camouflage. Surprisingly, he was the consummate extrovert and thus a wonderful colleague at single events. Bob and I would meet at these single events and eventually became good friends with Stan Crockett, whom we saw frequently at these happenings.

Stan was tall and good looking with a full head of hair and winning smile. He had been widowed for five years. He was an extremely kind, recently retired, well spoken, but generally naive, man in his late 50s. He had been an office supplies salesman and had never been outside the USA. On occasion he required adult supervision! At one dance he returned from the dance floor and informed Bob and me that he was embarrassed because it had been necessary to apologized to the woman he'd just been dancing with because he had left his car keys in his pants pocket and she might have felt them while dancing and assumed he was getting excited. He even thought it necessary to take his keys from his pocket and show them to her. On another occasion he informed us that tonight he had met two women that he wanted to see again and that he had gotten telephone numbers from both of them. One especially held his interest and he planned to take her to dinner and a play at the Kennedy Center in Washington, DC. He made the arrangements, called her to make the date, and boasted to us of his excitement for the entire week before the event. He arrived at her home with his dinner reservations, theater tickets, and a bouquet of flowers. When she answered the door, he realized that he had called the wrong woman. He innocently related such stories routinely and his episodes stopped surprising us.

The Cosmopolitans held their Black Tie dances once per month at a DC area embassy and invited one hundred single, professional men and a similar number of single, professional women. Many of my competitors at these dances looked distinguished, wealthy, and handsome. The competition was tough. But, then I noticed that few of them knew how to dance. Recognizing the potential advantage I would have if I learned to dance, I decided to take lessons and learn three or four steps in each of the popular dances. Alas, I had found my niche! I avoided the big name, high priced dance studios in favor of the inexpensive, close to home, dance classes offered by Arlington and Fairfax Counties.

I initially registered for an eight-week class that met in the evening, once per week, at a local K-8 school. Dance classes, for the uninitiated male, are populated by many more women than men. During each class the men rotate among the women so that everyone gets to dance. They are a single man's dream location for meeting women. The classes quickly became the highlight of my weekly activity. Why had this been kept a secret from me? It was possible, one was even encouraged, to repeat a class or take a similar class at a new location with a different teacher, and different women - I mean students. I continued to take lessons whenever it fit my schedule, was soon mastering the basic steps in several dances, and found that I could seamlessly lead a woman through most of them. The women loved it and I was having a marvelous time.

Two of the women I met while taking dance lessons were memorable. I met Janice in one of my earliest dance classes. Rotating among the women, I continually recognized that Janice moved with the polish of an athlete, but lacked some of the natural grace and rhythm normally detectable when dancing with a woman. (No, she was not a drag queen. Shame on you!) She was of slightly above average height with short, curly, blond hair and was amply endowed with all the curves and bumps that make a woman attractive. During one lesson, as we danced easily around the dance floor, I inquired, "I bet that you were an athlete in college. Perhaps a swimmer?"

She responded, "Yes. I was a college athlete, but not a swimmer."

"What sport did you play?"

After a brief pause, she replied, "I won't tell you."

I sensed that was the end of the conversation and we finished the dance in silence.

The last night of that dance class six of us, including Janice, retired to a local restaurant for coffee and dessert. At one point the conversation turned to job descriptions and Janice mentioned that she was in the midst of a career change. She had recently completed her training as a massage therapist and had quit her old job. She turned to me and revealed, "I'm sorry about not telling you about the sport I played in college; I was embarrassed to tell you while the class was ongoing. I went to Penn State and was the shot putter on the women's track team. I was also about forty pounds heavier and didn't have much of a social life. That's why I was in the dance class." I recognized this as an occasion when silence was my preferred response so I let others carry the conversation. Later, I wished her well in her career change, mentioned that I had never had a massage and asked her "If you are looking for business, would you consider me as a client?"

"Certainly," she answered reaching into her handbag, "here's my card. Give me a call for an appointment."

I made the appointment and she forewarned me that the address was her third floor apartment. She said that she had converted a spare bedroom into her massage studio and that I should come right up and knock on the door. I was surprised that a woman would invite clients to her apartment, but what did I know? I arrived precisely on time and my knock was answered immediately. Entering her apartment I could not help noticing the plaques and paraphernalia on the walls and my concerns about her safety immediately vanished. There were awards for achieving Black Belt status in Karate and Jujitsu, a sword with a five foot blade that I assumed was used in some oriental martial art, and a photograph of her receiving a trophy while dressed in the loose black pants and black belted shirt worn by a martial art master. I was certainly going to behave.

Her massage studio was soothingly decorated with pastel colors, large posters of serene scenes, the soft incantation music of the Far East, and a comfortably warm temperature. The message table occupied the center of the studio. I told her that I had no physical problems that should concern her and signed the waiver form. She then looked towards the certificates displayed on an adjacent wall and asked what type of massage I wanted? As she nodded towards each certificate in turn she mentioned that she was qualified to give Sacrocranial Massages, Swedish Massages, Sports Massages, Reflexology, and Deep Muscle Massages. She may have mentioned others, but I was a novice who thought a massage was a massage and stopped counting. Apparently because it was mentioned last and was therefore most prominent in my mind, I stated with the confidence of an expert, "A Deep Muscle Massage would be nice."

If you have never had a Deep Muscle Massage, don't expect to relax and fall asleep. Stretched out on my stomach with my face in the donut shaped pad at the end of the massage table, I soon had tears in my eyes from the pain. My testosterone wouldn't let me cry "Uncle" to a woman, but I couldn't help wondering: "Why does she hate me?" "How did this woman get so strong?" "Why does she want to hurt me so badly?" "She must have thrown the 12 pound rather than the 8 pound shot." "I'll bet she can crack open a lobster with her hands." To my great relief, the hour eventually ended. I paid, said, "Thank you" and left making certain that I did not try to lift my shoulders. Later that day, I felt amazingly limber, but not to the extent that I wanted to schedule another massage.

My second massage did not occur for several months. I went back to Janice following a very competitive racket ball game immediately upon returning from a two-week ski trip and my lower back was painfully stiff. I told her that I wanted her to loosen up my lower back and admitted that my first massage had been a very painful experience. She apologized and made me promise to tell her if she was being too strong and vigorous. I have since learned that is the correct thing to do. My second massage was a wonderful success. I am an advocate and have enjoyed many more massages, 'though none subsequently with Janice. When I have no specific ache or pain, I have had success answering the question, "What type of massage do you want?" with, "Just put me to sleep."

The other woman of note that I met dancing was Vicky. Ron Hinkel's wife, Barbara, was teaching Etiquette & Cotillion Classes for children. She told me of her friend and assistant who had begun taking dance lessons through the Fairfax County Park Authority with the goal of becoming a dance instructor, but who had stopped because, "The guys kept hitting on her." Barbara suggested that if I wanted simply to dance, she would arrange for me to meet Vicky. The offer was appealing because having a partner would significantly expand the available dance classes, because most evening and advanced classes specified, "couples only." I was mildly concerned about my reputation with women and queried Barbara about her, "If I simply wanted to dance," comment. Her reply was, "Vicky is married and has three children. Her husband is an Australian, rugby player, who refuses to dance because it's not macho."

Vicky and I met and we quickly became friends. She was tall, slim, energetic, and graceful. We danced together as partners, on and off, for three years. Neither of us was interested in competitive dancing; we simply wanted to learn additional and more advanced steps, and we enjoyed dancing together. Typically, I would join her once per week for a two-hour lesson at a County sponsored dance class. During the rest of the week she would pursue her dream of becoming a dance instructor by having at least one private lesson and several group lessons at the dance studio where she eventually became a dance instructor. During our classes together, we were usually able to perform a new dance step after only a few attempts and while the other couples in the class were trying to catch up, we would retire to a corner of the dance floor and she would show me the new steps she had learned during her private lesson the past week. She was becoming the dance teacher and it was a wonderful learning experience for me.

Eventually our dance time together was replaced by her schedule as a dance instructor with paying customers. I am proud to say that I was able to assist her on a couple of occasions when she began teaching and needed a partner/assistant. I even joined her once when she was hired to teach a one hour rumba and cha cha class to the staff of a large legal firm whose employees had requested the dance lesson instead of being taken out to lunch on Secretary's Day. I learned to love dancing in large part because of her. Several years after I had last seen her, I happened upon a book, on the history of ballroom dancing, that I was pleased to send her. I inscribed it with, "Thank you for teaching me the wisdom and accuracy of this book's title." The title was, "Dance: Three Minutes of Intimacy." I hope she still has it?

Alone again without a dance partner, I returned to the dance classes for singles whenever my schedule permitted. At the conclusion of one of these classes, the instructor informed the class that he was arranging a dance cruise. There would be dancing every evening and he would be giving dance lessons aboard ship. He continued with, "Don't you single women worry about coming unescorted because there will be dance hosts aboard the ship." Sensing another possible adventure, I approached the Instructor after class to inquire about this dance host thing? I was told that a man willing to dance with unescorted women could get a free cruise as a dance host. He also told me the web site where I could get more information. I checked it out and thought it would be an exciting adventure, not the least of which would be to see if I could pull it off. A short time later, at a Cosmopolitan Dance at the Embassy of Austria, I mentioned it to Bob and Stan. Stan knew about the program and revealed that he had tried to get into the program three years ago, but couldn't pass the dance test. I argued persuasively that he was a much better dancer now and how much fun we could have. He finally agreed that he needed a change (recently dumped by girlfriend) and would join me in my dance host adventure.

Dance Host Qualifications

The elite company providing dance hosts to cruise ships was Lauretta Blake's, Working Vacation, Inc. They had a contract to provide dance hosts to most of the quality cruise lines that used dance hosts, e.g., Radisson, Crystal, and Cunard Cruise Lines.

Their procedure for becoming a dance host involved three steps: submit a resume, pass a dance test, and be deemed acceptable after a personal interview. The resumes were meant to determine if the applicant would be able to converse intelligently with the cruise ship passengers. Both of our resumes were favorably received and we were directed to take the dance test.

The dance studio in our area that administered dance tests for the Working Vacation was the, In Step Dance Studio, in Fairfax, VA. The test consisted of recognizing the music (e.g., beats 3/4 or 4/4 time) and the dance (e.g., foxtrot or rumba or waltz, etc.); and demonstrating knowledge of proper dance hold, body position, frame, line of dance, and the ability to lead while dancing with the lead instructor/studio owner. During each of six dances, three smooth (foxtrot, waltz, and swing) and three Latin (rumba, cha-cha, and mambo or tango) we were to demonstrate a minimum of five Bronze (basic) Level steps in each of the dances. I made reservations for us to take the test two days later and learned that each test would take about 30 minutes and would cost each of us the standard price for a 30-minute private lesson. It was at this point that Stan reminded me that he had failed the Latin dance portion of his previous dance tests and that he didn't think he had improved sufficiently to pass the test now. The two nights before our dance test, in my back room, with all the blinds firmly closed and the draperies tied shut; I tried to help him learn five basic Latin dance steps. He could smoothly follow the rhythm and women enjoyed dancing Latin dances with him, but he did not know any of the required steps. I was concerned that he would not be able to join me on this adventure.

We arrived for our scheduled dance test and each paid $60 for the thirty minutes it would take to be tested. Grades were given on a scale of 1- 4 for each dance. We learned that a two was weak, a three was strong, and a four was given to potential dance instructors. I assume that a one meant that the ability of the applicant was limited to finding the dance floor? I volunteered to be tested first and at the conclusion was informed that I had passed nicely. I watched as Stan preformed the smooth dances like Fred Astaire and the Latin dances like Peter Sellers as Inspector Clouseau. When his test was finished he was informed that he had not done very well in the Latin dances. I appreciated that, "*his momma hadn't raise no dummy*," as he replied, "It will be quite some time before I am scheduled to go aboard ship as a dance host and until then I'd like to take private lessons from you. I'm certain that with you as my teacher I will improve; so why don't you tell them that I'm passable?" It was not long before we received notification that we should come to Chicago for our face-to-face interview.

We purchased a one day, round trip flight to Chicago, met the women president of Working Vacations, Inc. and were visually inspected - we were wearing our best suit, white shirt, matching socks, a neck tie, and shoes. (I was reminded how women must feel when ogled by guys.) Following inspection and a brief conversation, we were told that our background report was satisfactory, (Since 9/11 a record check from state motor vehicle, credit, and criminal agencies was required.) that we were now accepted as dance hosts, and that my dance test score qualified me to give basic dance lessons. Cruise ships using dance hosts request a minimum of two. The QE II that has two ballrooms, two orchestras, and was cruising between London and New York without a port stop, was requesting twelve dance hosts. I confidently and innocently announced that, "Stan and I are ready to go and we would like to go together on a ship cruising in the Mediterranean Sea."

"Everyone wants the Mediterranean cruises, neither of you are experienced as dance hosts, and Stan didn't score very well in the Latin dances," was the reply. "However", she continued while looking directly at me, "a dance host scheduled to go on the Alaska cruise aboard the Radisson's Seven Seas Navigator recently had to cancel. The ship leaves in three weeks from Los Angeles and the cruise ends 31 days later in Vancouver, BC. If you take the trip you will work with two different dance hosts, one during each 15-day period. You will then be experienced and I will assign you and Stan to a Mediterranean Cruise."

I accepted and signed a contract. In addition to agreeing to the cruise dates and port of embarkation, the contract specified that: I would assembled a wardrobe according to an attached list of required clothing (black tuxedo, white dinner jacket, blue blazer, tan dress trousers, white dress shirts, etc.), would provide a written biography for shipboard use, and would treat all female passenger equally with no display of favoritism, and I would avoid any romantic involvement. That last requirement was detailed in no less than five pages of text. My cost for the cruise was $25 per day payable to Lauretta Blake. In return I received round trip airfare (standard for all trips over 21 days long,) all meals and amenities, $15 per day bar allowance (wine was included with dinner,) $5 per day for laundry and dry cleaning, a 20% discount on anything purchased onboard, and free shore excursions if they did not involve a helicopter flight and space was available.

We were in the queue and my dancing adventure was about to begin.

Dance Cruise to Alaska

My first contract as a dance instructor & dance host was to Alaska aboard the Radisson's Seven Seas Navigator during May and June 2002. I boarded in Los Angeles sailed North to Anchorage and back down to Vancouver, BC where I disembarked.

I learned some interesting facts about life in the far north, saw some interesting sites, and had a pair of exciting adventures. Dancing was at a minimum because there were only three sea days during the 32-day trip, and the ship was small with a maximum of 530 passengers. There were two couples that made it interesting for me. The first was a young couple that wanted to develop and learn a dance routine for their upcoming wedding. They wanted to dance to a traditional waltz and we worked together. By the end of their cruise they were accomplished and confident. The second couple was older. I met them one evening in response to the rather abrupt request, "Hey, dancer. Will you please dance with my wife? She really wants to dance, keeps bugging me, and I don't dance." I complied - he had been in the Marine Corps - and we became friends. I spent considerable time with them at their table in the lounge and danced frequently with his lovely wife.

Alcatraz

The ship's first stop on the way north was San Francisco. I took a tour of Alcatraz, *"the Rock,"* found it interesting and highly recommend it. Some of America's hardest criminals were imprisoned there and I toured the cells occupied by Al *"Scarface"* Capone, George *"Machine Gun"* Kelly, and Robert Stroud, aka, *"the Bird Man of Alcatraz,"* but even more exciting was walking the escape routes of the fourteen escape attempts by a total of thirty-six men. Two inmates tried to escape twice and five were never seen or heard from again and are presumed to have drowned. Only one convict, John Paul Scott, is known to have survived the swim to San Francisco, but was captured on the rocks underneath the Golden Gate Bridge, near death from exhaustion and exposure, and too weak to crawl out of the water.

Ketchikan's Brown Bears

In Ketchikan I hiked with a native guide to the earliest settlement from the gold rush days. Many of the buildings are now native craft shops and boutiques, but a few maintain their original purpose. One old time establishment that I visited, but where I spent no money, was "Betty's House Of Negotiable Affection."

At Ketchikan's northern latitude the summer sunlight was lasting from 5 AM until 11 PM during my visit and consequently we passed many large plants. I had a photo taken standing behind a rhubarb plant and only my head is visible. We passed skunk cabbage plants that were sufficiently large and odorous to believe a skunk had recently sprayed the area. (More about skunk cabbage later.)

During the hike, we passed a bear's hibernation "cave," that was actually a hole dug under a large fallen tree and that prompted the guide to reveal some important knowledge about bears. The brown bear resembles its close relative the black bear, but is usually larger. The tern "brown bear" refers to the species found in coastal areas where salmon is the primary food source. Brown bears in Alaska that are living inland and in northern habitats are often called "grizzlies." In the wild, male brown bears live about 22 years and females about 26 years. Brown bears have an especially good sense of smell and under the right conditions can detect an odor a mile away. Their hearing and eyesight are about like humans. When a bear stands upright, it is not to get ready to charge, but to test the wind and see better.

In the summer, most mature, male bears weigh between 500 and 900 pounds, with females weighing half to three-quarters as much. When standing on it's hind feet, an Alaskan brown bear is about nine feet tall. Young are born in a winter den and weigh less than one pound. One to four cubs are common with two being most popular. Cubs separate from their mother as 2-year olds. Like humans, bears consume a wide variety of foods: berries, grasses, fish, ground squirrels, roots and plants. They can also kill and consume moose and caribou.

In the winter they spend 5 - 7 months hibernating in their winter den. Prior to hibernating a bear alters its diet to include bones, sticks, and dirt, to plug them up and avoid having a bowel movement in their cave. When hibernation ends, bear are ornery, not only because they are hungry, but because they are plugged up. The seedpods in the center of the skunk cabbage plant are a natural laxative and bears look for it. The plant's smell keeps animals other than bears away, so locals who go into the woods fishing or hunting in the springtime watch carefully to see if the pods of the skunk cabbage plants have been eaten to determine the presence of bears.

Sitka's Bald Eagles

In Sitka, I visited a salmon cannery to see eagles. Sounds strange, but 'tis so! The cannery, periodically dumped the unused parts of the canned salmons, e.g., heads, tails, and guts, into the bay. I counted 30 fish hunting, bald eagles in nearby trees, flying overhead, and diving for discarded salmon parts. Local citizens who had come to watch the feeding frenzy, claimed that some of the eagles have taken up permanent residence in the trees around the cannery, but agreed that most of the eagles had simply come for the dinning experience. I learned that the bald eagle, named for its conspicuous white head and tail, does not get those white feathers until age five years. Prior to that, its brown head often causes it to be misidentified as a soaring, golden eagle of the interior. The bald eagle is Alaska's largest resident bird of prey with wingspan reaching seven and one-half feet and weighing 10 - 14 pounds. Bald eagles are found only in North America, mate for life, and typically nest two eggs. Like most raptors, female eagles are about three times larger and more aggressive hunters than males.

Dog Mushing

From Juneau, I took a twenty-minute helicopter ride to the Juneau Ice Field, an area about the size of New Hampshire that has been the origin of over 40 glaciers, for a day of dog sledding. Six, independent, serious "mushers," living in tents, had flown in over 240 dogs to the site for summer training. Since everything had to be flown in, some of them relished the opportunity to make some money by hosting a tourist for half a day. I was paired with a 17-year-old Alaskan boy. He lived with his parents, "quite a few miles" further north, in a house that was 72 miles from the nearest neighbor and twelve miles from the nearest road - reached only by snowmobile or dog sled. He was home schooled for three hours per day. His father was a veterinarian who would travel to the main road twice a week, meet someone in a four wheeled drive vehicle for a ride to an airport, and fly to local villages to care for their animals. The boy was anxious to reach age 18 so he could participate in senior races like the Iditarod. (The Iditarod Sled Dog Race occurs annually in early March. It begins in downtown Anchorage and ends at Front Street in Nome, 1,100 miles and 10 - 17 days later. About 70 teams from around the world compete.) The boy claimed that his #1 dog team had taken him 120 miles in one day during a recent race. He rested his dogs for 15 - 20 minutes every forty miles and said that if he had a champion team it would be able to go 160 - 180 miles in a day. Having a father who was a veterinarian probably helped, but this boy really knew his dogs. He could tell when one of his dogs was not quite pulling its load, which was not apparent to me even when he pointed it out, and he would holler something meant specifically for that dog, and get a response. He also sensed when the dogs were getting hot and in need of a rest - "the amount or lack of frost on their muzzle", he told me. During rest periods the dogs would roll in the snow to cool down and eat snow to hydrate. With the two of us in a single sled, rotating periodically between sitting in the "basket" and standing on the sled runners, twelve dogs, harnessed as six pairs, were pulling us, over level ground, at about 15 miles per hour - according to the boy whom I found totally credible and knowledgeable. His orders to the lead dogs were sharp and clear, but unintelligible, e.g., RA, RA, RA or HE, HE, HE, but the dogs knew that one meant turn left and follow the trail and the other meant turn left and make a new trail. He had harnessed his current lead dog on the left, front side and an 18 month old "lead dog trainee" to its right. We traveled beyond site of the camp and with absolutely no landmarks, he always knew the direction and distance back to camp. The dogs undoubtedly knew their way back to camp also. I was completely lost. They probably could have returned to camp on their own while I saw only frozen, flat, white landscape in every direction. Sled dogs are well cared for and treated kindly, but like animals not house pets. They are not as large as I imagined, but much stronger than one would anticipate from the size of the animal. Returning to camp, I was invited to follow the young man to a pen with a mother and three, 7-week old pups. He said that he had bred them from two of his best and smartest dogs and hoped at least one of them would become a lead dog. He was very proud of what he was doing and clearly had a goal. It was a fascinating and educational day, in a very harsh environment, with an amazing young man.

Mendenhall Glacier Hiking

Glacier hiking also involved a helicopter ride, away from civilization. For this excursion I was outfitted with outerwear, hard shell boots, crampons, a harness, an ice axe, a helmet, and a hip pack with water and a snack. Three small tents had been set up at the helicopter-landing site on the Mendenhall Glacier and that's where guides checked our gear and gave safety instructions. *"When on a glacier, if you are with a group always walk in the footprints of the person in front of you. Never walk on snow, because it may be new and it may cover a chasm. There are two kinds of chasms, 'catchers' and 'keepers.' Guides carry 40 feet of rope. If you fall into a chasm and are within 40 feet of the surface, that's a 'catcher,' deeper than that and it's a 'keeper.'"* When we began our trek we selected a peak about 100 yards away as our target. The guide would poke the ground with the handle of his ice axe before every step that was not obviously, solid ice. We would be forced to change course every 15 - 20 feet because of a chasm. We walked for one full hour to get to the peak that was our target. It was slow, boring, and could be dangerous, but the blue colors that were visible when looking down onto a chasm were clear, bright, and unmatched. It was the heavily packed ice, under great compression forces that created the unique, blue colors. Been there, done that, no interest in another glacier hike.

Skagway, Alaska

A day in Skagway is a history lesson. I had an underwhelming lunch at a restaurant with opaque, smoked (dirty?) windows that advertised, "Cheap Food on Real Plates" and rode the train that now parallels the Chilkoot Trail, of Klondike Gold Rush fame. The train started in Liarsville at the foot of the Chilkoot Trail. The town was named by the gold seekers when they noticed that this was as far as the newspaper reporters went, but reported "from the gold-rush fields," anyway. The train ride ended at White Pass Summit, on the US - Canadian border, overlooking the Chilkoot Pass. Experienced hikers can hike the trail (16 miles from the trail head up to Chilkoot Pass) for a small fee. A maximum of fifty hiking permits are granted each day. Those seeking gold had to hike down the far side of the mountain to the gold fields.

Dance Cruise in the Mediterranean

Stan and I did get to cruise the Mediterranean together. It was aboard the Radisson's, Seven Seas Mariner from August 23 - September 29, 2002. The Mariner could host 750 passengers, a bit larger than the Navigator's 530, but was still a small ship. Our contract was for thirty-six days, that included several 7, 10, and 14-day passenger cruise segments. During the 36 days, we spent only two days without a port stop, when we had to provide a one-hour dance lesson. We boarded in Stockholm, Sweden and went as far south as Sicily with stops in Estonia, St. Petersburg, Germany, the Normandy Coast of France, Spain, Portugal, the French Riviera, Monaco, and Italy. From Sicily we backtracked finally disembarking in Nice, France.

Every day was a highlight and I did send e-mail reports back to friends, who in turn addressed their responses to "the Dancing Gigolo." (I think that got started after someone watched the humorous movie, Out To Sea, where Walter Matthau and Jack Lemon become dance hosts.) There were many unescorted women on this cruise - several who confessed that they only went on cruise ship that provided dance hosts - consequently Stan and I danced every night from the time the band began until it stopped.

We also complied with a request to host a "Singles Table" with seats for ten, each evening. The Maitre D used it if a person arrived alone for dinner because of a sick or otherwise detained spouse and did not want to dine alone, but mostly it was filled with the single women on board. We had a great table, allowed no bitching, and encouraged funny stories and jokes. During one dinner the women were discussing the availability (or lack thereof) of single men where they lived. One woman who was quoting statistics on the subject indicated a young women at the table who was known to be from Alaska and said, "Most places single men outnumber single women by about six or eight to one, but in Alaska you have it made with a ratio of ten or twelve to one."

The response was, "Where I come from in Alaska we say, 'The odds are good, but the goods are odd.' That's because the only men that come to Alaska are either escaped felons, hunters, fishermen, or gold miners."

Another woman, from Washington, DC added, "In DC they say the odds are pretty good, but they include in their count, gay men and men in prison. And DC has plenty of both."

Neither Stan nor I considered that bitching and simply enjoyed the repartee.

Other "highlights" include Stan getting lost in the Hermitage Museum in St. Petersburg, Russia and missing the tour bus back to the ship. In his defense the museum is one of the largest in the world, boasts over three million items on display and it has been estimated that it would take eleven years to spend one minute viewing each item. In one of the souvenir/gift shops, Stan selected an item he wanted to purchase then while he stood in a long line to pay for the item, the tour moved on. I looked for him after noticing that he was missing, but we never did reconnect.

On another occasion, while walking on a beach in northern Germany, Stan became mesmerized by the splendid sites during his first visit to a topless beach and inadvertently stepped on the extended leg of a large size, male sunbather who jumped up cursing and chased Stan several meters down the beach. We refer to this as, the German Giant episode.

Through all of our adventures together Stan and I remain loyal and trusted friends. He's a great guy who happens to be single at the moment and I wonder if he has recently considered a return to the adventures of cruise ship dancing? I will ask him the next time we speak.

The overall, singular highlight of my second, and final, cruise as a dance host was meeting Becky, my future wife. She came aboard in Nice with a girl friend for a two-week cruise segment during our southern excursion towards Sicily. She dined at our singles table a few times, and we crossed paths occasionally while sightseeing ashore, but we never danced. She was adamant about, "I will never wait in a line of women for a dance. There are a lot of other things I'd rather be doing." Her final night onboard, during a small gathering when Stan and I were saying our "good byes" to the departing passengers, she gave me her telephone number and offered to give me a city tour if I ever came to New York City. And that's a later story!

Ancestry
"My folks didn't come over on the *Mayflower*,
but they were there to meet the boat."
Will Rogers 1879 - 1935

PARISEAU

A great aunt in the Pariseau clan, whom I had never met, commissioned the Genealogical Society of Montreal, Canada to trace her family roots. The resulting report, written in 1946, is in French. My Dad inherited the book in the 1990s, after his aunt died, and I now have it in my possession.

The book indicates that the first Pariseau to come to North America was Jean Delpue dit Dalpe-Parisot-Pariseau. He was born in 1648, the son of Jean Delpue and Marguerite Delnat in Rodez, France. He arrived in Canada in 1665 as a seventeen-year-old soldier in the LaFreydiere Company of the Carignan Regiment that was sent to "New France" to fight the Iroquois, Indians. His company landed in Quebec and camped in Montreal during the winter of 1665-66. The campaign ended in 1668 and the regiment was discharged. He was one of 400 soldiers that remained in Canada and became settlers. On November 19, 1674, at age 26, he married 17 year old, Renee Lorion, in Montreal. They had eight children and two of the sons; Francois and Pierre married and are the ancestors of the Dalpe and Pariseau families. Jean Dalpue dit Pariseau was killed in combat with the Iroquois on July 2, 1690 and a monument has been erected at the battle site at Point-aux-Trembles. The battle occurred during the King William's War (1689 - 1697) that was the early round of the French and Indian Wars.

In June 2000, I went to France to visit the town of Rodez. The town is 335 miles South of Paris. I found no "Pariseaus" in the town's telephone book and was told that the "eau" ending came from Canada. The name Parisot (the "t" is silent, i.e., pronounced "pariso") was popular and I was directed to the town of Parisot about 10 miles west of Rodez. It is a charming, hilltop, town with a lake that is a popular site for an afternoon picnic.

On my "bucket list" is to follow up on Jean Delpue dit Pariseau's history, visit the battle monument where he died, and try to discover how my family came to settle in Massachusetts.

LeBLANC

What I know about my Mother's background is that she was born, Viola Elizabeth LeBlanc, in Cocagne, New Brunswick, Canada. Her mother's maiden name (and my namesake) was Delina Richard. She had five sisters (Julie, Sara, Arlene, Alida, and Sally) and two brothers (Philip and Al.) Her father, George LeBlanc was a farmer and lobsterman.

What I heard was that the boys wanted to come to America, her father said they would all go or no one would go, a family meeting was held around the kitchen table and as a result they came to America. They arrived in Boston aboard the ship, the Governor Dingley, in

September 1923. Mom was ten years old. Her father had a brother living in North Attleboro and they settled there.

My first attempt to learn more was an Elderhostel Course, called Acadian History & Culture that I took at the University of Maine at Presque Isle, Maine.

Acadia was a colony of New France in northeastern North America that included parts of eastern Quebec, the Maritime Provinces, and modern day Maine to the Kennebec River. In the 1600s, there was no famine, or plague in France and if you were catholic you had religious freedom. Life was good. Lords with money recruited skilled, literate people (e.g., bankers, hunters, bakers, builders) to come to America for adventure. If they organized a voyage the King would give them monopolistic rights, e.g., the fur trade in a large designated area for ten years. The Acadians came from the Loire River valley area of France, - the provinces of Poitou, Anjou, Tourane - and sailed to America from the port of La Rochelle. The French from the provinces along the Seine River, (Brittany, Normandy, and Isle de France, now Paris) sailed from the port of Le Havre and went to Quebec. Quebec has been a city since 1608, the British came to Jamestown, Virginia in 1607.

The early French settlers were men only. In 1636 families began arriving including a Scottish gentleman who had put together a trip and who settled in the area now called Nova Scotia. The Scotch and Irish were welcomed in Acadia because, like the French, neither liked the English.

The Micmac Indians in Acadia were friendly to the Acadians and according to the Canadian Mounted Policeman, dressed in a bright red uniform, who lectured the Elderhostel Class one day, there were several reasons the Indians preferred the French over the English. (1st) The French settled on the marshlands that the Indians did not use. The settlers from the Loire River area knew how to build dikes to keep the marsh area from flooding and wore wooden shoes to keep their feet dry. They planted sea grass to absorb the salt and discovered that young cattle that had not tasted sweet grass would eat it. After two years the French pulled the sea grass out by the roots and planted crops. They never had a crop failure and got very rich trading with the colonialists in Boston. The English went into the forest and cut down trees to build a settlement. (2nd) The French philosophy of colonization was to adapt to the land and local people. They mixed easily with the Indians, traded with them as equals, and even married them. The English philosophy was to make a little England wherever they went. They considered the Indians of lesser class and kept them at arms length. (3rd) The French made extensive use of water transportation while the English used the Indian's trails. The English acknowledged that Acadian women were better at handling and rowing a canoe than English men. (4th) While Captain Weymouth of the Royal Navy was capturing five Indians for the King's zoo and throwing a baby overboard to see if it had an innate ability to swim, the French Jesuits were converting the Indians and telling them that the Virgin Mary was French and that the English had crucified Christ.

In 1710, Acadia fell to the British for the final time.

In 1752, the Acadians refused to take an oath of allegiance to Britain because they feared they would have to fight against their brethren in Quebec. In fact, no Catholics were allowed in the British army at this time.

In 1755 the grand deportation of 14,000 Acadians from Nova Scotia began. To avoid deportation 6,500 escaped to New Brunswick.

Fearless Canadian Drivers

When the course ended my plan was to drive to see the home site in New Brunswick where my mother was born. I began my drive in the early morning well before sunrise in the rain. I knew that I was relatively close to the border and was watching for a sign indicating that I was crossing into Canada. I drove for over an hour along two lane, curving roads with dense forests on both sides surprised at the speed limits that I could barely maintain even though I was in a hurry. As the weather cleared and I was getting accustomed to the high speed Canadian driving, I passed a small sign that indicated the distance to the next town as 38 kilometers. It finally dawned on me; the speed limits had been in kilometers per hour not miles per hour. The 55 miles per hour limit that I was trying to maintain was really 55 kilometers per hour or 33 miles per hour. No wonder I thought these Canadians were heavy-footed, fearless drivers.

The LeBlanc House

The nearest city of size, to where my mother was born, is Moncton and the nearest town is Shediac. My immediate destination was the house that my mother's brother Alphonse (Al) had built. It was "across the street" from the original homestead. Al had recently died but his wife, Mary, was expecting me. I was following handwritten directions and a rough, pencil drawn map to her house, because I would not be asking for directions. No, in this case it was not, "a guy thing," it was because my brother was here several years ago, and stopped in at a store in Shediac to get directions to, "Alphonse LeBlanc's residence." The proprietor asked him if he wanted Alphonse LeBlanc the fireman, the fisherman, the barber, the lawyer, the carpenter, or the undertaker?

Mary's house was across the street from several acres of well-ordered and tended farmland hosting a crop of potatoes and other vegetables. The field extended from the road to a cliff overlooking the Northumberland Strait with Prince Edward Island a blur on the horizon. Mary walked with me to the back of the field by the cliff and showed me the remnants of a house foundation and chimney.

Mary had decided that we would have lobsters and green beans for dinner. I was given a cooking pan, directed to a trap door at the end of the hallway, and told to, "Go down into the cellar and get some green beans." It was an old fashion root cellar with a dirt floor and little headroom. Among the stored and well-marked items was a barrel of fresh green beans preserved in heavily salted brine. The beans would be soaked to remove the salt while we went for the lobsters.

With a bottle of Jack Daniel's Tennessee Whiskey in hand she drove to a small harbor crowded with boats unloading their catch. She took me to meet a friend who was unloading his boat behind a fish market. I was introduced, brief pleasantries and the bottle of whiskey were exchanged, and we were told, " All those baskets of lobsters with the blue tags are mine; help yourself." We each ate a three-pound lobster for dinner that evening.

A LeBlanc "cousin" resided in the house adjacent to the farmland. We enjoyed a very pleasant and informative visit to their house while food, drink, and stories flowed like a tidal bore.

Overall, I found the people friendly and the area fresh and healthy, but no one spoke much about their winters. It will be thrilling to return during a serious, genealogical hunt.

65th Wedding Anniversary

In April of 2001 we celebrated Mom and Dad's 65th wedding anniversary with a large contingent of Pariseaus and LeBlancs. On April 6th, Dad had his ninetieth birthday and on May 13th, we would celebrate the fourth anniversary of Mom's 22nd birthday. Prepared to go to the celebration we took a photograph in the family living room.

"Mom and Dad's 65th Wedding Anniversary"
Left to right, Bob, Mom, Lynne, Dad, Joan, Dick.
(Personal Photo)

Volunteer Tutor

"Everyone is ignorant, only in different subjects."
Will Rogers 1879 - 1935

Have you ever had so much fun that you felt guilty? In my case it led to an unexpected adventure.

About my third year as a middle-age bachelor, I was crossing items off my bucket list at a rapid pace and began feeling that my recent pleasures, e.g., attending a Rose Bowl Game in Pasadena, CA, skiing in St. Moritz, Switzerland, and going to Rio de Janeiro, Brazil for Carnival (Mardi Gras), were not being balanced by my recent volunteer work. I had been delivering Meals on Wheels for Our Lady of Lourdes Church and teaching a course at Arlington's Learning in Retirement program, but decided I should add something else. My search led me to volunteer as a tutor in the Alternative Education Program. The program covers a wide variety of learning, from helping adults learn to read or pass a high school equivalency exam, to tutoring school children who are missing classes because they are in a hospital or must remain at home because of an accident or are in a drug rehabilitation program.

After calling to volunteer, I appeared for two, lengthy, personal interviews, filled out the necessary mountain of government forms, agreed to another background check and to be fingerprinted, again. (I assumed that much of this was because I may be tutoring children.)

For at least six weeks I heard nothing. Late one afternoon while greeting the poker players for our monthly game, my house telephone rang. A poker player answered thinking it was another player calling to say he would be late. It was a gentleman from the Alternative Education Program. When I got the telephone he asked if I could teach math, including calculus. I assured him that I could and was then told, "We need you right away to tutor math in the Women's Juvenile Detention Center in Fairfax, VA. Can you begin tomorrow?"

"A Women's Prison? I come from a family of teachers and their worst nightmare is trying to teach a class where one or more students are disruptive and uninterested. I can't imagine what it's like in a prison."

"I assure you that will not be a problem. Tomorrow afternoon from 1 - 4. The building is adjacent to the Fairfax courthouse. Park under the building where the sign says, 'Police & Staff Only.' Get there a little early; someone will meet you. Can we count on you?"

I said, "Yes," and hung up the telephone.

Joining the players, now seated around the poker table, I was asked, "What was that all about?"

"They want me to tutor math in a women's prison."

Through the simultaneous eruption of laughter, comments, questions, and advise, that lasted for several minutes, I heard: "Are you kidding me?" "Your reputation with women is going to suffer when word gets out that you are doing this to find a date." "You should have asked for some pardons in case you see a woman you like." "You get yourself into more shit." "The alignment of your stars is really f_ _ _ ed up."

Any rebuttal on my part would have been weak.

I arrived shortly after noon and after driving down the ramp that said, Police & Staff Only, a barrier blocked my way and a chain link fence slid into place behind my car. While a uniformed policeman with a clipboard matched my name on his authorized access list with the name on my driver's license, a second officer circled my car with a large black German Sheppard. I was told to leave the car keys - guess I was getting valet parking - and that the head administrator would come and get me.

She was slender, of medium height, dressed in a dark suit, and with her tightly, pulled back, hair and clenched jaw clearly indicated that she booked no nonsense. On the way to her office she mentioned that I had expressed concern that a student might be disruptive and explained, "Everyone here goes to school from 9 - 4 PM. If anyone misbehaves they are taken to their cell and left there without paper, pencil, book, or audio devices. Here's a cell."

Looking through a narrow glass window in the cell door, I saw a small concrete room with a concrete slab about four feet above the ground with what appeared to be a thin, rolled up mattress at one end.

There was a tiny window at the top of a wall that was too high to reach to get a view of the outside. A stainless steel toilet with steel seat but no lid adorned another wall. Otherwise the room was totally bare and sterile. The entire place smelled of Clorox.

"As you can see, no one wants to spend time in here. You won't have any problems."

Her office was in the center of a corridor that had eight or nine wooden doors. I later learned that most of them were classrooms. Passing an opened card table with two adjacent folding chairs against the wall to her office she revealed, "You will work here. At the beginning of each class a teacher will bring you a student and at the end of the class will come and get the student. If you sense anything wrong or you're uncomfortable, tell the student you must leave early, take the student back to her classroom, and come talk to me." I actually felt rather safe because at each end of the hallway there was a huge, black man, weighing at least 290 pounds, with a shaven head, wearing a tight, white, Tee shirt that accentuated his biceps, standing with arms folded and ready for trouble. I assumed they were police.

Inside her small, nondescript office, she continued my education, "Some of the students are awaiting trial, others are waiting transfer to the "big house' when they reach age 18, some are spending a few days here for a relatively minor offense, and others are waiting for their parents to come and pick them up. Don't tell them your name, where you live, or engage them in any conversation. We had a tutor who made friends with a student that later escaped and ended up at the tutor's house. Also, don't touch them or encourage them with a pat on the back, because some have been abused and you may set them off." (What an environment! What have I gotten myself into?)

A bell sounded as she was giving me a pad of paper and a brilliantly color pencil with psychedelic designs. Trying to lighten the mood, before taking my place at the folding table in the hallway, I commented, "This is quite a pencil."

"Yes, and I want it back."

"Of course."

"No, I don't think you understand. See that block of wood on the blackboard chalk tray that has holes drilled in it and a number next to each hole. There is a numbered pencil that goes into each hole. Look at the names of the students on the blackboard; the number after their name is their pencil number. They check them in and out for each class. In here pencils are considered lethal weapons. A counselor was held hostage by an inmate who was holding a pencil to the counselor's jugular vein. If I don't get one back, including yours, all teachers and counselors begin searching for it while the students get strip-searched. (OK, now I felt a little less safe?)

The first student arrived carrying a notebook and a textbook, and was accompanied by a teacher who was carrying the student's psychedelic pencil. After the student was seated the teacher placed the pencil on the student's notebook. I asked the student what she wanted to work on and she opened her algebra textbook to some word problems. Trying to solve a word problem it became obvious that she had missed a lot of earlier material. I kept backing up in the book until she had at least a partial understanding of what was going on. We spent the session adding and subtracting fractions. When the bell rang, ending the session, the teacher came for the student, picked up the student's pencil, and then invited the student to return to the classroom. This process never varied and most of the students were at a similar level of math/arithmetic.

An exception was one student who wanted to continue with her advanced placement (AP) calculus and had a good grasp of the material. I assumed she must have been recently picked up for under age drinking or drugs, because she was either very smart or had not missed a lot of school. The teachers however, treated her just like all the others. And so did I.

The students changed periodically and there were sometimes more and other times fewer. I was on call two days per week, (Tuesdays & Thursdays) and told a day in advance, what hours between 9 AM and 4 PM I would be needed. This went on for about five weeks when suddenly I was told that a tutor was no longer needed. I assumed the ones I had been tutoring had turned eighteen years of age and moved to the Big House, been released, or escaped? I did immediately take the opportunity to call the Alternative Education Program office and rescind my volunteerism.

The poker players were disappointed that I didn't have any ribald tales to reveal from this adventure. I simply kept repeating that every child should visit a jail and witness what I saw. I believe it would make a positive impact and be remembered. The experience did me some good. It let me leave on my next trip with a clear conscience.

Baccalaureate Speaker

"The man who reads nothing at all is better educated
than the man who reads nothing but newspapers."
Thomas Jefferson 1743 - 1826

I was honored to be the Baccalaureate Service speaker at Avon Old Farms School in Avon, CT in May 1995. The Headmaster who invited me to speak was George Trautman. When he graduated from the University of Pennsylvania his first teaching and coaching job was at Tabor Academy. He arrived the same year I did and he was responsible for introducing me to the game of lacrosse.

Rather than prepare a speech, I compiled a list of one-liners that I thought were important and for which I had an example of how I had experience each one in sports, submarine duty, business, or life. I have included the list because I found them still pertinent almost twenty years later. I also enjoyed reading them again because many of them I had learned from my father. I selected the first four for my speech, kept it short, and received positive feedback from the students, parents, and faculty.

My list:

* Play a team sport. It teaches great lessons and your teammates will be friends for life.

* Have multiple interests. Play a musical instrument, paint, sing, write for the school paper, and learn to play cards and board games such as backgammon.

* Set goals and have a dream. Without a dream you can never have a dream come true.

* Make friends, keep your promises, and be known as someone they can depend on.

* Say "Thank you" a lot and say, "Please" a lot.

* Smile and laugh a lot. A good sense of humor cures most ills.

* Learn to play golf, tennis, and squash or racket ball while you are young. You will be able to play them forever.

* Never give up on yourself or anyone else. Miracles happen every day.

* Be punctual and insist on it in others.

* Never cheat.

* Your grades are important. You will be asked at least twice for a transcript during your lifetime, and they will make a difference.

* Your most valuable asset is your reputation. Guard it carefully; it is difficult to repair once damaged.

CHAPTER 12

Adventures With Becky

MUGSY - The City Dog

"Animals are such agreeable friends; they
ask no questions, they pass no criticism."
George Eliot (pen name of Mary Ann Evans) 1819 - 1880

Mugsy was a small, white haired, Bishon Frisee. He was Becky's dog when she lived in a tenth floor apartment in Trump Place along the Hudson River in New York City. A happy dog that was content to be left alone while Becky ran the Women's Justice Center and taught law courses at Pace University Law School.

I really got to know Mugsy on a crisp, fall, Friday afternoon soon after Becky and I had begun dating. I had arrived at Becky's apartment after a 255-mile drive from Arlington, VA to be with her for the weekend. Becky had made dinner reservations at a nice restaurant and purchased tickets to a Broadway play. When I arrived at her apartment, she had just returned from work and wanted to change clothes after a long day in court representing clients. She asked me if I would mind taking Mugsy out to do his business while she finished getting ready.

"He's very good and will finish quickly for you. There are plastic bags tied to his leash for picking up his mess," she added.

It sounded easy, I was familiar with dogs, and I agreed.

Across the street from the main entrance to Trump Place was a sloping grassy area that led down to a paved walkway along the Hudson

River. The area directly across the street was fenced because the slope was rather steep, but there was an access path to the river-walk one half block to the left. Becky and I had used it several times to enjoy an evening walk along the river. I was familiar with the path and the grassy area to which it allowed access.

Mugsy was leash trained and remained by my side without tension on his leash. Down the elevator and out the front door of the apartment building we went. The street was clear of traffic when we exited so I quickly led (pulled, I didn't want to be late for our dinner reservations,) him across the street and down the sidewalk to the path that provided access to the grassy slope. He was game and seemed happy to jog to keep up with me. We reached the grassy area in no time and I slowed to his pace. We walked in the grass, back and forth, and back and forth, and back and forth.

"Come on Mugsy, this is not a parade it's a business trip. Do something. I'm in a hurry." I pleaded.

He responded by wagging his tail to the sound of my voice and we walked back and forth a few more times. Checking my watch I saw that we had been gone almost fifteen minutes. I convince myself that despite the fact he had been in the apartment all day, he did not have to relieve himself and began leading him back to the apartment building. We exited the grassy area, walked to the edge of the sidewalk and stopped for automobile traffic. As soon as I stopped, Mugsy stepped into the gutter and relieved himself. I picked up his deposit and assumed that he'd sensed that this was his final opportunity and taken advantage of the moment. Not so dumb after all.

Upon our return to the apartment Becky was ready and waiting to leave for dinner. I happily reported that, "Mugsy did everything he was supposed to do, but it was not as easy as you suggested."

We left the apartment, and headed for the elevator. "What happened?" She asked.

I began telling her the story while we waited for the elevator and finished during our descent. I glanced at her, expecting words of praise and encouragement, but noticed that she was trying, unsuccessfully, to suppress a big smile on her face.

"What?" I inquired.

"That's because he's a city dog. He doesn't routinely walk on grass and would not want to foul it. Let him stop at the nearest gutter, he will know what's going on and be very prompt."

And that's what had occurred. He was a city dog. Well, I'll be darn. That was a new one on me! I don't recall the name of the restaurant, what we ate for dinner, whether or not it was good, or even the play we saw on Broadway that night, but Mugsy and I became friends and I have never forgotten how to walk a city dog.

Never Tell Your Mama a Fib

"After all, what is a lie?
'Tis but the truth in masquerade."
George Gordon Byron 1788 - 1824

The week of my birthday in 2005 was spent in Puerto Vallarta, Mexico with Becky, Dick and Joy Hamon, and Jim and Joan Lippold. Dick Hamon and I both have February 3rd birthdays. I have enjoying my travels to Mexico. I find the margaritas enjoyable and the people industrious, pragmatic, and possessing a terrific sense of humor. I don't think a store in the USA would have a sign on their door that said, "Sorry We're Open" or you would be invited into a souvenir shop by a salesman who touted, "Come on in and buy something from China."

While in Puerto Vallarta, Becky and I did a Rainforest Canopy Tour - climb a tree in the rain forest to a tiny, treetop platform, grab a pulley attached to a cable strung between distant trees, clip it to your safety belt, leap off the platform, and ride the cable to another tiny, treetop, platform. Repeat for another hour and a half while riding the cable across rivers, canyons, and over the top of lesser treetops. Not a well described adventure, but actually lots of fun. A professional guide is useful!

On my big day, Becky found somewhere to purchase a Mexican birthday piñata, carried it on the local city bus, and hung it from a rafter in the downtown restaurant where we had dinner. After dinner, I was blindfolded, given a large stick, spun around several times, and told to hit the donkey shaped piñata to release my birthday prize - it was filled with dark chocolate candy and a couple of cigars. Piñatas are an interesting Mexican birthday tradition.

Becky and I also toured a tequila factory and spent quite a bit of time in the tasting room after the tour. We learned that there are three grades of 100% blue agave tequila. The un-aged liquor, right out of the still, is called Tequila Silver/Blanco/Plata/Platinum or White. Reposado is 100% blue agave tequila that has been aged, often in oak barrels, for 2 - 11 months. Anejo is 100% blue agave tequila that has been aged from one to four years. Many brands of Reposado and Anejo are very smooth and can be sipped like brandy. Tequila Mixto or Gold is a mix, containing at least 51% tequila, sold for mixed drinks like margaritas. There is no worm in any of the good stuff and usually only in Mescal, although sometimes found in a tequila mixto in the USA. The worm is actually an agave worm that is a butterfly larva. Some times a plant being processed may have a worm. In 1950 one distiller decided that his Tequila Blanco going to the USA was so strong that it would only be consumed by macho males so why not maximize their machismo and put a worm in the bottle. A product, exported only to the USA, was born.

We each purchased a good bottle of 100% Blue Agave Anejo to take home. It was one that we had sampled and decided that it could be served "neat" either before or after dinner. Becky selected one in a beautifully shaped and carved bottle for $68 US dollars.

When the week ended, Becky flew home via Kansa City to visit her Mom who was battling cancer. With her suitcase open to retrieve a gift she had purchased, Becky's Mom saw the bottle of tequila and proclaimed, "You don't drink that stuff do you?"

Since her Mom had never wanted her to drink hard liquor, there was only one answer. "Oh no Mom. I bought it for the beautiful bottle. In fact I will leave it here on your mantle so you can enjoy the beautifully shaped bottle until my next visit." A harmless little fib to keep Mom happy; right?

On her next visit Becky did not see the bottle of tequila and asked where it was.

"Father Ron has been visiting me regularly while I've been sick and he noticed the bottle. He's from Mexico you know? Anyway, he commented on the high quality of the tequila and how much he enjoyed having a little tequila before bed at night. So I gave it to him. I told him you had purchased it for the bottle and he promised to return the bottle when it was empty."

Later, after her mother had died, Becky saw Father Ron at church one Sunday after Mass and asked, "Father Ron, how did you liked that tequila?"

"Oh, it was wonderful. It was the best I ever tasted. I saved the empty bottle for you."

She then told him the entire story.

With a sly smile, but without a hint of embarrassment or apology, the priest counseled, "That will teach you to never tell your Mama a fib."

Marriage Proposal to Becky ,

"As soon as you cannot keep anything from a woman, you love her."
Paul Geraldy 1885 - 1983

In 2008, I had been a midlife bachelor for over ten years and was enjoying my freedom every day. That in itself is not bad, but fortunately I was about to discover that my idea of freedom requiring bachelorhood was badly flawed.

Becky's last evening aboard the Radisson's Seven Seas Mariner in 2002, she gave me her telephone number and offered to show me New York City, if I was ever up that way. I accepted her invitation later that year and she was a most gracious hostess.

Becky was born and raised in Kansas. She graduated from the University of Kansas with a Masters of Science Degree in Cell Biology. After completing Nursing School at Cornell she worked at Sloan Kettering doing cancer research. She stopped working to become a stay-at-home Mom and raise two children, and then went to law school. She was teaching law at the Pace Law School and running the New York Women's Justice Center when I met her.

Our second date was in Virginia. She called to tell me that she would be attending a session of the Supreme Court in Washington, DC and wanted to know if I wanted to join her. I certainly did. At the Supreme Court the morning of the event, she presented her invitation and we were escorted to a room where a crowd of people was enjoying a large buffet breakfast of fresh fruit, biscuits, pastry, juices, and coffee. Our escort said we would be notified when to take our seats in the courtroom. I was impressed by the way attorneys were treated, but not overly surprised.

An escort led us into the Supreme Court and down the center aisle. The empty judges chairs were lined up on a high platform behind a long, polished, wooden table. Arriving at the fourth row from the front, Becky whispered, "Sit in this row. I'll see you when court is adjourned." I joined the majority of the people from the breakfast buffet while Becky continued forward and took a seat, front row, and center. Now I was getting suspicious, but Becky hadn't told me anything. The Supreme Court Judges entered, took seats and Chief Justice, Rehnquist, began the proceedings by announcing that the court wanted to recognize three attorneys who would henceforth be able to litigate before the Supreme Court and would they please stand. Becky and two others seated in the front row stood. Extolling the accomplishments of each one in turn, Chief Justice Rehnquist spoke of Becky's extensive effort in briefing and educating police officers to avoid a case being lost because of a technicality during an arrest, and her work related to spousal & child abuse including changes to the New York State laws. Wow. Yes. I was both surprised and impressed. The Justices did hear a case, but I found it anticlimactic. Becky remains among the smartest and most humble people I've ever met.

My contribution to the date was to take Becky on a three hour "Segway Tour of the Washington Mall and Monuments." Learning to ride a segway (a battery powered, two wheeled, self-balancing, personal transport) was facilitated by the tour organizer recommending that tour participants arrive thirty minutes early for a brief lesson on how to get on/off, ride, steer, control speed, and stop, and then ride the segway around the parking lot to practice. It's a great little vehicle and once tried, it is easy to understand why park police and mall security personnel have them. It was a sundown tour, on a temperate evening with a soothing breeze, and the tourist crowd had diminished from overwhelming to manageable. Our guide provided a wealth of information and we covered miles, traveling up and down the mall, to the Capital, White House, Lincoln and Jefferson Memorials, Library of Congress, etc., at a leisurely pace and without breaking a sweat. It was an out-of-the-box evening on the Washington Mall! What, you don't think that's romantic? Well, in November I took her on a guided "Full Moon Hike" at the National Arboretum. The guide was a park herbalist and lecturer whom we followed and listened to during four miles of hiking through the moonlighted gardens, meadows, and woods. Yes, I know, there are not many garden flowers blooming in November, but I though that was romantic. Oh well; something worked!

We dated, on and off, long distance, between New York City and Arlington, VA and made some wonderful trips together. She was kind, loving, generous, and clearly among the most intelligent people that I'd ever met. She initiated many of the adventures we shared, was the perfect companion, and easily became my best friend. Unfortunately, I remained stupidly paranoid about my independence for about six more years.

In August 2008 I was visiting Chuck and Louise Kiger in Santa Fe, NM. They were being wonderful hosts and showing me all the wonders in the area. Despite the fact that I had not seen Becky since the previous November, I apparently expressed my appreciation of the sites, artwork, and sunsets we were seeing by saying, "I wish Becky could see this." The Kigers got tired of hearing my comment and told me. "You'd better go marry this woman. She's all you talk about and we want to meet her."

Before I left New Mexico I called Becky, told her I was planning to drive from Virginia to Cape Cod, and asked if I could buy her lunch on my way through New York. She agreed and said that she would be working at the Hebrew Home in Riverdale, NY.

We met at the Hebrew Home and exchanged pleasantries while walking to a bench on the edge of the cliff overlooking the Hudson River. It was a warm summer day, the flowers were still in bloom, the sun glittered off the river, and I felt confident asking her, "Is there any chance we could get back together?"

"Maybe, but I don't want to just be a girlfriend or traveling companion again."

"What does that mean? Do you want to get married?"

"That would work."

"OK. Let's do it." I responded immediately, without conscious planning and totally surprising myself.

"Then you had better leave now, go to Cape Cod, take forty-eight hours to think about what you just said, then call me if you still feel the same way and are not in shock." (Always a lawyer!)

I left. No lunch. Total meeting time, about fifteen minutes.

I returned to New York on Monday, two days (forty-eight hours) later, comfortable, happy, and without regret. What I did not know until my return was that Becky had retired, sold her apartment in the city, purchased a house that was under construction in Cary, NC, and intended to move there. She had rented a small apartment in White Plains, NY where she was storing her furniture and possessions until her new house was completed, and was leaving for Mexico to attend an extended, Spanish language, immersion course in four days. The stars were aligned in my favor, because had it been four days later she would have been in Mexico and then North Carolina, and I may never have found her again. She later told me that after our brief meeting when she returned to her office to finish packing up her things, a colleague apparently noticed a change in her demeanor and asked, "What going on?"

"I think I'm getting married," was her reply.

On Tuesday, Becky completed her business in New York as planned. Wednesday she came to Virginia instead of flying to Mexico.

We decided to elope, get married immediately, and have parties later. I suggested the drive-through-chapel in Las Vegas with Elvis as a witness, but got no answer. We agreed to get married in Virginia. August 28, 2008 we went to the Arlington Court House about 11 AM to fill out forms and discovered that neither a blood test nor a witness was required to get married in Virginia. Is this a great State or what? The office clerk directed us to a computer where we filled out the forms on line and the clerk could immediately access and approve them. The clerk, a very helpful, Hispanic, woman then gave us a preprinted list of names and addresses of officials who could perform a marriage ceremony in Virginia. We asked if any of the officials were nearby and the clerk pointed out one whose office was across the street and whom she had seen earlier that morning. We went to his office unannounced and met a very pleasant, friendly, and available gentleman. He asked why we wanted to get married and we simultaneously responded, "Because we are in love." He approved of our response and married us in a simple but touching ceremony. We have spoken of the ceremony many times and both agree that the private ceremony without having to be concerned about the welfare of guests was lovely, personal, intimate, and absolutely perfect.

We decided to immediately return to the clerk's office in the Court House with our marriage certificate to obtain certified copies for passports, military identification cards, Becky's name change, etc. As we approached the clerk, she recognized us and said, "Oh. Oh. We made a mistake on the application didn't we?"

"No, " I said, "we're already married."

I heard her reply something like, "Holy shit!" Becky heard something like, "It's nice when two people really know what they want."

We got four certified copies of our marriage certificate and departed the Court House. That's when I remembered that I had only put money for one hour in the parking meter, anticipating that to be sufficient time to fill out the forms to get married. Now we would probably have a parking ticket as our first wedding present.

When we arrived at our car, surprise; surprise. We had eight minutes left on the parking meter. Talk about efficiency!

Becky still gets calls about consulting, but she has been good about declining. When she did accept a request from a friend who is teaching at Georgetown Law School to give a one-hour, video taped lecture on the laws relating to Spousal Abuse and Child Endangerment, she received $500 for her hour of work. About the same time I had accepted a request from an Adult Center to give my talk on, How To Discriminate Between Statistical Facts and Fiction. My talk lasted almost two hours and I was given a $50 stipend. Besides the obvious greater value of her expertise vis-à-vis mine, her requests are often so interesting I (almost) encourage her to accept them. Consider her call from a Medical Doctor who had examined a patient and, as requested by the man, written him a prescription for Viagra. Three days later the man was arrested for rape. The Doctor wanted Becky to assess his liability.

Tango Argentina
"Pleasure's a sin, and sometimes sin's a pleasure."
George Gordon Byron 1788 - 1824

At one of my dance classes I heard about the Annual International Argentinean Tango Festival held each spring in Buenos Aires, Argentina. There was a package deal that included fifteen, one-and-a-half hour dance lessons taught by Tango Masters who would be performing on stage at the evening shows. You could choose from various combinations of three experience levels (beginner, intermediate, and advanced) and a variety of techniques (e.g., kicks, turns, close embrace, milonga, etc.)

being taught concurrently in five different dance halls over the period of five days. We thought it would be fun to learn the Argentinean Tango and decided to go for a week of dancing followed by a week of sightseeing.

The earliest dance classes began at 1:00 PM. There were four classes in each dance hall every afternoon with thirty minutes between classes for students to relocate among the dance halls. If you do the math correctly, you'll discover that the dance lessons ended at 8:30 PM. Squeeze in dinner and get to the 10:00 PM Tango Show where Master Tango Dancers (many were our daytime instructors) performed before hundreds of people in large theaters around the city. Tickets to each night's tango show were included in our package. The shows were exotic and magnificent, and ended about midnight. The public dance halls and milonga cabarets were open from 1:00 AM - 4:00 AM and we were encouraged to spend at least a few hours practicing what we had been taught. Sleep generally occurred from 4:30 AM - 11:30 AM followed by a noontime meal (Breakfast or lunch? I never could figure out which I should be eating.) And a 1:00 PM dance class. Repeat for five days and you will find it an exhausting but spellbinding experience.

During our second week we went to a soccer game in a typically large South American stadium full of passionate fans, visited Evita's tomb, visited the suburbs via underground subway, and took a river boat ride, up the Rio de la Plato, with the mailman, to the Argentina - Uruguay border.

The most popular foods in Buenos Aires are beef, beef, beef, pasta, beef, and pizza. I made contact with our USNA classmate from Argentina, Mario Zambra, who lived in Buenos Aires. During our meeting at a cafe he invited me to his Argentinean Naval School Class' monthly dinner. It was held on the roof top floor of an apartment building and was attended by twenty-four of his classmates. Many of them spoke passable English. A large brick barbecue with two cooks held the center of the floor. Tables and chairs were spread around the room. Argentinean Malbec wine was plentiful. We each received a plate and a sharp knife and approached the barbecue (as often as desired) to receive generous pieces of beef sirloin, ribs, flank, rib eye, fillet, or sausage. The rest of the dinner was displayed on a tiny table close to the barbecue. On it was a small dish that held about fourteen olives and a larger dish that contained about two small handfuls of potato chips. As stated, Argentineans like to eat beef, (and drink wine.) I had a wonderful time.

The naval school dinner was a men only affair, but Becky insisted that I attend. I was a little bit concerned about leaving her alone and was anxious to hear how she had spent her evening. "Not to worry." She told me, "I went to a milonga and danced."

I often make decisions because I am afraid to miss something, but Becky's as bad as I am. I need never worry about her sitting and twiddling her thumbs.

Painting In Italy
"There are moments when art attains
almost the dignity of manual labor."
Oscar Wilde 1856 - 1900

We met Barvo and his wife Maureen during a lunch break while touring the Alhambra in Spain. The four of us were on a cruise ship cruising the coasts and visiting port cities in the Canary Islands, Morocco, Spain, and Portugal. Barvo declared himself a painter and sculptor from Dallas, Texas. Several months after we met he called to ask if I was interested in joining him for a two-week watercolor painting class in the Umbria region of Italy. He was looking for a roommate. I reminded him that I was simply a hobby painter and proposed that I visit him in Texas and that we paint at his studio a couple of days and then decide if going together on the trip was a good idea. He agreed and I flew to Dallas.

He had two easels set up in his studio, a palette with acrylic paints for each of us, and a photograph of Saint Peter's Basilica in Rome that we would paint. At the far end of his studio he was sculpting a life size horse being ridden by two young children. They were the children of the family that had commissioned Barvo (for thousands of dollars) to do the work. I also discovered that he had a solo exhibition of his paintings in Dallas and that several of the large sculptures on display in parks and in front of museums and office buildings around Dallas were his work. And even though he had a last name (Walker) everyone, including individuals taking dinner reservations in restaurants, knew him as Barvo. He is truly a professional and magnificent, artist and sculptor. He taught me a lot during our painting sessions and we both agreed that my painting of Saint Peter's Basilica should be framed and displayed.

I brought the painting to Cape Cod to show my siblings my latest work. At brother, Bob and his wife, Paula's house, I showed them my work, replaced it in my canvas, zippered, portfolio bag and joined them for lunch. Getting ready to drive away in my car they began laughing. In response to my puzzled expression they revealed that while feeding me lunch they had exchanged my painting for one from their living room wall. We returned to the house, observed the new décor, agreed that it fit nicely and I departed with pride that they would want to display my painting. The last time I visited it was still on display!

Barvo and I flew to Rome and spent a day before heading to Terni and our painting school. We were enjoying an early afternoon drink at a sunny, sidewalk table of a cafe that fronted a large open plaza in Rome. A young artist carrying a large sketchpad and pencils approached and asked if we wanted him to sketch our picture. We declined but a woman at an adjacent table responded affirmatively to the identical question. As the artist began to work, Barvo quietly opened his sketchpad removed a blank page and surreptitiously began to sketch a picture of the artist at work. Barvo finished several minutes before the young artist, but said nothing until the young man had completed his work and collected his money. As the young man was leaving Barvo offered him the sketch saying, "Here. You can have this."

After a quick look and a stiffening gesture of surprise he said, "Wow. This is really good." and after a pause "You should consider working in one of these plazas; you could make a lot of money." When

I hear about Barvo's latest painting sale or sculpting commission, I still ask him if he's thought recently about a career sketching in a Roman plaza?

The school site, in the hills above the town of Terni, was a converted monastery. The students and teachers stayed in the old monk's quarters with showers at each end of the hall. The well-lighted chapel with its stained glass windows had been converted into a painting studio. Each day we would board a van for a trip to a nearby town/city to paint. e.g., Orvieto, Todi, Perugia, San Gemini, Assisi, and Spoleto. We returned each evening for lively happy hours, dinner, and studio painting if the spirit (spirits?) moved you. I was laughed at for using a ruler to sketch a building, but it was among people who became good friends. As far as watercolor painting goes, uggh!

Hut-to-Hut Hiking in the Swiss Alps
"I do not approve of anything which tampers with natural ignorance."
Oscar Wilde 1856 - 1900

During May 2001, a USNA '60 classmate, Vance Fry called from Tennessee to ask if I was interested in joining him on a two week hiking adventure in the Swiss Alps. We went in late May and early June. It was such a terrific experience that I wanted to share a similar trip with my new wife, Becky. I planned the trip for June 2009.

It was clear right from the beginning, that this trip would be different. Heavy rains in Virginia delayed our flight to JFK and only a change of air carriers allowed us to make our connection. An hour into our flight from JFK to Zurich I was delighted to smell what I believed was our dinner being cooked -- a meal is still served on international flights. As the smell intensified I feared they might be burning our dinner. As the cabin began filling with smoke and flight attendants rushed up aisle with fire extinguishers, I began to ponder how cold the water might be in the Atlantic Ocean below us. It was an electrical fire in a bathroom and we diverted back to Halifax, Nova Scotia. We landed safely on an isolated runway lined with ambulances and fire trucks and walked to the terminal that had been closed for the night. No food, no water and six hours on the floor waiting for a replacement aircraft. We arrived Zurich nine hours late, at 3 PM instead of 6 AM.

Swiss Alps hiking is really hiking between small mountain farms/inns/huts called berghaus or berghotel. In the summer Swiss farmers take their herds into the mountains to feed, saving their farm grass for winter-feed. They typically have a small mountain house and spend the summer collecting milk and making cheese. When hikers began stopping for the night they were provided with a mat and pillow in the attic. Today several of these berghaus have a couple of private rooms, in addition to the co-ed attic sleeping, and serve family style dinner and breakfast. In most cases the bathroom is at the end of the hall. Every berghaus we visited to spend a night was clean and comfortable, and the food was always fresh, wholesome, and delicious. On the trail outside each berghaus is a signpost with directional arrows to other berghauses with distance, hiking time, or both recorded. As a warning to future visitors, the hiking time is for a member of the alpine hiking club. When only the time was listed on the signpost we learned to add quite a bit of extra time, otherwise we relied on the distance and made our own time calculations.

Our plan was to spend fifteen days hiking in two different areas of Switzerland: the Appenzell area in the northeast near the Austrian border where German is routinely spoken and the Bernese Oberland area in the southwest where French and Italian are frequently heard. Once in Switzerland, when not walking, we planned to travel by train. Swiss trains run on time. An agent assured us that three minutes was sufficient time to change trains because they ran from nearly adjacent tracks and would be on time. And the agent was correct. We learned to be comfortable napping or reading on a train if we set an alarm for the time the train was scheduled to arrive at our next station stop. When the alarm went off we disembarked, no need to verify the station name. Our routine also included leaving most of our baggage in a locker at the train station and hiking hut-to-hut with only a small backpack.

I had made reservations for our first night's lodging in one of their six private rooms at the Berghaus Seealp, where Vance Fry and I had spent a night on my first trip. I remembered it being an easy one-hour walk from the end of the train line in Wasseraun. From there we would be exploring new territory.

I was pleased to discover, since we were running late and were tired after our layover in Halifax, that a train was running directly to Wasseraun from the airport. I remembered having to change trains in the quaint, small town of Appenzell to get to the end of the line at Wasseraun. Was our luck improving? At the station in Wasseraun there were no storage lockers. I assumed the station had been remodeled and where I remembered the lockers being located was now a storage facility for a hang gliding club. (On my first trip we had left our suitcase at the station in Appenzell where we had to change trains and where a sign alerted hikers that there were no lockers at Wasseraun. But I did not remember that. Come on, it had been eight years.) Then, what I remembered as an easy one hour walk, uphill all the way, meant when one was rested and without baggage except for a small backpack. Becky was a trouper. She refused to let me carry (drag) her bags and she walked the entire way dragging her own suitcase and carrying her backpack. I lost a significant amount of credibility with my trip planning, but was smart enough to remain silent when she frequently decided to stop, "to admire the beautiful scenery." We eventually made it, were shown to our charming, pine walled room, ate dinner, chatted with other guests, and then slept for ten hours. We walked around Lake Seealpsee, found the Chapel in the Woods, and returned to the berghaus for a second night. It was a weekend and musicians and yodelers provided entertainment during and after dinner. We also discovered that town-folks thought nothing of making the forty-minute uphill walk to have dinner at this charming berghaus. (Yeah, forty minutes to them. It took us over an hour!) We hiked the area a second day then headed for Luzern - 2 hours and 45 minutes away by train.

We walked the Luzern city sites, found that our two-week "rail pass" included boat rides on Lake Luzern and we indulged before moving on.

It is a two-hour train ride from Luzern to Bernese Oberland via Interlocken. The Bernese Oberland area is bounded, on one side by three mountains: the Eiger, Monch, and Jungfrau. (Or as the local school children explain it, "The Monk stands between the Ogre and the Young Maiden.) We stayed at the Alpiglen Berghaus at the foot of the North Face of the Eiger. A few yards from the Alpiglen Berghaus we visited the site where climbers traditionally camp before they began an ascent and where a small monument to those who have died trying to climb the North Face of the Eiger is located. One dinner at the Alpiglen Berghaus that we very much enjoyed was a traditional "Kasenschitten Alpiglen -- a combination of seven cheeses melted over bread soaked in wine and served with tomatoes, garlic, parsley, pickles, and pickled onions.

We hiked from Alpiglen to Klein Scheidegg then rode the cogwheel Jungfrau Express for fifty minutes to the mountaintop. At the top of the Jungfrau Mountain there is an ice palace and an outdoor observatory where the wind was blowing at forty-one miles per hour, the temperature was thirty degrees F, and at 13,642 feet altitude it was difficult to breathe. It was seventy-five degrees F in the valley when we began hiking this same morning.

Next we went to the Lauderbrunnen Valley in the high country above Bern, the Swiss capital. One of the grandest valleys in the Alps, it is a deep cut between sheer, continuous walls of rock. The three mountains (Eiger, Monch, and Jungfrau) are now to the East and the Schilthorn forms the west wall of the valley. The valley has many waterfalls with the two most famous being the Staubbach and Trummelbach Falls. The latter drains snowmelt and rain from the Eiger, Monch, and Jungfrau at rates up to 5,200 gallons of water per second. A Swiss hiker we met translated the flow rate into metric units, "That's 20,000 liters per second," he said and then impressed us by adding, "Which is nearly double the local beer consumption rate during Oktoberfest." We hiked between Murren, Grindelwald, and Steckleberg, and stopped to enjoy a Swiss fondue where local tradition called for the addition of some cherry schnapps to the melted cheese.

We rode the world's longest cable car lift to the top of Schilthorn Mountain and the Piz Gloria solar-powered restaurant. From the top of the Schilthorn one reputedly can see two hundred mountain peaks. James Bond visited the Piz Gloria restaurant and skied down part of the Schilthorn in the movie "On Her Majesty's Secret Service."

We hiked terrain that varied from fields of colorful, alpenrose and edelweiss wildflowers in full bloom, to narrow paths through several inches of snow. After hiking up to Berghotel Gross Scheidegg in shorts and a tee shirt, we ate, watched a beautiful sunset, went to bed and woke up to a freezing temperature and falling snow with several inches of accumulation already on the ground. Weather in the mountains is truly unpredictable.

We made use of an overcast day to take the train to Bern and tour the city. Albert Einstein's apartment and museum were of special interest as was reading the Legend of William Tell. (He used a crossbow, not a bow and arrow, and the complete tale is fascinating.)

We visited Interlaken, toured Lake Thun by boat, and learned to appreciate the various Swiss housing styles through the ages at the "Ballenberg Museum." The "Museum" is a fifty-two acre site with eighty characteristic Swiss houses, from eighteen different counties, that were dismantled, transported to the museum, and rebuilt.

Our return flight home was from Zurich and we spent a day there before our uneventful flight home.

Becky used her Apple Computer Self-Publishing capability to create an exquisite hard cover book of our hiking adventure complete with text and color photographs. Reviewing the book recently, we had two comments. It is a worthwhile trip, and do it while you are "young," mobile, and in reasonably good aerobic condition. If you ever plan such an adventure, and you are encouraged to do so, you should begin with the book, <u>Switzerland's Mountain Inns: A Walking Vacation in a World Apart,</u> by Marcia & Philip Lieberman. It is an indispensable resource that lists, locates, and has contact information for every berghaus and berghotel in the Swiss Alps.

Across the USA in an RV
"The one serious conviction that a man should
have is that nothing is to be taken too seriously."
Samuel Butler 1835 - 1902

Groundhog Day

Groundhog Day, annually on February 2nd, is when Punxsutawney Phil emerges from hibernation and looks for his shadow. Tradition says that if he sees it, winter will continue for six more weeks, but if he does not see his shadow, spring is on the way.

With a February 3rd birthday, I developed a fascination with the February 2nd event and the animal that could predict the end or continuation of winter weather. I routinely reminded friends of my birthday by saying, "It's the day after groundhog day," and I truly enjoyed, and recommend, the 1993 movie *"Groundhog Day"* starring Bill Murray and Andie MacDowell. So, in June 2005, with my newly purchased Roadtrek recreation vehicle, an early stop on my cross-country trip with Becky was in Punxsutawney, Pennsylvania to see Phil.

Punxsutawney is a small, quaint, country town (population about 6,500) in the mountains of western Pennsylvania (at an elevation of 1,439 feet) that hosts as many as 40,000 visitors from around the world during its Groundhog Day festival. The locals call their town "Punxy."

Phil has two homes: a modern, glass, zoological enclosure in the city center's library, and a rustic home in an undisclosed location where he resides when the library is closed and where he is allowed to hibernate. I saw Phil in his downtown habitat from which he had a window to observe the well-manicured town square with the huge groundhog statue and, from the other side of his habitat, view the people in the main area of the library. During my visit, he didn't seem much interested in the library visitors and preferred lying in the sunlight coming through his library window. The majestic and well cared for statue in the town square is ostensibly modeled after the original Phil who forecasted in 1886 when the town newspaper, the *Punxsutawney Spirit,* declared that February 2nd would forever after be called Groundhog Day. Since groundhogs have a life span of only about five years the carved statue represents a lot of "Punxsutawney Phils."

A few miles from town center, atop a hill, is the gated, forest clearing called Gobbler's Knob. It is the location of the highlights of the annual February 2nd event. At one end of the clearing that has been packed by as many as 5,000 people, is a large stage. On the eventful day, the gates are opened at 3:00 AM when the lights are turned on, music is played and dancing begins. (In early February, in the mountains of Western PA there is usually snow on the ground.) At 6:30 AM there is a fireworks show and at 7:00 AM the members of the Inner Circle of the Punxsutawney Groundhog Club arrive in their long, black coats and top hats to take their place on the stage. They have Phil with them, peacefully sleeping in a "tree stump" shaped enclosure with a heated burrow inside. At 7:25 the music stops, the crowd grows quiet and his handler - wearing thick gloves in case the sleeping animal bites or scratches the intruding hand that awakens him - takes out Phil. Announcing the presence of, "Phil, the king of groundhogs, the seer of seers, the prognosticator of prognosticators, and weather prophet extraordinaire," the handler raises Phil in the air for all to see (and ostensibly to give Phil a chance to look for his shadow?) The Club President leans close to Phil to get the forecast and make the announcement. The crowd cheers, and the music and dancing resumes. During our visit on a sunny fall day, we were fortunate to find a member of the Groundhog Club repairing the stage at Gobbler's Knob, and who was willing to sit with us and proudly reveal intimate details of the event.

Many civilizations had spring festival including the Roman Empire and the Celts of ancient Ireland, and they generally fell between the winter solstice (the shortest day of the year - about December 21st) and the spring equinox (when day and night are the same length - about March 21st) and thus were celebrated on February 2nd. The Germans apparently observed that if an animal awakening from hibernation saw his shadow it would crawl back into its hole for six more weeks of winter hibernation. Many Germans settled in western Pennsylvania, groundhogs were plentiful, and a tradition was created.

As a tradition it is delightful and entertaining, but as a weather predictor it is a failure. From the data displayed beside Phil's library residence it was simple to calculate that he had only predicted the end/ continuation of winter correctly 39% of the time between 1887 and 2005.

It was a satisfying visit that prompted me to watch the movie, "Groundhog Day," at least one more time.

Frontier Cultural Museum

In Staunton, Virginia, in the Shenandoah Valley between the Blue Ridge and Allegheny Mountains there is a living Frontier Cultural Museum. It consists of a series of farms manned by costumed guides meant to depict and promote an understanding of how the American frontier homes and farms developed.

Since most of the early American settlers were from England, Ireland, and Germany, a visitor first wanders through a replica of the farm and buildings that a settler from each of those countries might have left behind when coming to America. Next is a farm typical of what a West African slave might have left when shipped to America and finally the farm and teepee of a local, native American Indian. The idea is to facilitate the observance of how the early settlers learned from each other by adapting and combining the best features of each culture to build the American frontier farms.

The museum then features an American farm circa 1740, one from the 1820s, and one from the 1850s complete with a one-room schoolhouse. An example of idea and crop sharing was the American farm garden with Irish potatoes, okra and black-eyed peas from West Africa, and the "three sisters" gardening technique used by the native Indians. The Indians planted corn, surrounded by a circle of green beans (so the beans could use the corn stalk for climbing and vertical support), and squash between the rows of corn to prevent weeds - the three sisters. It was a fascinating and extremely educational tour.

I noticed in the reproduction of the West African farm that it included a mud hut for eating, a hut for family gathering, a hut for wife number one, a smaller hut for wife number two, and a small hut called a "man cave." It makes me wonder if this was the origin of "the porch of no ambition?"

The Warther Carving Museum

At the Warther Carving Museum in Dover, Ohio, we saw intricately carved trains, movable figures, and witnessed Mr. Carver's son carve a working pair of wooden pliers in one minute. When the applause subsided he told the museum spectators that the record was twenty seconds and was held by his father, until . . . his father was invited to appear on the Johnny Carson Television Show. Examining a pair of wooden pliers his father had carved, Johnny proclaimed that it was impossible to do the carving in twenty seconds. So, his father carved a pair on live television in nine seconds, improving on his own world record.

Remnants of the Homestead Act

In the middle of a flat dry landscape, in western Kansas, we toured the remnants of an old sod hut build in response to the Homestead Act. Inside the sod hut whose roof was badly in need of a "lawn mowing," we read a note left by the last Homestead Act occupant that said, "The government is betting 160 acres vs. $18 that we will starve to death before five years."

General Custer's Last Stand

At the Little Big Horn Battlefield in Montana we had a morning tour with a Park Ranger. We followed the guide over the five miles from where general Custer arrived at the Big Horn River, split his forces and with 236 soldiers eventually fought the 800 - 1500 Sioux and Cheyenne warriors. We ate lunch at the memorial and were joined by a Park Ranger of obvious American Indian descent. Our conversation about the battle and what we had learned from our tour guide prompted our lunch companion to offer a repeat tour with "an Indian version of the battle." We accepted. The timeline of the battle was virtually the same, but some of the reasoning was quite different. For example, Custer's scout steadfastly estimated, "a few hundred Indians," despite seeing the dust cloud being made by over 1,200 Indian war ponies on the far side of the river. Additionally, the portrayal of the soldiers in a tight circle fighting off the Indians is now acknowledged as mostly fiction. A prairie fire uncovered belt buckles, weapons, and other military paraphernalia spread over a wide area strongly suggesting that many soldiers scattered and ran for their lives. Historical truth is often intentionally skewed by politics or a writer's agenda, and unintentionally varied by the incomplete memory of a witness or survivor. (Recall my warning in the Introduction?)

World Series of Poker

I stopped in Las Vegas during the World Series of Poker. Many of the past winners and big name stars were present. Most were pompous and unapproachable. By far the most congenial, likable, and approachable was Chris "Jesus" Ferguson. I stayed there alone for several days in July to watch the tournament and play some poker. (Not in the tournament.) I anticipated living in my Roadtrek RV that I parked in the parking lot in front of the Gold Coast Hotel & Casino. I quickly discovered that parked in the sun, with the outside temperature hovering around 100 degrees Fahrenheit, and heat radiating off the black tarmac of the parking lot, the water in my water tanks was so hot that I could not use it to take a shower. I had to get a room.

Tombstone, Arizona

In Tombstone, we toured the OK Corral and witnessed a reenactment of the famous fight between Doc Holliday and the Earp brothers (Virgil, Morgan, and Wyatt) against the McLaury brothers (Tom & Frank) and the Clanton brothers (Billy & Ike.)

We found the tombstones on Boot Hill to be entertaining as well as educational: "George Johnson Hanged By Mistake 1882," "Rook Killed by an Apache," "Unknown Found in a Mine 1882," "Kansas Kid," "Here Lies Lester Moore Four Slugs From A 44 No Less No More," "Six Shooter Jim Shot By Burt Alvord 1885," "John Heath Taken From The County Jail & Lynched 1884," and "Margarita Stabbed By Gold Dollar."

Along Main Street was Big Nose Kate's Saloon. Big Nose Kate became the wife of Doc Holliday. Further along Main Street were the Outlaws Social Club and the infamous Bird Cage Theater. The Bird Cage Theater was really a saloon that got its name because of the ladies that danced in cages hanging from the ceiling. In the basement of the Bird Cage Theater there was a single poker table where the longest running continuous poker game was played. The minimum buy in was $1,000, the dealer kept the list of people waiting to play, and for eight years, five months, and three days, the game never stopped. The basement room, poker table, chairs, cards and poker chips remain, as they were when the game ended. (I could not find out why it ended.)

Old Tucson Movie Studio

Many of the building in the western town that was built as a movie studio in Tucson, Arizona were recognizable from movie that we had seen. Not because we were serious movie fans, but because over 400 movie were made there. John Wayne worked there frequent and was the star in McLintock, El Dorado, and Rio Lobo all of which were made at the studio. Recognizable building from movies including the church, saloon, water tower, livery stables, general store, and barbershop were open for perusal and photographing. The studio/town will certainly generate movie scene recall of anyone who watched western movies starring John Wayne.

Graceland

I reluctantly visited Elvis' home in Memphis, TN, but came away with new respect for "The King." Did you know that he earned black belts in Tae Kwan Do and Karate while in the Army? That he had ninety-one albums that were Gold, Platinum, or Diamond? That he made thirty-one films as an actor? That after visiting the White House and seeing that the President had simultaneous access to news from NBC, CBS, and ABC, Elvis had three televisions installed in his den with each one tuned to one of the news stations? That he converted his garage into a pistol shooting range? And there is a lot more. It's worth a visit.

Roswell, New Mexico

Roswell NM is a very weird town with a strange unsettling atmosphere. The UFO Museum is the main draw and it becomes immediately obvious that these people really believe in aliens and visitors from outer space. The museum contains drawings and first-hand statements from people who were captured and taken aboard spaceships. People will gladly stop to relate how, when, and where they saw or heard a space ship land or pass overhead. Signs direct visitors to space ship landing sites in the nearby desert. We were anxious to leave town after a very brief stay and visit to the UFO Museum. I will concede that I could believe that some of our recent political luminaries escaped from a space ship in Roswell.

Appalachian Homestead and Working Museum

In Norris, Tennessee, a small Appalachian settlement is maintained the way it was in the 1800s. There is much to see and experience, but the highlight of our visit was our arrival on baking day. In the cookhouse a wood fire is made in the morning to heat a large brick oven. When the cook can put her hand in the oven and count slowly to ten, the oven temperature is perfect for baking bread. When the bread is done, the oven temperature is just right for baking cakes. When the caked are baked the oven temperature is perfect for pies. When the pies are cooked the oven temperature is right for baking rolls. When the rolls are done, the oven temperature is perfect for baking cookies. When the cookies are done the baker is finished until next week. Fascinating and very clever.

The Eastern Shore

Assateague Island is a thirty-seven mile long barrier island. Its northern end is part of Maryland and the rest is part of Virginia. The Island is home to herds of wild ponies that graze the channel side marshes and gallop along the pristine beaches. Annually, for the past ninety years, during the last week of July about 150 of the ponies are rounded up by Saltwater Cowboys and driven across the a narrow part of the channel to Chincoteague, VA. A pony auction is held to benefit the Chincoteague Volunteer Fire Department and the ponies not purchased make the return swim back to Assateague Island. We were not there for the pony swim and auction, that draws 30,000 - 50,000 people each year, but we roamed the Island and the town for several days while camping in our RV. We drove the Beach Road, hiked Black Duck Marsh and the Woodland Trail, and spent time on the beach with the ponies. The area is a wildlife refuge and advertised as, "home to 320 different types of birds." We did see lots of birds in addition to the ponies, but were eventually driven away after being up close and personal with a mosquito population of 1,000 per cubic inch, (my estimate.) The mosquitoes were relatively small, their growth probably stunted from consuming all the "deet" it took for them to become impervious to its presence. There small size enabled them to somehow squeeze through the screens on our camper's windows and overwhelm us even at night. I recommend a visit, but only in January when there is snow on the ground. Alternatively, read the children's book, Misty of Chincoteague, by Marguerite Henry, to visit the area vicariously.

Egypt and the Nile River

"Love is a wonderful thing and highly desirable in marriage."
Rupert Hughes 1872 - 1956

As a young girl Becky dreamed of sailing up the Nile River so I decided to make it a birthday present. We joined a two-week Smithsonian Institute led tour of Egypt that included a five-day sail up the Nile River. We even had time to add a hot air balloon ride over the Valley of the Kings, coastal monuments, and villages.

Before leaving, we took advantage of the opportunity to take a course at the North Carolina Museum of Art called, "Understanding Hieroglyphs." Most important was learning how to write our names in hieroglyphs in case we wanted our name on a Tee shirt, a tattoo, or jewelry cartouche. (A cartouche is the word for the oblong shape enclosing the names of pharaohs and gods in ancient Egypt. The French thought it looked like a gun cartridge (bullet) and thus, from the French, the word "cartouche.") Becky now has a gold cartouche pendant with my name on one side and her name on the other, both written in hieroglyphs. I resisted getting a hieroglyph tattoo.

The monuments are huge, the salesmen very, very aggressive and in your face, and we found it advisable to always count your change - even in the National Museum of Antiquity. In addition to the spectacular visuals some interesting customs were revealed.

Egypt flourished because the Nile overflowed each year dumping rich soil along its banks. Each temple had a "Nileometer" that measured the highest level of the Nile during the overflow. It was a stairwell dug to water level with marking along the wall. Access was limited to priests and pharaohs. Taxes were levied on peasants and farmers based on the flood level, i.e., how far inland the water spread. The Nileometer remained in use until the Aswan Dam was built.

We noticed, especially during our hot air balloon ride, that few of the houses were finished with a roof. Most appeared to be under construction with re-bars protruding from the top floor even though the lower floors were occupied and the top floor was being used for drying grain and hay storage. We learned that in Egypt one does not pay taxes on a house or building until it is finished. When a family member marries or more room is needed when more children are born, it is common to add a floor but always leave the top unfinished.

Our trip preparation included a visit to the "Travel Doc" at the military hospital. He looked at out itinerary and provided pills for potential illnesses. We were very careful about what we drank (only bottled water) and ate (no uncooked food) yet before the end of the Nile River sail I made use of some pills. I do not remember ever not being careful about what I ate and drank, and several other travelers got sick also. In retrospect I think the small boat with minimal electrical power that took us up the Nile River, was washing and rinsing the dishes in the Nile River after every meal.

Super Bowl Sunday in Las Vegas
"The urge to gamble is so universal and its practice
so pleasurable that I assume it must be evil."
Heywood Broun 1888 - 1939

For my birthday in February 2010, Becky arranged for a family get together in Las Vegas. For me, and most of the male family members, it was poker all day, dinner as a family, and a show at night. The women enjoyed the spas while the men played poker. The lone male exception to the routine was my brother, Bob, whose wife could not make the trip. He slept during the day so he would be fresh to play poker from 9 PM - 5 AM against the drunks and tourists looking for a little action after the shows. He did well. Everyone had a great week and I was disappointed when it ended.

The night before our departure from Las Vegas a snowstorm hit the east coast. Family members flying home to Providence, RI and Boston, MA were fine, but our flight to Baltimore, Maryland was cancelled. Go figure! Rescheduled for two days later, it was cancelled again because the airport was still closed. There was no vacancy at our plush hotel, but the Gold Coast recognized me as a favored client and gave us a room.

Because of the snowstorm we were in Las Vegas for Super Bowl Sunday, February 7th, Drew Brees and the New Orleans Saints vs. Peyton Manning and the Indianapolis Colts. The Sports Book at the Gold Coast was like a sports bar on steroids. It offered eighty-eight football bets and twelve "miscellaneous propositions" that kept us, and a ruckus crowd, interested in the game until the last play. Together, Becky and I had ten different $20 bets. The odds and payouts obviously differed from bet to bet, but consider this sample of options:

Team to receive opening kickoff. Saints or Colts?

Team to score first. Saints or Colts?

Team to punt first. Saints or Colts?

First team to get a first down. Saints or Colts?

Team to score last. Saints or Colts?

First score of the game. Touchdown or any other?

First offensive play will be. Pass or run?

Total interceptions by both teams. Over or under 2 and 1/2?

Total fumbles lost by both teams. Over or under 1 and 1/2?

Will either team score in the first 5 minutes of the game? Yes or No.

Will either team score in the last 2 minutes of first half? Yes or No.

Will either team score in the last 3 minutes of the game? Yes or No.

The shortest field goal made will be, Over or Under 24 and 1/2 yards?

The longest field goal made will be, Over or Under 43 and 1/2 yards?

Will there be a special team or defensive touchdown? Yes or No.

Total touchdowns by both teams will be, Over or Under 6 and 1/2?

Will at least one quarter be scoreless? Yes or No.

First turnover will be? Fumble or Interception.

Largest lead of game will be, Over or Under 16 and 1/2 points?

The team to use the coach's challenge first will be? Saints or Colts.

Drew Brees' first pass will be complete or incomplete?

Peyton Manning's first pass will be complete or incomplete?

Drew Brees' total number of completions will be, Over or Under 24 and 1/2?

Peyton Manning's total number of completions will be, Over or Under 24 and 1/2?

Drew Brees will throw an interception? Yes or No.

Peyton Manning will throw an interception? Yes or No.

Drew Brees' longest completion will be, Over or Under 38 and 1/2 yards?

Peyton Manning's longest completion will be, Over or Under 38 and 1/2 yards?

What will Drew Brees throw first. An Interception or a Touchdown?

What will Peyton Manning throw first? An Interception or a Touchdown?

Similar options for running backs. Over or Under yards gained and number of carries.

Same for pass receivers. Over or Under number of passes caught and receiving yards.

The largest lead of the game will be Over or Under 10, 12, 14, or 16 points?

Last score of game will be? Pass, field goal, run, safety, other.

Total points scored will be, Over or Under 56 and 1/2?

"Double bet." 1st half leader & game winner? Colts or Saints in any combination.

"Double bet." 1st to score & game winner? Colts or Saints in any combination.

"Miscellaneous propositions" or "off-game bets" included these offers:

Who will score more points, the Colts or Kobe Bryant on 2/6/10 vs. Blazers?

Who will score more points, the Saints or Kobe Bryant on 2/6/10 vs. Blazers?

Who will score more points, the Colts or Dwight Howard on 2/7/10 vs. Celtics?

Who will score more points, the Saints or Dwight Howard on 2/7/10 vs. Celtics?

Who will have more? Phil Mickelson 4th round birdies or Peyton Manning TD passes?

Who will have more? Phil Mickelson 4th round birdies or Drew Brees TD passes?

And finally, for scrabble players: Will the total number of scrabble points in the last name of the player scoring the first touchdown be Over or Under 10.5? (Scrabble letter points were listed, e.g., Q & Z =10 points; J & X = 8 points; K = 5 points; F, H, V, W, & Y = 4 points; etc.)

Becky had a bet with 40:1 odds that there would be a total of precisely five field goals made during the game. Four field goals had been made with about five minutes left in the game. The game was close. Fourth down, with 6 yards to go for a first down or 24 yards for a touchdown. Instead of taking the "automatic" field goal, the Saints threw an incomplete pass. Another field goal and Becky would have won $800 on her $20 bet. What a bummer!

If you ever get the opportunity to watch a super bowl game at a sports book/bar in Las Vegas, don't pass it up. Make a few "crazy" bets and have a great time.

Fantasy Fest, Key West, FL.
"The Anglo-Saxon conscience does not prevent
sinning it only prevents enjoying one's sins."
Salvador deMadariaga 1886 - 1978

Always searching for new art forms and painting ideas I heard about Fantasy Fest, billed as Key West's weeklong Halloween party with parades, parties, and body painting. I had not tried body painting before and it sounded like an adventure.

I included plans for a few stops on the way south to allay any hesitance Becky may have had to join me. We stopped and toured the Kennedy Space Center, an alligator farm in the Everglades, and the

World Chess Hall of Fame - which has a comprehensive history of the development of the game, unique chess sets from around the world, interesting insider stories, and videos such as the Kasparov vs. Fischer matches. I don't think Becky needed the inducement of the side trips to join me, but they each proved to be worth the time.

Fantasy Fest is much like Mardi Gras in New Orleans without the crime and drunks. People partied and had lots to drink but there were no drunken bodies passed out in the gutter and on the sidewalk. Women who wanted to be topless did so and others were never asked to show their boobs in exchange for some beads as is so popular in New Orleans. I have tried both Mardi Gras and Fantasy Fest and the latter is better. Besides it is a major body-painting exhibition and that's what I wanted to try.

Body painters set up inside stores, in display windows, and on the sidewalk along Duval Street. Painters each had their own style with some using various combinations of hand brushes, airbrushes, stencils, and free hand drawings while body painting. When a stencil that covered the upper-torso and could be held against the body to allow spray-painting was used, the cost was $30 - $75. Free hand, original paintings began at $45 for upper torso and cost much more for full body. Prices varied with the number of colors, size, and complexity of the painting, with creativity commanding more money.

I dusted off my brushes, purchased some body paint (it's water based so it can be washed off) and found a spot on the sidewalk near a body-painting tent that had a waiting line and was charging high prices. I had a sign that read, "FREE BODY PAINTING. ARTIST IN TRAINING. WOMEN ONLY." Not only did I get business, but before long I was invited inside a store to paint in their display window. One of my early creations, by request, was an upper body red octopus against a blue sea background.

"The Process Counts."
(Personal Photo by Becky)

"The Product is Free."
(Personal Photo by Becky)

I had satisfied customers, of course there was no cost, but regardless of what you might think of the quality of the art, I can truly say that the pleasure was in the process not the result.

I sent enough pictures to my fellow students and the instructor in the painting class I was attending at the Torpedo Factory in Old Town Alexandria to incentivize a few students and make the rest (at least the males) envious. I even became the class hero for the remainder of the semester -- if not for my artistic ability at least for my daring and bravado.

Fishing in Alaska
"It gets late early out here."
Yogi Berra 1925- 2014

In the summer of 2007, Becky and I along with Bob and Nanette Bell spent a week fishing in Alaska. We made arrangements with Tim Berg's Alaska Fishing Adventure to stay in his lodge for a week, go on a different fishing adventure with a guide each day, have all our fishing gear and bait provided, and be able to drop our daily catch at a processing plant near the lodge to be filleted, vacuumed sealed, flash frozen, and packaged in airline approved containers - up to 50 pounds of fish per person.

We flew from Virginia to Anchorage where we spent two nights. During the days we toured the city, visited the starting line for the Iditarod great dog sled race, and sampled the local fare. We drove 149 miles southwest to Tim Berg's lodge in Soldotna, on the Kenai River, nine miles inland from the Cook Inlet. We had a private room with a balcony on the second floor of a beautiful lodge. Large baskets of red, blooming, flowers hung from the balcony railing - for the first two days. Early in the morning on our third day we awoke to some noise and witnessed the final minutes of breakfast, of a very larger moose, standing in the driveway and enjoying the taste of the flowers that had adorned our second floor balcony.

We were served breakfast each morning and then directed to a pantry to make and pack our own lunch. The standard "goodbye" when leaving the lodge, no matter where you were headed was, "May the fish be with you." Returning at night a wonderful family style dinner was served, and the guests were allowed to tell stories of the ones that got away today!

Day 1 we were driven by our guide to an area of the Kenai River to fly fish from the riverbank for Sockeye (or Red Salmon.) We used a single hook with an un-weighted fly to catch sockeye that ran close to shore and averaged 4 - 8 pounds. Sockeyes are identified by their dark blue backs and absence of spots, on their back, tail or fin.

Day 2 we did a fly-out to fish for Coho (or Silver Salmon.) We flew west across the waters of the Cook Inlet for twenty minutes in a small, "Beaver" aircraft that had five seats. After landing in a lake and taxing to its edge, we exited into hip deep water with a soft mushy bottom and lots of marsh grass. (We had been provided with waist high wading gear.) While walking about 300 yards to a small river, we noticed lots of bear poop and were comforted to see that our guide carried a rifle.

(One does not run very fast in mud wearing waders.) The limit for Coho was three fish. We fished with a small sinker and a hook baited with "a hand full" of salmon eggs. Coho bleed when caught so there is no catch & release option while hoping to catch a trophy. Becky got her three fish and ended up with nine pounds of fillet. I only caught two, about two pounds of fillet, but I also caught a Dolly Vardin. It's a species of trout that's native to Alaska and provides a great fight when hooked, but has to be released.

Day 3 we went deep-sea ocean fishing out of the Cook Inlet for Halibut. A young man about twenty years old was our guide and boat captain. He had an assistant that was about eighteen years old. We fished the bottom from a drifting boat in water between 150 and 180 feet deep. The end of our line had an eight-pound weight and half a herring for bait. The first fish we caught weighed 106 pounds and the guide recommended throwing it back because it was "a small one." Reeling in the eight-pound weight in 150 feet of water, to see if you still have bait on your hook after a strike is labor intensive. Add a 106 pound fish and it's exhausting. It was the biggest fish I'd ever seen caught and couldn't believe the guide thought it was a small one. We were reminded that the limit was two fish each so we released the "monster." The four of us each caught our limit, the largest were all about 150 -160 pounds. We also caught some Link Cod, almost as large, that we kept despite their ugliness. Turns out we didn't think they tasted very good either, unlike Northeast Atlantic Cod.

"A Catch of Alaskan Halibut."
Left to right: Dick & Becky, Nanette & Bob Bell.
(Personal photo)

Day 4 we were driven to the Upper Kenai River to fish for Chinook or King Salmon. The limit is one if you are lucky enough to catch one. The river was running at about 8 -10 knots and we were in a boat heading into the current at five or six knots so that we drifted backwards with the current at about three to four knots, called back trolling or back-bouncing depending on what the sinker was doing. King salmon run deep and can weight 50 - 60 pounds. We were using 35-pound test line with a large sinker to get to the river bottom and a barrel swivel with a five-foot leader. The "bait" was a large plug and when bait is allowed a small slice of sardine is often added to give it a fishy smell. Becky was the only one of the four of us who caught one. It was within a few inches of being as long as Becky is tall and our guide estimated its weight at 40 pounds.

Day 5 was fly-fishing for rainbow trout. Trout fishing was catch and release only. Our guide took us down a shallow, lazy river, in a small boat. We stopped occasionally along the way to fish from the riverbank with moderate success. Finally the guide stopped at a "sand bar" about 20 yards wide and 30 yards long with enough brush to prevent seeing from one side to the other. Once we had all disembarked he told the women to wait for him while he took Bob & me to the other side of the sand bar. On the other side we were delighted to see swirling, rapidly flowing, bubbling white water rather than the very shallow, slow moving, wide river we had been on all morning. The guide told us we could fish here while he showed the women how to fish the slow, shallow side of the river. Oh. Yeah. Bob and I hurried to get that fly out into the deep, rushing water where the trophy fish hung out, while we discussed how this side of the river must be too dangerous for the women.

We were still excited when the guide returned about twenty minutes later and asked, "How are you guys doing?"

"We're having fun and optimistic about catching a big one, but so far haven't caught anything.

Well, the ladies have caught seven, so there are fish here. Show me what you're doing?"

We each had our favorite spot to place our fly near the middle of the swirling water and demonstrated with some self satisfying "skill" how we could land our fly right where we wanted it. The two flies drifted down stream as they had for the past twenty minutes, without being attacked by a hungry fish.

While preparing for the next cast, the guide said, "Drop it right here along the shore. No fish is going to fight that current and turbulence in the middle of the stream. It's too much work and . . ."

He couldn't even finish his explanation before I had a strike while following his advise. And before I had netted my fish Bob had a strike.

"I knew you men would not like fishing the slow, shallow side and would have trouble following my advise, unlike the women, that's why I brought you over here. I did assume however, that you would know a little bit about how to read a river for fishing!" As John Wayne might say, "What a couple of pilgrims."

That evening I purchased the book, The ABC's of Reading Alaska's Small Rivers and Streams, by Kelly Pinnell. I selected it because it has over forty illustrations and about fifty-five color photos. I think I get it now. I mean I think I know a little bit about how to "read a river," but I still don't understand "Why men are reluctant to take advise unless a task is macho or dangerous?"

It was an educational and enlightening trip. Alaska is amazing and its natural beauty is unequalled.

And, by the way, the freezer compartment of a traditional size refrigerator can only hold fifty pounds of fish if all else, including ice cubes, is removed. For several days after my return, my neighbors loved me while enjoying the smell, challenge, and reward of grilling the fresh salmon and halibut that I had given them.

Some Alaska Facts

Alaska is the size of 2 Texas, 4 Californias, 10 Floridas, 12 New Yorks, or 14 Virginias. Its flag consists of eight gold stars (representing the Big Dipper and the North Star) on a field of blue. Benny Benson designed the flag in 1926, when he was in the seventh grade. Alaska has twenty-seven species of mosquitoes and its official state sport is dog mushing. It has the only state capital not accessible by road - Juneau. It is the northern most, western most, and eastern most state in the Union. (The islands on the end of the Aleutian Chain are on the other side of the 180th meridian, putting them in the Eastern Hemisphere. The Aleutian Islands are closer to Tokyo, Japan than to Anchorage, Alaska.) In Anchorage, during Summer Solstice sunrise is at 3:21 AM and sunset is at 10:42 PM. (19 hours and 21 minutes of daylight.) During Winter Solstice sunrise is at 10:14 AM and sunset at 3:42 PM. (5 hours and 28 minutes of daylight.)

World Cruise

"Methods of locomotion have improved greatly in recent
years, but places to go remain about the same."
Don Herold 1889 - 1966

In 2012 between January and May we took a world cruise aboard the
Pacific Princess (formerly the Love Boat, maximum of 670 passengers),
108 days, 44 countries, and 32,197 nautical miles aboard ship. We would
call it the trip of a lifetime except it was so great; we want to do another,
with a different itinerary of course. From Ft. Lauderdale, Florida the
ship went to northern South America (e.g., Columbia), transited the
Panama Canal (a worthwhile experience), stopped in Central America
(e.g., Costa Rica, Nicaragua), then Hawaii, many Pacific Islands (e.g.,
Samoa, Fiji, Tonga), Australia, New Zealand, Tasmania, next was
Asia (e.g., Japan, Korea, China, Hong Kong, Vietnam, Thailand,
Singapore) then headed East to India, Oman, United Arab Emirates,
Bahrain, Egypt and Jordan, transited the Suez Canal to visit Adriatic
Sea countries (e.g., Croatia, Slovenia, and Italy.) We disembarked in
Venice and spent five days in a hotel on the Grand Canal before flying
home.

When asked for the "highlight" we can only respond by
discriminating:

Visually: The city of Petra carved into cliff sides in Jordan and still
being explored.

Acoustically: A lecture and concert in the Sydney Opera House,
1500 seats, no audio assist or microphones required by performers.

Physical Performance: (Dick) Throwing boomerangs and spears
at kangaroo targets and trying to get music from a didgeridoo at
Aboriginal Cultural Center in Australia. Gets it's own write-up, see
"Using a boomerang." (Becky) Riding bareback elephants in Thailand.

Easiest to Accept: Sea days. A new Sudoku puzzle each day with
breakfast on our stateroom balcony, ceramics painting - they had a kiln
onboard, - ballroom & belly dancing lessons; a ten week cooking course
by Alfredo Marzi, the Master Chef of Princess Cruise Lines complete

with certificate; historical and informational lectures by guest speakers; 3 PM tea, scones, fresh whipped cream, & jam served by a waiter with a cart as we sat in large deck chairs reading a book and watching dolphin, whales and flying fish disrupt the ocean surface; an evening stage show; beautiful sunsets - all interrupted by meals in the dinning room, or a visit to the "anytime buffet," or the hamburger & pizza bar. Yes, there was a full gym onboard; did I forget to mention that?

Most Amazing: The Mall of the Emirates in Dubai. Marble floors, stained glass ceilings, 588 stores, on three stories, large enough to have a McDonalds East and a McDonalds West, three car finding services, and a ski mountain with five ski runs over 400 meters long with over 60 meter descent, double chair lifts, penguins walking around, a snow board half-pipe, and a beginners slope. Temperature on the street was 102 degrees F, in the Mall 68 degrees F, and in the ski area, 26 degrees F.

Cleanest & Safest: Singapore where one is fined for eating, drinking or chewing gum on the street or in the metro and there is even a fine for failing to flush a public toilet. The city was immaculate and the people were well dressed, educated, orderly and friendly. Penalties for breaking the law are harsh, however it did allow a woman to join us in a crowed subway car, put her purse in the overhead rack and later go to the other end of the car to greet an acquaintance who had boarded, without the least concern that her purse would be touched.

Most Disappointing: The US press and media's propensity for blatantly exaggerating reports of trouble and horrific events where we were visiting. On several occasions the US reported "spectacular happenings" that the BBC found unworthy of mentioning and that we knew were false or extremely over exaggerated because we were there.

Best Souvenir: I collected a coin from each country we visited and had them attached to a bracelet as a trip souvenir for Becky.

Best Cemetery: The Dog Cemetery in Guam. Deserves and has its own write-up.

Best Market: The Marriage Market in a large park outside Shanghai where parents go, armed with pictures and a resume of their child, to find a marriage partner for their child. Eligible individuals are categorized from A - D based on education, wealth, appearance, and ability to speak English. Men marry below themselves to avoid competition from an "equal" woman. D level men and A level women probably leave China to find a marriage partner?

Best Haggler: Becky at a kiosk anywhere. Having learned that quantity sold was more important to most merchants than price, she would hold up two of an item and ask, "How much for the two?" Sample answer, "$20." Holding up one of the two she'd ask, "How much for this one?" Sample answer, "$14." Holding up the "other" one she'd say, "Ok, then I'll take this one for "$6." She either got a very good buy or, in confusion, they left her alone.

Best Primitive Efficiency: The Dhobi Ghat open-air laundry in Mumbai, India. A man standing in each of 14 concrete tubs, 4' x 4' in size, and mid-calf deep in water, beating laundry against the concrete wall of his tub to clean it. Loads arrived constantly on trucks, carts, and bicycles from hospitals, restaurants, and residences. Laundry drying on poles, rooftops, clotheslines strung between buildings, and on rocks. Becky managed to get up close and reported that the washed clothes smelled clean and fresh. Codification so efficient that loss rate is one item per million.

Best Bar: The Ice Bar in Sydney, Australia. Deserves and has its own write-up.

Best Monument: One evening before we left on the cruise, we saw and enjoyed the movie "Kachi" starring Richard Gere. It is based on a true story about a dog named, Kachi. The movie is set in US, but acknowledges that the original events took place in Tokyo. Movie credits mentioned a statue of Kachi outside Tokyo Central Railway Station. We had it on our "must see" list, found it, and took a picture. It's a great story of a dog's loyalty and a good movie.

Best Gotcha: Deserves its own write-up. See "100 Camels For Your Wife."

Best Purchase: Dick's Rolex Knockoff. Deserves its own write-up.

Dog Cemetery, Guam

We had heard rumors about a unique cemetery on the Island of Guam and when we stopped at the Island we set out to find it.

We discovered it on the US Naval Station (our military ID cards allowed us entry) and quickly learned that its location is unknown by most of the civilian and naval personnel working at the Naval Station. If you ever try to find it, ask directions from a Marine. It is a cemetery dedicated to the twenty-five Doberman, war dogs, that gave their lives helping the Marines capture the Island of Guam during WW II. It is located in an isolated corner of the naval station, in a clearing surrounded by dense tropical vegetation and is not visible from the paved road that allows automobile access to the area. A small, sign directs a visitor to a narrow path through the vegetation and ultimately to the beautifully manicured memorial, maintained by the Marines stationed at the naval station.

In the center of a circular area, is a dark grey, granite block, about three feet tall, with a casting of a life size Doberman, alertly resting, on top. On the west facing side of the granite memorial is carved:

"ALWAYS FAITHFUL" WAS INSPIRED
BY THE SPIRIT OF THESE
HEROIC DOGS WHO ARE THE EMBODIMENT
OF LOVE AND DEVOTION.
Sculptress: Susan Bahary Wilner

And the words carved on the east side read:

25 MARINE WAR DOGS GAVE THEIR
LIVES LIBERATING GUAM
IN 1944. THEY SERVED AS SENTRIES,
MESSENGERS, AND SCOUTS.
THEY EXPLORED CAVES, DETECTED
MINES AND BOOBY TRAPS.
SEMPER FIDELIS

And it list the names of these heroes:

KURT, SKIPPER, NIG, MISSY, BLITZ, BURSCH, YONNIE, PONCHO, PRINCE, CAPPY, ARNO, PEPPER, KOKO, TUBBY, FRITZ, DUKE, SILVER, LUDWIG, BUNKIE, HOBO, EMMY, MAX, BROCKIE, RICKEY, and TAM (buried at sea off Asan Point)

In a circle surrounding the granite memorial is a walkway with twenty-five evenly spaced, concrete headstones with the silhouette of the head of a Doberman and the name of the dog buried at the marker. An American flag flying at half-mast is raised by a Marine each morning at sunrise and lowered at sunset. Every morning, after raising the flag, the Marine places a fresh, bone shaped, dog biscuit (in lieu of flowers) in front of each dog's headstone.

The memorial was given in the memory and on behalf of the surviving men of the 2nd and 3rd Marine War Dog Platoons, many of whom owe their lives to the bravery and sacrifice of these gallant animals. It was dedicated on July 21, 1994 by William W. Putney, DVM CO 3rd Dog Platoon.

The serenity, beauty and dignity of the site simultaneously reminds a visitor of the devastation war reeks on all living things, the devotion of a dog to its master, and that once a Marine always a Marine. Semper Fi.

The Ice Bar

It took some time, thirty-four days and 6,059 miles aboard the Pacific Princess to be precise, but we were finally in Auckland, NZ. So we spent an afternoon having cocktails at the Ice Bar. Yeah, it's mostly a guy thing, but Becky had fun also, and besides what else should one do on their first visit to New Zealand?

The Ice Bar is the private, rear addition to a "drinking house" near the head of a pier in downtown Auckland. The main part of the establishment is a large, open, indoor room with an attached patio area. Both the indoor bar and the patio area have a bandstand, tables, stools, and each is dominated by a very long bar down the middle.

The Ice Bar has its own reception area where one must pay an entrance fee of $35 NZ or $29.50 in US dollars for admission. (The exchange rate was $1.19 NZ for $1 US.) Customers were given the following briefing.

"The price of admission includes one drink and the use of ski gloves, a fleece lined hooded parka, and boots if you are not wearing proper footwear. The temperature in the bar is kept between -5 and -7 degrees Celsius." (That's 19 to 22 degrees Fahrenheit. The temperature on the street was a sunny, 76 degrees Fahrenheit and we were wearing shorts, sandals, and sunglasses.) "We request that you hold your glass of liquor with both hands because the glass is made of ice and will be very slippery. You can have scotch, bourbon, gin, vodka, or select from a menu of vodka based mixed drinks. We cannot keep beer in the Ice Bar because it freezes.

And no picture taking is allowed. There will be a photographer inside taking pictures that you can purchase when you leave. The rule is partly for us to make some money, but also because we have a heated, protective covering for our camera to keep it from freezing. We highly recommend that you not take your cell or camera inside unless you keep them close to your body, because many have been ruined by the cold temperature. We have a secure area, continually occupied, that's available for anything you want to insure doesn't get frozen. We have thirty jackets and pairs of glove, so that's our occupancy limit. If the Ice Bar is full you can put your name on a waiting list and we will call you in the main bar when your turn comes up."

We paid and were each given a pair of disposable rubber gloves to wear inside the heavy gloves and disposable booties to wear inside the boots. Dressed and given the OK to enter the Ice Bar, we proceeded to a thick wooded door with a sign that stated, "Do Not Allow Both Doors to be Open at the Same Time." (Not unlike entering the bird or butterfly sanctuary at a zoo, except these doors were about 18" thick.)

Because we were dressed for the temperature, there was not the sudden burst of bone chilling, cold air that I expected upon entering the bar, but rather a pleasant and comfortable temperature change. Inside, the walls were covered with a thick layer of ice and all the furniture (tables, chairs, life size animal carvings, the bar, shuffle board, gaming tables, etc.) were all carved from ice. Among the animal ice carvings, all of which were life size, and to be used as seats, there was a llama with a white, llama wool, pad for a saddle. Becky mounted the llama long enough for a picture, but she found it difficult to keep her legs from touching the animal's body and, wearing shorts, found that was uncomfortably cold. There was a dartboard hanging on one wall with the appropriate chalkboard for scoring, but we were disappointed to discover that it, and the darts, were magnetic. Expressing my displeasure, I was told that the real darts had to be replaced because darts missing the target – it was a bar after all and people were drinking – were chipping the ice from the wall. In the center of the room there was an ice hockey table, carved from ice of course, with two plastic paddles and a plastic puck. In traditional fashion, if the puck was hit into a goal it would slide down an ice chute to an ice pocket for retrieval. We found the ice surface and sidewalls made for faster puck movement than the traditional, polished, plastic surface. The bar was at the end of the room furthest the entry door. A standard bar of proper height and width, about ten feet long with six bar stools – everything carved from ice. A variety of blend and named brand bottles, all glazed with ice, occupied the ice shelves behind the bartender. All drinks were $8 NZ or $7 US. The bar stools and all other seats, had small, flat animal skin covers to keep one's tush from freezing to the seat. The ice glass was about an inch thick and shaped like a goblet with a wide top making it possible to hold while wearing thick gloves. Drinking from it was easy. Drinks were served on small, black, rubber coasters to prevent the ice glass from sliding off the ice bar. We discovered that all adult beverages stored at 20 degrees Fahrenheit and served in an ice glass were velvety smooth, deliciously gentle and seemed non-alcoholic. (In truth, we did not try them "all", but the several we tried were definitely delicious and easy to swallow.) When finished with a drink, protocol directed that one proceed to what looked like an eight-foot long shuffleboard table – carved from ice of course – place the empty ice glass on the table upside down and slide it forcefully to the other end. When we did so, the ice glass shattered against the far end of the table and the pieces fell through an opening in the table into an ice bucket on the floor. (The Ice Bar version of throwing a champagne glass into the fireplace?) A new ice glass came with each drink; dishwashing was not an issues. Other furniture included several benches, small tables with facing stools, more animals and other creature carvings, and a chandelier – all of course carved from ice. The only non-ice items in the room were the small animal skins that covered to top of the seats, the ice hockey puck & paddles, the darts, and dartboard. It was a wonderful and exciting adventure.

Using a Boomerang

In Cairns, a tropical town in northeastern Australia, at the edge of the rain forest, we chose to spend a day at the Tjapukai Aboriginal Cultural Center. The aboriginal people originally arrived here via a land bridge from New Guinea. The sights were impressive and the presentations on the history, culture, and cuisine of the aboriginal people were most interesting. They demonstrated their dances to the sound of drums and a didgeridoo. (A didgeridoo is a 4 - 8 foot long, hollow, wooden instrument, without keys, that is blown like a horn.) Invited to try the didgeridoo, I could not make any kind of sound. To make continuous sounds/music one must simultaneously inhale through one's nose and exhale through one's mouth into the instrument. Try it! It's not natural and must be learned.

Concluding the presentation detailing their hunting methods and weapons, we were told that we would be taken to a field and shown how to throw a boomerang at a straw, kangaroo target. Before being led outside however, the audience was asked if anyone had experience throwing a boomerang?

I proudly raised my hand and noticed that I was the only one.

"What was your experience?" The aboriginal who had given the presentation asked me.

"Well my brother brought me a boomerang after he visited Australia. I spent time in a ball field trying to throw it and catch it's return. I got my hands on it once or twice, but never could catch it."

The presenter turned to face the adjoining room from which other men had been bringing and returning various weapons and paraphernalia, and shouted something in an unintelligible language. In response, another aboriginal in native dress and dread locks came out and joined the presenter. "See this man's face?" He said pointing to an angular scar that ran from above the man's right ear to the bridge of his nose. "That's what happens when a boomerang comes all the way back. And don't ever try to catch one." he said pointing my way. (So much for my pride and boomerang experience!) "Boomerangs are supposed to return towards the thrower, rather than continue into the brush and get lost," he continued, "but they should land between you and your target so that you can pick it up while following your target and throw it again if necessary or at least retrieve it for later use. Boomerangs are not easy to carve and not every one turns out to be good."

My boomerang practice back home did not help me to hit the target either. To throw and catch it, I was throwing it in high looping arc. To take down a kangaroo it is thrown low and straight at the target. The straw "roos" were safe with me throwing at them.

Today, the nicely painted boomerang, given to me by my brother, hanging safely and arrogantly on the wall of my poker room and I have deleted, "Throw and catch a boomerang," from my, 'To Do' list.

As an aside and not verified, a guide on the Hop-on Hop-off bus we used one afternoon to see Sydney, Australia, told us passengers the following story. When the British arrived in Australia and saw the large, reddish-brown, hopping animals they asked the aboriginals, "What do you call that strange animal?" They received no answer and shouted out the question a second and third time. There was still a language barrier, but after some silence and consultation among the aboriginals, the British thought they heard the word, "kangaroo." The animals were thus called kangaroos and the name stuck. Quite a bit later, when the British began learning the aboriginal language they discovered that the aboriginal word, "kangaroo" meant, "We have no idea what the f_ _ _ you're saying, mate."

A bit later, when approaching a beautiful, large building – that was identified on our tourist map as the Australian Office of Records where birth, marriage, divorce, and death certificates are kept – the same guide called our attention to the, "Hatch, Match, and Dispatch" building.

Ah! The beauty of language.

One Hundred Camels for Your Wife!

In mid-April, during our world cruise, the ship docked in Salalah, Oman. Oman is a Muslim country slightly smaller than Kansas with a population of 3.5 million people. The women wear black burkas with only their eyes showing. Men can have as many as four wives. Salalah, the second largest city in Oman, is located in the southern corner and is most famous as the perfume capital of Arabia. The afternoon heat in April was almost unbearable, but boswellia trees thrive here and their aromatic resin, frankincense, is the basis for incense and perfumes. In ancient times, Salalah merchants acquired fabulous wealth as caravan traders purchased large quantities of frankincense. It was burned in temples to mask the smell of sacrificed animals and in homes to repel mosquitoes.

We had witnessed the bleeding of a boswellia tree for its white sap (frankincense when dried), and then traveled to a souk (old market place) to purchase some frankincense. Our shopping completed, we were standing in the imperfect shade of a scraggly, palm tree waiting for a taxi and watching an Arab in a red turban trying to entice tourists onto one of his two camels for photographs or rides in the desert. During a lull in business he approached and I got a good look at his sun-wrinkled face, bushy grey mustache that appeared to begin in his nose and descended below his chin. As he got closer I saw that he had an easily countable number of teeth.

After briefly verifying that I was not interested in a camel ride, he said, in broken, but clearly understandable English, "Your wife very pretty. I give you one hundred camels for her."

While Becky rolled her eyes and drifted several feet away, I asked him, "How many wives do you have now?"

He said, "Only one that's why I need one more."

"Well, I don't know what I would do with 100 camels?" I confessed.

"Oh, sir. With 100 camels you make much money selling pictures and making desert rides. You can retire very fast."

I was telling him, "That's interesting, but I'm already retired and . . ." When Becky, who had edged back by my side interrupted me asking, "Why are you baiting him?"

I told her, "I was just trying to find out if he would add a few goats to his offer." It was worth the slap to the back of my head . . .. Gotcha.

Dick's Rolex Knock-off

In Shanghai, China, it is easy to become convinced that a copy of anything made anywhere in the world is locally availability for purchase. I was looking at Rolex watches. Walking along the sidewalks, vendors would approach with Rolex watches up both arms from their wrist to their elbow. Most were priced from $25 - $35. After passing several of these vendors I was approached by a Chinaman who was a little better dressed than the others who was selling his Rolex watches for $45 - $50. In response to my comment that I could have gotten a better price from his competitors he said, "Mine better. Seiko inside!" Fortunately I did not make a purchase that day; I waited and got a better deal aboard ship the day we left.

The wristwatch I purchased looks like a Rolex with its large face and thick, heavy, metal, wristband and fold-over closing mechanism. It has four sets of ten, diamond looking (glass) chips around the outer edge of the face. On the beveled outer-most edge, under the glass face, the twelve months are printed in white on a black background and each has some lines underneath suggesting a perpetual calendar. Over the black, main watch face, the hour hand and minute hand, both in white and edged with gold, rotate above a twenty-four hour clock face and five golden dials pointing to the ornate edges of three white and two gold graduated scales. One scale lists the days of the week, another - if you look very closely - has the words "on, off, hold" in tiny gold lettering. Another has the words, "Time, Cal, Alt" inscribed in gold oblique letters. The months and days of the week are all spelled correctly. The last two scales with pointers have tiny writing that I could not read with a magnifying glass, but serve to enhance the beauty, uniqueness, and splendor of the timepiece. (I think one scale is going to remind me when my car needs an oil change.) I have worn my watch to black tie formal affairs and must say that it was as pretentious and appeared as expensive as anything on any other man's wrist. (Some of the women had some rather gaudy baubles on their wrist that might have surpassed my timepiece in elegance and price!) The cool part is that my watch has only one small battery because only the hour and minute hands move, the others are for entertainment. The only downside is that there is so much (apparently) happening on the face it is difficult to tell the time. But that's OK because I only wear it on formal occasions, when time is of little importance. I hesitate to wear it routinely for fear of attracting a robber who could easily misjudge my worth upon seeing my wristwatch.

By the way, this superb timepiece cost me only $19.95 and it has been keeping the correct time for three months, six days, and fourteen hours. Did I get a great deal or what?

In case you wonder where I keep it when the plain, white faced, Timex, with the large numerals that I prefer to wear is on my wrist; I will reveal all! It resides in a small drawer alongside a few relics and an early battery powered watch with an alarm that I received after the high school basketball team went to the Boston Garden Tournament in 1955. (We didn't know how to work the "new" alarm and the sound of an alarm would occasionally embarrass one of us when it rang loudly during a high school class.) My latest watch also keeps company with a watch that has a cotton puff in the center and leaves as arms (from the Cotton Bowl Game); a watch with an "N Star" in the middle of the face and the letters "NAVY43ARMY12" around the rim where the numerals usually appear (it was the widest margin of victory in an Army-Navy game); a Gruen with gold roman numerals and a football oval surrounding the words, "NORTH SOUTH SHRINE GAME" in the center; and finally a travel watch with two faces for keeping time at home and local time when on a trip (practical but most often forgotten when traveling.) So, what's in your watch drawer?

Hawaiian Vacation
"Adventure before dementia."
(I made it up.)

I wanted to show Becky the charm and beauty of the Hawaiian Islands that I had enjoyed during my two, two-year submarine tours on Oahu at Pearl Harbor. Our schedule was for a week on Oahu, a week on the Big Island, and a week on Kauai. On the Big Island we stayed in a small, one bedroom cabin at the Kilauea Military Camp on the rim of the volcano. At various locations in the volcano complex, volcanic ash was flowing towards the sea, a steam vent smelling strongly of sulfur created a vertical cloud hundreds of feet into the air, and we walked down to and across a crater floor. We drove the Big Island in a rented car to enjoy unique sites such as Black Sand Beach. (The sand is clean, soft, and black having originated as black volcanic lava.) During our drives the scenery was frequently interrupted by signs warning, "Don't Hit The Nene." There were neither warning signs nor nenes on the well-developed island of Oahu and I had no idea what this State Bird looked like. Inquiries revealed that there were nenes at the local zoo and that we would pass the entrance road to the zoo on our way back to the airport. We departed early for our return trip to the airport to see a nene at the zoo. Traffic was heavy, the parking lot was congested and we ran through the zoo to where the nenes were penned. It was an unremarkable looking goose that looked much like one of the Canadian Geese that are popular on the mainland. It was not a memorable bird but finally we had seen one. QED!

We were on time for our flight and one hour later we were in Kauai. Ex-submarine shipmates, good friends, and our host and hostess, Mike and Claudia Salewske met us and drove us to the Hanalei Bay Resort. We had a first floor bedroom and noticed two large spray bottles with labels that read, "Use To Keep Out The Nene. If The Patio Door Is Left Open They Will Enter." We drew back the curtains that were keeping the afternoon sun from heating the room through the sliding glass patio-doors. Five nenes were on and alongside the patio eating grass and crumbs. As we exited to the patio, the closest goose honked and stretched its neck towards us in annoyance. We were interrupting his dining and he resented the disturbance. It was tempting to respond using the water spray bottle, but mutual glances between Becky and me resulted in laughter over our very recent expedition to the zoo to see one of these "elusive " animals. We opened some wine, joined our hosts and nenes on the patio and proceeded to narrate our morning experience.

Knowledge vs. Wisdom

"The older I grow, the more I distrust the
familiar doctrine that age brings wisdom."
H.L. Mencken 1880 - 1956

Three days prior to departure on a planned RV trip down the Blue Ridge highway I watched a neighborhood youngster trying unsuccessfully to jump from the sidewalk down to the road on his skateboard. He was failing to shift his weight to his back foot and the front of his board kept nosing into the road. Fit, capable, healthy, and only about 60 years older than the youngster, I decided to show him how to do it. My tibia is now fractured and my right leg is in toes to knee cast. The cast prevents driving; our trip has been postponed. My wife, now also my chauffeur, explained that my mistake was not differentiating between <u>knowledge</u> (how to do something) and <u>wisdom</u> (when not to do it.) Her analogy, to help me understand, was, "Knowledge is knowing that a tomato is a fruit. Wisdom is not putting tomato in fruit salad." I think I've got it now. Women are really smart!

Go to Sleep With a Smile

"Everything is funny, as long as it is
happening to somebody else."
Will Rogers 1879 – 1935

I have always enjoyed telling jokes and hearing a joke. Occasionally I would find a good joke in the newspaper, a magazine, or among my e-mails and would share it with Becky at night, in bed, before we went to sleep. In bed, sharing a pillow in the dark, our routine is to briefly discuss our day, our plans for tomorrow, and new hopes or ideas for the future. If I had a joke it would precede our last, "I love you; sweet dreams."

One night early in February, Becky asked, "Mardi Gras is next week; what are your plans for Lent?"

Rather than give up something, e.g., chocolate or alcohol, we try to be positive and do something good each day during Lent, but I confessed to being without a plan.

"I enjoy going to sleep with a smile after laughing at one of your jokes, why don't you find a nice joke to tell me each of the forty nights between Fat Tuesday and Easter?" She suggested.

I agreed, despite immediately realizing two major issues: finding a joke book, or two, and a way to remember a joke until after our nighttime ritual ended and it was time to go to sleep. The lights would be out and there would be no reading from a joke book or crib sheet.

It did not take long to ascertain that my personal library would offer little hope. The closest I had to a useful joke book was a 200-page compilation of stupid people doing stupid things, titled <u>The Darwin Awards</u>. Not something to go to sleep thinking about, so it was off to the local Barnes & Noble Bookstore.

My library now includes, <u>Milton Berle's Private Joke File</u> (somewhat useful, but too many one liners,) <u>Pretty Good Joke Book</u> (a Prairie Home Companion with an especially funny section of, "Yo Mama Jokes") and the Reader's Digest books that came through day after day. Reader's Digest has published four books of the jokes that appeared in their magazine under the titles: <u>Humor in Uniform</u>, <u>Laughter, the Best Medicine @ Work</u>, <u>Laughter, the Best Medicine - Those Lovable Pets</u>, and <u>Laughter Really is the Best Medicine</u>. It took several books because many of the jokes were old, i.e., we had heard them before, too long or short, only funny if read, accompanied by a cartoon drawing, or setting specific.

I never missed a night, even when we were traveling, and I often shared two or three jokes. Actually, I found that if I used a one-word reminder of each punch-line and combined them into a sentence (of sorts) my memory was better than when I tried to remember a single punch-line. My memory was only pretty good however, because on more that one night I had to get out of bed in the dark, go to my desk, turn on a light, find my book, and refresh my memory of a joke, before returning to bed and sharing a laugh.

It became such an enjoyable occurrence that we continued after Easter until I had exhausted all the useful jokes in the books.

Since this event occurred a number of years ago and since our memory is fading because it contains so many facts and so much knowledge, (it couldn't be age?) I could probably do it again using the same books? Hmmm! When is Mardi Gras this year?

CHAPTER 13

Reflections and Thoughts Going Forward

What Is Retirement?

"The brain is a wonderful organ; it starts working
the moment you get up in the morning and
does not stop until you get into the office."
Robert Frost 1874 - 1963

In 2011, Tom Winant, a good friend and Operations Research colleague from the Naval Postgraduate School was retiring from a large aerospace company in the San Francisco-San Jose area of California. His wife asked me to provide input to the retirement ceremony. I had been retired for over a decade and the request caused me to ponder what retirement really meant. I sent her the following letter. She told me that the Master of Ceremony read it to a large audience.

Retirement Advice and Congratulations

Congratulations Tom on finally summoning the courage to begin your final career, i.e., RETIREMENT. You should promise yourself that you will make it your final career and not accept any of the tempting offers you will undoubtedly receive. For example, you may be solicited to run for governor of California on the Tea Party ticket.

The first thing you will notice about retirement is that it's true what you have been hearing from retired friends, but never quite believed. "You will be busier in retirement than when working." For starters, much of your retired time will be occupied responding to correspondence, paying bills, forwarding jokes on the Internet, and talking on the telephone with old friends. You know, all that stuff you did every day at the office. You will be surprised how much time it takes. In my case, I had been Naval Academy Class President for ten years, and had to resign when I retired because it was taking up an excessive amount of my "free" time.

The next think you will discover is that power naps are great. I don't mean those 20 minute naps you've been taking at your work desk, I mean a 45 - 60 minute uninterrupted snooze. Medical science has recently discovered that it is the best way to relieve any stress that you may have built up after being up for three or four hours.

It is very important that you make a list of things you've wanted to do and begin doing them. Include travel, both near and far. Don't overlook the local museums, college athletic events, and local strip club you've been longing to visit. Include hobbies you have wanted to pursue, but for lack of time have been neglecting. You can never tell where they may lead and what new adventures might result. I took group dance lessons at the local community center and ended up as a dance instructor/dance host on a cruise ship. I began oil painting as a new hobby and last year spent four days at Fantasy Fest in Key West, FL. body painting naked women. It was truly an unforgettable adventure. I can send you e-mail pictures if you have any doubts and if you have your own, private, e-mail address. It is important that you make and keep a list of things you want to do because during retirement your mind becomes so cluttered with "stuff" that you will begin to forget things. It's unlikely that it applies to you, but I've been told that some people even begin to forget things just from thinking about retirement as the big day approaches.

You should also establish a place or area of your home and designate it as your, "_____ of no ambition." My friend who began this wonderful idea, has an entire second floor porch (his porch of no ambition), I have a gazebo of no ambition, and a colleague has designated a corner of his garage. In the designated area absolutely no work of any kind should be attempted.

No laptops, professional reading, cell phones, or loud music allowed. I use my area for light reading when I'm alone, Michael Connelly is a favorite author. When I'm with like-minded friends, we typically include cigars and adult beverages – they are, of course, allowed in "the area" of no ambition. With friends, jokes are rampant, we discuss important subjects, e.g., women and sports, and we attempt to find answers or solutions to world problems and ponderable issues such as, "Why didn't Tarzan have a beard?" We recently made an interesting list of, "Statements that would be fun to put in fortune cookies." We are now looking for a Chinese fortune cookie maker with a large pair of – – – – (you know whats), who might want to purchase our wit.

So enjoy your new freedom, not only from a work schedule, but also from the need to constantly appear technically sophisticated. Once retired, if you're in a store and bothered by a clerk who asks, "Would you like to buy a colored TV?" You can answer, without fear of losing your job, "Do you have any red ones?"

And don't let people think that you are becoming a couch potato. If you enjoy exercise have at it, just don't overdo it. Otherwise, begin calling your bathroom the Jim instead of the John, so you can tell people that you go the "Jim/gym" every morning. You may also want to rename your pet. If you renamed your dog, "Five Miles," you could tell people that you walk five miles every day.

I hope you are now beginning to appreciate how much fun you can have in retirement. You have made the correct decision. Enjoy your new adventure. Welcome to the club.

Dick

On The Porch With Dad

"Everyone sets out to do something, and everybody
does something, but no one does what he sets out to do."
George Moore 1852 - 1933

One summer afternoon, Dad and I sat on the porch of the family's Cape Cod cottage exchanging tales about our experiences. He told me a story that impressed me so much that I put it in writing. When it was finished, I thought it should appear in a sports magazine or a magazine for teenagers, but its length did not suit the requirements of the magazines I thought might be interested. Dad was able to deliver a copy to the brother of the story's main character, but the story was never submitted for publication. I offer it to you now under the title, The Team Manager.

The Team Manager

He was pleased to be part of the High School football team, even if it was only as team manager. Coach Rollie had seen Frankie hanging around the football field during practice, inquired about his interests, and that very same day invited him to be the team's manager. Frankie loved sports but realized that being team manager was the best he could do. In fact, being team manager was a real accomplishment, a goal he'd only dreamed about, because since the accident he'd only been told, and frequently reminded, of the things that he would be unable to do. Frankie was pleased that he had been given some significant responsibilities and he fondly remembered several occasions when players had gone to the coaches with equipment problems and been told, "Go see Frankie, he will take care of it for you." It was important to Frankie to feel like a contributor and the sparkle in his eyes, whenever he was with the team, revealed his pride and sense of worth. Two Pariseau brothers coached the football team. They had established a winning tradition at Tolman Senior High School, in Pawtucket, RI and Frankie was part of the team during these banner years.

Youthful curiosity and a sense of challenge induced him to attempt to refill the cigarette lighter with lighter fluid. The refill hole was small and required a great deal of concentration for a young boy. By the time he had finished he was unaware of the amount of the fluid that he had spilled on himself. Frankie did not remember flicking the lighter to see if it would light, he only remembered the pain that followed. He overheard the doctors say that he had burns over 90% of this body and that he would probably never walk again. He did not disbelieve that assessment; his mind simply chose to purge the entire event, from the agony of the frequent operations to the boredom of the two years he had to spend in the hospital. He did learn to walk, but it was an ungraceful gait that gave the appearance of a limp followed by dragging one leg along behind the other. Actually, his ambulation was ungainly because he had bad balance. Something to do with the accident he had been told. He did not mind the stare he frequently received when he walked at school or out in public, because it simply reminded him of what he had accomplished. He was especially proud that the coaches let him run out onto the field with the football team before each game. Obviously no one expected him to run at their pace, but he managed. He knew where to position himself to get a head start and from where he could almost keep up with the players all the way to the team bench. Everyone on the team treated him with respect and no one on the team paid any attention to his awkward gait. If it was not a natural reaction for a new player, there was no doubt from the coaches' actions that it was the only attitude they would tolerate. On a team with these coaches, everyone received respect.

Frankie was deceptively strong for someone who would have been below average in height even before the accident and now appeared even shorter because he had to remain hunched over to maintain his balance. He had no trouble lifting and carrying a bag of footballs, a medical kit, and the assorted equipment that the team manager was responsible for having constantly on hand. His face was not disfigured, but his upper and lower jaws did not mesh exactly. He looked a little strange when he opened and closed his mouth while chewing his food, but he never missed an opportunity to eat with the team. After all, the players did not care, they were his friends, and the doctors had also told him he would never be able to eat solid food.

Being with the team was clearly the highlight of Frankie's day. He especially enjoyed participating in the singing and hollering that always went on during the short bus ride from the team's dressing room at the High School to the stadium on game days. This was Frankie's second year as the football team manager and he had shared in the thrill of victory and the humiliation of defeat as intensely as anyone associated with the team. A few weeks before the football season ended, Coach Rollie, who coached the swimming team during the winter semester, asked, "Frankie, you are the best team manager I've ever had. Will you be the swim team manager?"

The answer, as he straightened to his maximum height and a perceptible twinkle appeared in his eyes, was a proud "Sure Coach. Thank you."

"Tolman High School Swim Team"
(Back row far left Coach Rollie Pariseau; far right Frankie Folan.)
(Photo from the Tolman High School Yearbook, "The Redjackets")
(Used with permission)

The swimming pool at Tolman Senior High School is in a small room with tiled walls, less than adequate lighting and left one smelling of chlorine for hours after leaving the area. The pool itself has four, 25-meter lanes and is about 15 meters wide. One day during swimming team practice, near the end of the season, Frankie approached Coach Rollie and asked, "Coach, I think I could swim across the pool, not the long way, but from side to side. The doctors told me that I'd never be able to swim, but I really think I can do it. Do you think I could try?"

"You know where the bathing suits are Frankie. Go get ready and you can try/"

While Frankie was in the dressing room, the coach told the swimmers that Frankie was going to try to swim across the four lanes of the pool and that they would get out of the pool and take a break while he tried. He also told them not to try to help because it was important that Frankie did it by himself. If Frankie needed to be saved from drowning; the coach would do it.

Frankie reappeared wearing a sweatshirt and his khaki pants. Coach Rollie blew his whistle and told his swimmers to take a break. The young men exited the pool with a considerable amount of pushing, hollering, and fooling around; it was rare to take a break during practice. Frankie approached the edge of the pool and removed his khaki trousers. Almost instantly a deafening silence descended over the pool and all eyes focused with astonishment at the quilt-work of small patches of skin sown together over Frankie's legs from his ankles to the bottom of his bathing suit. The shocked witnesses continued to stare in silent disbelief as Frankie removed the sweatshirt and revealed a similar pattern of small squares of grafted skin from the top of his bathing suit to the base of his neck.

There had been word around the school that Frankie had had an accident as a child, but neither the swimmers nor the coach was prepared for what they saw. Perhaps it had taken as much courage to disrobe in front of his classmates as it did to attempt the swim, or perhaps it was simply the intensity of his desire to accomplish the feat, but without hesitation Frankie stepped forward and let himself fall headfirst into the pool. It was a feeble attempt at a dive and he met the water with a thud and a splash that made the swimmers grimace. He struggled awkwardly to reach the surface and his head finally emerged at the very edge of the pool where he'd entered the water. Frankie stretched his body out toward the far side of the pool and began an irregular windmill motion with his arms and occasionally kicked out with one of his legs. His movement in the water more closely resembled the thrashing of a drowning man than any swimming stroke and under other circumstance, any witness who could swim would have jumped into the pool to save this obviously drowning man. It was difficult to even imagine that he would resurface between his flailing strokes yet it appeared that he was actually making progress across the pool. His journey was agonizingly slow and anything except direct, but there was progress nonetheless.

Suddenly the splashing in the pool was punctuated by a shout of encouragement from one of the swimmers standing at the edge of the pool. That shout was like a catalyst that provided an outlet for the awkward and helpless gaze of amazement from the observers and provided them with the opportunity to become part of this courageous display. They all began shouting words of encouragement. As Frankie continued to slowly make progress across the pool, the noise level grew steadily louder and more passionate. By the time Frankie approached the far side of the pool, a passerby hearing the noise, could easily have believed that the room was packed with hundreds of spectators and that it was the final event of the State Championship Swim Meet. Finally Frankie was able to reach out and grab the side of the pool. Despite his desperate effort to regain his breath, a broad smile of satisfaction beamed from his face as he acknowledged the applause and cheers from all those who had witnessed his accomplishment. He was helped from the pool by an enthusiastic and astonished group of young swimmers whose continued cheering showed that they appreciated the significance of what they had just witnessed. For many, including the Coach, it would become a valuable lifelong lesson in one's ability to conquer incredible odds with a combination of intense desire and courage.

That summer, between his junior and senior year of High School, Frankie died. It was unexpected by his classmates and the school faculty. There were the inevitable rumors. Some said that an early death had been predicted as a result of the accident. Others theorized that his inability to properly chew food had a critical effect on his diet, but the truth was never known at the school.

The next football season, the team was undefeated going into the final game of the season, on Thanksgiving Day, against St. Raphael

Academy, a private, Catholic school, and cross-town rival. The outcome would decide the State Championship and all predictions were for an extremely close game that either team could win. The coaches at Tolman Senior High School had a tradition of briefly stopping the bus at a church on the way to each game. The players were invited to thank god for the opportunity to play in today's game, and to pray that they played well and that no one would be seriously injured. The players knew that they did not have to leave the bus if they preferred not to pray, but no one can recall an occasion when the entire team in full football uniform except for helmet and cleats, did not go into the church. For this championship game, Coach Rollie suggested to his coaching brother that instead of stopping at the church they should stop briefly at the cemetery and visit Frankie's grave. Coach Rollie volunteered to prepare an appropriate message that he would read at the gravesite. The message would applaud Frankie's courage and they would dedicate the game to his memory. Both coaches agreed that it could be the motivation that the team needed to play their best in the big game.

The bus ride began with the loud songs, random cheers, and shouts of encouragement that were typical of Tolman Senior High School teams under their current coaches. The noise was not unlike that made by an army, building up its courage, and overcoming anxiety, before going into battle. When the bus stopped at the cemetery, the surprised players were told to gather at Frankie's gravesite. Once the team had gathered, Coach Rollie began to read his notes, "Frankie was a proud, courageous, and loyal teammate who always regarded the team's success more highly than his own success. Yet his courage and personal accomplishment are undeniable. They told him that he would never walk, but he learned how to walk. They told him he'd never run, but he led us onto the filed. They told him he'd never swim, but many of you have heard how he . . ." Overcome with emotion, the coach could not continue to read what he had written. His coaching brother told the team to re-board the bus.

During the remainder of the bus ride to the stadium there was a compelling silence in the bus. Coach Rollie whispered to his brother, "I really goofed this time. They are all so caught up in their own thoughts they may not be able to refocus on the game."

With a silent nod, his brother admitted that conditions did not look good.

The atmosphere in and around the stadium was charged with anticipation and loud with the release of tension. The school bands, cheerleaders, and fans, many wearing yellow mums, were noisily celebrating in anticipation of the upcoming event on this clear, cool Thanksgiving Day in New England. A long line of people waited to purchase tickets. It would be a packed stadium.

The atmosphere in the team dressing room before the game was tense and somber, in stark contrast; not only to the outside, but also to the pre-game dressing room at every other game this team had played. When the referee knocked on the dressing room door and called for the team to take the field, Coach Rollie said, "This is the game you have all been waiting for, the one you will always remember, make it one that will make you proud. And if you make an especially good play - a nifty run, hard tackle, great block, or difficult catch - point to me on the sideline and say, 'That was for you Frankie.' Now let's go out there and have some fun."

The coaches did not know what kind of game to expect from the team, but it didn't take long for the first player to make a play that he considered exceptional, point to Coach Rollie and say, "That was for Frankie." It became obvious that no player wanted to be left out by not doing something that was worthy of dedicating to Frankie, so each one began to hit harder, run faster, and play smarter. They fed off one another's great plays for the entire game and Coach Rollie acknowledged each and every dedication to Frankie. The opposition had no idea why they were literally being mauled and the next day the sports writers reported Tolman's lopsided victory without a clue to Frankie's impact. Frankie definitely helped the team win the big game his senior year. His pride and courage were clearly remembered by his teammates. The coaches need not have worried.

Later that year, his senior class dedicated their yearbook to Frankie's memory. There is also an annual Frankie Folan award, given for courage and being respectful of the dignity of others. Coach Rollie Pariseau, my Dad, won the award the first year it was awarded.

Athletics: Then and Now

"Everything comes to him who hustles while he waits."
Thomas Edison 1847 - 1931

One Sport or Two?

Growing up if I felt like playing a sport, depending on the season, I simply got on my bike and went to the vacant lot across the street from St. Joseph's Church to play baseball, to the green field below Olive Street bridge to play football, to the YMCA to play basketball, or if there was ice, to LaSalette to play hockey. Games began after school during the week, about 9 AM on Saturdays, and after church on Sundays. Two "captains" would be chosen, or self-elected and would alternately select players for their team. Among the baseball players up until high school, were two girls who were almost always ready to play and who were chosen before most of the boys because of their capability. One, now in her mid 70s, remains an avid baseball fan that uses every one of her season Red Sox tickets. The other, whose whereabouts is unknown, graduated with me from grammar school missing two front teeth that had been lost to a fly ball coming in from the direction of the sun.

Sports were organized in high school and college but playing more than one sport was not discouraged. Today, a youngster must select a sport, a position and a specialty if he is to compete. Sports are organized beginning at the Pee Wee level and forever after. Teams have players that are individually better than when I played, but the problem of melding players into a team remains. Instead of splitting practice time between run blocking, pass blocking, pass catching, carrying the football, and playing defense, a specialized player need only concentrate on one aspect of the game. Additionally, his playing time is significantly reduced so his opportunities to impress and make a big play are minimal thus forcing him to play with reckless abandon on every play. As a result injuries have increased and violent collisions are commonplace. Conversely when one was playing both offense and defense you hit and ran hard, but not with the intent of making every play spectacular because you were going to get action on many more plays.

Today NFL teams have begun outfitting players with 3.5 oz, GPS-like sensors in their shoulder pads that can detect and measure variables such as lateral and transverse acceleration, speed, and hitting force. The data is being used to position players (can an individual generate significantly more hitting power going to one side rather than the other?), to program pass routes (fast acceleration and good speed is crucial for a receiver on long downfield passes while transverse acceleration and rapid direction change is preferred on crossing routes.)

And, specialization and technology are common in other sports besides football. For several years now there have been defensive midfielders and offensive midfielders in lacrosse. When possession of the ball changes the midfielders change. Another player may enter the game only for face-offs or if someone has a good shot but is very weak on defense he may only play when his team has a man advantage because of a penalty.

The level of competition and income generated by winning will continue to motivate teams to look for an edge so specialization and technological innovation will continue to flourish. The players will be more polished in their specialty and the level of play may increase from a spectator's point of view, but I cannot believe the players are having as much fun as we did when I was going to school and playing sports.

Do Your Job

Today's players show off and celebrate every tackle, catch, or whenever a camera may be on them. They want applause for simply doing their job and in many cases getting paid enormous amounts of money to do it. I recall my Dad telling a player, "If you're lucky enough to carry the ball into the end zone, act like you have been there before."

Physical Appearance

The most notable thing about meeting great athletes is that they don't look imposing. They look like everyone else you see on the street. There are exceptions of course. I suspect that if I had the pleasure of meeting LeBron James, I would say he looked like an athlete. But, arguably some of the greatest in their sport, Wayne Gretzky (ice hockey), Jimmy Lewis (lacrosse), Johnny Unitas (football), Joe Dimagio (baseball), and Jimmy Conners (tennis) were not physically imposing individuals. My point is that making judgment about an individual's capability based on appearance is fraught with peril. And it is not limited to athletics or to males. From a lineup of sailors one could not identify the SEALs and from a lineup of men and women in business attire the most successful could not be identified. Success in any endeavor comes equally from the mind, the heart, and the body and only one third is revealed by appearance. Looks are deceiving.

Athletic Toughness

I made light of the physical prowess of the some of the elite classmates I met at Tabor and championed the toughness of the middle class athletes I met at the Academy. It was not the money that made the difference per se; it was the lack of motivation and consequences of failure. Family money opens doors to provide opportunities and is a cushion when things go bad. When athletic performance is necessary to provide academic or lifetime opportunities there is a bit of desperation that is motivating and toughens an athlete. There are exceptions of course, but most of the hard-nosed athletes and performers that I have met either had something to prove or were motivated to succeed because of the other opportunities athletic success would provide.

Winning May Not Be Everything

In northern Virginia there is a high school named, The Thomas Jefferson Magnet School for Science and Technology. They have athletic teams and the students play to win and to have fun. They are not competitive with the very large, public high schools in their vicinity yet filling a schedule sometimes requires such a match. I attended one such football game. The local public school was ahead by a good margin and their supporters never ceased ringing bells, tooting horns, and cheering. The Thomas Jefferson school supporters, undermanned and without horns and bell had been relatively quiet for most of the game. I felt a bit heavyhearted about their plight, but they eventually put me at ease when the entire student body responded with the chant, "Hey, hey, that's OK. You'll all work for us someday." They knew why they were playing and they knew that winning - at this level - was not everything.

My Greatest Sports Disappointment

"A brother is a friend given by Nature."
Jean Baptise Legouve 1729 - 1783

My brother, Bob, was born four years and nine months after I was born. During our early years we were the best of buddies, but such an age difference becomes significance during teen-age years. By the time I began high school at age 14, we each had our own circle of friends. When I played football at Attleboro High School, Bob was too young to come to games alone and Dad was busy coaching at Pawtucket East High School (later renamed Tolman High School) in Pawtucket, RI. During basketball season, Dad coached ice hockey or swimming. When my brother was starring at Attleboro High, I was away being a midshipman at the Naval Academy in Annapolis. In fact, I graduated from the Naval Academy and Bob graduated from Attleboro High School on the very same day. (After my senior year, the Attleboro High School basketball team did not earn another invitation to the State Championship Tournament at the Boston Garden until

Bob was playing. He went in both his junior and senior years.) When Bob was setting a variety of lacrosse records at Bryant College and then playing for the University of Maryland on a lacrosse scholarship, I was a Naval Officer at sea on a nuclear powered submarine. (I made him play - lacrosse - catch with me at the beach during my Naval Academy vacations.) Later, when he played semi-pro football, I was stationed in Pearl Harbor, Hawaii.

My greatest sports disappointment was not being able to routinely play on the same football, basketball, or lacrosse team with my brother. My second greatest disappointment was not even being able to watch him play.

The sole exception was one lacrosse game when we played on the same team. It occurred at a Tabor Academy's alumni homecoming. Bob had graduated from the University of Maryland and I had just arrived at my new east coast duty station, in New London, CT. When I registered as a homecoming attendee, I was informed that they were trying to organize a Varsity vs. Alumni lacrosse game and would I play. I had been playing with the San Francisco Lacrosse Club and the Camp Pendleton Marine Lacrosse Club, during my tours out West. I was in pretty good shape, it sounded like fun, and I agreed.

A week before the homecoming, I was contacted and asked, "Could you recruit a player or two, because the alumni team is very shorthanded?"

"My brother did not attend Tabor Academy, but played lacrosse a little bit, can I invite him?" I responded with excitement.

"Certainly, that would be fine."

Bob was available and agreed to play.

The game day was a spectacular example of a Massachusetts spring day. The field was manicured as only a private school can afford to do. We were both listed on the announcer's program as "R. Pariseau" without distinction between "R" for Robert and "R" for Richard. We played our usual positions, Bob played attack and I was a midfielder. The first time I came down field with the ball, Bob eluded his defender, I passed him the ball, and he shot and scored. "Goal by Pariseau." Was announced to the crowd. Bob scored another one "Goal by Pariseau" or two, "Goal by Pariseau", before he began to get embarrassed at how easy it was and started passing the ball back to me or another teammate rather than take an open shot. I score a goal, "Goal by Pariseau." and also stopped shooting. We continued trying to include other players, but they couldn't seem to get open for a feed and seemed reluctant to take shots. Because we were shorthanded we had to play most of the game and we certainly were not going to let the other team win. Overall, I think Bob scored five or six goals and I had two or three. We had a wonderful time even though the competition was less capable than we were used to playing against.

I was complemented several times during reunion weekend about my goal-scoring prowess. Apparently it sounded even more spectacular than it was, because many people were busy greeting and talking with old friends in the homecoming tradition and were not paying particularly good attention to the actual play on the field, only to the announcer's interruptions of their conversation. Eventually, I tired of trying to explain that I had a partner and simply took credit for being an extraordinary good scorer.

When I am reminded of that game, rather than smile at how often everyone heard the announcer declare, "Goal by Pariseau." I recall how good an athlete Bob was and how much I missed not being able to routinely play on the same team with him. We would have done well together.

What if not USNA?
"Nobody goes there anymore, it's too crowded."
Yogi Berra 1925 - 2014

For me, the Naval Academy was a wonderful opportunity for which I am extremely grateful. The education I received at the Academy perhaps could have been acquired elsewhere, but the friends I have made and the concepts of duty, honor, loyalty, and integrity that were instilled on each of us are unique and have guided me through life. Uncle Joe's son Robert, "Rollo," also went to the Naval Academy. There was an occasion when the three of us met in Memorial Hall in our navy uniforms: Captain Joe, Lieutenant Commander Dick, and Midshipman Second Class Rollo.

"The Pariseau's Navy Reunion at the Naval Academy"
Dick, Joe, & Rollo
(Personal Photo)

What if not USNA?

If I had not attended the Naval Academy I would have gone to Brown University. I would have thoroughly enjoyed fraternity life and I would have had fun. I'm uncertain about the school's ultra-liberal attitude, but as a student it may have been easy to accept and a pleasure to exploit. The fact that Brown University was only eighteen miles from home may have stifled my experiences a little. I would have taken an engineering curriculum, realized I didn't enjoy engineering work and probably switched to business. I could easily have ended up as a teacher or coach. However, unlike Dad, who didn't even include money in his equation for happiness, I may have been distressed with my level of income as a high school teacher. I probably would have remained in the New England area. Alternatively, while taking courses in disciplines other than engineering I could have found a profession I enjoyed. Or, I may have befriended a classmate who would introduce me to a business possibility. I would have been happy doing some type of analysis (stock market analysis?) but I would have had to learn the details of such professions.

It is also possible that I could have been drafted and ended up on the ground in Vietnam.

I did not seriously consider a career other than the navy until after I had qualified for military retirement. I did not love every job I had in the navy, but I was not passionate about a different field and a military career is very seductive. It is a seductive career in the sense that once you get in it is easy to remain. The military makes ones life easy. The military provides free medical with a focus on prevention, pays for or furnishes room and board, provides built-in friends at each new duty station, offers vacations with pay, and world travel. What's not to like except your current boss (changes every two years), your duty station (changes every two years), or your job (in many cases it can be changed.)

So I guess I would have been a teacher. Without the Navy sending me to school to get a Masters Degree (two years of obligated service for each year of school) and the GI Bill paying for my PhD, I likely would have ended up as a high school teacher. Coaching would have been the obvious way to increase income assuming that I had a reasonably successful athletic career at Brown.

I think I should increase my annual donation to the Naval Academy!

Favorite Child?

"When children are doing nothing, they are doing mischief."
Henry Fielding 1707 - 1754

My siblings have, during occasional conversations, identified me as being Mom's favorite child. I initially thought it was simply a jesting regurgitation of the idea that a mother loves her first child the most. I do not think that's true, but on my returns home from the Naval Academy or as a naval officer, Mom always made my favorite meal and I guess I did get some "special" treatment. Mostly I think it's because Attleboro is a small town, I stayed out of trouble, had athletic and academic success, and my siblings were suppose to continue that legacy. My sisters were excused, at least outside of our home, because they were girls and my accomplishments had been largely forgotten by the time they attended Attleboro High School. For my brother, Bob, it was a different story. He was stubborn, a rebel of sorts, and did not worry about pleasing everyone like I did.

I was generally aware and periodically reminded that I had created an unintended handicap for Bob. For example, he found a report that I had submitted in Mr. Cooper's biology class four years earlier and asked me if he could use it since Mr. Cooper was again asking the identical question. I was pleased that he had found my paper useful and quickly agreed. Later when I asked him about his paper he said, "They still like you better. I replaced the cover sheet and submitted the same report. You got an A- and I got a B."

During a recent gathering he was asked if an exasperated teacher, coach or parent ever asked him, "Why can't you be more like your brother?"

"Yes. I was asked that." he replied.

I interjected, "Is that true? Did you hear that often?"

"About 300 times per day." was his reply.

I feel badly that I added an obstacle to what was expected of him during his school years in Attleboro and thankful that he remains a best friend and trusted brother.

In Memory of Mom and Dad

As the oldest sibling I gave the eulogies at the funeral Mass for each of my parents. They are included in honor of two kind, loving, and generous people. Dad died at age 94 and Mom died two and a half years later, one month before her 94th birthday.

Eulogy
Roland J. Pariseau
November 17, 2005

There is a danger inherent in giving a eulogy because most of the audience has typically known only one facet of the deceased's character and is likely to assume that the speaker is exaggerating. In the other extreme, there is the story of a wife listening to her husband's eulogy being given by his best friend and golfing buddy. In the middle of the eulogy she turns to her young son sitting next to her and says, "Go up there and peek in the casket; make sure it is your father that's in there."

In this case, I have no reservations because any one who knew Rollie, either as a mentor, coach, teacher, friend, teammate, or relative, will have experienced many of his best attributes. You didn't have to know him for long before he was offering to help you fix a plumbing problem in your home, sharpen your ice skates, help you understand a mathematical concept, cheer you up with a card trick, or offer you the shirt off his back. You will hear some stories about Rollie from the perspective of one of his children, but the characteristics attributed to him will be familiar to all of you.

An early lesson he provided was that hard work would not kill you. He would get a telephone wake-up call at 2 AM to go to work in the family bakery, leave there about 6 AM to teach high school math until 3 PM, then coach football for three hours before coming home tired. Except on Friday and Saturday nights when he would play the saxophone in an orchestra until midnight. We didn't understand how he could do all that, but it was an indelible example of how most people underestimate their capability. And because he knew that there was more to life than earning a living, Sundays were family days. Visiting a relative, a drive to the country for a picnic, a trip to the zoo, or ice-skating at LaSalette, it was a family affair.

I recall him teaching me to ice skate at LaSalette when I was 5 or 6 years old. He had made me a pair of double runners and insisted that I wear the thick woolen knit hat my mother had made for me. He held me up between his legs and skated across the pond. "Feel the wind, you can go as fast as you want, isn't it great." It was and I wanted to learn. He showed me how to push off with either foot and glide in between pushes. He said it was important to count how many times I fell, because when I had fallen 100 times I would know how to ice skate. That was cool. I could do that. Periodically he would take a break from his hockey game to ask how I was doing. "Great, I fell 17 times." He would ask to see what I could do, give me some guidance, a lot of encouragement, and tell me to keep counting. He was demonstrating a lesson in leadership. Identify the goal, demonstrate the thrill of success, provide the means of accomplishment, offer periodic advice and encouragement, and let the person earn it.

He placed a great value on education. Several years ago he mentioned to me that his will specified that if any of his children wanted to attend school he wanted that paid for first and then we should divide the remaining assets equally. He would occasionally reinforce the benefit of education and I recall an instance while watching a football game when he pointed out an exceptional athlete who was big and fast, but frequently would not know his assignment and would go the strong way. He commented that, "It was no good to be as strong as a bull if you are only as smart as a tractor."

He had a thirst for knowledge beyond formal education. During summers at Cape Cod he would get a different job each year so he could learn something new. A carpenter, a plumber, a roofer, working for a gas company, driving wells, he tried them all. Eventually he was getting so many calls from people that wanted him back the next summer that he relented and concentrated on learning all he could about the technology and business of a natural gas company that sold bottled gas. One summer I was having a fanciful discussion with teenage friends about what we would do if we found a complex machine into which we could insert a penny and get a $100 bill as output. In the mist of our daydreaming, one friend who had apparently seen my father's workbench said, "You had better find the machine before your father, because he would take it apart to see how it worked."

My father also preached winning with humility and losing with dignity. The more successful we became the more frequently he would remind us that we would lose sometime. He insisted on no excuses when we did lose, especially not to blame others. He taught that, whether it was play or work it was only important that we could look in the mirror after it was over and truthfully say, "I did my best." He did not like trash talk and the self-promoting dancing that goes on in the end zone during today's professional football games. He often said that if you had the good fortune of ending up in the end zone, you should act like you have been there before.

By example my Dad taught us to have good people as friends. My brother and sisters have selected their spouse wisely and they are loved and accepted like brothers and sisters. I recently heard of a father who telephoned his daughter to say, "Your mother and I are breaking up, we can no longer live together and we will likely be getting a divorce." The daughter responded, "'Dad don't do anything until I talk to you. I will call my brother and we will both be there next week. Promise you won't do anything until we get there." The father promised, turned to his wife, gave her a big hug and said, "It's all arranged, they will both be here next week for Thanksgiving." For our extended family and cousins there are not enough holidays for getting together. We can't seem to have enough reunions; we even make some up. One cousin has an annual Yankee Swap Meet after Christmas and a few weeks ago my sister had a costume-required Halloween party at which there were 92 relatives and friends. The next generation also attends and they are a great bunch. The traditions will go on but we will sadly miss the man who presided over these affairs for so many years.

The morning after a family reunion a couple of us were up early, drinking coffee, and wondering where Dad was, when he entered through the front door. In response to questions about where he had been he said that he had had such a good time last night with all the family and friends, and felt so happy when he got up this morning that he decided to go to Mass. I wonder how many people go to church when it's not Sunday or to celebrate happiness instead of asking God for a favor.

I grew up with a lot of support from my family, not from their pockets; those were not very deep, but from the heart where there was an unlimited supply. We learned a lot from Rollie, our Dad, the Coach. He led and taught with deeds not words and I know that he is embarrassed about all these kind words in his behalf. But, I have thought of something that I think he would appreciate. I suggest that each of us go out of our way to perform an act of kindness or complete a project that we know we should have done, but are putting off because it looks hard or it's something that we don't look forward to doing, and when it is complete, look up, point to the sky and say, "That was for you Rollie." I know that he will hear you and I guarantee that he will give you a warm and fuzzy feeling for having done it.

Thank you.

Eulogy
Viola E. Pariseau
March 23, 2007

We are here to honor a woman who made being a good mother a great occupation; who raised four children enabling Dad to be a baker, teacher, coach, and musician; and who taught us that being a loving, faithful wife is a man's great treasure.

It was not always easy raising four children. As first-born I began making it difficult by crying instead of sleeping when I was tired. The way it was told to me, Mom noticed that I would fall asleep quickly when riding in a car. So, it apparently became a frequent ritual that at bedtime I would get a ride around the block in the family car. It only took that three or four minutes to put me to sleep for the night. Creative parenting. Of course there are some side effects. I have taken many airline flights and have seldom been awake for take-off. When the airplane begins pushing back from the jet-way, I can immediately fall asleep. That's rather nice. However, on the down side, I have real trouble driving long distances in my car. I have been known to stop twice for naps between Attleboro and Cape Cod.

She had a health plan for the four of us; I think she brought it from Canada. Perhaps some of you will recognize it. It was called a daily dose of Cod Liver Oil. The name alone, the oil from fish livers, tells one that it will taste terrible and therefore must be good for you.

Even though she never liked sports, she gave up her flower gardens without complaint for a backyard basketball hoop. The basket had to be placed alongside the driveway, because that was the best place to dribble the ball. Consequently, the petunia garden became the foul line; the lilac bush marked the three-point line and air balls, those that missed the basket and backboard, landed in her rose garden. We tried, as hard as teen-age boys chasing a ball can try, to avoid the flowers, but none of the flowers were brave enough to attempt returning for a second year.

Even after I left for the Naval Academy in Annapolis I caused her stress. After plebe year they do a background investigation on all midshipmen as part of the procedure for granting a Secret Security Clearance. Well, in my case, they found out Mom was not a US citizen. It had apparently been assumed that when the family came to the United States and the parents became US citizens, all the children automatically became US citizens. Not the case. So, Mom had to expedite the citizenship process, including studying and passing the exam, not a stress free endeavor for a woman with three other children at home. Once again she did it for us.

Mom was great at celebrating holidays and that has endured as a family tradition. During the Christmas season she showed us how to string cranberries and popcorn for the Christmas tree and treated us to homemade molasses popcorn balls. The night before Christmas we slept at grandmother Pariseau's house along with our cousins, the Gurns'. After midnight Mass and a big breakfast, about three in the morning, we would hear Santa's heavy footsteps and jingling bells from his sleigh (my father upstairs above our bedroom) and everyone hanging out opened windows and yelling good wishes to the departing Santa. Great and memorable Christmas holidays thanks to Mom. Easter was as good. Easter morning we would each find a string attached to the foot of our bed. We had to follow the string to our hidden Easter basket. We followed our string under doors, in and out of closets, upstairs and down, all around the house. We had great fun and there was lots of shouting as we raced to be first to find our basket. Mom even made a day of cranberry picking at the Cape into a holiday and that's another tradition that continues.

For discipline, she had a knack for making us feel guilty for having disappointed her when we misbehaved. It usually worked. That is until my brother, Bob, began developing his magnificent stubborn streak. The rule was that we must eat everything on our plate before leaving the table. You know, because of those people in China, or somewhere, who were starving. Well, one day, Bob decided that he was not going to finish the peas that were on his plate. He didn't care about those people somewhere who were starving. He sat, with arms folded, staring at the peas for almost two hours, as I recall. I know I came in several times to see if he could come out and play and found the situation unresolved. Eventually, he was allowed to leave the table and his peas uneaten, "this one time". Mom knew how to pick her battles; I don't ever remember hearing about the starving Chinese again. She did have one other, stick and carrot, punishment that worked for me. It was our sitter. When Bob was four or five and I was eight or nine, we lived across the street from Carol Ganci. She was a beautiful high school cheerleader with shoulder length blond hair and her brother played quarterback and third base on the high school teams. When she was our sitter, I was content to just sit and stare at her. Bob, on the other hand, didn't appreciate her beauty and would run off and hide or make noise somewhere so that she would have to go look for him instead of sitting with me. Sometime she would even hold him in her lap while reading to us. I remember all my confessions during those years being about jealousy over my brother getting more of her attention that I was getting. Carol was the carrot, Hazel was the stick. Hazel was not pretty, she was mean, and she was old. I think she was nearly thirty years old and was so mean that she would actually make us go to bed on time. When I misbehaved, the threat that Hazel would be our next sitter instead of Carol was all that was needed to calm me down.

Mom taught us that there is nothing as good as food that you had picked from your own garden. Alternatively, if you had to purchase fruit or vegetable at a market, you should look over each item carefully to find the only good one among the crate full that was available. I though this was a LeBlanc gene until I started going to buy wood with my father. When buying fruit, a melon for example, I learned from my mother to carefully smell, feel, shake and listen to every one that is available before making my selection. I still have no clue what I am looking, listening, or feeling for, but if that is what Mom did it must be the correct way to do it, and that's what I do.

She was a loving mother and grandmother who especially loved to read to children and teach them to use a coloring book. She loved to play card games, Kitty Whist in particular, and remains the only person I know who never got a kitty that helped her hand. At a lobster dinner she would make a meal out of the lobster bodies discarded by the unknowing and save the tail and claws of her lobster for the next day's breakfast. She was an oil painter, could knit and sew with the most talented, made hooked rugs, and became a legend to all who tasted her chocolate chip or hermit cookies.

You can measure the success of a woman's life by the happiness of her husband and the interaction of her children and grandchildren. Dad was a happy man and the rest of us, her children and grandchildren, love one another without exception, are proud to call one another best friends, and cherish the times when we can get together. Thus we celebrate the wonderful achievements of a proud, classy, and successful woman, Viola Pariseau.

Thank you,

My Bucket List

"The great pleasure in life is doing
what people say you cannot do."
Walter Bagehot 1826 - 1877

My bucket list includes two old items that I wish I had done, but didn't. The first was to run a marathon. I've always admired those who had completed such a race and put it on my list many years ago. I didn't enjoyed running and never could generate enough enthusiasm to go through the training regime required. Now it's like an old shoe, I'm too old to wear it but I'd feel guilty throwing it out without wearing it.

The second item that will remain forever on my list is to earn a black belt in Karate. I took lesson with a Japanese Instructor during my tours in Hawaii and was ready to test for my brown belt when I left the Island. Too late to start over, but that is something that I wish that I had accomplished.

Run a marathon.

Earn a black belt in Karate.

Visit the Norman Rockwell Museum in Stockbridge, MA.

Write a novel.

Find an archery club and buy another bow.

Visit the French Foreign Legion Museum in Aubagne, France.

Have an exhibition of my paintings.

Complete a detailed ancestry for Pariseau & LeBlanc.

Visit the "Corpus" exhibit in Oegstgust, Netherlands.

Teach or help build on an American Indian reservation.

Co-author a children's book with Becky, using photos of our paintings as visuals.

Create a website for my paintings.

Visit Ellis Island.

See a Duke vs. North Carolina basketball game.

Return to Cherokee, NC to witness their annual Inter Tribal Lacrosse Game.

Create a list of famous/traditional/historical events (e.g., frog jumping, marble shooting, watermelon seed spitting, egg throwing, hog calling), and attend as many as possible.

Appendix A. Publications, Papers, and Reports

"If I cannot overwhelm with my quality,
I will overwhelm with my quantity."
Emile Zola 1840 - 1902

Listed below, with the most recent first, are the titles of publications, papers, and contract reports that I completed or to which I had a significant input.

Magazine & Journal Articles

Pariseau, Richard. "Operations Research: Decision Support Analysis at Work." *The SPINNAKER,* Advanced Marine Enterprises, Arlington, VA *Volume XVI, Number 1* Spring 1996.

Pariseau, Richard Dr. and Oswalt, Ivar Dr. "Using Data Types and Scales For Analysis and Decision Making." *Acquisition Review Quarterly, Volume 1, Number 2, Spring 1994: 145-159.*

Pariseau, Richard, Dr. Technical Consultant for the Book, <u>Hunters of the Deep</u>, A Volume of *The New Face of War* Series, Time-Life Books, Alexandria, VA. 1992.

Pariseau, Richard. "Underwater Management." *International Military and Defense Encyclopedia,* Pergamon-Brassey International Defense Publishers, Inc. 1992.

Pariseau, Richard Dr. and Gunn, Lee Captain USN. "Alternative Use of Volume: A Warship Design Concept." *Naval Engineers Journal*, January 1990: 82-83.

Pariseau, Richard Dr. and Gunn, Lee Captain USN. "Increasing Ordnance on Target in the Revolution at Sea." *Armed Forces Journal International, April* 1989: 59-61.

Pariseau, Richard and Gunn, Lee Captain USN. "What Submarine Quieting Means to the Soviets." U.S. Naval Institute *Proceedings*, April 1989: 46-48.

Pariseau, Richard Dr. "Unconventional Warfare Against Quieter Soviet Submarines." *Armed Forces Journal International.* April 1987: 66-67.

Pariseau, Richard. "Submarine Atmospheric Habitability." *The Submarine Review. A publication of The Submarine League. January 1987: 68-71.*

Pariseau, Richard Dr. "How Silent the Silent Service?" U.S. Naval Institute *Proceedings, July* 1983: 40-44.

Pariseau, Richard. "Stock Market States: A New Approach to Investment Timing for the Average Investor." Doctoral Dissertation, The George Washington University, Washington, DC. 1980.

Pariseau, Richard Lieutenant Commander USN. "The Role of the Submarine in Chinese Naval Strategy." U.S. Naval Institute *Proceedings.* October 1979: 66-69.

Pariseau, Richard. "The Reverse Ekelund: A Passive Ranging Technique." *Advanced Submarine Tactics Manual,* Submarine Training Center, Pearl Harbor, HA. 1972.

Pariseau, Richard. "United States Military Involvements Since 1775 Modeled as a Markov Process." United States Naval Postgraduate School, Monterey, CA. September 1970.

Conference Papers and Contract Reports

Chiles, Admiral H.G. Jr. USN (Retired) Chairman. *Commission on Maintaining United States Nuclear Weapons Expertise. Report to the Congress and Secretary of Energy. General Services Administration, Washington, DC. March 1, 1999.* (R.R. Pariseau designed and conducted the survey, and wrote the report published as Appendix C.1-32.) Http// www.dp.doe.gov/public/chilesrpt.htm

Pariseau, R. "Survey of Requirements and Shortfalls in Support of the Submarine Communications Master Plan." Chief of Naval Operations for Submarine Operations. June 1997.

Pariseau, Richard. "The Inflated Diesel Submarine Threat." Written for and presented at the Joint US-Russia Conference at The Aspen Institute's Wye Woods Center, sponsored by The Research Center of Geopolitics and Security Problems of the Russian Academy of Natural Sciences and US Defense Group Incorporated. June 1994.

Alnwick, K., Pariseau, R., and Oswalt, I. "Identifying and Prioritizing R&D Options for Enhancing Airport Security." U.S. Department of Transportation, Federal Aviation Administration, FAA Technical Center. October 1993.

Pariseau, Richard Dr., and Oswalt, Ivar Dr. " A Competitive Index For Evaluating Technologies Relative to DOD Operational Goals." Written for and presented at The 61st Military Operational Research Society's Symposium. June 1993

Pariseau, Richard. "Methodology for Assessing Alternative Ship Service Generator System Options." Advanced Marine Enterprises, Arlington, VA. May 1993.

Pariseau, R., Oswalt, I., and Turnquist, G. "Logistics Transportability: Analysis in Support of a Strategic Sealift Master Plan." Deputy Chief of Naval Operations, (Logistics), Strategic Sealift Mobility Branch, September 1992.

Pariseau, R., Oswalt, I., and Turnquist, G. "Comparative Analysis of Alameda County, Facilities for Fleet Operations on the West Coast: Training costs and Quality of Life." Director of Economic Development, Alameda County, CA. September 1992.

Pariseau, R., Oswalt, I., and Turnquist, G. "Strategic Sealift Needs and Available Technology Assessment." Naval Sea Systems Command, (Advanced Ship Development Division.) June 1992.

Pariseau, R., and Oswalt, I. "An Analysis of the Applicability and Potential Capability Enhancement from Using Unmanned Undersea Vehicles for Mine Countermeasure Missions." Lockheed Marine Systems. February 1992.

Pariseau, R. and Oswalt, I. "A Methodology for Determining a Figure of Merit and Prioritizing Strategic Concepts and Systems." Deputy Chief of Naval Operations, (Strategic and Theater Nuclear Warfare.) August 1991.

Pariseau, R., and Watkins, W. "Strategic Initiatives in Theater Warfare and Space Control." Deputy Chief of Naval Operations, (Strategic and Theater Nuclear Warfare.) April 1991.

Pariseau, R., and Oswalt, I. "A Methodology for Determining an Undersea Warfare Investment Strategy Based on Operational Utility" and "The Operational Utility of an Unmanned Undersea Vehicle for Remote Surveillance Missions." Defense Advanced Research Programs Agency. March 1991.

Pariseau, R. "Strategic Target Definition and Vulnerability Analysis." Deputy Chief of Naval Operations (Strategic and Theater Nuclear Warfare.) December 1990.

Pariseau, R., and Watkins, W. "Implications of Geopolitical Changes from Bi-Polar to Multi-Polar World on Strategic Warfare." Deputy Chief of Naval Operations (Strategic and Theater Nuclear Warfare.) December 1990.

Pariseau, R., and Watkins, W. "U.S. National Military Objectives - Deter, Repel, Defeat, Destroy - in Strategic Theater Warfare." Deputy Chief of Naval Operations (Strategic and Theater Nuclear Warfare.) December 1990.

Pariseau, R., and Turnquist, G. "U.S. Naval Special Forces (SEAL) Manpower Requirements Analysis." Commander, Naval Special Warfare. July 1990.

Pariseau, R. and Turnquist, G. "Analysis of the Organizational Structure, Legal Issues, NATO and Secret Service Support Functions, and Use of Mammals for Mine Detection, by Explosive Ordnance Demolition (EOD) Group Two." Commander, Naval Special Warfare. July 1990.

Pariseau, R., Hinkel, R., and Oswalt, I. "Operational Utility and Effectiveness Analysis to Support an Advanced Interdiction Weapon System Design. McDonnell Douglas Missile Systems Company, St. Louis, MO, April 1990.

Pariseau, R., and Cullen, C. "Operational Capability Appraisal of Explosive Ordnance Demolition (EOD) Group One." Commander EOD Group One, San Diego, CA. February 1990.

Pariseau, R., and Bailey, S. "Unmanned Undersea Vehicle Mission and Capability Analysis." Defense Advanced Research Programs Agency. November 1989.

Pariseau, R. "Is there a Role for Surface Effect Ship Hull Forms in the U.S. Navy?" Deputy Chief of Naval Operations (Strike and Amphibious Warfare.) September 1988.

Gunn, Lee Captain USN and Pariseau, R. Dr. "The Operational Characteristics of the Surface Combatant of the Year 2010." Assistant Chief of Naval Operations (Surface Warfare.) April 1988.

Pariseau, R. "The Cognitive Decision Process of a Submarine Commanding Officer During a Torpedo Attack." Office of Naval Research, Engineering Psychology Division. September 1985.

Pariseau, R., "Soviet Submarine Torpedo Firing Tactics and Training." Naval Operational Intelligence Center, Suitland, MD. May 1984.

Pariseau, R. "The Role of Air Cushioned Vehicles in Support of Arctic Submarine Operations." Naval Ships Research & Development Center, Carderock, MD. December 21, 1983.

Hansult, C., and Pariseau, R. "Advanced Cruise Missile Technologies: Where Should DARPA Go From Here." Defense Advanced Research Programs Agency Tactical Technology Office. December 1983.

Pariseau, R. "Soviet Motivation for Submarine Launched, Land Attack Cruise Missile Development." Written for and presented at Naval War College Conference on Prospective Threats to U.S. Naval Strategies.

U.S. Naval War College, Center for the Naval Warfare Studies, Newport, RI. January 20, 1983.

Pariseau, R. "Soviet Acoustic Capability and Trends in Anti-Submarine Warfare." Written for and presented at Brookings Institute's Foreign Policy Studies Program. May 21, 1981.

CPSIA information can be obtained at www.ICGtesting.com
Printed in the USA
BVOW08s0341040315

389933BV00009B/10/P